Living for Change

Living for Change

An Autobiography

Grace Lee Boggs

Foreword by Ossie Davis

University of Minnesota Press
Minneapolis
London

Published by the University of Minnesota Press, 111 Third Avenue South, Suite 290, Minneapolis, MN 55401-2520

http://www.upress.umn.edu

Library of Congress Cataloging-in-Publication Data

Boggs, Grace Lee.

Living for change : an autobiography / Grace Lee Boggs ; foreword by Ossie Davis.

p. cm.

Includes index.

ISBN 0-8166-2954-4 (hc : alk. paper). — ISBN 0-8166-2955-2 (pb : alk. paper)

1. Boggs, Grace Lee. 2. Chinese American women—Michigan—Detroit—Biography. 3. Political activists—Michigan—Detroit—Biography. 4. Chinese Americans—Michigan—Detroit—Biography. 5. Detroit (Mich.)—Biography. 6. Boggs, James. I. Title.

F574.D49C53 1998

303.48'4'092—dc21 97-27296

[B]

Printed in the United States of America on acid-free paper

The University of Minnesota is an equal-opportunity educator and employer.

10 09 08 07 10 9 8 7 6 5

Dedicated to

Jimmy Boggs *1919–1993*

W. H. (Ping) Ferry *1910–1995*

Dorothy Garner *1929–1995*

Kathleen Gough *1925–1990*

Freddy Paine *1912–1999*

Lyman Paine *1901–1978*

and

Detroit Summer Youth Volunteers

"Shaking the World with a New Dream"

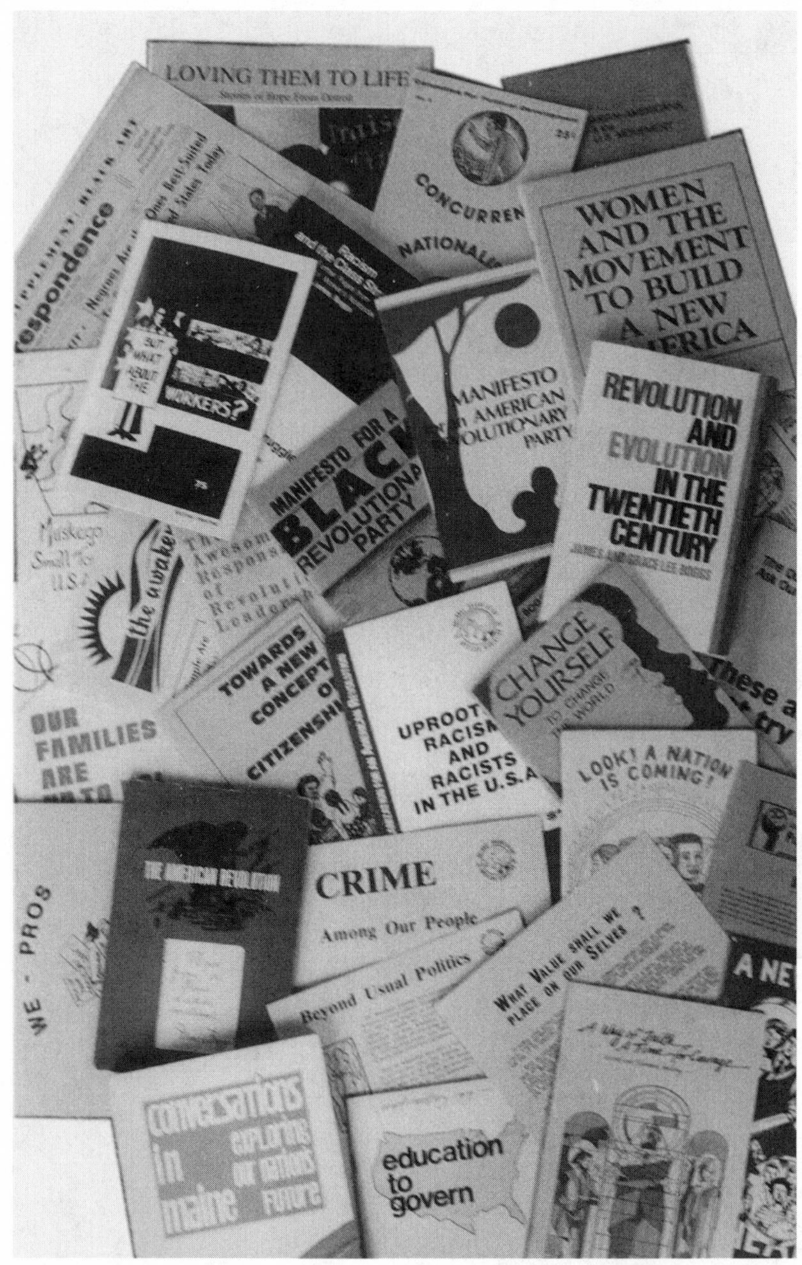

Books, pamphlets, and newsletters by Grace and Jimmy Boggs and associates.
Photo by Rebecca Cook

Contents

Foreword

Ossie Davis

Life is not easy, and like most who are perpetual students I need help. My logic limps; my conclusions stumble and fall; the truth I seek has been known to bear false witness. So when most in need of clarification, or to get confusions mended, I come to Jim and Grace to sit and listen. The fountain is always flowing, the welcome generous. They share their thinking gladly. I never leave without learning something new. This book by Grace is no exception. I read it, my cup runneth over.

For here is more than a feast for the hungering heart, or even a picnic—here is a life stating its case in eloquent summation, the journey now in sight of the setting sun. Grace is the voice, but you'll hear Jimmy, too, caught in midflight, never at rest except for ammunition. Time does not stand still, and neither do our two mentors. This book records two lives still up and growing. They search for truth as flowers search for sunlight, as hunters search for game, and whatever they find they bring and put on the table.

Through these pages walk causes, gatherings, confrontations, movements, and the men and women who made them: workers and students and committees of the People; Christians, Black Muslims, Black Panthers, labor unions; C. L. R. James, Rev. Cleage, Rev. Franklin, Coleman Young, Malcolm and Martin; artists, musicians, poets, actors, strikers, and seekers of revolution; members of both their families; and Jimmy, the flaming sword as much as Grace: his energy, his urgency, his dedication, his honesty, his patience, as well as his egregious lack of patience.

And Grace, and Grace, and Grace, constant as steel in all her moods and modes, yet supple and embracing. She takes us into the privacy of her past, filled as it is with family, and books, and study, with struggling, like an outsider, to grasp her "native tongue," and never quite making it. Going home at last to China, but finding her ultimate citizenship in Struggle, her proper setting. That's where she belongs, there in the lines of march with all the People. Growing, changing, and developing fast as the daily headlines, yet ever constant—I say it again—and therefore good for goals and for guidance, like Harriet Tubman and the North Star. Journeying into the past in search of the future. This book is the pilot's log.

From beginning to end, I could not read the words without hearing her voice—or seeing her face before me as she said them, especially when she spoke of Jimmy and his dying. It was almost as if she turned and, finding the reader crying, paused until he or she caught up, and then returned to talking—talking and teaching, until the final page.

玉平

Introduction

I consider myself blessed to have been born a Chinese American female with two first names: Grace and Jade Peace, which is 玉平 in Chinese. Had I not been born female and Chinese American, I would not have realized from early on that fundamental changes were necessary in our society. Had I not been born female and Chinese American, I might have ended up teaching philosophy at a university, an observer rather than an active participant in the humanity-stretching movements that have defined the last half of the twentieth century.

I never thought I'd be writing my autobiography. As late as the spring of 1994, when Shirley Cloyes of Lawrence Hill Books suggested it, my response was that I would rather continue my movement-building activities.

At that time Jimmy had been dead for less than a year and I was still trying to figure out what I was going to do on my own or, indeed, whether there was any "my own." That is what often happens when you lose the person with whom you have lived and worked closely for decades. Especially if you are a woman, you need time to re-create yourself, to discover who you are. In my case this need was even more acute because for most of the forty years that I was married to Jimmy, the black movement was the most important movement in the country. So I borrowed a lot of my identity from him—to such a degree that some FBI records describe me as probably Afro-Chinese.

In the three years since Jimmy's death I have been creating my own identity chiefly by my active participation in the ongoing movement to rebuild, redefine, and respirit Detroit from the ground up. As I gradually acquired more confidence in my ability to make decisions on my own, I also became more interested in discovering my own history.

Through writing this book I have learned things about myself that I find fascinating. For example, I discovered that my tendency toward nonconformity probably comes from my mother from whom I was estranged during the last fifteen years of her life. I also learned that one reason I am so critical of the victim mentality is that it made my mother's life so miserable and contributed to our estrangement.

I decided that the main reason I married Jimmy was that I needed to become whole. When we first met in 1952, I was a city girl from a middle-class Chinese American family. Despite the fact that I had already been involved in the radical movement for more than a decade and had even worked in a defense plant during World War II, I was still essentially a product of Ivy League women's colleges, a New York intellectual whose understanding of revolutionary struggle came mainly from books. Jimmy had been born and raised in a small town in Alabama where there were only a couple of stores on the main street. Even though at that time he had lived and worked in Detroit for fifteen years, he was still the kind of person about whom people joke, "You can take him out of the country but you can't take the country out of him." The main thing I like to do with my fingers is move them around on a keyboard. He loved to write and would dash off an article or a letter to the editor in minutes, but most of the time he had his hands in some kind of manual work, under the hood of a car or fixing something around the house. I was a Chinese American, an ethnic minority so small as to be almost invisible. He was an African American who was very conscious that the blood and sweat of his ancestors had made possible the rapid economic development of this country and who had already embarked on the struggle to ensure that his people would be among those deciding its economic and political future.

Ten years after our marriage Jimmy's first book, *The American Revolution: Pages from a Negro Worker's Notebook*, was published. To our amazement it brought a letter of congratulations from the British philosopher Bertrand Russell, initiating a correspondence during which Jimmy did not hesitate to lecture Russell, who was at the time probably the West's best-known philosopher, respectfully but firmly pointing out his ignorance of the ongoing struggle in the United States. As he wrote in the introduction to *The American Revolution*, "I am a factory worker but I know more than just factory work. I know the difference between what would sound right if one lived in a society of logical people and what *is* right when you live in a society of real people with real differences."

I believe that the story of how Jimmy and I, coming from such different backgrounds, were able to enjoy such a productive life together can be instructive to other Americans, especially in light of the rapidly changing ethnic composition of this country. In the past few decades the majority of immigrants entering this country are no longer Europeans but people of color from the Third World, especially Asia and Latin America. In some cities Hispanics and Asians are already the majority, and it is widely predicted that by the middle of the twenty-first century both Europeans and African Americans will be among the many minorities that make up the majority of the American population. With this new situation will inevitably come new stresses and strains. If the new immigrants are viewed as a threat, these tensions can explode as they did in South Central Los Angeles in 1992. On the other hand, if older migrants—and except for Native Americans, we have all migrated to this country, by choice or in chains—can see the new arrivals as people on whose backs we have prospered and whom we now need to make ourselves whole, we can embark together on the struggles necessary to make the United States of America what it was meant to be—a country that all of us, regardless of national or ethnic origin, will be proud to call our own.

This book is not only my autobiography. It is also inevitably a biography of Jimmy. In writing about who he was and what he did I have deliberately focused on his strengths, not because he was a saint but because I have found these strengths in other individuals. Like Jimmy, these individuals may seem quite ordinary and undistinguished, but when, like Jimmy, they have emerged from lives of hardship secure in the knowledge that their struggles have contributed not only to their own survival but to the continuing evolution of the human race, they are an invaluable resource. I hope that my focus on these qualities will contribute to their being recognized and nurtured in other individuals because of their importance to the future evolution of this country.

I have also devoted a full chapter to C. L. R. James, with whom I worked closely for twenty years from 1942 to 1962. Since his death in 1989 at the age of eighty-eight a flood of books and articles are coming out about this West Indian Marxist who many regard as one of the most brilliant men of the twentieth century. Most of these publications are by people who knew him only in his declining years, after he had become a globe-trotter and after a near-fatal auto accident in the early 1960s. He was still brilliant but nowhere near his old self, a person whose natural and acquired powers were constantly expanding because his life and the lives of the members of the Johnson-Forest Tendency were so intertwined. Inevitably as time passes,

James's biographers and critics will be basing themselves less and less on firsthand knowledge, particularly of his original stay in the United States, which he himself considered his most productive years. We came to a parting of the ways in 1962, but I have always cherished the years we worked together because it was during this period that my concept of revolution as a great leap forward in the evolution of the human race began to take shape. At the end of the chapter on Jimmy I describe how and why our break took place.

Through my association with C. L. R. James I met some of the outstanding leaders of Third World independence struggles, among them Kwame Nkrumah who became the first president of Ghana, the first African nation to win independence in the post-World War II years. Our first meeting was in New York City in 1945 when he had just finished his studies at Lincoln University and was preparing to go back to what was then known as the Gold Coast to participate in the struggle for independence. Our last meeting was in 1968 in Conakry where he was in exile after being overthrown in a 1966 coup. As Nkrumah, Jimmy, and I were toasting each other at the end of a week of thoughtful discussion, Nkrumah turned to Jimmy and said, "I hope you don't mind my saying this, but if Grace had married me, together we would have changed all Africa." The remark has stuck in my mind as an example of the headiness of the period.

Jimmy was always reminding us that in ourselves we are nobodies. "It is only in relation to other bodies and many somebodies that anybody is somebody. Don't get it into your cotton-picking mind that you are somebody in yourself." In these pages, besides my family, Jimmy, and C. L. R. James, you will meet the many somebodies who have profoundly influenced my life: somebodies like Lyman and Freddy Paine, Ping and Carol Ferry, Jim Jackson, Ossie Davis and Ruby Dee, Rosemary and Vincent Harding, Kathleen Gough Aberle, and Chung-lu (Louis) Tsen, with whom I exchanged and developed ideas over many decades; others like Clementine Barfield, Dorothy Garner, John Gruchala, Gerald Hairston, Shea Howell, Norma Mayfield, Donele Wilkins, and Nkenge Zola who have been my comrades in our day-to-day struggles to recivilize Detroit. I wish I could name them all.

Writing about myself hasn't been easy. Even though in most ways I am more American than Chinese, I was brought up in a Chinese family and socialized to think of myself in relationship to others rather than as an individual. For example, when I was about six years old, my siblings and I were all in the hospital having our tonsils removed. I was the last to come out of the anesthesia. As the American nurses and doctors hovered over my bed, they could hardly believe their ears when the first words out of my mouth were "How are the others?" Later, as the only Chinese American present at political meetings, I tried not to draw attention to myself and was visibly embarrassed whenever I was singled out for praise. During the turbulent 1960s people used to joke about my "passion for anonymity." This habit of self-effacement was reflected in my first draft, which was heavily criticized for its lack of "subjectivity." I am especially indebted to Stanley Aronowitz for not pulling his punches. "When Jim dies and Grace is for the first time in years on her own," he wrote in his review as an outside reader for the University of Minnesota Press, "we become convinced that, in the words of a favorite Gilbert and Sullivan song, until then she 'never thought of thinking of herself at all.' In effect, on the evidence of this book Grace Lee Boggs from age 20 was the intelligent supplicant of two great men." That really shook some of the insides out of me.

A lot of folks have helped in the writing and production of this book. Everyone at and associated with the University of Minnesota Press has been most cooperative. I am especially grateful to my editor, Micah Kleit, for his willingness, early on, to see beyond the limitations of my first draft and for his continuing encouragement and suggestions. As an outside reader, Professor Christopher Phelps of the University of Oregon did two close readings of early drafts. His corrections, suggestions, and enthusiasm were invaluable. University of Minnesota professor August Nimtz's suggestions were also very helpful. Copy editor Louisa Castner checked the manuscript so carefully and raised such thoughtful questions that making the final corrections at my end was almost a pleasure. Editorial assistant Jennifer Moore has patiently followed through on countless details. A number of friends and comrades struggled with me through several drafts, especially Michelle Brown, Itty Chan, Rick Feldman, Shea Howell, Jim Jackson, Alice Jennings, Gwyn Kirk, Xavier Nicholas, Freddy Paine, Peter Putnam, and Frances Reid.

Occasional comments from Louis Tsen in Geneva provided perspective from a distance; for example, this paragraph from his May 22, 1996, letter:

> It seems to me that the life of Grace Boggs has been an exercise of will. Through sheer will, without waiting for social conditions to come around and without waiting to explore her identity, she turned her back on who she was and barged into new territories. She was a woman who barged into men's territory; she was a Chinese who barged into black territory; she was an intellectual who barged into workers' territory. It is right

> for her to call herself a "revolutionist" because she has revolved and never ceased to revolve. Neither is it wrong to apply to her the heretical labels "voluntarism" and "transcendence," because she has no patience for any given, material or otherwise, and always insists on going beyond the limits of reality. Probably this is why she finds Mao a kindred spirit. Impatience is the hallmark of both.

Sunday dinners with my brother Eddie provided an opportunity to share recollections. We rarely agreed, but when you are approaching your mideighties, the number of people with whom you can discuss events going back six and seven decades is so small that everyone is precious.

The eagerness with which my good friends and comrades Alice Jennings and Carl Edwards awaited each chapter was a continuing incentive. They also made available the faxing and copying facilities of their office. I am especially indebted to Brenda Boyd, Ranae Mignon Griffin, Cora Radford, and Troy Tatum of their staff for their patience in faxing correspondence and unsnarling the copying machine for me.

Martin Glaberman has been an invaluable resource for checking dates and persons, always forthcoming when I phoned with a question or to borrow a book, a model of how comrades with political differences should relate to one another. He is, of course, not responsible for any inaccuracies. Without the help of the librarians at the Archives of Labor History and Urban Affairs at the Walter Reuther Library of Wayne State University, this project would have been inconceivable.

Finally, I thank my parents for the genes that have enabled me to remain actively engaged in projecting new dreams for the twenty-first century after living through most of the twentieth.

I am often asked what keeps me going after all these years. I think it is the realization that there is no final struggle. Whether you win or lose, each struggle brings forth new contradictions, new and more challenging questions. As Alice Walker put it in one of my favorite poems:

> I must love the questions
> themselves
> as Rilke said
> like locked rooms
> full of treasures
> to which my blind
> and groping key
> does not yet fit.[1]

玉平

Living for Change

1
East Is East—Or Is It?

I was born above my father's Chinese American restaurant in downtown Providence, Rhode Island, on June 27, 1915. When I cried, the waiters used to say, "Leave her on the hillside to die. She's only a girl." Later they told me this as a kind of joke. But for me, even as a child, it was no laughing matter. Early on, it gave me an inkling that all is not right with this world. It also made me wonder whether going back to China was such a good idea.

In those days it was assumed that the Chinese in this country were only "sojourners," that we/they would be going back home after making and saving enough money. In fact, as a child I thought *goingback* was one word. Because my head was so big, my brothers used to say that I would not be able to "go back" with the rest of the family because it would tip the boat.

My parents, like most Chinese immigrants in that period, were from Toishan, a county of peasant villages in Guangdong Province along the coast of the South China Sea, approximately two hundred miles west of Guangzhou, the provincial capital, formerly known as Canton. Like the Mexicans and Central Americans coming to the United States today, the Toishanese came to the United States because life at home had become impossible. Following the defeat of China by the British in the Opium War of 1839–42, the old economic and social structure had broken down. Forced to pay huge indemnities to the British victors, the Chinese government increased taxes on the peasantry. Unable to pay the high taxes and exorbitant interest rates to their landlords, millions of peasant families lost their land and became beggars, drifting around the countryside. Many joined bandit gangs or secret revolutionary societies. At the same time the influx of cheap textiles from Britain and the United States, mandated by the 1842 peace treaty, ruined traditional Chinese cottage industries, displacing millions of weavers and other handicraftspersons. Hard-pressed to survive, the people rebelled and kept rebelling. Between 1841 and 1849 more than one hundred uprisings took place. The Taiping (Great Peace) Rebellion, whose avowed aim was to create the Heavenly Kingdom of equal free men on earth, mobilized tens of millions and lasted nearly fifteen years, from 1851–1864. But unending, unsuccessful uprisings only increased the turmoil and chaos of people's lives. Millions found refuge in dope. Between 1838 and 1858, the amount of imported opium, although still illegal, doubled.

For many, especially the most enterprising, leaving the country became the only solution. Beginning in the 1850s, tens of thousands of Chinese left for America, which was known as the "Golden Mountain." In 1849 the Chinese population of California was fifty-four. By 1851 it was twenty-five thousand. At the turn of the century there were approximately one hundred thousand Chinese in the United States. Unlike those who came to this country from Europe, the Chinese did not consider themselves immigrants because they did not plan to stay. Little did they realize that the revolutionary turmoil of China would continue for another century, into the lives of their grandchildren and great-grandchildren.

My father was one of the enterprising ones. There were no schools in the village of Zhouzhong where he was born in 1870, but he was so bright that the elders sent him to school in the county seat for a few years. In his teens, like other youngsters in that period, he started going to Singapore to work. It was a long trip, but you could make your way on the boats plying the South China Sea. Eventually he was able to save enough to see himself crossing the Pacific Ocean, and in the early 1900s he was ready to embark on his first trip to the United States. It was not easy for Chinese to get into the country. In 1882 Congress had passed a law suspending the entry of Chinese laborers and "all persons of the Chinese race" except officials, teachers, students, tourists, and merchants, at the same time formally prohibiting the naturalization of Chinese. The 1882 Act was the culmination of decades of anti-Chinese propaganda and discrimination. In 1852 California Governor John Bigler described Chinese immigrants as "contract coolies, avaricious, ignorant of moral obligations, incapable of being assimilated and dangerous to the welfare of the state." In 1854 the California Supreme Court reversed the conviction of a white man for killing a Chinese miner by invoking Section 14 of the California Criminal Act, which specified that "no Black or mulatto person, or Indian shall be allowed to give evidence in favor of, or against a white man." In support of the decision Chief Justice Hugh Murray declared that "to let Chinese testify in a court of law would admit them to all the equal rights of citizenship. And then we might see them at the polls, in the jury box, upon the bench, and in our legislative halls." In 1879 the California State constitution prohibited corporations and municipal works from hiring Chinese and authorized cities to remove Chinese from their boundaries.[1]

My father never told us how he got around the restrictions of the Exclusion Act, and we knew better than to probe because it was generally understood that the distinction between being here legally and illegally was a shadowy one. He may have claimed to be a merchant, one of the categories exempted in the Exclusion Act. More likely he used the "paper son" stratagem, a common practice in which a Chinese man legally in the country sold a prospective immigrant a document swearing that the individual was his son. Like many other Chinese, he might have claimed that he was born in the United States but that his birth certificate had been destroyed in the 1906 San Francisco earthquake. He would sometimes tell people that he had been born here, although he never claimed that his mother, to whom he was very devoted, had ever left China. (She died in her village in 1937 at the age of 104 and was credited with three more years because she had borne three sons. A picture of her at 101, looking very regal, hangs in my living room.) My father always professed to be an American citizen, although I don't remember his ever going through the naturalization process. Whatever course he chose, after seeing the way he played cat-and-mouse with officials over the years, I suspect he used the confusion around Chinese names and his own limited English to maximum advantage, to the point where his interviewers finally gave up trying to make sense out of his inconsistencies.

Arriving in California with only fifty cents in his pocket, he worked first as a laborer and then as a supervisor of laborers. In Chinatown he attended an English language class taught by an American missionary named Grace, picking up enough English to work in hotels and restaurants and as a cook on a ranch. Eventually he was able to start a small business of his own and hire a few employees. "The only way to make money is by having people work for you," he used to say. He was speaking from experience. By hiring a few workers, he was able to make enough money to go back to China, marry a second wife, and bring her back with him to the United States.

It was an extraordinary achievement. Most Chinese in this country at the time were men living as bachelors because marrying Caucasians was out of the question. It had been declared illegal in California in 1857. If they had married and conceived children before they came to this country, the best they could hope for was arranging for a son to make the journey. Only officials and wealthy merchants had the money and power to travel with their wives and families.

In 1911 my father landed in Seattle, Washington, with his second wife, Yin Lan. She was twenty-one; he was twenty years her senior. He had left behind his first wife who was pregnant with their third child probably because Yin Lan was younger, prettier, and also pregnant—with a boy, he hoped, since his first wife had only given birth to girls. They had traveled in steerage on the P M Steamship Company's *Siberia* for more than a month. Shortly before they landed, Yin Lan gave birth to her first child, my sister Katharine, on the floor in steerage with the help of an American doctor. Katharine was also given a Chinese name, Hoy Gem or Ocean Jewel.

The name on my father's entry permit was Chin Dong Goon. His surname was Chin (sometimes Anglicized as "Chen") and the first name he had been given at birth was Dong Goon. When he came of age, in accordance with Chinese custom, he had given himself a new first name, Lee, meaning interest or profit. Most Americans called him Mr. Chin Lee or Mr. Lee because it was shorter and sounded more American, and eventually Chin Lee and then Lee became our surname.

My mother had been born into the Ng family. Her mother had been a widow who made a meager living by teaching sewing to girls in her village. She never knew her father who was probably a Hakka, a migratory people in southern China whose origins are uncertain. They may have descended from the Burmese or Siamese or from the aboriginal inhabitants of northern China. She and her little brother were hungry so often, my mother used to tell us, that they would steal the food from the graves of the ancestors. At one point the family was in such desperate straits that her uncle sold her as a slave to the people in the "big house," but she was able to escape. Her marriage to my father had been arranged by this same uncle. Although she despised this uncle, she accepted the marriage because it was her way of escaping the dead end of Chinese village life.

Once in the United States Yin Lan had no reason to want to "go back." Her mother and brother were both dead. Only her wicked uncle was still alive. She never spoke of any friends in China, and even if they existed, she could not correspond with them because she could neither read nor write. There were no schools for female children in her village. When I rode by bus through small villages in China during my first and only visit in 1984, I imagined my mother living in one of the dark hovels we saw, and I could understand why she had so relentlessly turned her back on China.

My mother often spoke with gratitude of the American doctor who helped her give birth to my sister on the steerage floor. From this encounter she concluded that American men treat women with a respect completely unknown back in China. As a result, she fell in love with America and began dreaming of the day when her children would be grown so that she could go to school to learn how to read and write enough English to become an American citizen in her own right. Meanwhile, she soon began dressing and conducting herself as if she had been born and raised in the United States. When I was a toddler, she would sing Chinese folk songs to us. But these were soon replaced by Christian hymns like "Jesus Loves Me, This I Know," sung at first in Chinese and later in English. At some point she decided to rename herself Esther from the character in the Old Testament. An attractive and vivacious woman, my mother was also a charmer. After she died in Hawaii in 1978, I put together a little album of her photos, from her arrival in this country in Chinese dress at twenty-one to her death at the age of eighty-eight. Two pictures, one of her on horseback at sixty-three and another of her in a bathing suit in her seventies, leave people breathless. Dining in a Chinese restaurant, she would soon become the center of attention as the owner and waiters fluttered around her.

My father never saw my mother as an individual, never understood why she was so unhappy or why learning to read and write English and becoming an American in her own name meant so much to her. I don't remember ever hearing him address her by her given name. He never spoke to her directly unless he was shouting back at her. Usually he spoke of her in the third person as "Mother." Believing in the Confucian concept of roles, he assumed that providing for her in her role as the mother of his children and insisting that her children respect her in this role were all that was required of him. When we were growing up, he used to tell us, "Your mother is a good woman who tends you, feeds you, loves you, and cares for you when you are sick. But she is a woman. When you need advice and guidance for the outside world, come to me. She only knows what is inside the boundaries of the house, while I meet all kinds." In old China a wife was called *nei ren* or inside person.

As a result, my mother was very unhappy. Comparing her life with that of American women, especially as portrayed in the movies, she saw herself as a victim and her loveless marriage and domesticity as a continuation of her oppression in China. My father had put the deed to our house in her name so that it could not be confiscated in case his business failed. So in the middle 1930s she locked him out of the house and refused to allow him to return. Long before the "Speak Bitterness" campaigns of Chinese women during the revolution in China, my mother would go downtown to my father's restaurant and denounce him in front of his customers and employees. My father would run into the kitchen and hide. Nevertheless, for thirty years, until he died in the mid-1960s, he used to write long letters to her, asking why they couldn't get back together, sending carbon copies to each of the children. The letters always began "Dear Mother."

My mother and I were never close. When I was small, she used to complain about how she had suffered in giving birth to me because my head was so big, implying that it was my fault. I don't know the circumstances under which I was conceived. They were probably what we would today call marital rape. But I never understood why, of all her children, I was the one who became the symbol of her oppression. Maybe it began with my giving her so much pain in birthing me. Maybe she saw it as a put-down that early on I began to assume the role of greeting people who came to our house because she couldn't speak English. Maybe it was because I was no help around the house. I hated housework as much as she did, but it was not all on her shoulders; a day worker came in once or twice a week to take care of the cleaning, washing, and ironing. (Usually, this was a European immigrant woman. I don't recall any nonwhites, but my brother Eddie remembers a black woman with whom he says my mother got along best.) Whatever the reason, the more unhappy she became with her life, the more envious she became of mine. The more I lived my own life, the angrier she became with the hand that she had been dealt. When I did well in school and buried my head in books, it seemed to remind her of the opportunities she had been denied. Because I was a feminist, in the late 1930s she demanded that I take a public stand with her against my father, and she never forgave me because I refused.

My father, on the other hand, never saw himself as a victim. Life to him was an adventure through which you are constantly learning and growing from your failures as well as your successes. Accepting setbacks and difficulties as part of the price one pays for living, he was constantly on the go, always thinking of new ways to expand his business and his mind. Taking maximum advantage of his few years of schooling, he read a Chinese-language paper every day and carried on an active correspondence with his family in China. He never stopped learning from his experiences and was always enlarging both his Chinese and English vocabularies. I can still see him, an old man in his nineties, sitting at his desk in the back bedroom of our house, looking up words in Chinese-English and English-Chinese dictionaries and compiling his own dictionary.

Every problem, large or small, was a challenge to his ingenuity. For example, in 1938, as a graduate assistant at Bryn Mawr College, I was living off campus and trying to survive on $400 a year. So every Tuesday morning he would put together a package with enough food from the restaurant to last me a week and mail it special delivery from the main post office on 34th Street, confident that it would be on the noon train from New York and arrive in Bryn Mawr before dinner that evening. To him, figuring out how to solve a difficult problem was half the fun. He was always working on ways to help other Chinese bring their sons or wives from China. In the late 1920s a story in one of the New York tabloids, the *Daily News* or *Daily Mirror,* alleged that he was part of an illegal scheme to smuggle Chinese into the country, in collaboration with Vice President Charles Curtis and, if I recall correctly, a man named Matt Glaser.

By the time my father arrived in the United States for the second time in 1911, there were few opportunities for Chinese to work on farms or in factories on the West Coast. In the 1850s Chinese immigrants had become miners, filing their claims like everyone else. Others were engaged in agriculture, as tenant farmers or laborers, teaching their white employers the skills of planting, cultivating, and harvesting orchards and garden crops that Chinese had acquired over the centuries. Later, large numbers worked on the railroads, performing the dangerous tasks that white workers refused to do, working (and dying) in snowslides and landslides. That is how the phrase "a Chinaman's chance" originated. Although Chinese could not become citizens because a federal law, passed in 1890, reserved naturalized citizenship for "white persons," there was stoop work for them to do.

As times got harder, however, white workers began taking out their frustrations on Chinese workers. In 1860 an estimated forty thousand Chinese miners were driven off their claims by whites. In the wake of the 1873 economic depression, white workers in the West exploded in anti-Chinese uprisings, beating and attacking Chinese laborers and merchants and destroying their homes and businesses. From then on, no Chinese felt safe either in person or property.

Confronted with this hostility from whites, Chinese workers in the West left the labor force and headed East, developing means of self-employment along the way. Because laundries and restaurants could be worked by the whole family and required relatively little knowledge of English and an outlay of only a few hundred dollars for equipment, Chinese became laundrymen and restaurateurs. By the mid-1890s "chop suey" had become popular in the United States, and cartoons of Chinese laundrymen saying, "No tickee, no laundry," were a familiar feature in American newspapers.

Recognizing this new reality, my father decided to take his wife and infant child East and go into the restaurant business, building on the skills he had acquired as a supervisor, a hotel and restaurant worker, and a cook on his first stay in the country. By 1913 he was operating a restaurant in Lawrence, Massachusetts, where my brother Philip was born. Thirteen months later he had sold the Lawrence restaurant and opened a new one in Boston where my brother Robert was born. Sixteen months later I was born above Chin Lee's Restaurant on Westminister Street in downtown Providence, Rhode Island. My father was headed South on his way to the Big Apple. After my birth in 1915, we moved to a house on Somerset Street where my two younger brothers, Harry and Edward, were born in 1918 and 1920, respectively.

During this period my father was often away from home traveling to Buffalo, New York, where he opened another restaurant and then to New York City to explore the possibilities for a really large establishment. It was the Roaring Twenties when thinking big was the rule rather than the exception. A man peddling rags from a cart could own a dry goods store in a year and a department store after two years. My father had moved up from small neighborhood restaurants to a downtown restaurant in a small city like Providence. Now his goal was to open up a Chin Lee Restaurant on Broadway. In 1924 he achieved his dream, and we moved to New York. I was eight years old.

In a 1949 book published in Los Angeles, Mr. Chin Lee is described as the "king of restaurant businessmen among the Chinese."[2] Chin Lee's was a huge establishment occupying the second and third floors at 1604 Broadway, seating nearly a thousand people. There were two entrances for patrons, one on Broadway with a big marquee, another on 49th Street with a smaller marquee, plus a delivery entrance on 7th Avenue. When Chin Lee's opened, Mayor Jimmy Walker publicly congratulated my father for lighting up the area north of Times Square. Movies of that period sometimes show the Broadway marquee. In a Cole Porter documentary there is a shot of it all by itself in the middle of the film. The obituary of Guy Raymond, dancer, stand-up comedian, and venerable character actor for seven decades in movies and TV, notes that "he began his career as a solo comedy dancer at Chin Lee's Restaurant in New York City."[3]

Encouraged by the success of Chin Lee's, my father opened up another equally large restaurant, Chin's, at 44th and Broadway in 1928. At both places patrons could dance to a live band and watch a floor show. Because it provided food and entertainment at such ridiculously low prices—for less than a dollar you could get a six-course dinner from a fruit cup to subgum chow mein or filet mignon to homemade pie and coffee—Chin Lee's over the years became a household name to tens of thousands of New Yorkers. Once I was stopped by a cop while making a U-turn on 7th Avenue in the Times Square area. When he saw from my license that I was Chin Lee's daughter, he let me go. Incredible as it may seem today, in that period Chin Lee's represented a kind of center of Chinese culture to many New Yorkers. Prior to World War II, most ordinary Americans had little idea of the world at large. Few had traveled to Europe, let alone to China. The books and films about China and the rest of the world that we take for granted today were not available. So people would often address their inquiries about Chinese culture to Chin Lee's. It was not until after World War II that Americans became sophisticated about Chinese cooking. During the war many GIs had been in the Pacific arena. Books and articles about China became more easily available. People began patronizing restaurants serving, first, Cantonese-style Chinese dishes, and then Mandarin, Szechuan, and Hunan styles.

It was only after we moved to New York that I began to face racial discrimination and the necessity of creating defenses against it. It was exciting to see the bright lights of Times Square and to look forward to moving into our new three-story house in Jackson Heights, which was in a neighborhood of one- and two-family houses and less than fifty yards from the subway, the El, and the Fifth Avenue bus. But it was painful to learn that my father had only been able to buy the land for the house by putting the deed in the name of his Irish contractor because restricted covenants prohibited sale to persons who were not Caucasian.

In Providence I had moved about in a very limited environment. I had never taken public transportation. Friendship Street Elementary School was just around the corner from our house on Somerset Street, and my father's downtown restaurant was close enough so that even as toddlers we could walk to and fro. Trinity Methodist Episcopal Church where we attended Sunday School was a block away. At the church we had been befriended by a British-born couple who, realizing that we had no grandparents in this country, told us to call them Grandpa and Grandma Pickles.

When we arrived in New York, we had to live for several months in the Hotel Bristol near my father's restaurant because the new house in Jackson Heights was not ready for occupancy. So my sisters, brothers, and I found ourselves riding the subway every day to P.S. 69, the elementary school near our new home. It was only an eighteen-minute ride, but it was an ordeal because people would stare at us as if they had never seen anyone like us before, making us feel that there was something wrong with us. To make them feel that there was something wrong with *them*, we would stare back at their feet.

We were the only Chinese in our neighborhood, and everyone we met or had anything to do with—our neighbors, classmates, and teachers—was Caucasian, a good many of them immigrants from Europe or their children. During this period it used to infuriate me when not only my peers but teachers and other adults would ask me, "What is your nationality?" I would reply patiently, as if giving them a civics lesson, that my nationality was American because I was born in the United States but that my parents were Chinese. But no matter how often or how carefully I explained, I would be asked the question again and again, as if to say that I could not be Chinese and American at the same time. Often the questioner, having heard my explanation, would go on to say, "But you speak English so well." It was said sweetly, as if I were being paid a compliment. But the message behind the sweetness was that being Chinese and speaking English well were just as incompatible as being Chinese and American.

Now that we were settled in New York, my father began to play a more important role in our upbringing. Unlike my mother, he was proud of his Chinese background. He drew up rules of conduct for us, spelling out in detail the role that each of us should play in relationship to my mother and to our siblings and how we should take care of our rooms. He had a host of favorite homilies, which he said came from Confucius. One of them was "gen mak ji hak" (if you go near ink, you'll get smeared); another was "beng guy doy lao ow yu" (a sick chicken infects other chickens). Even though he obviously enjoyed being a businessman, he was Confucian in his respect for intellectuals and peasants and in his distrust of merchants. So he was always emphasizing the importance of education and hard work and warning against the commercialism of American culture, especially in a big city like New York.

Anxious that we grow up with a knowledge of the Chinese language, he hired a Chinese tutor to come once a week to teach us reading and writing. To this day the Chinese characters that I remember best are the ones I learned then. But on the whole the tutoring was a fiasco. Teaching seven Chinese children, ages six to fourteen, together in one room might have worked in China. But we were Chinese Americans who were more American than Chinese in our behavior. We thought it was a huge joke to lock our tutor in the bathroom. We had no great desire to learn Chinese. When we were very young, we spoke it at home because my mother did not know any English. But as soon as she knew enough English to understand us, we stopped speaking Chinese. It was also easy to forget what we learned because we had little or no contact with Chinese people and no opportunities to speak, read, or write Chinese.

Unlike other Chinese families, we never went to Chinatown. On Sundays New York's Chinatown was alive with Chinese laundry and restaurant men who, after spending six days surrounded by "foreign devils," looked forward to one day of conviviality with people from their village. In contrast, my father didn't need to go to Chinatown to associate with Chinese because he had spent the week with a couple of dozen Chinese waiters and cooks (among whom were many relatives) in his restaurants.

There was an element of safety in our staying away from Chinatown. In the '20s from time to time there were tong wars, which I did not understand. All I knew was that they represented enough of a danger so that periodically my father was accompanied by a bodyguard when he came home in the early morning hours after the restaurant closed. I wasn't familiar enough with Chinatown then to know that tongs were secret societies in this country comparable to the ones that had emerged in China to oppose the Qing dynasty but that here ran drugs, gambling, and prostitution. My father used to explain to us that Chinese people had their own rules about renting property and other business matters. For example, if a Chinese person started a restaurant at a site previously occupied by another Chinese restaurant, he had to pay a fee to the former operator and not just rent to the landlord. These rules were enforced by traditional family and district organizations in Chinatown. If these failed, the tongs stepped in, bringing with them the violence with which they ran their operations.

Until I went to college my social milieu was very narrow, limited to my family, the neighbors on the block, the workers at my father's restaurants, the girls and boys at school, and the people we met at church. Every Sunday we went to Sunday School and the Community Church about a mile from our house because my mother thought that women were treated more equally in the Christian church than in other circles. But I don't recall people from the church visiting us or our having any friends among the young people at the church. In Sunday School we were given little white paper diamonds for memorizing passages from the Bible, which we attached to a ribbon pinned to our clothes. I memorized so many that my ribbon was two to three feet long. I liked going to church because I enjoyed singing hymns and Christmas carols and was proud to put the first two dollars I earned in the collection plate.

At school I was not particularly outgoing. I was too conscious of being Chinese to engage in teenage socializing and more interested in books than in boys and clothes. At home our family did not demonstrate affection in the American way by touching and kissing, and I was not comfortable around people who did. I was so shy that I was ashamed to change my clothes in the locker room. So even though our house in Jackson Heights was about a mile from Newtown High School in Elmhurst, I would run home before gym class to change into my white middy and navy-blue serge bloomers and run back to school in time for gym. In the dorm at college my friends used to tease me because gossip and dirty jokes made me so uncomfortable that I would leave the room when the conversation took this turn.

Our house at 3739 73rd Street in Jackson Heights was the largest on the block. The downstairs flat with seven large rooms was rented out. We lived in the eleven rooms on the second and third floors. My sister and I, and our half-brother, George, each had our own rooms on the third floor. Our furniture, except for two Chinese tables and two chairs of ebony inlaid with ivory, was much like that in any lower-middle-class home of that period. Next to the house was a fenced-in area big enough for a somewhat foreshortened tennis court. In the winter we flooded it for ice hockey. I was a tomboy; my brothers boasted that I didn't throw like a girl and that when we played baseball I often hit the ball over the fence.

Our neighbors were mainly lower middle class: workers, small shopkeepers, clerks, all Caucasians. (We referred to them as *fan gui*, meaning foreign devils. Blacks were referred to as *hak gui*, or black devils.) I don't remember any incidents of discrimination, although Eddie says he recalls one woman dragging her children into the house to stop them from playing with us. Only one man on the block, a reporter at a Long Island daily, was a real WASP who had graduated from college. He was always called "Mr. Kappler." For some years our downstairs flat was rented to a French Canadian family who owned a wholesale dress business in the garment district. Later it was used for doctors' offices. Living in the house behind us was a German American carpenter with his family. Across the street two southern white families, joint owners of a small laundry with children my age, lived for a few years. I stopped visiting them because the men were always groping me in the hall. Next door was an older couple, also from the South. The man, a civil service worker, would try to pull me onto his lap whenever his wife left the room. My best friend as a child was the girl across the street, Mary Abbruscato, whose parents had come from southern Italy. Her father was a barber. Her mother, like mine, had never been to school, and for a period I conducted a class in reading and writing English for both of our mothers. Her brother Nick became a lawyer and changed his name from Abbruscato to Scott. In high school my best friend was another Italian girl, Alvira Russo, whose parents spoke very little English. Her brothers, who were laborers, expected her to wait on them hand and foot, something that would never have been tolerated in our home. Because of my friendship with Alvira, I hung out socially with Italians. In those years, the stars of the high school basketball team were Italians who were barely considered Americans. They were only accepted as such after the election of Fiorello La Guardia as mayor in the early 1930s.

In the late 1920s we began to spend our summers in Island Park, a little village in Nassau County on the south shore of Long Island, one mile from Long Beach and nineteen miles from Penn Station in Manhattan, close enough so that my father could commute. For two years we rented a house, but in 1929 my father had a house built for us right on the beach. In those days Island Park was "country." At low tide we could dive for clams from the float in front of our house and swim or row across the bay to pick up blue shell crabs and fill a bag with clams. The Labor Day swimming meet every year included a mile swim from Long Beach. One year my brother Harry won and I came in second among the women. As we grew older, however, we no longer wanted to spend our summers together, and in the 1930s the house remained vacant and was finally confiscated because of unpaid taxes.

During the week my mother prepared our meals, consisting of rice and some Chinese dish like stir-fry or salt fish, which we ate family style around the dining room table. Later, as she became more Americanized, she would prepare a roast. But rice, which my father bought in one hundred-pound bags, was always on the table, even if we were eating spaghetti or potatoes. Sunday was a very special day, the only day that my father was home because the restaurants did not open until 4 P.M. It began with a breakfast of pork chops and French fries, which he had brought home from the restaurant the night before. After breakfast we went to Sunday School and church. By the time we came home my father was up and cooking Sunday dinner, which we all ate together. Until I went away to school in the 1930s, I cannot remember a single Sunday when any one of us was excused from this ritual. Some Sundays the whole family would go out for a drive in our seven-passenger La Salle, driven by a chauffeur because the children were all too young to drive. When I was learning to drive, my brother Bob used to pile five of his teenage friends in the backseat of the La Salle and make me do U-turns on a narrow street while his friends made disparaging comments.

Until my mother and father separated, my mother never had to cook Thanksgiving, Christmas, or New Year's Day dinners because on these holidays a huge package containing a twenty-pound turkey, chestnut dressing, gravy, cranberry sauce, and vegetables was delivered from the restaurant to our home and the homes of about a dozen business friends of my father. After my parents separated, we used to eat two Thanksgiving and Christmas dinners—one at home with my mother and another in the restaurant with my father.

Chin Lee's and Chin's were both closed down in 1949 by the federal government for nonpayment of taxes. During and after World War II establishments featuring live music were required to collect a 30 percent federal amusement tax from customers. My father collected the tax, but when business fell off after the war he used the money to pay his suppliers. As the federal officials padlocked the doors, they were almost in tears. Moved by the pleas of my father, they had delayed the closing time and again, hoping that he would be able to come up with the funds. The demise of Chin Lee's and Chin's foreshadowed the decline of Times Square as the center of popular entertainment, where ordinary New Yorkers congregated on Wednesday and Saturday nights to go to the movies and hear the big bands at the Rivoli, Capitol, Paramount, and Radio City Music Hall, preceded or followed by chop suey and chow mein at Chin Lee's or Chin's. By the 1970s the main businesses in the area were adult movies and bookshops.

When Chin Lee's and Chin's were closed down, I was almost more inconsolable than my father, who at the age of seventy-nine began making plans to start all over again. For twenty-five years since 1924, the restaurant had been like my second home. Every time I walked up the twenty or more broad marble steps from the street level and entered the dining room, I was greeted by waiters and headwaiters who had known me since I was a child. It was heartwarming to see so many people enjoying themselves at lunch or dinner. Chatting with the entertainers and musicians in the band made me feel worldly. From the time that I was a child I used to spend hours at the restaurant, helping out with cashiering and making reservations for parties, particularly during the busiest hours at lunch or dinner or on Saturday nights and New Year's Eve. I loved watching my father as he sat behind the rolltop desk from which he could see everything going on or as he welcomed people and urged them to "Eat, drink, and be merry!" He took pride in his handiwork, loved being a host and arranging all kinds of parties—sweet sixteen parties, going away parties, wedding parties. I still marvel at the way he used to organize the serving of thousands of people in a few hours on a busy Saturday night.

At home my father was an old-fashioned tyrant. He left for work in the mornings at 10 A.M., came home every afternoon from 3 to 5 P.M. for a nap and at 1 A.M., after Chin Lee's closed, to go to bed. While he was in the house everyone tiptoed around. He was very old-fashioned in his views about how we should conduct ourselves. For example, as a teenager I was not allowed to wear a bathing suit or shorts as I rode my bike around Island Park. One Labor Day, when I was fifteen and getting ready to swim the mile race from Long Beach to Island Park, he gave me a beating when he discovered that I had signed up for a correspondence sewing course costing about $150. But at the restaurant my father was cheerful and cordial, always ready to help folks with their problems. For example, in those days butcher shops did not carry the chicken livers that Jews used for chopped liver. So my father would put them aside and give them to total strangers. He was almost always in good spirits, incapable of holding a grudge or complaining of being wronged, even when things were not going well. His energy and enthusiasm never abated—in good times and bad. And there were many bad times, especially in the 1930s.

Until the restaurants were closed down in 1949, he continued to work seventeen to eighteen hours a day. After my sister died in 1962 and there was no one in New York to look in on him, he came to Detroit to live, spending a few months in each of our three households: Harry's, Eddie's, and mine. By this time he was ninety-two, but he would still travel by bus on Saturday nights to a local Chinese restaurant to lend a hand as a headwaiter or cashier. The day before he died in May 1965 at the age of ninety-five he walked two miles. The morning of his death he called me into his room and said that his legs had buckled while he was walking. So he had strengthened them with an elastic bandage and was going out to circulate a petition asking for benches along the streets so elderly pedestrians could sit and rest. As he walked out of the house, he lost consciousness and fell, hitting his head on the cement. Rushed to the emergency room, he died without regaining consciousness. We celebrated his life with a party attended by neighbors from all three neighborhoods—Ed's, Harry's, and mine.

My father's interests in the United States were selfish. He wanted money in the pockets of Americans so that his restaurants would prosper. During World War I he bought Liberty bonds, and the Providence newspaper published a picture of our whole family (I was the youngest at the time) as a gimmick to encourage other immigrant families to support the war to "save the world for democracy." His social and political consciousness was reserved for China. Like most overseas Chinese, he supported the Chinese Revolution of 1911 and its leader, Sun Yat-sen, founder of the Kuomintang or Chinese Nationalist Party. On the wall in Chin Lee's, as in other Chinese businesses, there hung a certificate of appreciation from the Kuomintang with Sun's picture on it. Over the years my father dreamed of how to modernize his village, and in the 1930s he commissioned Henri LeMothe, a commercial artist, to make a sketch of the village complete with schools, a railroad station, and an airport. In the 1960s, shortly before his death, my father attended a meeting in our home at which Felix Greene described the changes that the Chinese revolution had brought to Chinese villages. My father was overjoyed by the news. "Mao did what I wanted to do," he said. When I talk to young Asian Americans, I often credit my revolutionary activism to a combination of my mother's rebelliousness and my father's commitment to country and community.

In Asia today, especially in China and South Korea, there are millions of people with the entrepreneurial energies and indefatigability of my father. Many overseas Chinese, including entrepreneurs and skilled technicians, viewing China as today's "Golden Mountain," have gone back to stay. When China watchers predict that by 2050 China's economy may be the most powerful in the world, I suspect it is because they see a lot of Chin Lees in China.

At the same time, ever since the McCarren Act of 1952 and the Hart-Celler Act of 1965 liberalized immigration from Asia, Chinese have been coming here in growing numbers. Today Asians are the fastest-growing minority in the United States. They come from many different countries—China, South Korea, Southeast Asia, India, Pakistan, the Philippines—with very different histories, and also from many different classes. Although they are lumped together as Asians, English is the only language that many of them have in common.

In 1930 there were approximately seventy-five thousand Chinese in the United States. By 1980 the number had increased more than tenfold to 812,000. Since then hundreds of thousands more have arrived, both legally and illegally. Chinese immigrants are no longer mainly peasants from Toishan. They include upper-class political refugees from the Chinese Communist Revolution, professionals from Taiwan, Chinese businesspeople from Vietnam and Hong Kong, and untold numbers of poor and unskilled farmers and workers who toil in New York and California garment sweatshops and Silicon Valley chip manufacturing plants. Living from hand to mouth and under constant threat of deportation are those who have paid tens of thousands of dollars to smugglers to bring them in on ships like the *Golden Venture*, which was carrying 271 illegal Chinese immigrants when it ran aground in 1993 near Rockaway Beach, New York. At the same time tens of thousands of Korean and Chinese infants have been adopted into American middle-class families.

The influx of Asians to this country has transformed many neighborhoods and cities. For example, in 1990 the population of Monterey Park in Los Angeles was 56 percent Asian, mostly Chinese. On buildings and lawns you see more For Rent signs in Chinese than in English. In Los Angeles, signs with bold Korean characters advertise a Korean presence extending far beyond Olympic Boulevard. Between 1980 and 1990 the Asian population of Houston, Texas, the fourth largest city in the United States, rose by 139 percent to 110,000. It now has two distinct Chinatowns, three local Asian American banks, and an egg-roll factory, employing mostly Latinos and owned by a Taiwan native who holds a doctorate in engineering. The factory produces 80 percent of the egg rolls sold in the nation's grocery stores.

Restaurants serving Chinese, Thai, or Japanese food are in malls all over the country. Bruce Lee movies are favorites among teenagers. The top U.S. Table Tennis Tournament players were born in China, and Caucasians are flocking to ping pong parlors to be coached by them. When I was growing up, I had to keep my eyes riveted on the movie screen to catch a glimpse of someone who looked a little like me. Now newscasters of Asian origin appear nightly on the six o'clock news.

Last May, I visited my old Jackson Heights neighborhood where seventy years ago restricted covenants forced my father to buy the land on which to build our house in the name of his Irish contractor. Today it is home to one of the largest Asian communities in the United States. Walking along 37th Avenue, not far from where we used to live, I approached an elderly Caucasian woman walking with a white cane, told her that I used to live in the neighborhood, and asked her what she thought of it now. Unable to see well and assuming from my lack of an accent that I was also Caucasian, she replied, "I'm working on a way to move out of here soon. In my apartment house there are too many dirty foreigners."

The flood of Asian immigrants has created a new tension in depressed communities where many residents are unemployed or underemployed. The best-known example is the 1992 explosion in South Central Los Angeles, where African Americans and Latinos, enraged by the acquittal of the police officers in the Rodney King beating, burned and looted Korean stores. Less well known is the hostility toward Cambodians that is developing in Lowell, Massachusetts. During the nineteenth century Lowell was a flourishing textile town that welcomed Irish immigrants when the mills were booming and attacked them in times of depression. After World War II, Lowell, like many other New England mill towns, virtually died. In 1976 the decision of An Wang, a Chinese immigrant, to relocate Wang Laboratories in the city created a new economic base for Lowell, attracting not only technicians but unskilled immigrants. As a result, the number of Cambodians rose from one hundred to twenty-five thousand, one-fifth of the city's population. But An Wang died in 1990 and in 1992 Wang Laboratories filed for bankruptcy. The result has been unemployment, homelessness, as well as youth gang and drug activities—and the same kind of scapegoating of Cambodians that was inflicted on Irish immigrants during nineteenth-century depressions.[4]

At the same time Asian Americans are beginning to enter into alliances with other people of color, especially Hispanics. In San Gabriel Valley, California, a predominantly middle-class area, they have formed an effective alliance with Hispanics. In Los Angeles Hispanic and Asian garment workers have joined together in struggles against management. In California and elsewhere Asians are active in campaigns against anti-immigration legislation. In Washington State Gary Locke, the son of Chinese immigrants, who did not speak English until after his fifth birthday, became the first Asian American governor in the contiguous United States in 1996. The continuing furor over the Democratic fund-raising activities of John Huang reflects the potential influence of Asian Americans in American politics.

When I was in the class of 1935 at Barnard the only people of color on campus were Louise Chin and I, and a Japanese woman, Grace Ijima, of the class of 1934. In the spring of 1995 Louise and I attended our alumnae reunion. It was my sixtieth—and also my first. One of the reasons I decided to attend was that a special alumnae of color reception was on the program. At the reception I learned that today more than 25 percent of Barnard students are Asian and that there are similar percentages at many other colleges and universities. Asian students are now the largest ethnic minority on the University of Michigan campus, and the West Lounge in the South Quad Residence Hall has been renamed in honor of Yuri Kochiyama, the Japanese-American human rights activist who cradled Malcolm's head in her lap as he lay dying on the stage at the Audubon Ballroom in February 1965. Equally interesting, an estimated 50 percent of Asian young people now marry non-Asians, mostly Caucasian but sometimes African American or Hispanic.[5] What that means for the future of this country I cannot begin to imagine. But one thing is for sure: whoever still believes that East is East and West is West and never the twain shall meet is not ready for the twenty-first century.

2
From Philosophy to Politics

There were seven children in our family. Katharine (Kay), Philip, Robert, myself, Harry, and Edward—in that order—were the offspring of my mother and father. My half-brother, George, the son of my father and his first wife, and the same age as Kay, also lived with us. We all had Chinese first names. Mine was Yuk Ping or Jade Peace. At home or at my father's restaurant I was called Ping. My American name, Grace, was given to me by my father in honor of the American churchwoman who gave him lessons in English when he first came to this country, and it was what they called me at school.

Our family name was Chin, but we used the surname Chin Lee or Lee. At college I was known as Grace Chin Lee. Before I got married, Grace Chin was the name on my passport.

As first-generation Chinese Americans we had to create our own identities. We had no role models. In those days many immigrant families in the New York area struggled to send at least one child to college, usually a son, so that he could become a professional. The parents of Louise Chin, my classmate at Barnard, owned a small laundry in Corona, not far from our house in Jackson Heights, in which the whole family worked. Yet they were able to send all four children to college, and all became professionals. Three married Chinese; one married a Caucasian.

My siblings and I had little interest in upward mobility or convention. I am not sure why. My father was very entrepreneurial. Very early on he had set his sights on owning a restaurant on Broadway, and he not only worked hard but took a lot of risks to achieve his goal. My mother was always a rebel. At a time when few American—let alone Chinese—women defied their husbands, she took on my father. We also came of age during the Great Depression, when more people were headed down than up the ladder. Each of us followed a different path. George, Phil, and Kay married Chinese. Bob and Eddie married Caucasians. Harry married a Japanese American. I married an African American.

George was the only one who became a restaurant man. Born in China and brought here at the age of six or seven, he was an outsider from the start. Because he was the son of my father's first wife, conceived at approximately the same time as Kay, my mother resented him and treated him like a Cinderella, burdening him with the most menial household tasks. I am ashamed to say that we also treated him like a pariah. Physically he looked very different from the rest of us. Bigger than most of the kids in his class, speaking English with an accent, and overworked at home, he went only intermittently to school and dreamed of becoming an airplane pilot. It was the age of Charles Lindbergh. My father felt bad about the way George was being treated but didn't see any way to change the situation. So when George was eighteen, my father sent him to air mechanics school. In the 1930s George went to China and flew first in the air force of Chen Dai-hong, the Guangdong Province warlord, and then for the Chiang Kai-shek government in Nanking. Returning to the United States he served in the U.S. Army during World War II. After the war he worked as a headwaiter in Polynesian and Chinese restaurants, including my father's, and married an American-born Chinese woman with whom he had two children, Richard, who became a news photographer, and Lorraine, who became a lawyer.

My sister, Kay, was the oldest child. As such, she suffered most from the clash between my father's Chinese ideas and the Flapper Age culture that appealed to her as a teenager. People were always telling her how pretty she was and that she should be in the movies. So how she looked became very important to her. Eventually she changed her name to Kay Kim and became a model. She was very thin, and I suspect that she was bulimic because I can remember overhearing her regurgitating her food after enjoying a hearty meal. When she was seventeen and eighteen, she would drop me, her kid sister, at the movies and go off with her boyfriend. At eighteen she eloped with one of my father's headwaiters. My father forced her to annul the marriage. But she continued to see the man she had married and, although he married again, he always considered Kay his wife and insisted that his children treat her as such. They drank together regularly, and she died of cirrhosis of the liver in 1962 when she was only fifty.

As the oldest son born in this country, Phil was the one most attracted to Chinese culture. While the rest of us eventually adopted Lee as our surname, he called himself Philip Chen. Even as a youngster he was an enigma. He seemed to remain in the background, observing and manipulating the rest of us like puppets. We finished elementary and high school at the same time, and he went to Columbia College, which was just across the street from Barnard where I was an undergraduate. But during the whole four years we never got together. After graduation he went to medical school but left after two years to travel in Europe and China. Every now and then we would hear from him. In the late 1930s, for example, we learned that he had been kidnapped in China and would be released only on the payment of several thousand dollars, which my mother put together by pawning some jewelry. After that, he spent a year in isolation on the third floor of our house in Jackson Heights, shunning visitors and reading the *Encyclopaedia Brittanica* from cover to cover. In 1943 he asked me to meet him in a Childs restaurant on Seventh Avenue across the street from Chin Lee's. To my surprise he showed up in the uniform of a U.S. Military Intelligence Service officer and proceeded to ask me questions about my radical activities that showed he had access to FBI files. Around that time he was married to a Chinese air stewardess whom he later divorced. They had a son, Darwin, who as an infant spent some time with my mother in Jackson Heights. Some years ago Darwin sent my brother Ed pictures of Phil with his second wife, a Chinese woman working for the United Nations in Europe, and their adopted daughter.

Bob was the peacemaker, always trying to be helpful and to cheer everyone up. He was about six feet tall, very good-looking, and persuasive. After graduating from high school in 1932, he attended the University of Wisconsin and Virginia Polytechnic Institute for a couple of years, but then, like so many young men of that period, hit the road, doing all kinds of odd jobs for a living. At one point he biked to Florida. At another he rained thousands of Job Wanted flyers with his photograph from the top of the Empire State Building down on Fifth Avenue and 34th Street. Unable to find work, he tried to enlist in the armed services, only to be met with laughter. "Except for Filipino mess boys in the Navy," he was told, "we don't have Orientals in the military." Moving to Los Angeles, he signed a contract with MGM and played a fleeting role as a peasant resistance fighter in *Dragon Seed,* a 1944 film about the Sino-Japanese War starring Katharine Hepburn and Walter Huston made up to look Chinese. I used to call him my beachcomber brother because for years he worked as a lifeguard and a health and recreation instructor at resorts in Florida, Las Vegas, Santa Monica, and Honolulu. In Honolulu he became a salesman and in his late fifties married a young Caucasian woman from Idaho with whom he had two children, Sondra and Jonathan.

Harry was a tournament swimmer, tennis and soccer player, and a YMCA camp counselor who was so good with kids that they would assemble at the subway exit near our house and wait for him. While studying for his master's degree during World War II at Springfield College, a YMCA institution in Massachusetts, he enlisted in the U.S. Army and was assigned to the Chinese Service Unit because he was anxious to learn Chinese. Later he received a discharge from that unit and reenlisted in the Air Corps. After the war he married Julie, a Japanese girl from California who had been in an internment camp, and together they moved to Detroit. After working and organizing in the factory for several years Harry was fired, allegedly because he had not included his master's degree on his job application, and he became a public schoolteacher in a Detroit suburb. Julie, who also worked in the plant for a while, is an artist. Their two daughters are both married to Caucasians.

Over the past forty years I have remained in closest contact with Eddie. Five years younger than I, he attended Lafayette College in Easton, Pennsylvania, but left after a year to work at odd jobs with Bob and then as a photographer at the New York World's Fair in 1938–39. During World War II he served in the U.S. Army in Japan. After the war he also moved to Detroit. A Chrysler worker for thirty years, most of that time as a skilled worker, he has a passion for gardening, cooking, creative writing, and figuring out how things work. In the plant Ed met Averis, who was born and raised in a little mill town in Georgia and who shared his interest in gardening. They got married around the same time as Jimmy and I. Jimmy and Averis really enjoyed one another, and they were both devoted to my father. Sometimes, watching the three of them together, Averis with her Georgia accent, Jimmy with his Alabama accent, and Pa with his pidgin English, I would marvel at their closeness and wonder what bonded them. Was it that all three had been raised in the country while Eddie and I were city folk? Jimmy and Averis especially were proud of our being what they called a United Nations family.

I was the most intellectual. In school I was skipped a lot and eventually graduated from the eighth grade before my twelfth birthday. In my last term in high school, with only one class to attend, I decided to go to Merchants and Bankers School to learn typing and shorthand so that I would always be able to make a living. At home I was always reading and staying as far away as possible from the kitchen and housework. We had no books in our home in Providence. As we were leaving for New York, my Sunday School teacher, Mary Smith, gave me *The Secret Garden* by Frances Hodgson Burnett as a going-away present. It was the first book I ever owned. After we moved to New York, someone gave us a ten-volume *Wonder World* set that I read again and again. As soon as I was old enough to use the library, I would bring home an armful of books, devour them, and go back for more. I still do. For years I especially looked for novels on Chinese people. I found a couple by Pearl Buck, the American author of *The Good Earth*. One that I recall revolved around the dilemma of the two offspring of an interracial marriage between a Chinese and an American. The one who was interested in Chinese heritage looked like a Westerner; the other who was attracted to American culture looked Chinese. In those days there was only one Asian film actress, Anna May Wong. At the movies I used to keep my eyes peeled for her fleeting appearances on the screen.

As a good Confucian my father was a great believer in education and wanted all of us to go to college. Early on, it was clear that I was the one most likely to go. I was not a particularly good student because I felt it below my dignity to memorize facts and feed them back on tests. However, I was bright enough so that I was among the hundreds of New York high school graduates winning a Regents Scholarship worth $100 a year. That seems like pennies today, but in those days tuition at Barnard was only $700 a year, subway fare was a nickel, and you could commute for a dime a day. I was also raised to be frugal; my parents were always reminding us of the number of people starving in China. So with some help from my father, supplemented by money I made from typing papers for other students, I was able to make do.

When I became a Barnard freshman in 1931, I was sixteen years old and very immature. When people asked me what I planned to do with a college education, I had no answer. The only thing I was clear about was that I was not going to become a teacher. Somewhere along the way I had become convinced that "those who can, do; those who can't, teach."

My first two years at college were exciting. I wanted to try everything. I had never been around so many WASPs and middle-class Jews before. Most of the WASPs were from out of town. The Jews came from the Central Park West and West End Avenue neighborhood. Italians were few and far between. One of my friends was Yolanda Lipari, a fellow commuter from Queens, who, like me and Louise Chin, was the first girl in her family and neighborhood to go to college.

In my political science class I wrote my first paper on "The Japanese Invasion of Manchuria," which had just taken place, and I entertained the idea of a career in international diplomacy. I took classes in German (I had studied Spanish and French in high school) and was fascinated by the philosophic ideas implicit in the structure of the language. My most exciting class was in zoology, taught by Professor Crampton, who had grown up in the nineteenth century when Charles Darwin's theory of evolution had seized the imagination of scientists and intellectuals. Captivated by sweeping statements like "Ontology recapitulates Phylogeny" and by the opportunity to dissect dogfish in the laboratory, I contemplated becoming a scientist. But science classes meant a lot of lab hours in the afternoon when I would rather have been playing tennis or swimming. I was also anxious to test the waters of college politics. So I ran for treasurer and then for vice president of the Women's Athletic Association, a campus-wide organization, and won.

Then, suddenly, in the first semester of my junior year, both my classes and my student activities became boring and empty. Overnight, it seemed, ideas like those of Professor Crampton's on evolution seemed as irrelevant as the lessons I had been taught in Sunday School.

In part, this was because of the social crisis created by the Depression and the rise of Adolf Hitler in Europe. But unlike some of my classmates I did not feel moved to social action. I admired Eleanor Roosevelt and tried to get her for our keynote speaker at the annual Women's Athletic Association banquet in 1933, but I was not ready to follow her lead in visiting coal miners and people living in Hoovervilles. I recall participating in only one demonstration—a Briand Peace Pact march around the college. One speech from that demonstration, pointing out the imperialist roots of World War I, remained in my mind for years. The sister of one of my classmates, a Jewish girl, was a social worker with the Emergency Relief Bureau, and I became aware of the mass demonstrations and struggles going on, for example, to stop landlords from evicting tenants who could not pay their rent and to demand emergency relief stipends. I remember another one of my classmates, an Irish girl from Brooklyn, reporting proudly upon our return to school in the fall of 1934 that she had become a member of the Communist Party. Two of my friends went to meetings sponsored by the Young Communist League.

I did not accompany them because in those days I did not identify with the unemployed and homeless. We owned our home, and because my father was a restaurant man we never lacked for food, even when business was slow. During the Depression he was able to keep his restaurants open only by borrowing right and left to pay his suppliers. I can still remember the morning he had to borrow subway fare from one of my brothers to get to work. He worried, and I did too, that the wage requirements in the National Recovery Act might put him out of business. The waiters in his restaurants, who were mostly relatives, were only paid a dollar a day, which was supplemented by tips. But prices were also incredibly low. During the Depression forty cents was all you paid at Chin Lee's or Chin's for lunch. In the evening you could enjoy a full-course dinner for sixty-five cents.

Instead, I responded to the deepening crisis by turning inward. I began asking myself and my friends questions about the meaning of life and engaging in endless discussions. Not satisfied with these discussions, I suddenly decided to drop all or almost all of my classes and began auditing philosophy classes. When people asked me why I had become so interested in philosophy or what I was going to do with a major in philosophy, I was unable to explain. I could not even tell them what philosophy was about. All I knew was that I was feeling the need to think for myself. What other people had discovered, what other people thought was no longer enough for me.

Many years later, reading José Ortega y Gasset's *What Is Philosophy?* I discovered why at the age of eighteen I was attracted to philosophy. Truth is always changing, Ortega explained, and yesterday's truth is today's error. Every society lives by a concept of reality and the meaning of life that is based on assumptions. At a certain point these assumptions are no longer tenable, and the public begins to feel a need for a new concept of reality and the meaning of life. At that point those individuals who get an almost voluptuous pleasure from grappling with ideas begin philosophizing; they embark on the struggle to create a new philosophy.

One book from that period, *The Modern Temper* by Joseph Wood Krutch, sticks in my mind. I don't know how it came to my attention, but I vividly remember how it captured my unease. For two generations, said Krutch, the West had been living by the scientific optimism of the nineteenth century, willing to accept the meaninglessness and insignificance of the human spirit implicit in the scientific approach in exchange for the bourgeois comforts acquired through power over Nature. But now even physical scientists, like Albert Einstein and Sir Arthur Stanley Eddington, were acknowledging the critical role that the human mind plays in creating truth, including the truths of physics. At the same time the knowledge produced by scientists has become so specialized and couched in such jargon that it makes little sense to the ordinary person. As a result, confidence in science is oozing away.

As it turned out, the philosophy department at Barnard was more a part of the problem than the solution. The two professors, a man and a woman in their fifties and sixties, had been born in the nineteenth century and had studied in college with professors whose worldviews had been developed in the early part of that century. Their personalities had been shaped before World War I shattered the illusion that scientific and technological progress inevitably brought social progress. So they saw history essentially in terms of three periods: Ancient Greece and Rome; Medieval Europe (which they viewed as the Dark Ages); and the Modern Age, which they viewed as the end of history because man had finally been liberated from the superstitions and mysticism of the Middle Ages by philosophers like Francis Bacon, René Descartes, and John Locke. Philosophy to them was the professional activity of leisure-class individuals like themselves who in the tradition of Plato and Aristotle engaged in the pursuit of "the Good, the True and the Beautiful." It worried these professors that I was looking to philosophy to provide me with answers about the meaning of my own life and that I wasn't concerned with credits or a grade. What if I didn't find the answers I was looking for? Would I commit suicide? I can still see the anxiety and concern in their faces.

Somehow, despite dropping and signing up for courses right and left, I was able to graduate on schedule with a fairly decent grade point average, mainly because I was usually able to write a thoughtful exam. I had no idea what I would do after graduation. Philosophy was hardly a marketable skill. I knew shorthand and typing, but an office job, except perhaps with a church organization, was unlikely because most companies in those days would come right out and say, "We don't hire Orientals." A Chinese woman salesperson at Macy's or Gimbels was as unheard of as a black one. Then, fortuitously, I heard that a Chinese graduate scholarship was available at Bryn Mawr College because the civil war in China was making travel to this country difficult. So I drove down to Bryn Mawr for an interview and was accepted. The scholarship paid $400 a year, including tuition, room, and board. The next year I became a fellow in the philosophy department (which paid $700) and the year after that, a reader, which paid $400.

Life on the Bryn Mawr campus was close to idyllic. The Barnard campus was (and still is) tiny, occupying four blocks in the middle of upper Manhattan, from 116th to 120th Street, between Broadway and Claremont Avenues. Its facilities for about a thousand students consisted at the time of two dorms for resident students and two four-story buildings for classrooms, administration, gym, swimming pool, and a theater. About one-fourth of the space was allotted for a tiny park (we called it "The Jungle") and four tennis courts.

By contrast, the Bryn Mawr campus for approximately the same number of students sprawled over many acres of rolling hill country in heavily wooded Montgomery County in Pennsylvania, about fifteen miles west of Philadelphia and a hundred miles south of New York. In those days all the buildings, except the science building, were Gothic gray stone. As I recall, there were about ten buildings, including four to five dorms, a classroom building, a science building, library, the Deanery, the Inn, and gym. One of the dorms was named Rockefeller Hall. Graduate scholars and fellows, most of whom, like myself, were poor as church mice, lived in Radnor Hall, where our accommodations were as plush as those of the undergraduates, most of whom came from very affluent families. Black maids, dressed in gray uniforms with white collars, made our beds, cleaned our rooms, and served us our meals three times a day at tables with fine china, cutlery, and cloth napkins. After each meal we would rush upstairs to smoke, drink coffee, and play bridge for an hour before going to class or to our rooms to study. The "Village," a few minutes' walk from campus, consisted of one main street and a movie theater where we would go on Friday nights. Trips to Philadelphia on the Paoli Local and to New York City on the Pennsylvania Railroad were easy and cheap. Round-trip fare between New York and Philadelphia cost about $5.

Under these conditions, I was able to use my $400 scholarship money and later my $700 fellowship money for miscellaneous expenses, books, and trips to Philadelphia and New York. I supplemented the $400 by working thirty hours a month for $1 an hour in the graduate school office with my good friend Doris Sill Carland under the National Youth Administration program.

The most rewarding part of being at Bryn Mawr was the opportunity it gave me to study with Paul Weiss. Unlike my philosophy professors at Barnard who taught philosophy from books, Weiss philosophized as if his life depended on it. A young man, in his midthirties, and a new father, Weiss not only got an almost palpable pleasure from grappling with ideas but was passionately engaged in creating a new philosophy that would meet both his own needs and those of a society for whom science was no longer sacrosanct. At Harvard University he had studied under Alfred North Whitehead, whose *Science and the Modern World,* published in 1925, I still read and recommend for its priceless exposure of "the fallacy of misplaced concreteness" or the tendency of intellectuals to become so preoccupied with the abstractions necessary for scientific thinking that they lose sight of concrete reality, which is always many-sided.[1] Weiss was a living example of the "recurrence to the concrete for inspiration," which Whitehead recommended. Small of stature, feisty, and quick-witted, he jumped around the room as he asked hard questions about the meaning of the world around us, not only of his students but of himself. As the words tumbled from his mouth in a New York Jewish accent, you got the feeling that he did not know in advance what he was going to say and that what he said had never been said or thought before either by him or by anybody else. No wonder that in the 1970s he was a frequent guest on the late-night talk show of Dick Cavett, who had been one of his students at Yale.[2] In 1992 I came across an article on Weiss in *Modern Maturity*, the American Association of Retired People monthly magazine. By then he was ninety years old, but from the picture and article he was as perky as he had been when I was his student. Since our association at Bryn Mawr, he had written thirty books, taught at Yale, Rockefeller, and Catholic Universities, and been president of the American Philosophical Association. But combative as ever, he was suing Catholic University for age discrimination because after his two decades of teaching there, it had refused to renew his full-time contract and was only offering him a part-time job teaching two classes!

At Bryn Mawr I felt my mind stretching not only because of Weiss's approach to philosophizing but because he introduced me to the writings of the German philosophers Immanuel Kant and G. W. F. Hegel, who (I later discovered) had profoundly influenced Karl Marx.

Kant made a lot of sense to me. First of all, in his landmark work, the *Critique of Pure Reason*, first published in 1781 on the eve of the French Revolution, he denied that there is any such thing as Pure Reason. He exposed the pure mind, the starting point of traditional philosophy, as a myth concocted by the ivory tower intellectual in his own image. There is no Pure Reason searching for or contemplating some final, perfect, static, eternal truth. Our knowledge, Kant said, is the result of dynamic interaction between our selves and reality, in the course of which our minds impose forms or categories on reality. Kant's recognition that human minds supply the concepts that enable us to relate to reality produced a Copernican revolution in philosophic circles, as he himself noted in the preface to the second edition. It was also a watershed in my life. Slowly but surely I was being prepared to take my place in the world. For if we shape reality by how we think, we can also change reality by what we do.

Kant's famous "categorical imperative" as projected in his *Critique of Practical Reason*, published in 1788, also impressed me as down-to-earth. Instead of locating Virtue or "the Good" in some pure or mythical realm in which the traditional philosopher is rummaging, Kant based his concept of the Good on social conduct that respects the "dignity of man." Look on yourself as a citizen in a kingdom of persons, he advised. Act always as if the maxim of your action could become a universal law, always treating mankind, as much in your own person as in that of another, as an end, never as a means.[3]

From the study of Kant we moved on to Hegel's *Phenomenology of Mind* and *Science of Logic*, which I found excruciatingly difficult.[4] But I kept struggling with them because at a gut level I sensed that understanding Hegel was the key to the rest of my life. Often I would read and reread passages as if I were listening to a piece of music or poetry, unable to explain what was being said but feeling my humanity expanding and stretching as I read. As a result, when the day came for me to write an exam on Hegel for my M.A., I found myself staring at the blue book before me, unable to write a word. Had Weiss not taken me for a reassuring walk around the campus, I would have given up. To this day I have no idea what I actually wrote down, but it apparently made enough sense so that in 1937 I received my M.A. in philosophy.

Reading and rereading Hegel's *Phenomenology*, I began to understand why my philosophy professors at Barnard had been so unsatisfying. Because their concept of Truth was so static and sterile, they were in love with abstractions. Hegel, on the other hand, believed that the human spirit or "healthy human reason" is constantly evolving through a process of overcoming contradictions or inadequacies. Human beings are constantly struggling to make what they believe to be true, right, and just into a reality in their individual and social lives. Progress does not take place like "a shot out of a pistol." It requires the "labor, patience and suffering of the negative." In everything there is the duality of the positive and the negative. What is important is not any particular idea but the process of continuing development as the contradictions or limitations inherent in any idea surface and require the leap to a new idea or a new stage of Spirit. For Hegel, therefore, the abstract truths cherished by traditional philosophy are actually untrue because they represent ideas from the past that is already behind us.

Hegel helped me to see my own struggle for meaning as part of the continuing struggle of the individual to become a part of the universal struggle for Freedom. Empowered by these ideas, I began to view my unease and restlessness not as a weakness but as a strength, a sign that I was ready to move to a new and higher stage of being.

After receiving my M.A., I searched for a dissertation topic that would challenge me as I had been challenged by Hegel. Meanwhile, I moved off campus, making my living first as a reader in the Department of Philosophy and then as a secretary at the International House in nearby Philadelphia. Then one day in 1939, browsing in the philosophy library, my eye was caught by four bright-blue volumes with gold lettering. They turned out to be the posthumously published works of George Herbert Mead: *The Philosophy of the Act, The Philosophy of the Present, Mind, Self and Society*, and *Movements of Thought in the Nineteenth Century*.[5] It was one of those happy accidents that, in retrospect, seemed necessary if I was to continue to develop.

Until that moment I had never heard of Mead, who was one of the four founders of the distinctively American philosophy of pragmatism, along with John Dewey, William James, and Charles Sanders Peirce. Mead was less well-known, in part, because he was more a teacher than a writer. His lectures were not collected and published in book form until after his death in 1931. But an even more important reason for Mead's obscurity is that in those days pragmatism was not recognized in most philosophy departments as a philosophy because it was too down-to-earth for traditional philosophers. Its proponents challenged the kind of metaphysical speculation that the leisure class of Europe could afford to cultivate. Linking knowing to action, pragmatists asserted that the truth of an idea should be tested by its practical utility. They were more comfortable with the concept of mind as Intelligence than as Reason and had no use for the old dualisms of Fact versus Value, Mind versus Matter, Knowledge versus Action, and Thoughts versus Feeling that European philosophers had been arguing over for centuries. Dewey and Mead especially had little respect for those intellectuals and philosophers who prided themselves on the purity of their ideas, uncontaminated by contact with work or action or feelings. Over the years my dissatisfaction with American schools has been heavily influenced by Dewey's insistence that education be of the hand as well as the head and his allegation that the preoccupation of Western philosophers with the head has its roots in ancient Greece, where manual work was considered inferior because it was done by women and slaves.

Although both Dewey and Mead had been born in the Northeast, they were more Midwesterners than New Englanders. They had taught together at the University of Michigan and then moved to the University of Chicago. Conscious of the growing need for social knowledge, social action, and social change that was being generated by our rapidly developing urban and industrial society, they saw themselves as socialists. Mead had done three years of graduate work in Germany. Dewey came under the influence of Hegel while doing graduate work with the Hegelian G. S. Morris at Johns Hopkins University and did his dissertation on Kant. Both viewed ideas as evolving historically.

In his *Movements of Thought in the Nineteenth Century* Mead explained the connection between the French Revolution and the ideas of Kant and Hegel. Kant, he said, was the "philosopher of the French Revolution" because his "categorical imperative" was a development of Jean-Jacques Rousseau's concept of the "General Will," which projected the vision of every individual in the community seeing himself as a representative not only of himself but as if his will were identical with that of every member of the community. Hegel's dialectical philosophy, he said, reflects the process of continuing struggle. Progress does not take place in a straight line. Even though the French Revolution ended in the dictatorship of Napoleon and the Napoleonic Wars, it advanced society because human beings emerged from the struggles of the period with a heightened sense of themselves and their capacities. In his *Mind, Self and Society* Mead explored the process by which human beings normally and naturally create themselves both as individuals and as social beings through the use of language.

Although I did not know it at the time, Mead prepared me for the next stage in my own development by providing me with (1) a way to look at great ideas in their connection with great leaps forward in history, and (2) an analysis of how the self and society develop in relation to each other. I was so energized by these ideas that I sat down at once to write my thesis on *George Herbert Mead: The Philosopher of the Social Individual.*[6] My father came up with $400 so that I could quit work, and within a few months I had completed my dissertation in time to receive my Ph.D. in June 1940.

In retrospect, it seems clear that what attracted me to Mead was that he gave me what I needed in that period—a body of ideas that challenged and empowered me to move from a life of contemplation to a life of action. It was time for me to return to the concrete for inspiration. Since 1931 I had been living a sheltered existence in the ivory towers of Barnard and Bryn Mawr. I had no idea where I would go or what I would do once I left the university. But my love affair with Hegel had given me a sense of how protracted the struggle would be. Now the ideas of Mead were helping me to move into a world where doing had priority over knowing and where I was confident that my actions as an individual would reflect a social perspective.

After the commencement ceremony at Bryn Mawr in June 1940, I returned to my mother's house in Jackson Heights. I had no plans for the future. It would have been a waste of time for me, a Chinese woman with a Ph.D. in philosophy, to apply to a university for a teaching job. In any case I hadn't studied philosophy in order to teach it. Fortunately, I was able to put off making any major decision for a while because I was having trouble with my back. Some years earlier I had injured it making a three-point goal in a faculty-student basketball game, and a doctor had suggested an operation fusing the sacrum with the ileum. I spent the summer checking that out, finally rejecting the idea when my investigation showed that the operation was effective only 40 percent of the time.

What I wanted to do was to become active. Throughout the 1930s I had been aware of the Depression, the New Deal, and the emergence of the labor movement, but I had not felt the need to act. Now, recognizing how rapidly we were moving toward direct involvement in World War II, and recalling what I had learned about the imperialistic roots of World War I during the Briand Peace Pact march, I started to check out antiwar activities. I had been away at Bryn Mawr for five years and didn't know anyone who could give me a lead. Even when I lived in New York, I had never been to Greenwich Village or Union Square where left-wing groups had their headquarters and debated one another from soapboxes. While I was at Barnard there had been none of the heated confrontations between Stalinists and Trotskyists that I later learned made City College a hotbed of radicalism.

At a loss for where to begin, I sat down and wrote letters to Senators Joseph R. Knowland and Arthur H. Vandenberg who were opposed to involvement in the European war from the isolationist point of view. Then, after looking up the address in the phone book, I decided to go down to the Socialist Party headquarters. It didn't take me long to conclude that I didn't want to join them. After learning that I had a Ph.D. from Bryn Mawr, the young man I spoke to suggested that I speak at one of their upcoming meetings. Groucho Marx said he didn't need to be a member of any club that would have him as a member. In the same spirit I couldn't see myself joining a group that could overlook my obvious ignorance because of my academic credentials. Because of that experience, I have steadfastly refused over the years to identify myself as a Ph.D.

Somehow I learned about a social event being sponsored by the Communist Party. It was the summer of 1940 and Hitler's invasion of the

Soviet Union was still a year away. So the Communists were still antiwar. I didn't stay long at the social. I knew no one and I felt uncomfortable in a room jammed with strangers dancing, drinking, and shouting to be heard above the loud music. It also troubled me to see so many white women circulating through the mixed crowd and asking black men to dance. It made me suspect that the party was using white women to recruit black men. Later in Chicago I would learn about the tensions this was creating among black women in the community. One meeting I attended, for example, broke up when a black woman started knocking over chairs because of the presence of a black man with his white girlfriend. A few years ago I ran into the couple, Lillian and Alan Willis, in San Francisco. They had been married more than forty years.

My sense, although I don't remember discussing it with anyone, was that with the fall of France to the Nazis in June 1940, European civilization had collapsed. I also recalled that although both George Herbert Mead and John Dewey had been born in New England, they developed their distinctively American philosophy of pragmatism in Chicago. So thinking of my own New England roots, I decided to go to Chicago, which, seen through Carl Sandburg's eyes, was the opposite of European decadence:

> Hog Butcher for the World,
> Tool maker, Stacker of Wheat,
> Player with Railroads and the Nation's Freight Handler,
> Stormy, husky, brawling.
> City of the Big Shoulders.[7]

In the fall of 1940, with only a few dollars in my pocket and a suitcase containing a change of clothing and some books, I took the train to Chicago. I had no friends or relatives there. The only person with whom I had had any correspondence was Charles Morris, the University of Chicago professor who had edited and written introductions to Mead's works.

In Chicago I went door to door, looking for a room in the neighborhood of the university. At that time many homeowners were making ends meet by renting out rooms for about $2.50 a week. My mother was getting ready to do that in our Jackson Heights home. At every house I was told that they didn't rent to Orientals or that the room was already rented, which amounted to the same thing. Finally, when I was almost ready to give up, a little Jewish woman on South Ellis Avenue took pity on me. There was a couch in her basement, she said, and I could stay there for no rent. I leapt at the opportunity, even though the basement was damp and my space was separated only by a barricade of old doors from the huge coal furnace, which a black handyman checked every morning. I opened up a panel in one of the doors so that I could hand him a cup of coffee on his arrival. Like me, he had to face down a lineup of rats each time he entered the basement.

The day after my arrival I went to see Professor Morris, who helped me get a job in the philosophy library of the University for $10 a week. That is what I lived on for the next year and a half. It meant going without what we today consider necessities, like a refrigerator or a car. I wore the same blue corduroy jumper and saddle oxfords until it became a kind of uniform (worn under my leopard coat during the blustery winters). But you could ride the street car for a nickel or dime, and a glass of beer cost a nickel. Five hundred dollars a year seems like peanuts today but in those days the income of the average American was only $1000 a year, and I was young, in good health, and living rent free. I don't mean to romanticize poverty, but living simply gives you a freedom to make life choices that is lost when you begin to think you need everything that is for sale.

Having found a place to live and a job, I began to look around for opportunities for action. One day, walking through the hall of one of the university buildings, I happened on a meeting in a classroom where students were being asked to get involved in the struggle against rat-infested housing in the neighborhood. I signed up immediately and was soon busy with the group, calling itself the South Side Tenants Organization set up by the Workers Party, a small Trotskyist group that had split off from the Socialist Workers Party.

Working with the South Side Tenants Organization was an eye-opener for me. For the first time I was talking with people in the black community, getting a sense of what segregation and discrimination meant in people's lives, learning how to organize protest demonstrations and meetings. Up to that time I had had practically no contact with black people. There had been no blacks at Barnard. At Bryn Mawr there was one black graduate student, a French-speaking woman from Haiti. I still remember her name, Madelaine Sylvain, although I can't remember ever having had a conversation with her. I had had some experiences with racial discrimination, especially in trying to rent a room or an apartment. My most instructive experience was in the middle 1930s en route by train from Ohio to New York. I was sitting in a regular coach as we crossed the Ohio River, which at that point demarcates the Mason-Dixon line, when the conductor approached and asked me to move to the Jim Crow car. Later he returned and said that he had made a mistake and that I could move back, which I decided not to do. I have never forgotten that incident, because it brought home to me the qualitative difference between the discrimination Asians experience and the slavery and legalized brutality that blacks have endured for centuries. In 1932, as a freshman at Barnard, I had participated in a weeklong conference at Silver Bay near Lake George during which I had gotten some idea of the injustice of racial segregation and discrimination in the United States from Ira Reid of the Urban League. One Thanksgiving I invited a Korean doctor whom I had met at the International House in Philadelphia to have dinner with my mother and me in my Bryn Mawr apartment. During dinner he began making typically racist remarks about his Negro patients at the county hospital. When he continued despite my admonitions, I gave him his hat and showed him the door. But that had been the extent of my militancy. I had never intervened at my father's restaurant when headwaiters escorted the few black customers to corner booths. In 1951, during a layover at the Lexington, Kentucky, airport, I was refused service at the lunch counter and told to go to the back. I can still remember how scared, alone, and confused I felt until I decided to sit down in the space set aside for "Colored" to await the departure of my plane to California.

The Workers Party comrades invited me to go with them to Washington Park not far from the University of Chicago. It was where blacks from Chicago's South Side congregated. For that reason it was also where all the radical groups—Communists, Trotskyists, and others with only a handful of members—came to promote their ideas. Most of the time the blacks didn't even look up as radical speakers addressed them from their various soapboxes, in part because what was presumably being addressed to the people in the community actually had more to do with their differences and disputes with one another. But when I got up to speak some people would come around, mainly because as a Chinese woman I was a novelty and they were curious about where I had come from and what I thought. Their willingness to listen made me very conscious of how little I had to say.

The more I went out in the community and met people, the more inadequate I was beginning to feel. For example, in preparation for a big protest meeting, I was assigned to ask Horace Cayton, a well-known local black leader, to be our main speaker. A few years later Cayton coauthored the classic study *Black Metropolis* with St. Clair Drake.[8] He said that he couldn't be at the meeting but that we could use one of his speeches if I was the one who read it. It was a huge meeting, about a thousand people. Because I was moved by the speech, I presented it in a very moving way. As a result, at the end of the speech it seemed as if people were ready to follow me in a mass march downtown. It scared the living daylights out of me. Just out of university and getting my toes wet in radical politics, what did I know about leading masses of people? I was especially sensitive on the question because I had recently read an article saying that the reason why the French Communist Party was able to recruit so many intellectuals was that it gave them a mass audience and thus helped them overcome their alienation and isolation from the masses. I resolved to avoid speaking at mass meetings until I was a lot better informed.

Around this time black labor leader A. Phillip Randolph issued a call for blacks all over the country to march on Washington to demand jobs in the defense plants. The factories were booming, he said, and white workers were back at work. The Depression had ended for whites. Yet because of Jim Crow discrimination, blacks were still unemployed. "Only power can effect the enforcement and adoption of a given policy," Randolph proclaimed. "Power is the active principle of only the organized masses, the masses united for definite purpose."[9] His speech was a forerunner of the Black Power movement, which in the 1960s would electrify the country.

The response to Randolph's call exceeded all expectations. Overnight people who had been sitting listlessly under the trees in Washington Park and turning a deaf ear to radical agitation were galvanized by hope for a better future. By the hundreds and thousands they began attending meetings, testifying to their bitterness and frustration at the injustice of being jobless when the defense plants were begging for workers, getting ready to march on Washington. I remember particularly the response of Mary Harris, a young prostitute whom I had met in Washington Park. "I'm going home to iron my clothes to go to Washington," she told me.

All over the country, the momentum for the march was building. March on Washington headquarters were opened up in Harlem and Brooklyn in New York, and in Washington, D.C., Pittsburgh, Detroit, Chicago, St. Louis, and San Francisco. In January 1941 Randolph had called for ten thousand people to descend on Washington on July 1. By May people were talking about fifty thousand and even a hundred thousand marchers. There was practically nothing about the upcoming march in the mainstream press, but President Franklin D. Roosevelt was very conscious of the national and international embarrassment that a mass march on Washington would cause the United States at a time when he was getting the nation ready for a war against racist Germany. Even Eleanor Roosevelt, who had distinguished herself by bringing black suffering to the nation's attention, joined the administration's efforts to persuade Randolph to call off the march. Sidney Hillman, Roosevelt's conduit to labor, promised Randolph that there would be a radical change in the treatment of blacks. He was sending letters to defense contractors asking them not to discriminate, he said. But Randolph had learned from his many years of experience in struggle, and especially from his defeats and successes in organizing the Brotherhood of Sleeping Car Porters, that promises are cheap. Under enormous pressure he refused to call off the march, and one week before it was to take place President Roosevelt, having met his match, issued Executive Order 8802, banning racial discrimination in the defense industry.

American society was transformed as a result of the March on Washington movement. All over the nation blacks moved from the countryside to cities to take the newly opened-up jobs in industrial plants. Cities in the North became the Promised Land for southern blacks, precipitating the biggest migration of blacks in American history. For the first time in four hundred years black men could bring home a regular paycheck and see themselves as the head of the household. Black women as well as men were able to work on jobs for enough money and with enough security that they could buy homes and send their children to college. In turn, these children in the 1960s were the ones who guaranteed the success of the civil rights movement by organizing the Student Non-Violent Coordinating Committee. Throughout World War II the black community continued to exert pressure on the government and on industry, carrying on what was officially called the "Double V for Victory" but that most people I knew called "Double D for Democracy" at home and abroad.

Some people describe the March on Washington as "aborted." That was essentially my view at the time, which I expressed in an article for *The New International,* the Workers Party theoretical magazine, written under the name Ria Stone.[10] In fact, the movement not only transformed American society but taught me lessons that have shaped my activities ever since. From the March on Washington movement I learned that a movement begins when large numbers of people, having reached the point where they feel they can't take the way things are any longer, find hope for improving their daily lives in an action that they can take together. I also discovered the power that the black community has within itself to change this country when it begins to move. As a result, I decided that what I wanted to do with the rest of my life was to become a movement activist in the black community.

How to go about becoming that I had no idea. Joining the Workers Party seemed a good way to start since it was through the party that I had made contact with the black community. I assumed that the party would provide me with the political education that I needed to overcome my ignorance. It didn't trouble me that it was a Trotskyist party. Trotsky was little more than a name to me. I knew that he had led a worldwide opposition to Stalin's purges of Soviet dissidents and that he had been assassinated in Mexico recently, allegedly by an agent of Stalin. It had made headline news in *The New York Times*. I vaguely recalled the Commission to Investigate the Moscow Trials, headed by John Dewey, which the Trotskyists had initiated in the 1930s. But I had not been emotionally involved in the conflicts between the Stalinists and Trotskyists in the United States. In Washington Park I had paid about as much attention to their heated polemics as the picnickers from the black community.

To my surprise joining the party did not entail any elaborate procedures. All I had to do was say that I wanted to become a member. There was no orientation, no signing of any application forms. Beyond some minor dues payment, I wasn't asked to make any commitment. Getting a driver's license was more demanding.

The Chicago Local was made up of two small branches, one on the South Side and the other on the Northwest Side. In each branch there were six to seven members, all white. I soon discovered that the two branches did not get along. According to the comrades in the South Side branch, of which I became a member, the comrades on the Northwest Side were only interested in political debate, not in community activity. No one made any effort to educate me politically beyond recommending that I read Trotsky's *History of the Russian Revolution* and some pamphlets by Karl Marx. The comrades either didn't think it was necessary to give me a sense of the party's history or didn't know how to do it. No one talked to me about Trotsky, Lenin, or Marx.

I didn't have much in common with my new comrades. We never got together except for the organizing work and branch meetings, which consisted of two parts—one in which we discussed the organizing work we were doing in the community, and the other devoted to political discussion, either of current events or of the political debate going on in the national organization. I found nothing stimulating in the meetings and nothing particularly interesting about the comrades. I had a feeling that they didn't know what to do with me, that I was as strange to them as they were to me. Max Shachtman, the party leader (Workers Party members were known as Shachtmanites), came to town once for a speech. I don't remember what he talked about. All I recall is that he reminded me of the fast-talking New Yorkers against whom my father had warned us when we moved to the Big Apple from tiny Providence. When we went out to eat after the meeting, he and the Chicago comrades exchanged "in" stories and jokes.

I probably would have drifted away from the Workers Party and started looking elsewhere for my political development had it not been that Martin Abern, a member of the national committee of the party, came to Chicago around this time to help the two branches resolve their differences. A party functionary being paid $15 a week with a lot of time on his hands, Marty decided to use this time to share with me his experiences over two decades in the radical movement. Born in Eastern Europe, he had been a member of the American Socialist Party during World War I, spending time in prison for his opposition to the war. After the Russian Revolution he was among those who split from the Socialist Party to join the Communist Party. In 1923 as the national secretary of the Young Workers League (YWL) and the youngest member of the Communist Party Central Committee, he had been responsible for bringing Max Shachtman to Chicago to take over his role as YWL leader. In 1927, with James P. Cannon and Shachtman, he had been a leader of the International Labor Defense, which organized the defense of Sacco and Vanzetti. In 1928, after being expelled from the Communist Party along with Cannon, Shachtman, and about a hundred others for their defense of Trotsky, he helped organize the group known as the Communist League of America (Opposition) because of its opposition to Stalin's policies.

During the 1930s Abern had been a leading player in the many maneuvers and mergers by which the Trotskyists tried to develop themselves into a force to compete with the Communist Party for leadership of the workers nationally and internationally. These included a merger in 1934 with the American Workers Party, led by pacifist preacher A. J. Muste, to form the Workers Party. It was followed by the entry of the Workers Party into the Socialist Party two years later in what was known as the French Turn because it was patterned on a similar move proposed by Trotsky for the French group. The rationale was that as a result of the Depression, the Spanish Civil War, and the rise of Hitler, a left-leaning tendency was developing within the socialist parties that was producing potential recruits to Trotskyism. With these recruits the Socialist Workers Party was formed in 1938. Because each of these moves was supported by some and resisted by others, they entailed countless meetings and debates, causing strained relationships, shifting alignments, and splinter groups. For example, a new group, known as the Ohlerites because it was led by Hugo Ohler, was created by those who opposed the French Turn. Out of each move the Trotskyists lost a few members but gained a few dozen or a few hundred, until by the late 1930s the national membership was probably about one thousand. This was ten times the number who had been expelled from the

Communist International in 1928, but it was still no serious rival to the American Communist Party with its tens of thousands of members.

Throughout the 1930s Trotsky and his followers had been harshly critical of the Soviet Union both for its domestic policies and for the role that the Communist International played in revolutionary struggles around the world, in China, Spain, and so on. But they had always defended the Soviet Union as a workers' state because the Russian Revolution had nationalized the economy, removing one-sixth of the world from the capitalist orbit. However, with the invasion of Finland by the Soviet Union in 1938 and the Stalin-Hitler Pact in 1939, defense of the Soviet Union was no longer an abstract question. As a result, the Socialist Workers Party split almost in half. The majority, led by James P. Cannon, followed Trotsky in maintaining the need to support the Soviet Union unconditionally as a "degenerated workers' state." The minority, led by Max Shachtman and including Marty Abern and C. L. R. James, having concluded that they could no longer defend the Soviet Union and that the radical movement needed a serious reexamination of what constituted a workers' state, organized themselves into the Workers Party.

I found Marty's stories fascinating. I recognized that it was an extraordinary privilege for a young person like me to be receiving an account of such a critical period in the history of the radical movement in the United States from one of its leading participants. His stories about the foibles of leaders like Cannon and Shachtman were also refreshing, saving me from the pitfall of leadership worship lying in wait for new recruits. But Marty had always been an organizer rather than a theoretician. He was a storehouse of information,[11] but his stories were mainly about schemes and maneuvers and personalities, not the development of ideas. The more he told me about what had transpired in the past, the more I began to suspect that the era I was being introduced to was already over. I sensed that although he was only in his midforties, Marty Abern had been burned out by the internal struggles that had constituted his life for more than twenty years and that one of the main reasons he was spending so much time with me was that he needed an infusion of new energy. This became obvious when what was for me a relatively casual affair became an obsession for him, forcing me to break off all contact.

The lack of spirit in the Chicago comrades was also troubling. Even though they were longtime residents of the city and had been in the organization for years, they knew as little about the black community and the history of black struggle as I did. I began to wonder whether our paths had intersected at a time when we were moving in different directions, when they were on their way out of a movement that I was just entering. We had no social ties in common, and I lost touch with them after I left for New York in 1942, so I have no idea what happened to them. Before I left, two comrades had already resigned because they disagreed with the party's decision not to support the war after the Japanese bombing of Pearl Harbor on December 7, 1941.

Despite my growing suspicions that my new comrades represented the past rather than the future, the Workers Party's decision to oppose World War II reassured me that I was in the right organization. My main reason for remaining in the party, however, was that I had met C. L. R. James when he stopped in Chicago to talk to the comrades on his way back from organizing sharecroppers in southeast Missouri. Tall, black, and strikingly handsome, C. L. R. was everything that the Chicago branch was not. He was bursting with enthusiasm about the potential for an American revolution inherent in the emergence of the labor movement and the escalating militancy of blacks. When together with another comrade I met him at the train station, he was carrying two thick books, volume 1 of Marx's *Capital* and Hegel's *Science of Logic*, both heavily underlined. When he discovered that I had studied Hegel and knew German, we withdrew to my basement room where we spent hours sitting on my old red couch comparing passages in Marx and Hegel, checking the English against the original German. It was the beginning of a theoretical and practical collaboration that lasted twenty years, until we went our separate ways in 1962.

3
C. L. R. James

Working with C. L. R. James during the years he spent in the United States was more exciting intellectually than anything I had known at Barnard or even at Bryn Mawr with Paul Weiss. James had a special gift for making ideas come alive. He helped you to see how ideas that matter are created by individuals in particular historical circumstances to explain or to cope with their conditions of life. So whether or not you were an intellectual, you felt that when you participated in a demonstration or asked probing questions about life and society, you were helping to create important ideas. History as he told and interpreted it became a weapon in the ongoing struggle because he openly and unabashedly studied the past with a view to creating the future. Thus, as he put it, he wrote his book on the San Domingo Revolution in 1938 in order "to stimulate the coming emancipation of Africa."[1] For CLR[2] the "groundlings" in Shakespeare's audiences, the Levellers and Diggers in the seventeenth-century English Revolution, the sansculottes in the French Revolution, the African American slaves who brought on the Civil War by rebelling and running away—all were forerunners of today's revolutionary social forces. By studying and making known how these early activists organized themselves, the revolutionary historian can inspire and strengthen those at the bottom of our society in their ongoing struggle to change things from the way they are to the way they ought to be.

At the same time, CLR emphasized the importance of combining practical struggles with continuing exploration of the most profound philosophical questions because reality is constantly changing and we must be wary of becoming stuck in ideas that have come out of past experiences and have lost their usefulness in the struggle to create the future. So over the years I have always kept my ears close to the ground, testing ideas in practice and listening closely to the grass roots for new questions that require new paradigms. As a result, new unforeseen contradictions have challenged rather than discouraged me, and I have never felt burned out.

CLR was born in Tunapuna, Trinidad, in 1901. His father was a schoolteacher and his mother an avid reader of English and American novels—Shakespeare, Thackeray, Dickens, Scott, Charlotte Brontë, Hawthorne, among others. His bedroom window overlooked the Tunapuna cricket field. With this background he grew up both a voracious reader and a cricket enthusiast. After graduating from Queens Royal College, the government secondary school modeled on the British public school, he became a teacher at the college where one of his pupils was Eric Williams, later the Prime Minister of Trinidad and Tobago.

In those days West Indians who needed a wider range for their talents went to England. CLR took this step in 1932, taking with him the manuscript of his recently completed *The Case for West Indian Self-Government*. In London he was prodigiously productive. In six and a half years he wrote *Minty Alley*, a novel of West Indian backyard life as seen by a black middle-class intellectual like himself; *World Revolution, 1917–1936: The Rise and Fall of the Communist International*; *Toussaint L'Ouverture*, a play starring Paul Robeson in the title role; *The History of Negro Revolt*; and *The Black Jacobins*, probably his best-known work. He also translated *Stalin* by Boris Souveraine from the French.[3]

At the same time he was politically active in a small Marxist group organized around the ideas of Trotsky. After the Italian invasion of Ethiopia he organized and became the chief spokesman for the International African Friends of Ethiopia. This group later became the International African Service Bureau, led by CLR's childhood friend George Padmore. In the 1920s Padmore had gone to Moscow to work with the Communist International in organizing anticolonial struggles for independence in Africa but left for London in 1935 when the Soviet policy of cooperating with the Western democracies (the Popular Front period) meant decreased support by the Soviets for these struggles. For a quarter of a century, between 1935 and his death in 1959, Padmore trained a whole generation of future African leaders, including Jomo Kenyatta of Kenya and Kwame Nkrumah of Ghana.

CLR's wide-ranging activities and his impact on radicals and liberals in London during these years have been captured in this passage from a book by his publisher, Frederic Warburg. CLR loved the passage and enjoyed reading it aloud to friends:

> Despite the atmosphere of hate and arid dispute in his writings James himself was one of the most delightful and easy-going personalities I have known, colourful in more senses than one. A dark-skinned West Indian negro [*sic*] from Trinidad, he stood six feet three in his socks and was noticeably good-looking. His memory was extraordinary. He could quote, not only passages from the Marxist classics but long extracts from Shakespeare, in a soft lilting English which was a delight to hear. Immensely amiable, he loved the fleshpots of capitalism, fine cooking, fine clothes, fine furniture and beautiful women, without a trace of the guilty remorse to be expected from a seasoned warrior of the class war. He was brave. Night after night he would address meetings in London and the provinces, denouncing the crimes of the blood-thirsty Stalin, until he was hoarse and his wonderful voice a mere croaking in the throat. The communists who heckled him would have torn him limb from limb, had it not been for the ubiquity of the police and their insensitivity to propaganda of whatever hue. . . .
>
> If politics was his religion and Marx his god, if literature was his passion and Shakespeare his prince among writers, cricket was his beloved activity. He wrote splendid articles on county matches for the *Manchester Guardian* during the summer. Indeed it was only between April and October that he was in funds. Sometimes he came for the weekend to our cottage near West Hoathly in Sussex and turned out for the local team. He was a demon bowler and a powerful if erratic batsman. The village loved him, referring to him affectionately as "the black bastard." In Sussex politics were forgotten. Instead, I can hear today the opening words of *Twelfth Night*, delivered beautifully from his full sensitive lips. "If music be the food of love, play on, give me excess of it." Excess, perhaps, was James' crime, an excess of words whose relevance to the contemporary tragedy was less than he supposed.[4]

In 1938 Socialist Workers Party leader James P. Cannon met CLR at a Trotskyist conference in Europe and invited him to visit the United States in order to give members a sense of what was happening in Europe and at the same time help the party develop a position on the Negro struggle. In the United States CLR was even more productive than he had been in England. England had provided an outlet for his huge talents, but the

United States immeasurably enlarged his view of revolution. In his own words, "I experienced a sense of expansion which has permanently altered my attitude to the world."[5] He was amazed by the zest and confidence with which individual Americans pursued both individual happiness and community. Arriving in the United States as the Congress of Industrial Organizations (CIO) was being organized, he saw the sit-in strikes that built the union as a sign of both the American passion for community and the prescience of Karl Marx. He was always quoting the passage in *Capital* where Marx describes "the revolt of the working class, a class always increasing in numbers and disciplined, united, organized by the very mechanism of the process of capitalist production itself."[6] To him it was almost a prescription for the sit-down by the auto workers at the General Motors plant in Flint, Michigan, in 1937.

In the United States, however, CLR's creativity had to take a different form. Admitted on a visitor's visa, he could not agitate in public as he had done in England. So for more than a decade he poured his prodigious energies into the internal struggles in the Trotskyist movement *and* into his courtship of Constance Webb, a woman of southern parentage who was eighteen when they met in California on his first nationwide speaking tour in 1938. They were finally married in 1948 and separated in 1951. The courtship was carried out mainly through handwritten letters, many of them thousands of words long, discussing not only personal matters but a wide range of subjects, including Michelangelo, Shakespeare, Shelley, Marx, Lenin, life in the West Indies, and American movies and comic strips. As interest in CLR has grown in recent years, these letters have become a treasure trove for scholars and voyeurs.[7]

Between 1938 and 1953, when CLR returned to London, he maintained apartments in Harlem, the East Bronx, the Lower East Side, and Greenwich Village but spent much of his time at 629 Hudson Street in Greenwich Village, not far from 14th Street and University Place, where most of the radical groups had their headquarters. Six-twenty-nine Hudson Street was the home of Workers Party members Freddy and Lyman Paine. Lyman, a Harvard graduate and prizewinning architect, was a descendant of Robert Treat Paine, one of the signers of the Declaration of Independence. Freddy, a self-educated and street-smart labor organizer, had been in the radical movement ever since she joined A. J. Muste's American Workers Party in the early 1930s. Together, Freddy and Lyman had a genius for hosting small gatherings where people from many different walks of life could eat, drink, hold far-reaching conversations, and listen to the music of Louis Armstrong or Beethoven. CLR, who had a somewhat peculiar view of the relationship between his political and his personal lives, shared with Freddy the trials and tribulations of his courtship of Constance and some of the correspondence.

I attended my first Workers Party convention in 1942, coming in from Chicago. It was a strange and bewildering experience to be in a hall on the Lower East Side of New York City with several hundred people, most of whom seemed to be Jewish and all of whom seemed to know each other. People were caucusing all over the place. The main bone of contention was the nature of the Soviet Union or what was called the "Russian Question." At only one point did I feel at home—when two sharecroppers from southeast Missouri were introduced to thunderous applause.

The Russian Question did not particularly engage me, because unlike those who had been around since the 1920s and 1930s I had been drawn to the radical movement—not by the Russian Revolution but by the black struggle. On the one hand, most party members were still struggling with how to understand and relate to the Soviet Union, which had been created by the first successful socialist revolution but had since purged many of the revolution's leaders, invaded Finland, signed the Stalin-Hitler Pact, and was now allied with the Western imperialist powers. On the other hand, during the Great Depression when millions of unemployed walked the streets in capitalist America, ill-fed, ill-clothed, and ill-housed, Soviet workers had enjoyed full employment because property there was nationalized. The bodies of these comrades were in the United States, but like Trotsky their hearts and minds were preoccupied with what was happening in the Soviet Union. I was not really a Trotskyist. I had been moved by his history of the Russian Revolution because it described so eloquently the movement of masses and their impact on leaders, but I had not been shaped by the hopes aroused by the Russian Revolution or by the heated debates that Stalinists and Trotskyists had carried on for years over Soviet policies at home and abroad. Actually I found most of Trotsky's writings boring. They struck me as essentially polemics against Stalin and the Communist Party over strategy and tactics for situations in the Soviet Union and other countries in Europe that were before my time and already behind us.

Inside the parties affiliated with the Communist International there was no debate on the Soviet Union. You toed the party line or you were expelled. The Trotskyist groups, on the other hand, prided themselves on their internal democracy. They had split from the Communist Party not only because they were outraged by the actions of Stalin but because these could not be questioned or discussed in the party. Now, confronted with the Soviet invasion of Finland and the signing of the pact with Hitler, they were also faced with the theoretical question of the nature of the Soviet Union. There were three options: (1) either state ownership of the means of production or nationalization made the Soviet Union a workers' state; or (2) nationalization made it a new formation, neither capitalist nor socialist; or (3) it was a form of state capitalism where, even though property was publicly owned, production took place in accordance with the laws of capitalist accumulation. Trotsky and the Socialist Workers Party stuck to the first position. The majority of the newly formed Workers Party, led by Shachtman, chose the second, calling the new formation "bureaucratic collectivism." CLR espoused the third. He was joined by Raya Dunayevskaya, a Russian-born and self-educated comrade who had been a radical since she was a child in the 1920s. In those days most radical party members went by pseudonyms, a holdover from the 1920s when the Communist Party was driven virtually underground. CLR's party name was J. R. Johnson; Raya's was Freddie Forest. Their agreement on this and later questions led to the creation of the Johnson-Forest Tendency whose members were known as Johnsonites. My party name, given to me by Marty Abern, was Ria Stone.

I was attracted to the state capitalist position because its proponents, tracing Marx's views back to their roots in Hegelianism, viewed socialist revolution as the release of the "natural and acquired powers" of workers rather than in terms of property relations. When Marx turned Hegel "right side up," they insisted, he didn't abandon Hegel's vision of the continuing evolution of humanity toward greater self-determination or the ability to assume greater control over our lives. He was extending its application beyond intellectuals to workers in production. The crime of capitalism, according to the Johnsonites, is that it denies this self-activity and self-determination to the worker in production, mutilates the laborer into a fragment of a man, degrades him to the level of the appendage of a machine. This alienation or estrangement from our human essence is what creates the antagonism of the worker to capitalism, "be his payment high or low."[8]

At the convention I discovered that radicals use the writings of Marx, Lenin, and Trotsky in much the same way that Christians use the Bible. Proponents of opposing positions had no difficulty in finding quotation from the masters to support their particular stands. This was not surprising since the views of Marx, Lenin, and Trotsky, like those of all great leaders, had not been monolithic. At different stages in their development, under differing circumstances, they had said contradictory things. Some of

Marx's projections are very mechanistic, as, for example, when he writes that "capitalistic production begets, with the inexorability of a law of Nature, its own negation."[9] On the other hand, the Marx I love to quote is the humanist prophet who in the *Communist Manifesto* warns,

> Constant revolutionizing of production, uninterrupted disturbance of all social conditions, everlasting uncertainty and agitation distinguish the bourgeois epoch from all earlier ones. All fixed, fast-frozen relations, with their train of ancient and venerable prejudices and opinions, are swept away, all new-formed ones become antiquated before they can ossify. All that is solid melts into air, all that is holy is profaned, and man is at last compelled to face with sober senses his real conditions of life and his relations with his kind.[10]

The debate on the Russian Question provided me with the incentive to read Marx and Lenin for myself. Incredible as it may seem to those who have gone to college within the past thirty years, I had gone through nine years of university without reading either one of them.

To study Marx and Lenin and to work with CLR I moved back to New York after the Workers Party convention. For a while I lived in my mother's house in Jackson Heights. Later, when she began renting out rooms, I rented apartments in different parts of the city. In the 1940s you could live in New York for very little money. The monthly rent for an apartment was a fraction of what you would have to pay today for just one night. Of course, wages were also very low. I started out by renting a room with a bath and tiny kitchen on 114th Street near Broadway for $15 a week. Then for three years, from 1948 to 1951, I lived in a fifth-floor, walk-up, cold-water flat with the bathtub in the kitchen. It was in an old tenement on Orchard Street on the Lower East side and cost me $20 a month. Today, that same apartment probably rents for twenty times that much. For a while my brother Harry and his wife, Julie, lived in the apartment across the hall. When they moved to Detroit, CLR, Constance, and their infant son took over their place, but it was too depressing for them and they soon moved to Greenwich Village. It was also getting me down. To enter and leave the building I had to get past the gypsies living on the first floor who pulled at my clothes in an effort to persuade me to pay them to tell my fortune. When I finally reached my fifth-floor apartment, I could hear the mice rattling in the walls day and night. I remember one night in particular when I spent more than an hour on my hands and knees trying to capture a mouse whose tail had been caught in a trap I had set. It was clip-clopping all over the place, slipping and sliding under desks, bookcases, and papers so that I couldn't get at it. To avoid a repeat of that humiliating experience, I bought a newly invented mouse-catching contraption from a door-to-door salesman. Made of tin, it was about the size and shape of a bread box in which you placed rice to lure the mice. But then you had to drown the critters to kill them! That, I can testify, is much easier said than done.

Fortunately, around that time I got a call from Adelaide Schulkind of the League for Mutual Aid, an organization that lent radicals small sums to tide them over crises, informing me of a job as secretary to James McDonald, the first U.S. ambassador to Israel. The job was in an office on the fifty-ninth floor of the Empire State Building, starting at $60 a week, which he later raised to $100. It was more money than I had ever made. All I had to do was arrange McDonald's speaking schedule. He was out of town most of the time, and I could read, write, and and hold meetings with comrades during working hours in the office. Making all that money, I was able to leave Orchard Street in 1951 and move to a basement apartment on East 17th Street in Gramercy Park where another comrade and I shared two huge rooms for $50 each or $100 a month. It was a much pleasanter neighborhood, but I wasn't happy about the field mice who popped up through holes in the floor. So I found another place on West 19th Street near Ninth Avenue for $60 a month. When I left New York in 1953, Constance, who by this time had separated from CLR, took over my apartment.

In the 1940s and 1950s transportation around the city was inexpensive, convenient, and safe. Subway fare was still only a nickel, and there were so many people traveling at all times that I thought nothing of traveling home by subway late at night to Jackson Heights or Orchard Street after working all day with CLR in the Bronx, Harlem, or at 629 Hudson Street. In the 1940s I supported myself by working part-time in my father's restaurant and/or doing secretarial work as a Kelly girl. For a brief period in 1945 I worked in a defense plant wiring and soldering small electrical parts for sixty cents an hour, which netted me about $20 a week.

Living in New York and working with the Johnson-Forest Tendency inside the Workers Party opened me up to a whole new world of people, ideas, and activity. I visited the Schomburg Collection in Harlem and read Amy Garvey's compilation of her husband's philosophy and opinions. It was exciting to discover that Marcus Garvey's Back to Africa movement had been inspired in part by the Russian Revolution. Lenin, said Garvey, had seized the opportunity of the crisis of the Western powers caused by World War I to make the October Revolution. People of African descent scattered all over the world, he thought, should follow Lenin's example and exploit the postwar crisis to recover Africa for themselves. The Workers Party had organized an Interracial Club with an office on 125th Street in Harlem where we held regular forums. They were chaired by Lyman Paine, who took the name of Tom Brown. After meetings we would go to the Apollo Theater, the Savoy (where I heard Count Basie one night), or Small's Paradise. Connie Williams, a West Indian friend of CLR's, owned a calypso restaurant in the Village where James Baldwin and Richard Wright hung out. Another West Indian friend, Beryl McBurnie, was a dancer who at one time played a leading role in a show at the Copacabana on 52nd Street and Broadway, where Carmen Miranda often performed. Pearl Primus, who danced at the Village Vanguard, was a friend of Freddy's. Katharine Dunham, one of the founders of the ethnic dance movement, invited me to give a class in philosophy to her dance company. But my own ideas were changing so rapidly in my new milieu that I couldn't imagine myself teaching anybody anything. A regular visitor at 629 Hudson Street was Henry Pelham, an elderly black worker. He kept us in touch with the rumblings in Harlem, which he expected to erupt into a full-scale rebellion at any time. The workers who wired and soldered electrical parts with me in the plant were mainly young black women. Before the war most of them had only done domestic work. Now they came into work every day laughing and joking, not only because they were looking forward to the security of a check at the end of the week but because it was exciting to work with modern machinery and to be producing goods that you felt would help your country win the war. On weekends we would get together and party.

Life in New York and all over the United States was exhilarating during World War II. It was a transcending time. The insecurity and despair of the Depression years had been replaced by full employment and a sense of common purpose and hope for a better future. People had been torn from their traditional moorings to fight in the armed services or to work in defense plants. Fourteen million men and women from all walks of life and from all over the country had been thrust overnight into close relationships in army camps in the South, on battleships and destroyers, in European trenches, and on the beaches of Pacific islands. Irrespective of their former occupations, they

> found themselves assigned to function not only in combat but in transport, ordnance, office and hospital. A farmboy was transformed into a signal corps specialist, a clerk in a shoe store became a combat medic among whose functions was the administration of morphine or plasma to the wounded in accordance with his judgment of the nature of their injuries and the possi-

> bility of their recovery. All this was part of the routine experience of every enlisted man. And equally routine but more dramatic was the expendability of any one of them.[11]

The armed services were segregated. But because of the March on Washington movement Americans of all ethnic groups worked side by side in the defense plants. Women left their kitchens and offices to work on the assembly lines. Radicals and intellectuals seized the opportunity to become "proletarianized." So the workforce became a new mix of whites, blacks, Latinos, and Asians, women and men, ex-farmers, intellectuals, and radicals, each with their own experiences and their own views of what was going on in the world. People from different backgrounds exchanged stories of where they had come from and how they viewed their lives, lent each other books, went bowling and drinking after work. The plant was like one big school. This was the first time in U.S. history that racial, educational, sex, class, and age barriers had ever been broken down to such a degree.

Because corporations in the defense industry were guaranteed profits after cost through what were known as cost-plus contracts, plant managers did not bear down on workers to produce and were in fact notoriously wasteful and inefficient. The demand for workers was so great that you could quit a job in the morning and be hired in at another plant in the afternoon. There were abundant opportunities for socializing. In some plants during hunting season workers thought nothing of bringing in a bear or deer to roast and share. In my plant in Brooklyn, we conducted Negro history study groups during our coffee breaks, straggling back to our places after the bell rang. There was so much we had to learn from each other. Lyman, who had left his architectural job to work in the shipyards, spent hours night after night talking with his workmate, Whitey, who had a high school education.

The war opened up the possibility not only of new relationships between Americans of different social and ethnic backgrounds but also for reorganizing production on a more human basis, building on the recognition of the dignity of labor that had been won by the labor movement during the 1930s and the conviviality of the war years. Working in the plant became more attractive than it had ever been. Thus, after they returned from serving in the army my two younger brothers, Harry and Eddie, decided to leave New York and go to Detroit to work in the factory as members of the Johnson-Forest Tendency.

The 1940s had begun with Wendell Willkie's concept of "One World." But at the beginning of the war most of us knew very little about the world outside our own city and sometimes our own neighborhood. Lyman Paine was the only one among us who had ever been to Europe. Nowadays high school students in the inner city — and sometimes even elementary and middle school students — go on trips to France, Italy, Spain, Japan, China, the Caribbean, Africa, and Latin America. In my day some students at the more elite colleges spent their junior year abroad in Europe, but no one with whom I associated at Barnard ever considered doing this. During the war years most of us received letters from our friends and family members serving in Europe and the Far East. At home we were reading about what was taking place in Europe and Asia. But we didn't know enough about the political situation abroad to discuss what was taking place, let alone future perspectives. CLR shared with us his knowledge of European history and gave us an insight into what was happening, focusing especially on how the Resistance movement against Nazism was expanding and creating the foundation for a Socialist United States of Europe.

The Workers Party was also transformed by the war. Most members who were not in the armed services worked in the plant. Party debates began to center on what was taking place in the United States rather than in the Soviet Union or Spain or Nazi Germany. One of the most important debates was over how to relate to the black struggle. American radicals have always had difficulties with this question. The participation of American blacks was obviously critical to a revolution in the United States. But because the radical parties were founded on the conviction that the working class is the leader of all the oppressed in the struggle against capitalism and because their overwhelmingly white membership saw the working class as white, they could not figure out what role blacks would play. That is why the black struggle began to be referred to in the radical movement as "the Negro Question," which some blacks found offensive and others hilarious.

The Negro Question included the following issues: Should blacks be viewed primarily in terms of their race or in terms of their class? Should the independent struggle of blacks be encouraged or should their struggle be subordinated to the class struggle of workers? Should the main effort of revolutionists be to create solidarity between blacks and whites, under the slogan "Black and white, unite and fight!"? This was essentially the approach of the Socialist parties and of progressive unionists. It was also the view of Ernest McKinney, a black leader in the Workers Party who had come to radical politics from a labor organizing background. His party name was David Coolidge.

Or should blacks in the United States be viewed as a nationally oppressed minority or an internal "colony"? Lenin leaned toward this position, as did Trotsky. In the 1920s the American Communist Party, trying to implement this approach, had called for self-determination for the so-called Black Belt in the South. In 1939 CLR visited Trotsky in Mexico, where he was in exile, to discuss this question.[12]

Until World War II the Trotskyists had been able to pose the Negro Question in these abstract terms because it had not been a pressing question for them. In most locals there were no blacks. Few locals did organizing in the black community or had any contact with blacks. But ever since 1941 blacks had been on the move. Their refusal to tolerate racism at home while fighting against it overseas was creating havoc in many units of the armed services and threatening uprisings at home.[13] It was no longer a question of white radicals discussing whether or how blacks should struggle; blacks were already struggling.

Traveling around the United States and experiencing discrimination much crueler and cruder than anything he had known either in the West Indies or in Europe and sensing the revolutionary potential in the independent black struggle, CLR refused to yield to the fears of white radicals, which made it so difficult for them to respond unreservedly to the spontaneous black struggle. Confident that the independent struggle of blacks would act as a catalyst to set workers into revolutionary motion, he urged party members to recognize the revolutionary potential of the black struggle. As he wrote in "The Revolutionary Answer to the Negro Problem in the U.S.,"

> Let us not forget that in the Negro people there sleep and are now awakening passions of a violence exceeding, perhaps, as far as these things can be compared, anything among the tremendous forces that capitalism has created.... Although their social force may not be able to compare with the social force of a corresponding number of organized workers, the hatred of bourgeois society and the readiness to destroy it when the opportunity should present itself, rests among them to a degree greater than in any other section of the population in the United States.[14]

Armed with this sensibility, the Johnsonites took the position that, instead of waiting for "Black and White" to "Unite and Fight," revolutionists should encourage and support independent black struggles. Instead of trying to control or incorporate this struggle, whether it be nationalist or reformist or capitalist, revolutionists should trust that the momentum of the struggle will bring out the hatred of bourgeois society that is latent in the black experience. Instead of labeling black eruptions as "riots," we should recognize them as uprisings for justice. This approach to the Negro Question brought us into conflict with Shachtman and the Workers Party leadership who had adopted the more cautious Black and White, Unite and Fight position espoused by Coolidge.

My own experience with the March on Washington movement made me a passionate defender of the Johnson-Forest position on this issue. We soon had an opportunity to put our convictions into practice. In 1943, as Henry Pelham had anticipated, Harlem exploded in the wake of an incident involving discrimination against a black soldier. Tens of thousands filled the streets. Police stood by helplessly as white-owned stores were looted and torched. Chinese laundries and restaurants were spared. The eruption was not unexpected. For months, people in Harlem and in other black communities across the country had been warning that they were fed up with fighting for democracy in Europe and being denied democracy at home. The media, as usual, labeled the explosion a "riot." CLR, who wrote the column "One Tenth of a Nation" for *Labor Action*, the Workers Party's weekly paper, was assigned to write the lead article. I was working with him. We decided that our headline, splashed across the top of the front page, would be MASS DEMONSTRATION IN HARLEM.

Another issue repeatedly debated in the American radical movement was the question of whether to advocate an independent Labor Party. European radicals generally regarded the American workers as backward because they had not formed their own party, and most American radicals shared that view. By contrast, the Johnsonites, basing ourselves on Marx's analysis of the organization, discipline, and unity of the workers inside production and the explosion of labor struggles of the 1930s, insisted that the key to overthrowing capitalism was encouraging and expanding the struggles that American workers were already carrying on inside the plant to gain control of their lives and work.

Despite our political differences with the Shachtmanites, the members of the Johnson-Forest Tendency carried out our responsibilities as party members diligently, paying our dues, distributing thousands of copies of *Labor Action* at plant and shipyard gates, organizing street-corner meetings, systematically acquiring the organizational skills and discipline that make even a few radicals so influential in mass organizations. But otherwise we didn't spend much time socializing with the members of the majority, among whom were intellectuals like Irving Howe, who was the editor of *Labor Action* and would later make a national reputation for himself as a literary critic. We poured our energies instead into the weekly classes in *Capital* taught by Raya. We read Hegel and struggled with what Marx meant when he said that we need "to grasp the positive aspects of the Hegelian dialectic within the realm of estrangement."[15] We also read a lot of Lenin, especially his speeches and position papers in the period between the February and the October Revolutions and in the 1920s when he struggled desperately to mobilize the workers and peasants to take over control of production and distribution in order to counteract the mushrooming power of the state. We studied the great revolutions of the past in order to make clear that in every great revolution it was always the deepest layers of the society that drove the revolution forward. Thus we decided that our spiritual ancestors in the English Revolution of the seventeeth century were not Oliver Cromwell and Henry Ireton but John Lilburne and Richard Overton who expressed the democratic aspirations of the urban artisans and yeoman farmers. In the French Revolution we identified not with Robespierre and the Jacobins but with Jacques Roux, Theophile Leclerc, and Jean Varlet who lived among the sansculottes and helped them to organize to fight for price controls and other concrete needs of the masses. In mid-nineteenth century America we identified with the slaves whose revolts and escapes made a compromise impossible between the rising capitalists in the North and the southern plantocracy, thus making the Civil War and their own eventual emancipation inevitable.

We went to see again and again the stage and movie versions of *Hamlet*, *Henry V*, *Julius Caesar*, and *King Lear*, in the process developing a deeper understanding of the new social forces emerging in Shakespeare's England and an appreciation of the power of the creative imagination to uncover contradictions of a complexity and at a depth that logic cannot reach.

Raya spent hours in the New York Public Library reading the collected works of Marx and Engels in Russian, while I bought and pored over the fourteen-volume set in German. We made exciting discoveries, which we immediately shared with other Johnsonites around the country. For example, I will never forget the day that Raya came back from the library with the news that she had found a Russian translation of the *Economic and Philosophic Manuscripts* written by Marx in 1843–44 when he was twenty-four years old. Unknown in the United States at the time, these essays make it unmistakably clear that Marx's overriding concern was the human essence of the workers, not property relations. Subsequently,

I translated three of the essays from the original German into English, and in 1947 the Johnson-Forest Tendency published the first English translation in the United States.[16]

On another occasion we celebrated Raya's translation from the Russian of Lenin's notes on Hegel, which convey his excitement when he first read Hegel's *Philosophy of Mind* and *Science of Logic*.[17] In 1915 Lenin, at a very low point because the German Socialist Party, despite the international solidarity to which it had committed itself, was supporting its own government in World War I, turned to Hegel to try to understand his own crisis and the crisis of the international movement. By internalizing Hegel's dialectical method, he was able to recognize the new contradiction that had emerged inside the labor movement. One had divided into two: on the one hand, the labor aristocracy that had been bought off by the superprofits from imperialism, and on the other, the great masses of workers. Hegel's analysis of the importance of "leaps" in any transition and of the "ideal passing into the real" inspired Lenin to reconceptualize socialism on the eve of the October Revolution as a society in which "every cook can govern." This is the vision he put forward in *The State and Revolution*.[18]

In turn, Raya's translation of Lenin's notes on Hegel inspired CLR's *Notes on Dialectics*, which he sent from Nevada in 1948.[19] CLR's notes are a priceless analysis of the difference between Trotsky's and Lenin's way of thinking. (CLR is careful to make clear that he is questioning Trotsky's methodology, *not* his willingness to throw himself on the side of the masses in the heat of the class struggle.) In his assessment of party leaders shortly before his death, Lenin had pointed to Trotsky's "excessive preoccupation with the purely administrative side of the work."[20] Lenin's notes on Hegel helped CLR to understand that Trotsky's "administrative" tendency was not accidental but rooted in a way of thinking that is very common. Whitehead called it the "fallacy of misplaced concreteness." Hegel called it the thinking that makes "a finite into an infinite or Absolute." Thus Trotsky took a finite act—that is, the nationalizing of property by the workers' state after the October Revolution—and made it into "a universal law" defining a workers' state. By contrast, Lenin was always returning to the concrete—what workers and peasants were doing at the grassroots level—to inspire a new Universal or a new Vision. Thus the Soviets created spontaneously by the Russian workers in 1917 became the core of Lenin's new vision of socialism and the inspiration for his projections for concrete steps to achieve this vision after the seizure of state power: for example, Workers and Peasants Inspection, universal accounting and control of production and distribution, and nationwide peasant cooperatives.[21]

I will always be grateful to Raya for making Lenin's notes on Hegel accessible. Until I read them, my respect for Lenin as a philosopher, based on his 1908 *Materialism and Empirico-Criticism*, had been pretty low.[22] The 1915 notes provide an unprecedented opportunity to observe a great mind changing before your very eyes. In the countless exclamation points, underlinings, and marginal comments (leaps! leaps! leaps!) you can almost see the light bulbs going on in Lenin's head as he recognizes that what he had written in 1908 was crude and vulgar materialism.[23] With every year CLR's use of Lenin's notes to explain the difference between Trotskyism and Leninism has meant more to me. Together Lenin's notes on Hegel and CLR's *Notes on Dialectics* taught me that, in times of crisis or transition in any organization, movement, or society, it is a matter of life and death for the organization, movement, or society to recognize that reality is constantly changing, that the contradictions present in everything are bound to develop and become antagonistic, and therefore that ideas or strategies that were progressive and mind-opening at one point have become abstractions and fixations. At such times revolutionary leadership must have the audacity to break free of old ideas or strategies and create a new vision or visions based on concrete actions by the masses that suggest a forward leap in their self-determination or ability to assume greater control and responsibility for their own lives. So instead of being disheartened when I have had to give up ideas, associates, and organizations to which I have whole-heartedly committed myself, I have seen these breaks as an integral part of my evolution as a movement activist.

CLR, Raya, and I were inseparable. In today's New York the sight of us together—a tall, handsome black man flanked by two women, one a somewhat stooped and scholarly Jew and the other a round-faced Asian—might not attract much attention. But in the 1940s a lot of people must have wondered where we came from and what we were about, especially as we entered and left Raya's swank Sutton Place apartment where we often worked. At other times we worked at 629 Hudson Street or in CLR's apartment way up in the East Bronx, which I reached by subway or in the old Packard touring car that my brother Eddie had left behind when he went into the army. It was a twenty-five-minute drive over the Triborough Bridge from the Bronx to Queens, and I often drove home late at night. I shall never forget one night when the transmission in the Packard died, and I had to make the trip nonstop, red lights and all.

Our energy was fantastic. We would spend a morning or afternoon writing, talking, and eating and then go home and write voluminous letters to one another extending or enlarging on what we had discussed, sending these around to other members of our tendency in barely legible carbon copies. (This was long before photocopying.) Most of this material is accessible in the Dunayevskaya and Glaberman collections in the Wayne State University Archives of Labor and Urban Affairs in Detroit. When occasionally I look up something in the collections, I find it hard to believe that we wrote so much and took on so many literary critics and historians.

The Johnson-Forest Tendency consisted of a small number of members—never more than sixty to seventy in an organization of several hundred. But the fervor with which we supported the independent black struggle and attacked the alienation of human beings in the process of capitalist production made us stand out in any gathering. Most members of the Johnson-Forest Tendency were part of the new generation who had joined the radical movement in the 1940s because we wanted to make a second American Revolution—which to us meant mainly encouraging the struggles of rank-and-file workers to take over control of production inside the plant and supporting the black struggle for full social, economic, and political equality. Black, white, Asian, and Chicano, workers and intellectuals, living on the East Coast, West Coast, and in the Midwest, we were a representative sample of the new human forces that were emerging in the United States during World War II. Because CLR could not be publicly active, we acted as his transmission belt to the larger American community. Our little organization was a collective way to know reality.

We were not discouraged by the smallness of our group. Energized by our contact with the workers in the plant and the ideas that we were absorbing from our studies of Marx, Hegel, Lenin, and past revolutions, we moved about as if we had discovered the secret of the universe. In any gathering you could tell us by the stars in our eyes. The Shachtmanites scoffed at our sweeping historical generalizations. But we were convinced that by being in tune with what the American workers were thinking and doing we had become part of the continuing historical movement of those at the bottom of society to take control over their own lives. The workers, CLR used to insist, didn't need an organization to organize them. They would organize themselves. In *Notes on Dialectics* CLR took this idea of spontaneity to the extreme limit. "The task is to abolish organization," he wrote. "The task is to call for, to teach, to illustrate, to develop *spontaneity*—the free creative activity of the proletariat."[24]

One of CLR's great gifts was that he could detect the special abilities and interests of individuals and encourage them to use these to enrich the movement and at the same time enlarge themselves. In those days most radical women worked at secretarial jobs so that their men could be full-time party functionaries. We were proud that in our tendency Raya Dunayevskaya was a coleader with CLR. I was sometimes considered the third leader of the tendency because I did so much of the research, wrote some of the documents, and typed even more of them, but I saw myself as a junior and a learner, and both CLR and Raya treated me as such. Filomena Daddario, the daughter of Italian immigrants who lived in Astoria (her father and brothers were New York City sanitation workers), sold records in a music shop. She had a marvelous ear for popular lyrics and a love for the spoken word. So CLR introduced her to Shakespeare, and before long she was reciting and interpreting Shakespeare for popular audiences. Selma Weinstein, later Selma James, was a young mother who from her life in the plant and at home had developed an insight into the subtle forms that male chauvinism takes in the United States. CLR encouraged her to write the pamphlet *A Women's Place* with Filomena. Phil Singer, a young GM worker, was always talking about the frustrations of the rank-and-file worker in the plant. CLR proposed that he keep a journal of his experiences. These were subsequently published in *The American Worker* along with an analytical essay I wrote as Ria Stone. Si Owens's stories of his life as a black worker from the South were edited into the book *Indignant Heart* by Constance Webb James, who went on to write the first full-length study of Richard Wright. Willie Gorman, an intellectual with a Talmudic background and a flair for sweeping historical generalizations, was assigned to write and speak on the antislavery movement and the Civil War. Martin Glaberman who worked in the Flint auto plants wrote *Punching Out*, a pamphlet on wildcat strikes.

As World War II was coming to an end in 1944 and 1945, people in the plant began wondering about the future. They knew that it was the war that had put them back to work. Would the war's end put them back on the streets? In the early years of the war, workers had felt it their patriotic duty to keep producing for the men at the front. But as Nazi Germany went down to defeat and layoffs began to take place, workers felt freer to act out their differences with management. As a result, in 1944 and 1945 a wave of wildcat or unauthorized strikes swept the country. This was the only way in which workers could make their concerns felt because early in the war, in order to assure uninterrupted production for the war effort, the union leadership had made a no-strike pledge and joined the War Production Board. After Hitler invaded the Soviet Union in 1941, they were joined by the Communists who had provided a lot of the leadership for the labor movement in the 1930s but who were now doing their best to suppress the militancy of the workers. This created a leadership vacuum in the factories that Workers Party comrades began to fill. Week after week *Labor Action* exposed the huge profits being made by the defense industry, called for an end to the no-strike pledge and to cost-plus contracts, and warned of the dangers of mass unemployment after the war ended. Party members, including Johnsonites, stood outside plant gates handing out hundreds of thousands of these papers.

Inside the party, comrades began wondering what kind of leadership we should give to the new wave of unrest. We Johnsonites hailed the wildcats. We viewed them as the self-activity of the workers, providing a magnificent opportunity for the American workers to create a new movement that would continue where the labor movement of the 1930s had left off, mobilizing the workers not only to control production but to decide what and how to produce. Shachtman and his supporters, on the other hand, proposed "Plenty for All" as the theme for the postwar struggle and published a pamphlet with that title. It was the straw that broke the camel's back. For five years the party leadership had demonstrated its conservatism on the Russian Question and the Negro Question. Now the best they could come up with as the goal of an American revolution was an abundance of goods for everybody. They could not even imagine—let alone project to the workers in the plant and to the American people—that they should and could take over control of production in the plant as the first step toward controlling their own destiny.

The differences between us were brought home to me the week of V-J Day when the war with Japan came to an end. At the time a number of Workers Party comrades, including me and another Johnsonite, were working in a plant in Brooklyn where members of the party majority were the leaders of the local union. When we came in to work after V-J Day, the Johnsonite comrade and I decided to organize a sit-in to demand that we be kept on the payroll to help reconvert the plant to peacetime production. While we were agitating the workers, who were very responsive, and running from department to department organizing discussions of how to reorganize production, our comrades as union leaders were meeting with management to work out how to get us to leave the plant peacefully!

In order to make clear how far apart we had grown, the Johnson-Forest Tendency submitted a resolution stating that "no revolutionary can deny the possibility that two years from today the American proletariat could cover the nation with soviets or their equivalent in a nation-wide strike against the bourgeoisie."

Shachtmanites called us romantic idealists, carrying on "politics in the stratosphere." The statement was admittedly somewhat excessive. But from all accounts the atmosphere in defense plants all over the country was electric. Workers were determined not to return to the unemployment and despair of the 1930s. Black workers especially were talking about the need to go beyond the union and engage in revolutionary struggle. Also, inside the organization we were sick and tired of arguing with the Shachtmanites. For years we had been trying to convince them that Marxism and revolutionary struggle were not about property relations and acquiring more things but about encouraging the self-activity of those at the bottom of our society and the expansion of their natural and acquired powers. The debate on the Russian Question had been theoretical; there was nothing that we could do about the direction of the Soviet Union. The differences on the Negro Question struck closer to home, but there were few blacks in the Trotskyist organizations, and the civil rights and Black Power movements were still years away. On the other hand, we felt that how we lived our daily lives and what we said to those we worked with were at stake in the dispute over the American Question.

At the end of the debate it was no longer possible for us to remain in the same party. So recognizing that we were too few and too inexperienced to exist on our own, we began to look for another political home. Fortuitously, during this period the Socialist Workers Party issued a pamphlet titled *The Coming American Revolution* by James P. Cannon, the veteran working-class leader who had supported Trotsky in 1928 and led the split of the Left Opposition from the American Communist Party. CLR and Raya went to see Cannon with the proposal that the Johnson-Forest Tendency enter the Socialist Workers Party as an organized tendency with ideas of our own and a willingness to function as disciplined party members. Cannon, recognizing that he didn't know much about blacks and also that his party could use some fresh blood and new ideas, welcomed us.

So in the fall of 1947 the Johnson-Forest Tendency became a group inside the Socialist Workers Party. Before entering, we enjoyed an interim period of about two months during which we rented an office in midtown Manhattan and published a number of pamphlets summarizing the views we had arrived at during five years of struggle inside the Workers' Party. These included *The Balance Sheet,* summing up our experiences in the party; *The Invading Socialist Society*; *Dialectical Materialism and the Fate of Humanity*; *The American Worker* by Paul Romano and Ria Stone, *State Capitalism and World Revolution*; *Marx's Economic and Philosophic Manuscripts of 1844*.[25] It cost us about $5,000 to issue all these publications. Most of it came from contributions by comrades who had served in World War II and had just received a lump-sum bonus.

The concluding paragraph of my essay in *The American Worker*, written in 1947, sums up what I was thinking after nearly six years of working in the Johnson-Forest Tendency inside the Workers Party (I was thirty-two years old):

> The American bourgeoisie is organically incapable of assuring any perspective of economic and social stability and progress on the one world scale axiomatic in our time. Already its political front, which had seemed so imposing, is beginning to show signs of great strain. Today, more and more workers say, with that simple directness which requires no proof, "Sure, we could do it better." In their words, there is contained the workers' recognition of the enormous scope of their natural and acquired powers, and the distorted and wasteful abuse of these powers within the existing society. In these words is contained also the overwhelming anger of the workers against the capitalist barriers stifling their energies and hence victimizing the whole world. Never has society so needed the direct intervention of the workers. Never have the workers been so ready to come to grips with the fundamental problems of society. The destinies of the two are indissolubly united. When the workers take their fate into their own hands, when they seize the power and begin their reconstruction of society, all of mankind will leap from the realm of necessity into the realm of freedom.

Shortly after we entered the Socialist Workers Party, I went to Paris to attend the Second World Congress of the Fourth International as a representative of the Johnson-Forest Tendency. I found the gathering very dull and pretentious. The thirty to forty people who had assembled to debate the Russian Question, the main purpose of the congress, seemed to me holdovers from the 1920s and 1930s. The only exception was P. Chaulieu, the party name of Cornelius Castoriadis, who had joined the movement in Greece at the age of fifteen, had translated Hegel's *Science of Logic* into French, and now in his twenties was the leader of a small group in Paris calling itself Socialisme ou Barbarie.[26] We soon discovered that we had the same interest in the daily lives of workers in the capitalist process of production and similar views about revolution as the liberation of human creativity. I spent a wonderful four months in Paris, mostly socializing with Chaulieu and the members of his group. I spoke French poorly but I could read and understand it fairly well, and it was a pleasure to hear discussions about political and philosophical ideas in French. In fact, I enjoyed these comrades so much that when Richard Wright invited me to spend a day with him and his wife visiting the flea market, I declined because I was looking forward to an afternoon with Chaulieu's group. I have always felt more comfortable around rank and filers than around celebrities.

Before returning to the United States I traveled for two weeks in Europe in order to get a sense of the devastation from World War II. With two briefcases containing hard-boiled eggs, cheese, and bread, a prepaid train ticket, and $20 (U.S.) in my pocket, I went from Belgium to Germany and on to Denmark, England, and Ireland, staying with comrades wherever I could and determined not to break my $20—or if I had to break it, to receive my change in U.S. dollars rather than in the local currency. In Copenhagen I knew no one. But fortunately a young policeman to whom I told my story was an aspiring writer who wanted to make contact with Americans. He took me to the inn where he was staying, asked the landlord to put me up for the night, fed me dinner, and saw me off the next morning.

Returning to the United States, I found the Socialist Workers Party even more stultifying than the Workers Party had been. Party members were civil and cordial, but they talked and acted as if World War II had never taken place. Mostly men and women in their late forties and fifties, they had no sense of the new energies and new social forces of rank-and-file workers, blacks, women, and youth that had emerged during the war. Their concept of revolution came from the Russian Revolution of 1917 and their concept of the working class came from the Minneapolis Teamsters Strike in 1934 in which party members had played a leading role. Their views on the Negro Question, flowing from Trotsky's support of "Self-Determination if the Negroes themselves want it," were closer to ours than the Shachtmanite position had been. But the black movement was still years away, and party members did not share our passionate conviction that the independent black struggle was a formidable threat to the U.S. power structure. On one occasion, for example, I was reprimanded for my use of the phrase *white cops* to describe the enemy during a public meeting on the situation in the black community. George Breitman was the only exception. Later, in the 1960s, he was the one chiefly responsible for inviting Malcolm X to speak at party forums following his break with Elijah Muhammad. Pathfinder Press, the publishing house initiated by the Socialist Workers Party, was the only one publishing Malcolm's speeches until commercial publishers recognized the huge market for books by and on Malcolm.

Johnson-Forest comrades in California and Detroit were experiencing the same frustrations. It was as if we and the Cannonites were living in two different eras. So in 1951 we decided that the time had come for us to leave the Trotskyists completely behind, and after issuing a document titled *The Balance Sheet Completed* summarizing our experiences with the Socialist Workers Party, we set out on our own with the view toward publishing our own newspaper and pamphlets that would mainly recognize and record the views and activities of rank-and-file workers, blacks, women, and youth—the four groups that we identified as the revolutionary social forces.

Again, considering how few we were and that we were doing this long before computers made desktop publishing a snap, our achievements were fantastic. Within a few months of our split from the Socialist Workers Party, we published *Indignant Heart* by Matthew Ward, the pen name of Si Owens,[27] *A Woman's Place*, *Punching Out*, and *Artie Cuts Out* (a pamphlet by and about youth). At the same time, in order to complete our break with Old Left politics, mainly fought on the Lower East Side of New York, Raya moved to Detroit to set up our new office in that city, and we asked Johnny Zupan, a Ford worker and a member of the Johnson-Forest Tendency, to leave his job and become full-time editor of *Correspondence*, named after the Committees of Correspondence of the first American Revolution.

To prepare ourselves for the publication of *Correspondence* we organized a school where members of the four groups identified as the new revolutionary social forces would be the teachers and the older members and intellectuals would be the students, ready with "full fountain pens" to write down the views of our "teachers." We called it the Third Layer School, based on Lenin's efforts in 1921 to mobilize a "third layer" of workers and peasants because the first layer of Bolshevik leaders and the second layer of trade unionists had not been sufficient to keep state capitalism from overtaking the fledgling workers' state. The school was held in New York in the fall of 1952. Among the third layer comrades who came to the school were James Boggs from Detroit and Selma Weinstein, later Selma James, from Los Angeles.

Meanwhile, the Immigration and Naturalization Service was hounding CLR for overstaying his visitor's visa. He had been admitted in 1938 and had registered every year as he was required to do under the Alien Registration Act. While the war was going on, the Immigration Service had allowed him to stay. But the war had now been over for nearly seven years. CLR desperately wanted to become an American citizen. He loved this country. He had married an American woman and had an American son. As an intellectual he also realized how lucky he was to be surrounded by such a diverse group of committed and supportive activists and intellectuals and that it was highly unlikely that a similar group could be created in another place and time. His lawyers applied for an extension of his visa. When his application was denied, they appealed again and again. Finally, after five years of legal maneuvering, he was incarcerated on Ellis Island in June 1952 pending a final determination on his appeal.

While on Ellis Island CLR wrote *Mariners, Renegades and Castaways: The Story of Herman Melville and the World We Live In*. Earlier, during Workers Party discussions on the goals of an American revolution, CLR had characteristically begun a study of the period between 1851 and 1865, when the railroad, the iron ship, the factory, and the labor union all began to be dominant forces within the United States, and when this country had also produced its greatest writers—Ralph Waldo Emerson, Walt Whitman, Herman Melville, Nathaniel Hawthorne, and Edgar Allan Poe. Looking at *Moby Dick* as a mid-twentieth century revolutionist who was also a lover of Shakespeare, he had come to the conclusion that Melville's masterpiece was the "first comprehensive statement in literature of the conditions and perspectives for the survival of Western civilization."[28] He saw Ahab, the mad captain taking the *Pequod* to the bottom of the ocean in pursuit of the white whale, as the forerunner of the totalitarian dictators of our epoch. The crew and the harpooners represented the creative power of the masses; the two officers, Starbuck and Stubb, the helplessness of labor and liberal leaders; while Ishmael symbolized the powerlessness and isolation of the intellectual.

Upon CLR's release on bail from Ellis Island in October 1952 we published *Mariners, Renegades and Castaways* as a paperback, with a final chapter describing CLR's experiences on Ellis Island and emphasizing his qualifications to become a U.S. citizen.[29] Then we sent the book to all the members of Congress in a last, desperate effort to win their support for his application to remain in the United States.

In vain. His appeal denied, CLR was given the option of being deported or leaving voluntarily, which left open the possibility that he could later return. He chose the second option and in the spring left for England, where he eventually became known as the dean of the Pan-African movement. At the same time he continued to see himself as the leader of the Johnson-Forest Tendency in the United States, now called *Correspondence,* sending long letters from London, full of both political analysis and detailed directions. The result was increasing friction between him and the leadership in Detroit, culminating in the split, first, with Raya Dunayevskaya in 1956 and then with Jimmy and me in 1962 around a document written by Jimmy. In the next chapter I will tell the story of when and how these splits developed.

Meanwhile, in 1954 I spent four months with CLR in London, working mainly with Mbiyu Koinange on an account of the struggle against British colonialism in Kenya. I found London interesting enough, but my heart was back in Detroit. Working with CLR was becoming something of a chore. Selma, whom he was planning to marry, was still in the United States, and he was at loose ends, trying to find his way after fifteen years out of the country. He subscribed to all the newspapers (*London Times*, *Daily Telegraph*, *Manchester Guardian*, *News of the World*), and we read them religiously. We went to cricket matches and he wrote a few articles. He managed to establish contact with a worker from the shop floor movement, which was developing in England, and with a few recent West Indian immigrants. George Padmore was in Africa, but we went to Manchester two or three times to talk to T. Ras Makonnen who with Padmore and Kwame Nkrumah had organized the Fifth Pan-African Congress in 1945 while CLR was in the United States.

Upon my return to Detroit, we established the Kenya Publication Fund to raise money for publication of *The People of Kenya Speak for Themselves* by Mbiyu Koinange and also as a way to organize Kenya Sunday, a special Sunday on which Detroit ministers agreed to talk to their congregations about the significance of the independence struggle in Kenya. The Kenya Sunday project brought me into contact with a number of the most politically conscious preachers in Detroit, including Revs. C. L. Franklin, pastor of New Bethel Baptist; Horace B. White of Plymouth Congregational; and Henry Hitt Crane of Central Methodist. C. L. Franklin, the father of Aretha Franklin, was one of the most enthusiastic supporters of the Kenya project. On Kenya Sunday Jimmy and I sold more than four hundred copies of the Kenya booklet to members of New Bethel from the pulpit.

In 1957 I again spent five months in London, partly to work on a book on Nkrumah and the revolution in Ghana (CLR and Selma had just returned from the independence celebrations in Accra), but mainly to work on *Facing Reality*,[30] written to celebrate the Hungarian Revolution as the most recent confirmation of our conviction that a new socialist democracy was inherent in the spontaneous rebellions of the modern working class. The title was suggested by Jimmy Boggs who was spending his vacation from Chrysler with me in London. But the book is pure C. L. R. James in its celebration of spontaneous rebellion and its insistence that the main role of socialist revolutionaries is to recognize and record the rebellions of ordinary working people.[31] It also draws heavily on the experiences of Selma, who with her son Sam had come to London and married CLR in 1956.[32] I did not share CLR's excitement about the Hungarian Revolution, and after living in Detroit for three years I was beginning to have some reservations about his celebration of spontaneity. But I did not challenge him, and although I did little of the actual writing, I went along with including my name with Chaulieu's as a coauthor.

In 1960 Jimmy and I spent five weeks with CLR in Trinidad, where he had gone to edit *The Nation*, the newspaper of the Peoples National Movement led by Eric Williams. Subsequently, CLR was involved in a very serious auto accident in Jamaica.

In the wake of the black rebellions in the late 1960s CLR was allowed to return to the United States, where he held teaching positions at a number of colleges and lectured at many others including Harvard and Princeton, gaining a following among the many black students who were avidly reading *Black Jacobins*. But he was never able to build another group of collaborators and supporters like the Johnson-Forest Tendency, and, especially after his separation from Selma, he was always on the go, traveling from country to country and city to city.[33]

After our break in 1962 I saw CLR only three more times. The first time was in 1968 when he showed up at a rally at the Shrine of the Black Madonna in Detroit and addressed the audience briefly. We exchanged perfunctory greetings. The second time was in November 1976 when Freddy and Lyman Paine invited him to Los Angeles to celebrate his seventy-fifth birthday with Lyman who had been born the same year. When Freddy and I met him at the airport, he was rejoicing at the role that blacks had recently played in electing Jimmy Carter president. The political distance between us had clearly deepened. CLR was still excited about blacks getting into the system. Jimmy had just made a speech at the University of Michigan exposing the emptiness of the electoral system and calling for a "new concept of citizenship."

The third time was in 1986 when I was invited to London to speak at the weeklong tribute to him sponsored by the Greater London Council.[34] By then C. L. R. James had become quite famous, appearing often on British TV. Over the years he had traveled all over the world lecturing and attending conferences in Ghana, Nigeria, Tanzania, Cuba, the West Indies. In 1976 he had been instrumental in persuading Tanzanian President Julius K. Nyerere to host the Sixth Pan-African Congress in Dar es Salaam and in stirring up interest for the Congress in Africa, the West

Indies, and the United States. In the end, he did not attend himself because two weeks before the opening he was informed that organizations not officially sanctioned by their governments would not be allowed to participate.

The 1986 tribute included a production of his play on Toussaint L'Ouverture and presentations by individuals who had played a role in his life or who had been strongly influenced by him. I visited him a couple of times at his lodgings on the top floor of the Race Today Collective in South Brixton. His surroundings were much the same as I had known them in the past except when he had been married to Constance or Selma. He was lying on his bed. There were books all over the place. A female assistant (in this case, Anna Grimshaw) was typing away in a corner, and in the tiny kitchen next door there were dirty dishes and leftovers. Each time we spent about half an hour chatting, but there were periods when the conversation noticeably lapsed. Before he died, he sent a note to me through Marty Glaberman asking if I would come to London to work with him on his autobiography. Characteristically, it had apparently not occurred to him that I might be engaged in activities in Detroit that I could not or would not want to leave.

In May 1989 C. L. R. James died in his home in South Brixton, London. His body was returned to Trinidad for burial. Since that time, there has been an outpouring of books and articles about him.

Through my association with CLR I came into contact with a number of black writers and political leaders, some of whom were or would become famous. Eric Williams, whom we called Bill, often came up to New York from D.C. to consult with CLR on strategy for the Caribbean Commission on which he was working. Williams struck me as a rather fussy academic type. I must have been somewhat ungracious because when his book *Capitalism and Slavery*, a major achievement, was published, he inscribed my copy, "To Grace, my dear enemy, from Bill, her dear friend."[35] In 1955 Williams returned to Trinidad and began speaking to thousands of Trinidadians about their right to independence at what was called the University of Woodford Square. People called him The Doctor and wrote calypso songs about him. As a result, he became prime minister of independent Trinidad and Tobago and came to London in 1957 to attend his first Commonwealth Prime Ministers Conference. I was surprised to see how much he had changed. He seemed like a new person, joking and telling anecdotes about prostitutes who wouldn't do business while the Doctor was talking. During the five weeks that Jimmy and I spent visiting CLR in Trinidad in 1960 I didn't see

Williams at all. I knew that he was very busy with the oil strike, but I also noticed that he didn't respond to the messages and instructions sent to him by CLR sometimes two and three times a day through Selma's son Sam. Later, Williams and CLR became estranged after CLR accused him of selling out to the United States because he permitted the Americans to maintain a base at Chaguaramas; Williams then placed CLR under house arrest as a dangerous radical. In 1965 CLR returned to Trinidad and organized an opposition Workers and Farmers Party to oppose Williams. The party "had no organic ties to the working communities on whose behalf it claimed to speak" and soon faded away.[36]

Mbiyu Koinange, with whom I spent a lot of time in London in 1954 working on the little booklet *The People of Kenya Speak for Themselves*, was president of Kenya Teachers College, an independent institution organized by Kenyans to educate their own children. Together with Jomo Kenyatta, he had organized the Kenya African Union. After Kenyatta was imprisoned by the British, Koinange came to London as the delegate of the union to tell the true story of the Kenya independence struggle, which the British had labeled "Mau Mau" in order to give the impression that Kenya freedom fighters were nothing but terrorists. Koinange was a somewhat pedestrian type, not at all charismatic. He hated living in England, not only because of the climate but because being surrounded by whites he never felt free to speak and had begun to feel tongue-tied. After Kenya gained independence we didn't stay in touch, but I understand that he became minister of state in the new government.

I first met Kwame Nkrumah in 1945 after Raya Dunayevskaya encountered him in a Harlem library and arranged for him to talk to CLR at 629 Hudson Street. Nkrumah had just finished his studies at Lincoln University and had written an essay against colonialism that was later published as *Towards Colonial Freedom*.[37] He was preparing to go to London, so CLR gave him a letter of introduction to George Padmore. I invited him to a party that some friends who worked with me in the plant were giving that night. Subsequently, he wrote me a number of letters from England, and after he returned to the Gold Coast and became Leader of Government Business, he wrote to ask me to come to Africa and marry him. I was completely taken by surprise. I don't have a copy of my reply, but as I recall I declined because I couldn't imagine myself being politically active in a country where I was totally ignorant of the history, geography, and culture.

In 1957 Nkrumah was also in London to attend the Commonwealth Prime Ministers Conference. One afternoon CLR, Selma, George Padmore, Bill Williams, and I went to visit him at the Dorchester Hotel where he was staying. During the visit he completely ignored everyone else and spoke only to me. His behavior was so strange that in the taxi on the way home I asked CLR why he had paid so much attention to me. CLR's reply was characteristic: "Because he knows that you work closely with me."

In 1968, following the coup d'état that had overthrown him while he was in China, Nkrumah was in exile in Conakry, Guinea, where Sekou Toure had conferred on him the honorary title of copresident in appreciation of the aid that Ghana had given Guinea after its breakaway from France. Jimmy had just completed a speaking tour in Italy, and I contacted Nkrumah suggesting that we visit him to talk over developments in the United States and Africa. Nkrumah was living in a villa on the coast and appeared in excellent spirits, confident that it was only a matter of months before he would be summoned back to Ghana by the people. We stayed a week in Conakry. Every day we were taken by limousine to a gazebo in the hills where we talked and were served an elaborate meal.

Certain things from our discussions stand out in my mind. Nkrumah had married a woman from Egypt. When I asked him where she and the children were, he replied, "I sent her back to Nasser." I was also concerned about the men in Nkrumah's entourage, some of whom had been talking with Jimmy and me. There were about fifteen of them—journalists and aides who had been in China with Nkrumah when the coup had taken place. Now through no fault of their own they were living in exile in a country where they were unfamiliar with the language and culture and had no idea whether or when they would be reunited with their families. For example, although Guinea is only a few hundred miles from Ghana and on the coast, the people do not eat fish or use dairy products even though they raise cows. One of the men told Jimmy how much he missed butter, and Jimmy made a sketch for him of how to turn milk into butter. I told Nkrumah that he ought to develop a program of activities to make the lives of the men more meaningful and outlined one such plan for him.

The day before our departure when we were making our final toasts, Nkrumah turned to Jimmy and said, "I hope you won't mind if I say this, but if Grace had married me we would have changed all Africa." It was only then that I understood why he had paid so much attention to me in London. It was with the same dynastic perspective that he had married a woman from Nasser's Egypt.

For mementos of our visit Nkrumah gave me an African necklace and a bust of W. E. B. Du Bois and Jimmy a white Nkrumah jacket and cap in which Jimmy took great pride.

George Padmore was the only one of these black leaders who impressed me as being at ease with what he had accomplished in his life. He was also the only one whom CLR treated as a peer. Over the years Padmore and his wife, Dorothy, had welcomed hundreds of African students to London and made them feel at home in their Camden Town apartment. For more than twenty years he had been training Africans to go back and become freedom fighters in the anti-imperialist struggle. His books analyzing colonialism were studied widely, and his columns appeared in black newspapers all over the United States. He had organized his life to meet a historical need, and by the middle and late 1950s his mission was about to be achieved. When Padmore died in 1959, drums beating out his name were heard all over Africa.

Jimmy Boggs was different from all of them including CLR. He always stayed close to his roots and never lived in exile.

玉平

4
Jimmy

When people asked Jimmy how we got together, he would pause, smile broadly, and say, "Grace got *me*." The story behind those three little words goes back a long way.

I never thought of getting married. My mother's unhappiness may have had something to do with it. But the main reason, I believe, is that when I was fifteen I read *Women and Economics* by the feminist writer Charlotte Perkins Gilman and was impressed with her thesis that wives are like prostitutes because they exchange sex for economic support.[1] According to Gilman, a girl learns early on that she can get a new doll or a new dress by sitting on her father's knees and tickling him under the chin. That is how girls are socialized for marriage. The edition I read was not illustrated, but that image of a little girl on her father's knees never left me. That was not where I was going to end up.

As I got older, my father from time to time would bring home an overseas Chinese student to test out the waters. I wasn't interested. We had nothing in common except the slant of our eyes and the color of our skin. I suspect that they took one look at me and decided that I would be plenty of trouble. Most overseas Chinese students were from the upper classes and looked down on Chinese born and raised in the United States. Our parents came from peasant stock and had little education. Most of us didn't know how to read and write Chinese. So they called us *Jook Sing*, which means bamboo head or having nothing between the ears.

I was repelled by their air of superiority. In 1935, I had an experience that reinforced my distaste. At Harvard Summer School, where I was spending a few weeks after graduation from Barnard, I met Dollie Sah, who really looked like a Chinese doll and whose father was an official in Chiang Kai-shek's Kuomintang (Chinese Nationalist Party) government. One night she arranged a double date for us with two brothers. They turned out to be the sons of former Shanghai Mayor Wu and were so arrogant and overbearing in their behavior to taxicab drivers and waiters that I wanted to throw something in their faces and leave. Many years later I learned that their father had been responsible for the 1927 massacre of Shanghai workers that precipitated the civil war between the Kuomintang and the Chinese Communists.

At the time I didn't know anything about the civil war in China. It was before the publication of Edgar Snow's *Red Star over China,* with its electrifying account of the Long March and the pioneering struggles of Mao Tse-tung and the Chinese Communists to build a workers' and peasants' government in remote Yenan as a base from which to challenge the Kuomintang.[2] Among overseas Chinese students in this country there were a few Communist sympathizers, but they were understandably cautious about disclosing their views for fear of ending up in a Chinese prison. My mother knew a Chinese woman student who had narrowly escaped being arrested and imprisoned by the Kuomintang for her progressive ideas. When she was at our house and the front door bell rang, she would run and hide in the corner of a bedroom closet.

Over the years, consciously or unconsciously, the men I chose to be intimate with were individuals who, for one reason or another, I would not consider marrying. Only once, on a moonlit summer night during World War II, did I deviate from this pattern when I found myself discussing marriage with a merchant seaman whom I had just met and who reminded me of the boy next door in Island Park on whom I had had a teenage crush. For a couple of months it was like something out of a storybook. He sent me gifts and flowers from the various ports where his ship was docked. His mother came to New York and we cooed over his baby pictures. The next time he came to town, I had regained my senses and we agreed that we should just be friends. After that I was involved with a married comrade for nearly six years. It was one of those extremely exciting physical relationships that everyone should enjoy at least once in a lifetime. But he was a fast-talking public relations man, and even if he had been single I would never have considered marrying him. The relationship wasn't going anywhere, and there wasn't anywhere that I wanted it to go. This dawned on me when he moved in one year and I got a case of hives that didn't go away until he moved out. One of the reasons I left New York in 1953 was that I needed physical distance to terminate the relationship.

I first met Jimmy in the fall of 1952. We were both members of *Correspondence*. I was living in New York City. He was living in Detroit. In 1948, while the Johnson-Forest Tendency was still in the Socialist Workers Party, we heard that a number of black auto workers in Detroit were coming around the party looking for an organization more radical than the union *and* the Communist Party. This was the period when UAW (United Auto Workers) President Walter Reuther and his followers were red-baiting and purging the Communist Party-supported Frankensteen-Addes caucus in the union. The main purpose of CLR's 1948 Detroit speech, "The Revolutionary Answer to the Negro Problem in the United States," was to attract these workers to the Socialist Workers Party. It worked. Jimmy and his good friend and fellow Chrysler worker Willie Lewis came to several public meetings but did not join. Then, at a meeting in 1950–51 they discovered that "Orientals" from New York had become part of the local and that they were members of a tendency, led by C. L. R. James, that was splitting from the Socialist Workers Party and forming an independent organization to publish a newsletter written and edited by rank-and-file workers, blacks, women, and youth. The "Orientals" were my brothers Eddie and Harry and Harry's wife, Julie. The newsletter we were getting ready to publish was *Correspondence*.

The *Correspondence* comrades in Detroit recognized immediately that in Jimmy Boggs they had found (or been found by) someone who was a prototype of the kind of individual for whom the newsletter was being created. A rank-and-file black Chrysler-Jefferson worker and community activist, Jimmy had very definite positions on everything—locally, nationally, and internationally—and could dash off an article on any subject at the drop of a hat. Soon after he became a member, he was so highly regarded by the Detroit comrades that when he caught pneumonia, they caused near-panic in the organization by sending out a telegram to all the locals reading, "Jimmy has pneumonia." Outside of Detroit we thought that the telegram referred to CLR whom we called Jimmie. One of the main reasons we organized the Third Layer School in the fall of 1952 was to give rank-and-file black workers like Jimmy the opportunity to teach trade unionists and intellectuals like myself. To make it possible for him to attend the school in New York, the Detroit comrades raised the money to support his family for two weeks.

The Third Layer School was held in two sessions; Jimmy was in the first and I was in the second. So I didn't meet him until we held a social one night, although I had already heard that he had practically taken over leadership of the school, for example, volunteering to write the reports of the discussions and actually doing so from day to day. When I asked him to dance, he declined because, as he said, he had already made clear to the comrades in Detroit that he "didn't come around the radical movement to get himself a woman."

After the social I didn't think anymore about Jimmy. I heard later that his sister had died during the school session and that he was also going through a painful divorce, initiated by his wife, Annie. He and Annie had grown up together in Marion Junction, Alabama, and like almost everyone in that little community they were distant relatives. They had been married since they were teenagers and already had six children. Another was born after the divorce.

Then in June 1953 I came to Detroit to work on *Correspondence*. Soon after my arrival I bought myself a red 1938 Plymouth for $100. Jimmy, who by this time was a member of the editorial board, didn't own a car. So after meetings I would drive him home. In the car he would position himself as close to the passenger door as possible and give only monosyllabic answers to my questions. After a couple of months of this, I invited him for dinner and he accepted. When he had not arrived an hour after the scheduled time, I called my brother Harry and discovered that Jimmy was still at his house working on a car. When he finally showed up two hours late, he turned up his nose at the lamb chops I had prepared (he didn't eat "the lamb of God") and my Louis Armstrong album (Armstrong was an Uncle Tom because he kept saying "Yowsah"). It was not an auspicious beginning. But later in the evening, to my surprise, he asked me to marry him and, also to my surprise, I said yes.

Actually, my response was not so surprising. Until I married Jimmy, most of my major decisions—where to go to school, where to live, or whom to relate to—had been made in this way, without premeditation or consultation with anyone inside or outside my family. Early on I had realized that I would have to plot my own course. So I had become accustomed to trusting my own feelings to let me know what I needed to do at a particular time.

I don't know why Jimmy asked me to marry him. Maybe he was testing me. If he was surprised by my affirmative response, there was no indication. We never discussed it. It all happened so naturally that there was nothing to discuss. Jimmy radiated a personal and political energy that I found very attractive. He was also more rooted and more secure in his identity as a human being than any man I had ever met. At the same time

I was finding the life I was living increasingly unsatisfying. Between 1940, when I left Bryn Mawr, and 1953 I had been involved in nearly a half dozen relationships and lived in more than a half dozen places. The contradictions in this nomadic existence had been growing, and even though I had not said it to myself or anyone else, I needed to settle down in a place and in a relationship that would be both nurturing and challenging. I liked Detroit. It was much smaller than New York, people seemed to know one another, and it was a city of neighborhoods and beautiful trees. It also felt like a "Movement" city where radical history had been made and could be made again. Working with CLR had been exciting but also extremely intellectual. As Johnsonites we tried to remain close to the grass roots, but it was still secondhand. I needed to return to the concrete.

Nobody was happy about our decision. Nobody gave us a party or gifts. But only two people openly objected, both of them black. One man, who worked in the plant with Jimmy, told me that I didn't know what I was getting into. This was the early 1950s, and I must admit that I hadn't given the question any thought. I had to change the way I drove because I soon discovered that when Jimmy was in the passenger seat cops gave me tickets for what I used to get away with. We were married by a justice of the peace in Toledo, Ohio. Driving along Lake Huron on our way back from our honeymoon in the Upper Peninsula, we had to sleep in the car because no motel would rent us a room. I was living in an apartment on Blaine and 14th Street on the west side of Detroit that I had subleased from a comrade. After Jimmy started staying with me, I was evicted.

The other person who disapproved was CLR. He wrote me a letter from London warning that I would end up a "follower" of Jimmy's rather than leading him. It was a handwritten blue airgram. I was so ashamed of CLR for writing it that for years I didn't mention or show it to anyone, including Jimmy. Then one day in the 1980s, leafing through the Jessie and Martin Glaberman files in the Wayne State University Labor Archives, I came across a copy that CLR had sent to Marty Glaberman—and who knows how many others. Maybe that is why none of our comrades congratulated us. After discovering the note in the archives, I asked Marty what he thought about it. (He had lent us his car for our honeymoon.) He replied, somewhat shamefacedly, "I figured that the good things CLR did outweighed the others."

I did follow Jimmy at first, consciously and openly, because he was so rooted in reality and in his community and knew so many things about politics that you can't get out of books. After about ten years I began to struggle more with him because I had begun to feel more rooted myself and also because I was concerned that the young people around us would get the wrong idea about how women should relate to men. Then we began arguing so vigorously that people around us often had to switch their eyes from one side to the other as if at a tennis or Ping-Pong match.

The role of the black church in the community and in the movement was the main issue on which we could never agree. As a child, I had gone to Christian Sunday School and church because that was what my mother believed we should do. But I hadn't been to church for decades and didn't think of myself as religious. Nevertheless, it seemed to me obvious that the black church had played a critical role in helping blacks maintain the conviction of their humanity during centuries of slavery and Jim Crow. In the 1950s and 1960s the black church was clearly at the center of the civil rights struggle in the South. In the North it was one of the few places where radicals could almost always hold a meeting, even during the McCarthy period. Jimmy, on the other hand, viewed religion as the opiate of the people and the black church as one of the main obstacles to blacks rising up against their oppression. Black preachers, he maintained, were hypocrites and opportunists, focusing on their own aggrandizement as they kept blacks on their knees and milked them of their hard-earned money.

I can still remember my first argument on this issue with Jimmy and his buddy Willie Lewis. It was in 1953, shortly after we got together. We shouted and screamed at one another with a vehemence that was almost frightening. After a number of equally heated arguments, I began to realize that the bitterness and anger exhibited by Jimmy and Willie were rooted in personal and social experiences that I had not shared. I have seen the same explosiveness around this issue in other black men who were raised in the church and later drawn to radical politics, usually in arguments with their mothers or older sisters. It reminded me of what I have heard about the viciousness of the disputes between the Stalinists and the Trotskyists in the 1930s. In this case I suspect that it is because for centuries blatant racism made the black church the only place where talented black men could exercise their leadership capacities. When the radical movement began to offer another avenue for exercising these talents, the handful of blacks who joined the movement viewed those who didn't as opportunists and traitors. Interestingly, when Willie Lewis lost interest in radical politics in later years, he became a deacon in the church.

The issue remains thorny and extremely important. Recently I was involved in another heated discussion with Michelle Brown, a local community activist who was a Black Panther as a teenager and who is now one of the co-coordinators of Detroit Summer, and Jim Jackson, a close friend and comrade for more than thirty years. We were discussing the struggle to rebuild the black community, and I said that we have to find ways to involve the black church in this struggle because it is one of the few relatively stable institutions remaining in devastated black neighborhoods. Michelle and Jim responded with the usual litany of betrayals by black preachers. In the midst of the discussion Michelle, who has a knack for hitting the nail on the head, turned to me and said, "You may have lived in the black community, Grace, but you are not black." Later Jim elaborated. Black preachers, he said, "have robbed us of our souls. We trusted them to give us spiritual leadership, but they are only interested in their own power." To which, undaunted, I replied, "Then why don't you take back your souls? Why don't you struggle for a reformation in the black church like that which Martin Luther achieved in the Roman Catholic Church in the sixteenth century?" Increasingly I hear rumbles in the black community suggesting that a struggle of this magnitude may be brewing. At this point the movement toward Islam is the tip of the iceberg.

Jimmy's mother, brothers, nephews, and nieces (with one exception) not only accepted me, they welcomed me into the family. Overnight, in line with old southern custom, I became Daughter Grace, Sister Grace, and Auntie Grace. They all lived in Chicago and we visited back and forth. The exception was Jimmy's oldest niece, the daughter of his recently deceased sister. I made the mistake of letting her cut my hair, and she hacked away most of it on one side, saying that the scissors had slipped.

I also felt very comfortable with Jimmy's friends and coworkers in Detroit, a good many of whom were from the South, including some like Joe Johnson and Queenie Brown with whom he had grown up. In those days there were few signs in the Detroit black community of the black nationalism that would later make relationships with blacks so sensitive. I may have been more acceptable as a person of color, although I was always careful to keep clear the distinction between the discrimination experienced by Chinese Americans and the hell that African Americans had endured. I didn't feel that I was being seen as "exotic," probably because during World War II Americans had gotten used to working alongside Orientals, as they were still called. Many blacks had also served in Korea during the war that had recently ended without a victory for the United States. Some had returned with Korean wives. To children, however, I was still a novelty. They wanted to play with my hair because it was so straight. Recently, a middle-aged woman came up to me at a meeting and said that she still remembers when she first met me in the 1950s: "You were the prettiest thing I had ever seen."

My relations with Jimmy's first wife, Annie, and his children were more complicated. When we got together, Jimmy was divorced but he had not seen Annie or the children for months because of the bitterness over the breakup. At my suggestion we took presents to the children at Christmas. The older children adjusted to the situation better than the younger ones. For example, Feller, the oldest, who was fifteen when Jimmy and Annie divorced, understood that his mother and father had been estranged before I met Jimmy. For preschoolers Jacqueline and Thomasine it was confusing. All they knew was that their father was home with them one day, and the next time they saw him he was with me. In the stressful situations that have inevitably arisen over a period of more than forty years, that memory has sometimes surfaced. But over time we developed enough trust so that we would pick up the children and bring them to our house to stay, go to Annie's for Thanksgiving or Christmas dinner, or even invite the whole family to our house. After a number of years Annie would often say that Jimmy and I were her best friends whom she could always turn to for advice and help.

My oldest friend in Detroit has been Ellen Richardson, a black woman from Mississippi who in 1953 had recently married a Detroiter. Jimmy and I were the godparents of her daughter Stephanie, who was born in 1954. Over the years I have not felt the same tension in my relationships with black women that is often in the relationship between white women and black women. That tension is rooted in long years of black women serving as mammies and domestic workers, nurturing Miss Ann's children, doing her laundry, and mopping her floors. By contrast, Asian American and African American women have no history of relating to one another, antagonistic or amicable.

When people discover that my husband was African American, they almost always ask whether we had children. My reply has been that we had no children of our own but that Jimmy had plenty of children by his first marriage and that I have a lot of grandchildren and great-grandchildren. I sense that they are disappointed, partly because of natural curiosity about how our offspring would look. Personally, I never wanted to have children because raising children is a full-time job and I always saw myself out in the world rather than in the home. It has even occurred to me that one of the reasons I married Jimmy was that he wasn't likely to want children because it was tough enough to support the children he already had. For years after we were married he used to get up at 3 A.M. to walk to one job cleaning a bar, then take the streetcar at six to work on the line at Chrysler. The first thing he did every payday was send a money order to the Friend of the Court for child support.

Reactions in my own family varied. Harry and Eddie who lived in Detroit had been friends with Jimmy before I met him. Around the same time that Jimmy and I got together Eddie married Averis, a fellow worker from a small town in Georgia. He was welcomed into her close-knit poor white family the same way I was welcomed into Jimmy's. Averis and Jimmy got along famously, talking and laughing about the experiences they had shared in the South. Eddie, who had known CLR, especially respected Jimmy because he was "the kind of leader who didn't overwhelm you, who let you think for yourself, and who did not expect others to minister to his needs."

My sister Kay, who lived in New York, and my brother Bob, who eventually settled in Hawaii, only met Jimmy a few times but would always send best wishes to him in their letters. Bob said he knew Jimmy was a good man because he took such good care of our father. On my few visits to New York I never discussed my marriage with my father, and until he came to live in Detroit, he said nothing about it, having learned through long experience not to intervene in matters that he was powerless to influence. I don't think he ever anticipated that his children would marry anyone who was not Chinese. When we were young, he used to warn us that the only whites who would have anything to do with Chinese were lowlifes or riffraff. When Harry first began to date Julie in the late 1940s, we considered telling my father that she was really Chinese but didn't look it because she had been raised in Hawaii. Later, in Detroit, I marveled at the way that my father related to Julie, Averis, and Jimmy. It seemed to me that he trusted them as much or even more than he trusted us, his own children.

My mother never said that she approved or disapproved. I assumed it was all right with her because when I lived in her house in Jackson Heights, she used to make my friends, including CLR, feel at home. So I wasn't suspicious when she kept putting off my suggestions that I visit her in Florida where she was living in the late 1950s and early 1960s. In 1962 my sister Kay died, and my mother and I spent a week together in New York cleaning out her apartment and settling her affairs. She flew back to Florida and I came home by train with my sister's body for burial in Detroit where most of the family now lived. Soon after that, my mother began returning my letters and birthday and Christmas gifts unopened. My brothers said she was upset about my sister's death and I accepted the explanation, hoping that the estrangement would be temporary. But as the years passed and the situation remained unchanged, I began having a recurring nightmare in which I frantically wandered the deserted streets of New York near Grand Central Terminal in the wee hours of the morning, trying to find out where my mother was living and how I could get in touch with her. In 1976, when I went to Hawaii to visit her, she refused to see me, telling my brother Bob that she would send for the police if I appeared at her door. After her death in 1978, I put together a little album of her transformation, from a young woman arriving in this country, looking very Oriental in her Chinese dress, through her years as an attractive, very American-looking woman, fashionably dressed or on horseback or in a bathing suit, to a white-haired and fragile elder obviously enjoying herself with family and friends at a party the Christmas before she died, and, finally, her gravestone in Hawaii. I show this album proudly to friends as the story of a Chinese peasant woman who became a woman of the world, saying nothing about our sixteen-year estrangement, not only because it has been too painful but because it has been a mystery to me.

Recently, in the process of writing this book, I raised the question with Bob and Eddie. Bob's advice was to let sleeping dogs lie. Eddie recalled my mother's saying back in the early 1960s that I was jeopardizing her relations with her white neighbors in Florida by sending her copies of *Correspondence* with articles by Jimmy on the escalating black struggle and headlines declaring that "Negroes Are the Ones Best Suited to Govern the United States Today." So she must have decided to cut off all ties with me.

Jimmy and I came from such different backgrounds that if we hadn't both been so committed to the struggle to change this country, it is unlikely that we could have stayed together so long.

He was born in 1919 in Marion Junction, Alabama, a little town where, as he used to say, white people were gentlemen by day and Ku Klux Klan by night. Marion Junction is in Dallas County, where as late as 1963 only 130 blacks were registered voters, even though they made up 57 percent of the total county population of fifty-seven thousand. His father, Ernest, was a blacksmith and iron ore worker who died when Jimmy was eight years old. His mother, Lelia, was a cook. She was twelve when they married. They had four children: Betty, William, Jesse, and Jimmy. Jimmy went to elementary school in Marion Junction and then to Knox Presbyterian School and Dunbar High School fourteen miles away in Selma, Alabama. After graduating from Dunbar High School in 1937, he hopped a freight train north to Detroit where his brothers, William and Jesse, were already living. Unable to get a job in Detroit, he again hopped a freight train, bumming his way through the western part of the United States, working in the hop fields of Washington State, cutting ice in Minnesota, and finally landing back in Detroit where he worked on the WPA until World War II gave him a chance to enter the Chrysler-Jefferson plant. He worked there for twenty-eight years on the motor line and was active in the local and on the Fair Employment Practices Committee created by Executive Order 8802.

We couldn't have been more different. An attractive brown-skinned man of medium height with a powerful neck and shoulders and a slim body, Jimmy took pride in his personal appearance, spending a lot of time in front of the mirror trimming his mustache, combing his hair, and rubbing on lotion and cologne. I never wear makeup or cologne and would brush my hair, throw on some clothes, and be ready to go. I had been raised in New York City. Jimmy was raised in rural Alabama. The saying "You can take a person out of the country, but you can't take the country out of a person" might have been coined for him. I have a New England accent. He spoke what is usually called Black English, taking pride in his Alabamese and telling audiences that they had better struggle to understand him because one day they would have to understand a billion Chinese. I like my meat and vegetables crisp, Chinese style; he liked them cooked to death. Traveling along the highway, I would have my head in a book, while he was pointing out the cows and the sheep, counting the freight cars and trying to figure out what they were carrying based on his knowledge of industry and agriculture in the region. I hated housework; he actually enjoyed vacuuming and mopping and waxing the bathroom and kitchen floors. After working all day at Chrysler, he would take out his frustrations with a broom or a mop. My approach to political questions came more from books, his from experience. We struggled over almost every issue. But I felt myself growing from the struggle, and I could also see the growth in him.

In addition to our commitment to struggling for radical change, another thing Jimmy and I had in common was that his mother, like mine, had never been to school and could not read or write. But even here, there was an important difference. My mother had lived in a big house and rarely lacked money to buy whatever she wanted. But she was not part of a community. She had no one to talk to about her problems. So she saw them as personal, not social. Jimmy's mother, whom everyone called Mama Lelia, had worked in the white man's kitchen all her life, but like many southern blacks she saw herself not as a victim but as a survivor, someone who despite obstacles succeeded in winning self-respect and the respect of others. During the six years that Mama Lelia lived with us, I felt closer to her than I had ever felt to my mother. I think that is because their philosophies of life were so different. My mother had the American conviction that she had an inalienable right to happiness and that somehow I was to blame because she was not enjoying this right. By contrast, as Jimmy was growing up, his mother used to tell him to "do whatever makes you happy, but at the same time you should do things that make the world a little better for everybody." And that, Jimmy used to say, is "what I have been trying to do all my life."

From the moment that I began living in the black community, I was impressed by the high level of social and political consciousness on the part of grassroots blacks who had been born and raised in the segregated South before the civil rights movement opened up avenues of upward and outward mobility for the black middle class. Those who had gone to college and those like Mama Lelia who could not read or write had to live next door to one another. Year in and year out, people talked about who was doing what in the community, how black folks were being treated and how what was going on in the world affected blacks. In barber shops, on front porches, at funerals and weddings, folks testified from their own personal experiences, wondering collectively why white folks were so inhuman and usually concluding that it was because they were more interested in material gain than in human relationships. In small groups and large, they talked about and judged the actions of individuals in their community, rejecting the temptation to make racism an excuse for antisocial behavior. Through this tradition of face-to-face oral communication, now in danger of disappearing, black folks maintained the conviction of their own worth and saved their own souls by refusing to fall victim to fear or the hatred of their oppressors, which they recognized would have been more destructive to themselves than to their enemies. As the poet Lucille Clifton put it, "Ultimately if you fill yourself with venom you will be poisoned."[3] There were incidents of individual violence, usually crimes of passion committed by someone under the influence of alcohol and over a man or a woman. But despite the unimaginable cruelty that they suffered, blacks kept their sense of humor and created the art form of the blues as a way to work through and transcend the harshness of their lives. Living under the American equivalent of Nazism, they developed an oasis of civility in the spiritual desert of "me-firstism" that characterized the rest of the country.

I spent the first few years of our marriage getting to know Jimmy and his friends and the city of Detroit. Except for the time I was in London working with CLR in 1954 and 1957, I was mostly involved in meetings with Jimmy's coworkers and *Correspondence* readers, listening and learning, making good use of a "full fountain pen," as I had discovered how to do in the Third Layer School. During this period I also worked in a number of offices, first, for some automotive industry suppliers in the General Motors New Center area and then for lawyers in downtown Detroit. I liked working on these jobs because they gave me a sense of the city from different viewpoints. I would usually start out as a Kelly Girl, and after working as a temp for a few weeks I would be hired outright for about $50 a week. The New Center job was a snap. All I did was take phone messages when the salesmen were not in the office. When I told them that I was a writer, they set aside some file drawers and a typewriter and writing paper for me. From the New Center job I got a picture of the relationship between the Big Three automakers and their suppliers.

Donald Welday, the first lawyer I worked for downtown, was an older man and a public administrator who had been appointed by a Republican administration. He made a good living without having to hustle. Citron & Cole, my next employers, were relatively new to the profession. They did a lot of Common Pleas work, including garnishee cases, and oversaw the sale of homes (most of which were owned by their Jewish friends who were moving to the suburbs) to blacks on land contracts. So their clients were mostly Jewish and black. Later I worked for an older Jewish lawyer who made a comfortable living without overexerting himself, doing probate work for his peers. From there I moved to a job typing proposals for the Production Machinery Sales Corporation on St. Aubin Street about a mile from where we lived. When I was laid off from that job in the early 1960s, I taught elementary school for a few years. Because of the scarcity of teachers for inner city schools, the Detroit public schools put out a call for people with liberal arts degrees but without teaching certificates to serve as so-called resource teachers, provided that they took educational courses to get their certificates. So I took forty credits at Wayne State University to acquire my elementary school teaching certificate, meanwhile making about $200 a week, more money than I had ever made before or since, and getting a good idea of why American education needs a fundamental restructuring.

After we were evicted from the Blaine Street apartment, which was on the west side of Detroit, we moved to the east side where most of Jimmy's friends and coworkers lived, many of them within walking distance. For about nine months we lived on Chene and Lafayette in a one-room furnished apartment with a pullout bed for $20 a week. The apartment had just been vacated by Jimmy's ex-sister-in-law, Ruby, who was moving to Chicago. Most of the sheets, towels, pots, and pans that I am still using were left behind by her. Then we moved further east to a three-room apartment in a building on Townsend and Agnes that was renting to black people for the first time. The whites had been paying $40 a month. We paid $62.50. There were still a few poor whites living in the neighborhood who drank and partied a lot. One day, as we were going out the door, I noticed a white man lying unconscious on the front seat of a car parked in front of our apartment house with the motor running and the windows closed. Concerned that he might be overcome by carbon monoxide, I moved to open the door and check on him, only to be stopped by Jimmy. "Don't you know that you could be charged with robbing him?" he said. That is the kind of thing I had to learn.

From the apartment on Townsend Street we moved in 1957 to a house in the same neighborhood on the corner of Baldwin and Goethe that was owned by Jimmy's good friend and coworker Meredith Peterson. Mr. Pete, as everyone in the neighborhood called him, was a courtly gentlemen who had been born and raised in Mississippi. His daughter, Virginia, still lives around the corner from us. In 1962 the house on Baldwin was bulldozed to build Bell Elementary School and we moved three blocks over to the corner house at Field and Goethe where I still live in the downstairs flat. It consists of six rooms with one and a half baths, has leaded windows and beveled-glass French doors. About twenty years ago the 1½" thick oak front door and bordering beveled glass panels were whisked away in the middle of the night by burglars who specialized in supplying irreplaceable items like these to builders of new expensive homes. The living room is 20' x 14' with a pewabic tile fireplace. Our starting rent in 1962 was $70. The landlady wanted $75 but I told her we couldn't afford it. Thirty years later, when Jimmy died, we were paying $150. Friends from New York and California used to joke that it would be cheaper for them to live in Detroit and commute to work.

Our neighborhood, which is only a few blocks west of Indian Village with its palatial mansions, was at one time predominantly German and then Italian. Before the 1967 rebellion there were still a few white residents. Today, I know of only one, a seventy-five-year old friend of Rumanian descent, who lives in the Field House down the street, which was built in the 1840s. There are many neighborhoods in Detroit with beautiful houses built before World War II by artisans, many of them still in excellent condition. A few, like ours, have carriage houses in the rear. Some that have been empty for decades have been or are being restored for personal use or for nursing and funeral homes like those on East Grand Boulevard one block west of Field. Diagonally opposite 3061 is a big house with a beautiful backyard that has been empty and boarded up for more than a year. A dwelling like that in the suburbs would be a bargain at $100,000, but no one wants it at one-tenth that amount because the inner city of Detroit is perceived as dangerous. Recently, for example, a student who had made an appointment to interview me called to ask if she could bring her boyfriend because her father did not think it was safe to be driving alone in my neighborhood. My sense is that living where I do is no more hazardous than living almost anywhere in the United States. Like practically all Americans, we have had some unpleasant experiences with break-ins—in addition to the very professional theft of our front door and bordering glass panels. In 1962 some kids squeezed their way into the house through a small rear window and got away with our TV, stereo, floor lamps, electric typewriter, and Jimmy's precious jazz collection. In the summer of 1990, while we were in Maine, someone broke in through the back door and stole our VCR, microwave, and a lot of canned goods. Some years ago, as I was going out the back gate to get into my car, a kid snatched my purse. Jimmy, a neighbor, and I chased him for three blocks in vain. Later that day, however, someone phoned to say that they had found my purse with the money gone but all the papers intact. While I was in Cuba last spring, someone broke into the garage and stole my car. When the police drove up behind it a week later, the man who jumped out and ran off resembled a neighbor who has been in and out of prison ever since I can remember. When he is out, we have to be extra careful about where we park our cars or leave our snowblower.

Living with Jimmy I was constantly reminded of how I had internalized the white liberal and radical view of blacks chiefly as victims and protesters. Jimmy refused to romanticize either workers or blacks and insisted that everyone, regardless of race or class, be held to the same high standards of conduct. For example, in 1953 his nephew, returning from serving in the army in Korea, showed up at our door. We made him welcome, listening and learning from his account of his experiences in Asia. But he would stay out all night carousing and come home in the morning to sleep all day just as we were leaving for work. After two weeks of this Jimmy told him that we had had enough and gave him his bus fare back to Chicago. In Chicago he was arrested for committing a felony and sentenced to a year in prison. Instead of sympathizing with him, the family decided that the punishment was deserved and that serving his sentence was the best way for him to learn how to stay out of trouble in the future.

Jimmy was very conscious of black suffering and oppression. But precisely because blacks have been so oppressed, he insisted that they can least of all afford to wallow in their victimization. The more they use their oppression to justify antisocial behavior, the more they weaken their own forces. The more sorry they feel for themselves, the more likely they are to expect others to change their condition and therefore the more powerless they become. Instead of making excuses for blacks, he was always chiding and challenging them, just as he was always chiding and challenging workers. He was constantly reminding people that when the union movement started in the 1930s, only a minority were ready to risk getting involved. Most workers, he used to say, had to be "whipped into joining the union."

Jimmy resonated to the devastating critique of Irving Howe's liberalism by Ralph Ellison, a fellow Southerner. Howe had written an article in *Dissent* attacking James Baldwin and Ellison for their critique of "protest fiction" and instead projecting Richard Wright's *Native Son* and *Black Boy* as models of Negro literature. Ellison's reply appeared in two articles of *The New Leader*.[4] One gets the impression, wrote Ellison, that when Howe

> looks at a Negro he sees not a human being but an abstract embodiment of living hell. He seems never to have considered that American Negro life . . . is for the Negro who must live it not only a burden (and not always that) but a discipline teaching its own insights into the human condition, its own strategies of survival. . . . Crucial to this view is the belief that their resistance to provocation, their coolness under pressure, their sense of timing and their tenacious hold on the ideal of their ultimate freedom are indispensable values in the struggle and are at least as characteristic of American Negroes as the hatred, fear and vindictiveness which Wright chose to emphasize.

There were many occasions when Jimmy's coolness under pressure impressed me. One that sticks in my mind was in 1960 when a state trooper stopped us as we were driving to New York on the Ohio Turnpike with Kathleen Gough, our British anthropologist friend, to take a plane to visit CLR in Trinidad. Packed tighter than sardines in Kathleen's tiny Morris Minor, we were a curious trio. Jimmy was driving. Kathleen, a tall woman, heavier than Jimmy, with red hair, a ruddy complexion, and a strong resemblance to Queen Elizabeth II, was in the passenger seat. I was squeezed in a corner of the backseat, trying to avoid being swamped by enough baggage to serve the needs of three people for a five-week vacation. The trooper ordered Jimmy to get out of the car, made him spread-eagle, and frisked him for weapons, explaining that he was doing this because a black man had held up a bank in Toledo and he had to make sure that ours was not the getaway car. Kathleen and I were ready to explode. Jimmy's comment was "No use us being crazy just because white folks are crazy."

Living and doing political work with Jimmy in Detroit was unlike anything I had previously experienced. Organizational meetings in the Workers Party and the Socialist Workers Party revolved a lot around the question of how to reach out to workers in the community. For Jimmy that was no problem. During the war whole communities and extended families had transplanted themselves from Alabama to Detroit, usually settling within walking distance of one another. Jimmy's coworkers at the Chrysler-Jefferson plant lived all around us. Jimmy didn't have to go out to find them. People in the community came to him for advice on community issues, for example, how to get rid of a fence on Mack Avenue that the residents of Indian Village, at that time a predominantly white enclave, had obviously built to keep out blacks. They also came to him with their personal problems. Almost like a precinct captain of the old-time city political machine, he helped them write for their birth certificates or process a grievance at work. They listened to his advice on how to cope with their cars, their children, or their spouses as if he were their minister. He loved being a notary public so that he could certify documents for friends and neighbors, never accepting payment. Observing the scrupulousness with which he kept his word, I would sometimes be reminded of Kant's categorical imperative: "Act always as if the maxim of your action could become a universal law."

Meetings of all kinds took place in our house. Practically anyone who has been involved in movement politics in Detroit, even some that I don't remember, can recall sitting on the couch in our living room discussing issues and strategies. During the 1950s Jimmy was a member of a rank-and-file caucus of the local, consisting mainly of white workers trying to stop speedup on the line through shop floor actions. One of the white workers, Andy Kranson, was always running for election as shop steward, but Jimmy who was not interested in holding office was the political leader of the group, writing the leaflets that described conditions in the plant and projected actions by the rank and file. As the situation developed locally and nationally and the issues changed, so did the people who came to the house to learn what Jimmy (and later I) thought and to enlist our assistance in developing strategies and writing leaflets.

The membership and leadership of Chrysler-Jefferson Local 7 today is predominantly black, but in the early 1950s white workers were still the majority in the plant. The bar across the street was still Jim Crow and the "place" position reserved for blacks in the Local was recording secretary. We considered it a huge victory when we won our campaign to elect a black worker, Ted Griffin, as Local 7 vice president in 1957.

I never ceased to envy and marvel at the fluency with which Jimmy wrote and the speed with which his pen would travel from the left side of the page to the right. When he came home from work, he would lie down on his stomach on the living room floor with a yellow pad and start writing. He would wake up mornings and dash off letters to the editor before breakfast. In the course of a meeting he would start writing and by the end of the meeting be ready with a draft of a leaflet or letter. When he was asked where he acquired these skills, he would say that it came from writing letters for the mostly illiterate people in the little town where he grew up. Like other blacks who developed into writers, he began as the community scribe. Just as his childhood writing served his community, every speech he made, every article he wrote as an adult came out of his experiences in the ongoing struggle and was produced in order to advance the struggle. His passion for writing, I am convinced, played an important role in his development as a leader and a revolutionary theoretician. Blacks emphasize the importance of the oral tradition in African and African American history, and rightly so. But the continuing review, revision, and self-criticism that are necessary to the development of ideas depend on a written script.

CLR with all his brilliance would never have been so productive had it not been that so many people took care of him, supported him financially, ran his errands, did his research, deciphered and typed his manuscripts. By contrast, Jimmy was always taking care of others. If he looked out the window and saw someone trying to start his car, he was out there like a flash offering his help. He filled out income tax forms for people in the community and for his coworkers, white and black. They trusted him more than they trusted H & R Block and brought their friends and relatives to him. I especially recall Mike, an old Italian retiree with a throat ailment that made him barely audible. Playing the numbers was Mike's only recreation. One year, after Jimmy had done his taxes, Mike concluded that Jimmy had the inside dope on which number would come out each day. Jimmy didn't want to disillusion Mike because having someone to talk to every day obviously meant so much to him. So every evening until Mike died, he would call and they would go through the ritual of Jimmy telling him what number had come out that day and giving him a number to play tomorrow.

Jimmy was especially caring toward young people and elders. We watched three generations of young people grow up on Field Street, where we lived for more than thirty years. He called them "my girls" and "my boys," kept track of how they were doing in school, and was always ready to help them with their homework or with advice about a summer job or how to get a student loan. His boys used to drive me crazy by ringing the bell late at night and asking for a dollar for bus fare. They called him Mr. Jimmy and me Miss Grace. During the Vietnam War he counseled hundreds of young Detroiters on how to register as conscientious objectors. To this day I receive phone calls from some of those whom he counseled, asking if there is anything they can do for me because they have never forgotten what he did for them.

His concern for elders was even more remarkable. As a boy he had taken care of Big Ma, his great-grandmother, feeding and dressing her and emptying her bedpan. In the 1960s my father lived with us for several months of each year. He was in his nineties but was very active. Jimmy would spend hours talking with him about the 1930s and "that man in the White House." There was nothing Jimmy wouldn't do for him. After Mama Lelia had lived with us for six years, we had to put her in a nursing home on the far west side. Jimmy not only visited her every day at dinner time to make sure that she was well taken care of, but he made the rounds, spending a few minutes with each patient, white and black, especially with those who had no visitors. We used to visit regularly with Chrysler-Jefferson retiree Nick Digaetano and his wife Sophie who lived not far from us and made wine from the grapes in their garden. Sophie had come from Russia in the early part of this century, and Nick from Sicily. An ex-Wobbly and a Local 7 shop committeeman for many years, Nick had taken Jimmy under his wing during World War II, lending him books like Louis Adamic's *Dynamite* and teaching him how to process union grievances. Nick printed and bound books and papers in his basement (his bound volumes of political and union newspapers, including *Correspondence*, are in the Wayne State Labor Archives). When Nick and Sophie had to move out of their home into a senior residence, we transferred Nick's printing and binding equipment into our basement because we could not bear to throw it out.

Sometimes I had the feeling that Jimmy needed this regular contact with elders as much as they did because after one died, I noticed, he would always find a replacement. In retrospect, I suspect that his confidence in his own judgment and his boldness in making projections, which never ceased to amaze me, came in part from his relationship with elders. Constantly talking over the past with old folks apparently provided him with a solid foundation for evaluating the present and building the future.

Jimmy believed that revolutions should be made for love of people and place, not because of hate. In the poem "The Man Who Wouldn't Be

King," written for Jimmy's memorial celebration, local poet Willie Williams called him a "hate hater." He hated the speedup at Chrysler, but he took great pride in his work as a jitney driver responsible for getting the engines to the motor line. It was not just a job but a challenge to his "natural and acquired powers." He never missed a day's work, because he felt that the motor line depended on him for its smooth functioning. We didn't own the house on Field Street, but you would never have known it from the way that Jimmy painted the house and garage every two years, fixed the plumbing and the furnaces, mowed the lawn, and shoveled the snow. Every morning he would go outside and pick up the litter on the street and sidewalks that had been thrown out of cars during the night. After every rain he would rub down his car; the motor under the hood was so clean you could eat off it. This worked against us one year when we were coming in from Canada. At the time customs officials were being so vigilant against drug smugglers that they even searched some black-hatted Mennonites. When they saw how clean Jimmy's motor was, they suspected that it was a hiding place for drugs and almost took our car apart.

Until I married Jimmy I had never voted in any election, local or national, even when the Socialist Workers Party ran candidates. This was partly because I was moving around so much but mostly because I had internalized the radical rejection of reformist politics. Jimmy, on the other hand, had registered to vote immediately on his arrival in Detroit. He had no illusions about the electoral system, but voting for him was a confirmation and continuing reaffirmation of his citizenship and his readiness to take responsibility for running Detroit and American society. He chided radicals who talked about "this lousy country" for their narrowness, insisting that if you want to make a revolution in the United States, you have to love this country enough to change it. Referring often to the work that his ancestors had put into draining and clearing the land and growing the cotton that was the economic basis of this country's industrialization in the nineteenth century, he used to say, "I hate what they have done and are doing to this country, but I love this country not only because my ancestors' blood is in the soil but because I see the potential of what it can become."

Jimmy unabashedly described himself as a revolutionary theoretician. I would never have had the nerve to describe myself that way. I think that is because his ideas came out of his reality and the reality of the lives of his coworkers, friends, and family, and not out just of his head or from books. He read very selectively, as if determined not to be overwhelmed by the books and papers that grew up like weeds around me. For as long as

I can remember, I have been reading the *New York Times* every day. I also read the Detroit paper, but only after I have read the New York one. Jimmy refused to read the *Times* regularly. But he buried himself in the local paper, reading every word in the *Detroit Free Press* from beginning to end, including the classified ads. One of my greatest joys is surrounding myself with a half dozen books on a subject, sampling them one after another to determine which ones, if any, are worth gorging myself on. Jimmy had a few favorites to which he returned again and again. One of these was *The Ragged Trousered Philanthropists*, a novel by Robert Tressel describing his work as a house painter and the refusal of his fellow workers to entertain socialist ideas despite the harsh conditions of their lives. Another was *The Revolt of the Masses* by José Ortega y Gasset, which attributes the barbarism of modern society to the rise of the masses at one end and of the technicians and specialists at the other. Neither has any sense of historical development.[5]

His attitude toward the Communist Party also came out of his reality. It was very different from CLR's. Soon after his arrival in England in 1932, CLR read Trotsky's *History of the Russian Revolution*, joined a small Trotskyist group, and almost immediately, because of his oratorical skills and charisma, became a major spokesperson. It was a period when radicals in Europe and the United States fought one another verbally and sometimes physically over what should or should not have been done to make a successful revolution hundreds and thousands of miles away — in the Soviet Union, China, Germany, Spain. In the spirit of these battles CLR undertook the writing of *World Revolution: 1917–1936: The Rise and Fall of the Communist International*.[6] I have always found this book unreadable because of its rhetorical excess in portraying the revolutionary masses as the victims of Stalin. Stalin is accused throughout of "betraying" the Russian revolution, "killing" the German revolution, "ruining" the Chinese Revolution, abandoning the Spanish revolution, and allowing Hitler to come to power in Germany, while Trotsky is portrayed as the savior.

By contrast, Jimmy was always very measured in his attitude toward the Soviet Union and the Communist Party, always careful to avoid any association with the anti-Communism of the power structure. As he put it in an article in *Correspondence* in the spring of 1954, "The way I see it America is a place where they talk about democracy and don't practice it, and Russia is a place where they talk about Communism and don't practice it." Coming from New York City to Detroit, I was amazed at how clear the average black was about the positive contributions that the Communists had made to the struggle for justice for working and black people and how out of place the anti-Stalinism of Trotskyists would have been in a gathering of community people. In fact, when I came to Detroit, Coleman Young had just become a hero in the black community because he had stood up against the House Un-American Activities Committee, declaring, "If being for human rights makes me a Communist, then I'm a Communist." Like most of his friends Jimmy was aware that the American Communists had provided indispensable leadership in the struggle against Jim Crow and to create the unions: it was the intervention of the Communist Party that stopped the legal lynching of the Scottsboro Boys, and the CIO (Congress of Industrial Organizations) would probably not have been organized in the 1930s without the active participation of Communist Party members. At the shop and community level Jimmy worked with Communists as comrades; they were his coworkers, friends, and neighbors. During World War II he participated with black members of the Communist Party in sit-down strikes to protest union and management discrimination against black workers. During the Reuther-led witchhunt, when management and the union tried to get rid of radicals, he mobilized black workers to support Van Brooks, a Chrysler-Jefferson coworker and Communist Party member. He was very conscious that without the existence of the Soviet Union and its opposition to Western imperialism, the struggles of blacks in this country for civil rights and of Third World peoples for political independence would have been infinitely more difficult. Jimmy was not unaware of the atrocities that had been committed by the party and Stalin. However, what mattered to him was not the party's or the Soviet Union's record but where people stood on the concrete issue at hand, and he was grateful to the party because, as he used to say, "It gave me the fortitude to stand up against the odds." Like other politically conscious blacks of his generation he recognized that without the Communists it would have taken much longer for blacks to make the leap from being regarded as inferior to being feared as subversive, that is, as a social force. This attitude toward the Communists is beautifully conveyed in a poem written by Ruby Dee after the collapse of the Soviet Union in 1991, originally titled "I'm Going to Miss the Russians."[7]

Inside the Workers Party and the Socialist Workers Party I had had very little contact with members of the Communist Party. After I moved to Detroit I met a number of black Communists who worked in the plant with Jimmy. I never thought of them as Stalinists, and I had no difficulty relating to and working with them on local issues.[8]

Jimmy's discussions with those with whom he disagreed politically also sharply contrasted with the polemics of radicals. He never used abusive language, never attacked individuals or impugned their motives. His civility in these matters, I suspect, reflected his upbringing in the southern black community where unity against the common enemy was more important than ideological differences. Acknowledging complexity also came much more naturally to him than it did to me. Particularly when I was younger, I had a tendency to go overboard in my enthusiasms and antagonisms. Jimmy's life experiences had taught him to think dialectically, that is, to recognize that in everything there is the duality of both the positive and the negative, that things are constantly changing, and that ideas that were once liberating can become fixations that distort reality.

The radicals I had associated with were shaken up by visits from FBI agents. In contrast, Jimmy treated FBI agents like backward children. When they arrived at our door periodically to inquire about black militants like Max Stanford or Robert Williams, the Monroe, North Carolina, leader who had spearheaded armed resistance to the KKK in defense of his black community, Jimmy would first of all make clear that he was not an informant. Then he would chide the agents for allowing themselves to be pushed around by J. Edgar Hoover and invite them to his next public meeting to learn how to struggle against their own oppression.

Jimmy was so unlike other black and radical leaders I have known that it is almost as if we were dealing with different species. Seeing him in a room or working among other black workers, he was undistinguishable from the average worker and was determined not to "cut the cords that tie me to the rank and file," as described in one of his favorite poems by Countee Cullen. That is one of the main reasons why he refused to abandon his Alabamese. When we met, he had just resigned from the executive board of his UAW local because workers who were not board members were excluded from the meetings. But when he rose to speak his mind, he would speak with such passion, challenging all within hearing to stretch their humanity, that he would often bring down the house. Watching him work as a leader, I was reminded of Ellison's description of jazz:

> [Jazz] is an art of individual assertion within and against the group. Each true jazz moment (as distinct from the uninspired commercial performance) springs from a contest in which each artist challenges all the rest; each solo flight, or improvisation, represents (like the successive canvases of a painter) a definition of his identity: as individual, as member of the collectivity, and as a link in the chain of tradition. Thus, because jazz finds its very life in an endless improvisation upon traditional materials, the jazzman must lose his identity even as he finds it.[9]

That is how Jimmy gave leadership. He asserted himself as an individual, as a member of the collectivity and as a link in the chain of tradition. But in finding his identity, he also lost it. There was nothing of the egotism, the self-centeredness, the arrogance that I have seen in so many radical and black leaders. As Vincent Harding put it in his remarks at Jimmy's memorial celebration in 1993, "He was a warrior who didn't need to growl to prove that he was a warrior."

Jimmy had an unshakable faith in the ability of humanity to keep evolving. That is why he didn't need to growl. This faith was constantly being nurtured by the poetry and music of the Harlem Renaissance, whose unique optimism has been noted by cultural critics.[10] He was always listening to the music of Duke Ellington and much more inclined to quote Countee Cullen or Langston Hughes than Karl Marx. He frequently startled his audiences by talking grandly about himself. It was his way of expressing confidence in the ability of others, particularly those at the bottom of society, to achieve grandeur. Addressing a class at the University of Michigan in 1991, for example, he declared, "I don't believe nobody can run this country better than me." Responding to the nervous laughter of the students, he continued, "I'm saying that you'd better think that way. You need to stop thinking of yourself as a minority because thinking like a minority means you're thinking like an underling. Everyone is capable of going beyond where you are."[11]

I don't want to give the impression that Jimmy was a saint. He cussed a lot, and he had a tendency to exaggerate. I sometimes had to play the bad guy and say no because he found it impossible to turn anyone down. Like his brothers Bill and Jesse, he was terribly long-winded; we used to joke that in order to make a point about capitalism, he had to go all the way back to the beginning of feudalism. He infuriated me with his backseat driving. On all too many occasions it made me so angry that I would stop the car, get into the passenger seat, and refuse to talk to him or have anything to do with him for days. We also had ferocious fights over the way that periodically, without saying a word to me, he would sweep up the clutter of notes and papers that I had allowed to pile up all over the house and throw it into the Dumpster.

But I have put so much emphasis on the contrast between his leadership and that of other political leaders because I believe he was the kind of organic leader, at one with and serving his community and at the same time challenging his coworkers, friends, and neighbors, that the movement needs to discover and nurture. I have also emphasized his love for this country and his caring qualities because over the years I have found these same qualities, in varying degrees, in a number of blacks from Jimmy's generation who were raised in the South and who are now in their twilight years. In the wake of the black nationalist tide in the 1960s and 1970s, black militants repudiated their southern forebears as Uncle Toms, replacing them with African kings and queens with whom they had no personal connections. In the process intergenerational relationships were ruptured and precious human qualities were lost. Anyone who is concerned about the future of this country needs to be thinking about how to restore these relationships. It would be a calamity for everyone in this country if these qualities were allowed to die out with Jimmy's generation.

Jimmy was fond of saying that he had lived through three different eras: agriculture, industry, and automation. His caring can be traced, I think, to his having grown up as part of a small agricultural community as a boy. In the country he had learned to cherish and nurture life and to function as a member of a community that was like an extended family. He had learned the basic skills necessary to meet the elementary needs of food, clothing, and shelter and to make do with very little so that he felt free to make political choices. Coming to Detroit to live and make his living in the period when the labor movement was gathering momentum, he discovered the tremendous leap in their humanity that the oppressed experience when they come together in militant struggle. Working on the line at Chrysler and taking pride in himself as a worker and citizen of Detroit, he was constantly challenged by the variety of people he encountered and the speed and energy of developments inside and outside the plant to see himself as an agent of change and to conclude that everyone is capable of being more than we are if we believe in ourselves and in our capacity to do what has not yet been done. I have often felt that all of us, and especially our young people, need this combination of city and country for our continuing human development.[12] Why did Jimmy become a leader when others with the same background, for example, his brothers, did not? Questions like that are, in the words of poet Alice Walker, "like locked rooms / full of treasures / to which my blind / and groping key / does not yet fit."[13]

In the 1950s our main political activity was publishing *Correspondence*. After CLR left the country Raya Dunayevskaya took over leadership of the organization. Johnny Zupan, a Ford worker, was the worker-editor who wrote a column titled "Workers Journal." Under the pen name of Al Whitney, Jimmy wrote a column titled "The Half That Hasn't Been Told." He was also the comrade chiefly responsible for reporting what people in the plant and the community were saying for the six columns of "Readers Views," the main feature distinguishing our newsletter from other radical papers. Meanwhile, CLR continued to send weekly and often daily directives from London on how to run the organization and the paper.

In 1954 and 1955 McCarthyism was at its height. All over the country radicals were burning their copies of the *Communist Manifesto* and hiding their Paul Robeson albums. Raya, whose history in the radical movement went back to the 1920s when the Communist Party under FBI pressure split over whether or not to remain above ground, had us changing our names every few months to the point where we ourselves often could not identify who was who in our letters and minutes. The situation became even more confused when CLR sent an article from England titled "Is McCarthy a Communist?" for front-page publication in the April 4, 1954, *Correspondence*. In 1955 the Subversive Activities Board brought the developing crisis in the organization to a head when it included *Correspondence* on its list of subversive organizations. Raya proposed that we go underground. Jimmy and Lyman took the position that as Americans we had a perfect right to continue doing what we were doing. They were supported by CLR, who said that the real reason why Raya wanted to go underground was that she wanted to write a book and "leave the movement." In those days differences serious enough to cause a split were often accompanied by such allegations. The assumption was that what *you* thought and did was "the truth, the whole truth, and nothing but the truth." Therefore, anyone who disagreed with you was probably leaving the movement. In any case, we parted company. Approximately half the group of about fifty members, including Johnny Zupan and Si Owens, whose pen name became Charles Denby, went with Raya. The rest stayed with *Correspondence*.

Far from leaving the movement, Raya's group went on to found a newsletter called *News and Letters* with exactly the same format as *Correspondence*, except that it also contained long philosophical and historical articles by Raya. Moreover, *News and Letters* has continued publication to this day, while after the split *Correspondence* appeared irregularly and finally suspended publication in 1964. Zupan wrote the "Workers Journal" column of *News and Letters* and acted as worker-editor. After he left, Charles Denby became editor and also took over "Workers Journal."

CLR had been right on target when he said that Raya was eager to write a book. In 1958 her book *Marxism and Freedom: From 1776 until Today* appeared with an introduction by Herbert Marcuse.[14] Up until the last few pages it recapitulated practically verbatim the work that the three of us had done together in the Johnson-Forest Tendency in the 1940s and 1950s on the philosophy of Hegel, the political economy of Adam Smith and David Ricardo, and how Marx went beyond them. At the same time, incredibly, there was no mention of the Johnson-Forest Tendency, of CLR, or of me, and no hint that the ideas in the book were the product of our collaboration. Not until many years later was the record of our collaboration included in the Raya Dunayevskaya Collection in the Wayne State University Archives, accompanied by documents tracing the split back to "philosophic divisions" that had been implicit for some time.[15]

After the split Raya forbade the members of her group to have any contact with the members of *Correspondence*. It was a hangover from her radical past when having anything to do with members of an opposing group, including attending the funeral of someone with whom you had split, was frowned on. For more than thirteen years Raya and I had been closer than sisters. But after the split if we met one another at a meeting—which was natural and normal since the *News and Letters* headquarters was in Detroit—she would look right past me. I couldn't believe my eyes when this happened in a Wayne State University restroom on a couple of occasions.

The main reason for the 1956 split, I believe, is that CLR underestimated Raya. He treated her as a subordinate, not understanding that she had always seen herself as a coleader, both theoretically and organizationally, of the Johnson-Forest Tendency. He found it hard to accept that those whom he had mentored had to sink or swim on their own. CLR's misjudgment in this situation was not a momentary lapse. The same pattern would repeat itself time and again—with Lyman Paine, Eric Williams, and Jimmy Boggs.

Raya's genius, in my opinion, was not so much in the ideas she developed and espoused but in the audacity with which she conceived of herself as a revolutionary philosopher and leader in the tradition of Hegel, Marx, Lenin, Trotsky, and Rosa Luxemburg, and the single-mindedness with which she organized all her personal and political relationships toward the goal of making a reality of this self-concept. She was probably the most powerful woman I ever met. Jimmy used to call her "the old Bolshevik." Born in Russia in 1912, she came to this country in the early 1920s with her family and soon thereafter, at the age of twelve or thereabouts, became a radical activist, working on the *Negro Champion*, the organ of the Communist-sponsored American Negro Labor Congress. After joining the Trotskyist Left Opposition, she taught herself Russian so that she could become Trotsky's secretary in Mexico. Studying Marx's *Capital* on her own, she arrived at the state-capitalist analysis of the Soviet Union independently. The more she developed herself as a theoretician, the more she began to see herself not only as the equal but possibly the superior to

CLR because she had been born in poverty, was self-educated, and had a longer history in the movement, having experienced the Russian Revolution as a five-year-old.

Raya had a deep distrust of petit bourgeois intellectuals. For example, when I received a raise in pay to $100 a week from James G. McDonald, she was so afraid that it would corrupt me that she took me away for a weekend to lecture me on my class origins. This was at a time when she was married to a man with a high-paying job, living in a luxurious apartment on Sutton Place!

In an earlier chapter I described our jubilation when Raya discovered Marx's early *Economic and Philosophic Manuscripts* and Lenin's notes on Hegel. To me Marx's early essays were important because they reinforced the Johnson-Forest view that the essence of socialist revolution is the expansion of the natural and acquired powers of human beings, not the nationalization of property. To Raya they also meant an opportunity to become the heir to Marx's humanist ideas and the national and international spokeswoman for Marxist humanism as "the philosophy of liberation for our age." Lenin's notes on Hegel were and still are significant to me because they emphasize that contradictions inevitably arise in the process of struggle and also the importance of creating a vision of human expansion for the revolution that you are struggling to make. For Raya, Lenin's enthusiastic comments on passages in Hegel were an inspiration to begin writing like Hegel. As the years passed, she began more and more to use Hegelian language to interpret current events of all kinds, speaking and writing in terms of self-transcendence, negative self-relation, living and spiritual self-movement toward the Absolute Idea or Notion where the universal, the particular, and the singular are united, and so on. I tried for a while to carry on a discussion with her in this vein, but I have to confess that half the time I could not follow what she was saying. For me it was going back to the abstractions of my university days. By contrast, having just discovered Hegel's Absolute Idea, Raya fell in love with it, as she said more than once. Our paths had intersected but we were moving in different directions.

Raya's belief in herself as larger than life has been persuasive. For more than thirty years, until her death in 1987, she maintained the loyalty of comrades who devoted their lives to promoting her as the revolutionary philosopher of our age and who to this day faithfully publish *News and Letters* and collect her notes and articles for posthumous publication. Friends of mine who have gone to her lectures say that listening to her was like taking a walk through history. Members of her group say that her enthusiasm for Hegel and her emphasis on the need to think dialectically have helped them to evaluate developing movements, to anticipate the inevitable contradictions, and to keep their eyes on the ultimate goal. With their help she collected and systematized tens of thousands of documents for deposit in the Wayne State Archives, including not only every speech she ever made and every article and letter she ever wrote but even her most casual notes, all carefully organized to demonstrate that whatever she did or thought from the time she was twelve years old was an integral part of the development of a historic world figure. Two large books listing the materials in the collection, with introductions and notes by Raya, are available from *News and Letters*.[16] An instructive example of how she saw herself is this sentence accompanying the documents from her trip to Europe in 1947 as representative of the state-capitalist tendency: "She also met a Camerounian, and that dialogue anticipated the whole Third World founded in the 1950s."

After the split with Raya, I became the editor of *Correspondence*, continuing in that role until 1964 when we finally disbanded. We established an office on the East Side at 7737 Mack Avenue, not far from where Jimmy and I lived. Jimmy's columns and the "Readers Views" articles in *Correspondence* give a good idea of what was happening all around us.

In the 1950s Detroit was undergoing changes in the city and factories with enormous political consequences. When I arrived in Detroit the city had just begun Urban Renewal (which blacks renamed "Negro Removal") in the area near downtown where most blacks were concentrated. Hastings Street and John R, the two main thoroughfares that were the hub of the commerce and nightlife of the black community, were still alive with pedestrians. Large sections of the inner city, however, were being bulldozed to build the Ford Freeway crisscrossing the city from east to west, the Lodge Freeway bisecting the city from north to south, and the Fisher and Chrysler Freeways coming from Toledo and proceeding all the way north to the Upper Peninsula. These freeways were built to make it easy to live in the suburbs and work in the city and at the same time to expand the car market. So in 1957 whites began pouring out of the city by the tens of thousands until by the end of the decade one out of every four whites who had lived in the city had left. Their exodus left behind thousands of houses and apartments for sale and rental to blacks who had formerly been confined inside Grand Boulevard, a horseshoe-shaped avenue delimiting the inner city, many of whom had been uprooted by Negro Removal. Blacks who had been living on the East Side, among them Annie Boggs, began buying homes on the West Side and the North End. The black community was not only expanding but losing the cohesiveness it had enjoyed (or endured) when it was jammed together on the Lower East Side. New neighbors no longer served as extended family to the young people growing up in the new black neighborhoods. Small businesses owned by blacks and depending on black customers went bankrupt, eliminating an entrepreneurial middle class that had played a key role in stabilizing the community. By the end of the 1950s one-fourth of the buildings inside the Boulevard stood vacant. At the same time all Americans, regardless of race, creed, or national origin, were being seduced by the consumerism being fostered by large corporations so that they could sell the abundance of goods coming off the American assembly lines. All around us in the black community parents were determined to give their children "the things I didn't have."

Changes of a similar magnitude were taking place in industry.[17] The end of the Korean War brought on the recession of 1954. In the midfifties Packard Motor Company merged with Studebaker and moved to the Studebaker plant in South Bend, Indiana, where production soon came to a halt. Hudson Motor Company merged with Nash to become American Motors and moved to Wisconsin. Meanwhile, because of speedup and advancing technology, the auto companies were able to produce more cars and trucks with fewer workers. Employment for unskilled and lower-skilled workers dropped more than 13 percent in the decade of the 1950s. In 1961 automation enabled 641,000 auto workers to produce a half million more cars and trucks than 735,000 had produced in 1949. Chrysler employed the largest number of auto workers in the city at its four plants. Between 1955 and 1958 the workforce at these plants was cut by more than half, from forty-six thousand to twenty-two thousand. No longer seeing a future for themselves in the auto industry, high school dropouts and graduates alike, were beginning to enlist in the armed services. This is what Feller, Jimmy's oldest son, did after graduating from Miller High School in 1957.

In an attempt to force the UAW to take action against speedup and to slow down layoffs, Jimmy and his friends formed a group of unemployed and employed autoworkers to picket Solidarity House, the UAW national headquarters not far from the Chrysler-Jefferson plant and our house. But to no avail. Old friends and shopmates, whose lives had once been given order and purpose by the work routine, were overtaken by despair. Some were turning to drink. In 1961, Jimmy's boyhood friend, Joe Johnson, choked to death on his own vomit. Jimmy was too broken up to speak at the funeral. So I gave the eulogy, describing the hopes and dreams that working folks like Joe once had and blaming his death on the inability of the union to keep these hopes alive. That was my first eulogy. Since then I have given many more in a city where more and more people die not of old age but because the system has failed them. Detroit has become a city where there are too many funerals and where community people use funeral services to say that we can't keep living and dying this way and that there has got to be a change.

Meanwhile, the Emmett Till murder in 1955, the Montgomery Bus Boycott in 1955–56, Ghana independence in March 1957, and the Cuban Revolution in 1959 were arousing new hopes in the community.

The Emmett Till murder shattered the complacency and pursuit of private happiness into which many in Detroit's black community had settled. Until then, it seemed to me that most black Detroiters who had been born and raised in the South were feeling somewhat superior to those who had stayed behind, viewing them with the arrogance that city folk often feel toward country folk, seeing them as too backward and apathetic to get up and leave. At the same time black parents often sent their children south to stay with relatives during the summer to maintain the extended family. I vividly recall Donald, Jimmy's youngest son, scoffing at his southern cousins who were so "country" that they said "Yes, sir" and "Yes, ma'am" to whites. Now the sight of the swollen, battered body of a fourteen-year-old Chicago boy who had been beaten and drowned by some white men because he had allegedly whistled at a white woman, ripped through their self-absorption. In the wake of a NAACP-sponsored tour by Emmett Till's mother, one could feel a national social consciousness reemerging among blacks, recalling that of the World War II years when blacks saw themselves as fighting for "Double D—Democracy at home and abroad." When a colitis attack sent President Eisenhower to the hospital, folks said, "Ike is ill because of Till."

A few months later the Montgomery Bus Boycott began, continuing for more than a year into 1956. Instead of looking down on their southern brothers and sisters, Detroit blacks began to talk about them with pride and envy: "They stick together down there a lot better than we do up here." Their mood was captured in a song, "Stop That Alabama Bus!" written by Will Hairston, a coworker of Jimmy's. Somewhere around the house I must still have the seventy-eight of Will's song.

In 1957 Ghana gained its independence under the leadership of Kwame Nkrumah. In 1959 the Cuban Revolution, under Fidel Castro's leadership, overthrew the U.S.-sponsored Batista regime. Blacks in the plant and the community were jubilant. They saw the Cuban Revolution as ousting the same corporations who at home were introducing automation and throwing them out of work. Blacks were beginning to see themselves as part of a world revolution and of a world majority of colored people and beginning to wonder how they could bring the struggle home. "Africans will be running their own countries, and we still won't be able to drink a cup of coffee at Woolworth's," people were saying.

On February 1, 1960, students sat down in the Woolworth's in Greensboro, North Carolina, to demand that they be served a cup of coffee. Anxious to do something to show our support, a few of us marched up and down Woodward Avenue in front of the downtown Woolworth's. People thought we were crazy because they could get a cup of coffee and a hot dog there anytime. Few of them had any idea of the struggles it had taken to end discrimination in bars and restaurants on Woodward Avenue in the late 1940s and early 1950s after the passage of the Michigan Public Accommodations Act. Jimmy had participated in these struggles with Arthur Johnson, who later served on the Wayne State University Board of Governors, and other members of the NAACP. They would sit down in a coffee shop or bar, citing the new law and refusing to leave until they were served. The owner would call a policeman, charging that they were drunk and disorderly. After a while the cops got to the point where they would tell the owner, "We know Jimmy Boggs. He doesn't drink." Prior to these sit-ins, discrimination in Detroit was accepted as part of the natural order of things, even by radicals. For example, when I came from New York to Detroit to attend an Active Workers conference in 1945, a black comrade was a member of our delegation. One day the Detroit comrades suggested that we go downtown to the Brass Rail for lunch. As we drove down John R, they told the black comrade, without blinking an eye, that they were dropping her en route at a restaurant in the black community because the Brass Rail didn't serve Negroes. They would pick her up later, they said.

When the Freedom Riders were viciously beaten in Anniston, Alabama, in 1961, white workers in the plant from the South, many of whom were still going back to Kentucky and Tennessee on weekends, applauded the violence by the White Citizens Councils and the southern police. The union leadership was willing to assist the civil rights movement with money, but it was not ready to challenge these workers. Jimmy seized the opportunity to criticize the union leadership for not organizing in the South and for not giving more support to the Freedom Riders. Acting for the Fair Practices Committee of Chrysler Local 7, he sent a telegram to Walter Reuther: "In the name of common humanity and as an expression of labor's support of the cause of freedom and equality at home, urgently request that

UAW-AFL-CIO immediately organize and send a fleet of integrated buses of freedom riders to Alabama."

When the Women Strike for Peace (WSP) movement developed in 1961, we formed a group called the Independent Negro Committee to Ban the Bomb and Racism. At the time most blacks saw the bomb as a "white issue," while WSP leaders hesitated to raise civil rights issues for fear of alienating their white middle-class constituency. I recall one white woman at a WSP march trying to rip up my sign calling for a struggle against both racism and the bomb. Our aim was to stretch the humanity of both groups. On a bitter cold day in December 1961 we organized a march in downtown Detroit that included Filomena Daddario from *Correspondence* and black educators Gwendolyn and Conrad Mallett and Delores and Reggie Wilson who had begun to work with us on *Correspondence*.[18] Also among the marchers was Alice Herz, a Jewish refugee from Hitler's Germany, who in 1965 burned herself to death on a busy Detroit intersection to protest the Vietnam War. A few WSP members, including Frances Herring, Eunice Dean Armstrong, and Kathleen Gough, welcomed our initiative, and we made some new friends. Later, as the struggle against racism became more popular, the WSP leadership changed its mind.

This was what was happening all around us in the fall of 1961 when Jimmy, as the chairperson of *Correspondence*, sat down to write the annual "State of the Organization, State of the Nation" document. The document, which would later be published by Monthly Review Press, first as a special summer issue of the magazine and then as a book,[19] began by describing the death of the union because of its failure to grapple with the question of automation. It went on to say that the rapid development of the productive forces by capitalism and the diminishing number of workers resulting from high technology were forcing us to go beyond Marx because Marx's analyses and projections had been made in the springtime of capitalism, a period of scarcity rather than of abundance. The document projected blacks replacing workers as the revolutionary social force in the 1960s. It concluded by insisting that no group is automatically revolutionary:

> People in every stratum [must] clash not only with the agents of the silent police state but with their own prejudices, their own outmoded ideas, their own fears which keep them from grappling with the new realities of our age. The American people must find a way to insist upon their own right and responsibility to make political decisions and to determine policy in all

> spheres of social existence—whether it is foreign policy, the work process, education, race relations, community life. The coming struggle is a political struggle to take political power out of the hands of the few and put it into the hands of the many. But in order to get this power into the hands of the many, it will be necessary for the many not only to fight the powerful few but to fight and clash among themselves as well.[20]

While Jimmy was writing the document, we had a discussion that I often refer to as an example of the process by which Jimmy developed his ideas, which often included turning to me for information that comes out of books. One morning, out of the blue he asked me to explain Marx's concept of Socialism. I replied that Marx had conceived Socialism as the period after the workers seized state power during which they used their power to rapidly develop the productive forces in order to create the abundance that would make possible Communism or the classless society in which everyone contributed according to his talents and received according to his needs. Hearing this, Jimmy immediately had his answer to the question that he had never raised with me but that had been worrying him ever since he became interested in radical politics. What he had never been able to understand, he said, is why Marxists in the plant go blank when a worker asks them, "What is Socialism and why should I fight for it?" His answer is spelled out in chapter 3 of *The American Revolution*, titled "The Classless Society." In it Jimmy writes:

> Marx in the 19th century said that there would have to be a transitional society between the class society of *capitalism* and the classless society of *communism*. This transitional society, which he called *socialism*, would still be a class society but instead of the capitalists being the ruling class, the workers would rule. It was this rule by the workers which, for Marx, would make the society socialist. As the ruling class, the workers would then develop the productive forces to the stage where there could be all-around development of each individual and the principle of "each according to his needs" could be realized. At this point there could be the classless society or communism.
>
> In the United States the forces of production have already been developed to the point where there could be the classless society which Marx said could come only under communism. Yet ever since the Russian Revolution all kinds of socialists have differentiated themselves from the Communists in terms of political policy and political organization but have never tackled this question of Marxist theory that socialism is just a

> transitional society on the way to communism and that only under communism can there be a classless society.[21]

This passage reveals Jimmy's unique and, I believe, exemplary relationship to Marx and Marxists. He respected Marx as a revolutionary theoretician. But unlike many Marxists, he did not revere Marx's ideas as the gospel truth. Recognizing instead that Marx was developing his ideas at a particular time in history and that our reality is not Marx's reality, he was ready to assume the awesome responsibility of doing for our time what Marx did for his.

As usual, we sent the manuscript to CLR in London for his comments. CLR's immediate response was to denounce the document and to declare that what the organization needed was education in Marxism. Toward this end he proposed that *Correspondence* publish a series of articles by him on Marxism. Jimmy replied that what the organization needed was "not a reaffirmation or education in Marxism but a serious study of the development of American capitalism, the most advanced capitalism in the world." To reach that goal he offered a resolution that "CLR's articles on Marxism and his views be discussed inside the organization along with other documents before the organization." CLR's response was an ultimatum: "From henceforth," he declared, "I break all relations, political and personal, with all who subscribe to this resolution."

That is how the split with CLR took place. Faced with this ultimatum from CLR, only four comrades, Freddy and Lyman Paine, Filomena Daddario, and I, were ready to support Jimmy's resolution that CLR's views be discussed inside the organization on a par with those of other comrades. It all happened within a few weeks, but in retrospect it became clear that the tensions had been developing ever since CLR left the country. No longer in continuing contact with the members of the group, living in isolation, but still trying to run the organization from a distance, CLR responded to Jimmy's document not as a serious effort to come to grips with the new realities but as a personal challenge to his leadership and an ideological betrayal of Marxism. Under the impact of the rapid changes taking place in American industry and American society in the 1950s and 1960s after CLR left the country, the differences between the revolutionary intellectual whose ideas came mostly from books and the organic intellectual whose ideas were rooted in the ongoing struggle and the realities around him became antagonistic, culminating in a break that was probably inevitable.

After the split I realized that the relationship between Jimmy and CLR, although always scrupulously correct, had never been warm. Returning from trips to Detroit in 1951–52 CLR had not had anything to say about Jimmy despite the strong impression he was making on the Detroit comrades. Instead, CLR talked only about Si Owens and the need to send Constance to Detroit immediately so that she could turn Si's story of how he came North into a book. In the United States Jimmy had known CLR only at a distance. His contact with CLR was mainly through CLR's speeches and books, especially *Mariners, Renegades and Castaways,* which was Jimmy's favorite. I do not recall any one-on-one political discussions between them either in the United States or later in England or Trinidad. I had never shown or told Jimmy about the letter in which CLR attempted to dissuade me from marrying him. In fact, I barely read it myself, probably because I didn't want to draw the conclusion, which was clearly implied, that CLR was viewing Jimmy as his rival for political leadership. When Jimmy spent his vacation with me in London in 1957, we stayed at CLR's house, but I don't recall any political conversations between them. I didn't pay that any mind at the time because it was Jimmy's first trip abroad and he was intrigued by what was happening all around him. We went to African independence rallies, visited Windsor Castle in London and Cardiff Castle in Wales, and flew to Paris to visit Chaulieu on a rickety plane that we thought would never make it across the Channel. In London Jimmy was fascinated by the fact that plumbing pipes were still outside the building and therefore much more accessible than the enclosed ones in the United States. In Paris it was exciting to see the city through his eyes as we walked all over town. On the Left Bank one day we ran into a woman from Martinique who could have been Jimmy's twin. She didn't speak much English, but she knew something about the section of West Africa from which her family had come, which suggested that Jimmy's ancestors might also have come from there. When we stayed with CLR and Selma in Trinidad for five weeks in 1960, Jimmy again spent most of his time outdoors, enjoying the bread fresh-baked in little alley ovens, trying to learn how to swim in the balmy waters of the Caribbean, marveling at the red snappers covering the bottoms of the fishermen's longboats and sold at the beach for practically nothing, teaching local people how to fry fish Southern style.

After the split Jimmy never attacked CLR personally but continued to speak and write about him respectfully for his role in "creating the new, different and challenging ideas without which no mass uprising can go beyond rebellion to revolution." CLR's contradiction, he said, was that "his only roots were in Trinidad which was too limited an arena for his fantastic talents."[22]

Despite the arbitrariness with which CLR had severed "all relations, personal and political," Lyman and Freddy continued to support CLR financially after the split as they had been doing for twenty-five years. During his stay in the United States CLR had practically lived at their home at 629 Hudson Street. He had been very much a part of their lives and they of his. Lyman's brother had died during World War II, and sometimes it seemed that CLR was filling the void. They were the godparents to C. L. R. James Jr., born to CLR and Constance in 1949. Freddy especially remained deeply attached to CLR. He had shared with her his courtship of Constance and introduced her to Beethoven while she introduced him to jazz.

The comrades who had sided with CLR in the struggle continued to function for a few years, calling their organization Facing Reality, with Martin Glaberman assuming the responsibility for leadership. CLR wanted to continue the organization, but in 1970 Marty decided that it had outlived its usefulness, even though to this day he essentially adheres to CLR's ideas on the working class and writes articles in their defense. Marty worked in the auto plants for many years and after leaving the plant taught American Studies at the College of Lifelong Learning of Wayne State University, from which he retired as professor emeritus in 1989. He has functioned as CLR's literary representative in the United States, setting up Bewick Press to reprint and distribute books and pamphlets by CLR and other members of the Johnson-Forest Tendency. Marty and I keep in touch both because he has never based his treatment of a person on political agreement or disagreement and because we share an interest in keeping the historical record straight. For example, if we find a factual error in an article or book about CLR, we will consult each other on how to correct it. I rely on the Glaberman files in the Wayne State Labor Archives to check my memory because I threw out most of my papers for that period. For anyone interested in CLR's activities and associates in the United States, they are an invaluable resource.

For me the separation from CLR came as a relief. Our relationship had become increasingly uncomfortable. His letter trying to discourage me from marrying Jimmy had shocked and pained me by its crudeness. Working with him in London in 1954 and 1957 had been like a tour of duty. His ideas, while still brilliant, struck me as increasingly abstract because he was not rooted in any place or any ongoing struggle. After living in Detroit and getting a sense of the diversity among workers and blacks and the need for both to struggle to transform themselves, I found his celebrations of spontaneity idealistic and romantic. They reminded me of Hegel's warning against trying to "get to the Absolute like a shot out of a pistol" without the labor, patience, and suffering of the negative. As the movements for national independence gained momentum in Africa and the West Indies, led by younger men who had been his protégés and were unquestionably not his equal in learning and eloquence, I began to wonder whether CLR's criticisms and directives to them stemmed in part from frustration that he had been born twenty years too soon. In 1956 Lyman had gone to London at CLR's request to discuss the organization. Upon his return he reported that the visit had been a disaster; CLR simply would not listen to anything that did not confirm his own views. In 1960 when Kathleen Gough accompanied us to Trinidad and met CLR for the first time, she found him so overbearing and self-centered that she moved out of the house the very next morning.[23] During that same visit it was painful to watch CLR persist in sending directives several times a day to Bill Williams in the Prime Minister's office, despite the lack of response. All this had been troubling, but in the male world in which I had learned my radical politics, you were supposed to make organizational decisions based on ideological agreement or differences, not on feelings. So I didn't articulate my feelings even to myself. Now CLR had freed me by initiating the break not only because of ideological differences but because he was unwilling to honor the process of democratic decision making, which we had upheld in the Workers Party and Socialist Workers Party and which has been the pride of anti-Stalinist socialist groups.

For years I didn't talk to anyone about the split. Periodically, Lyman, Freddy, Jimmy, and I would refer to CLR affectionately, regretting his isolation and decline after his departure from the United States.[24] In Detroit where we were busy with our various movement activities, the folks we worked with had no knowledge or interest in CLR, and the cottage industry that has grown up around his life and work since his death in 1989 was still years away. When I was invited to London in 1986 to talk about our years of collaboration during CLR's first sojourn in the United States, I meant it when I began my speech by saying,

> I am glad to be among those participating in this tribute to C. L. R. James. Over the last quarter of a century our paths have diverged, but I shall always cherish the years that we worked together because it was during that period that my philosophy of revolution as a great leap forward in the evolution of the human race began to take shape.

It was not until the spring of 1993 when I was invited to speak at an International Conference on C. L. R. James at Brown University that I decided the time had come to tell the story of the split and make it a part of the public record.[25]

After the split I took a copy of Jimmy's manuscript to W. H. (Ping) Ferry who was then vice president of the Center for the Study of Democratic Institutions in Santa Barbara, California, which he had cofounded with Robert Hutchins. Earlier I had sent Ferry some copies of *Correspondence* and he had responded with a few clippings. I didn't know it at the time, but Ferry had recently written *Caught on the Horn of Plenty* in which he warned that "conceptions of work" and "economic theories adequate for an industrial revolution are not good enough for the conditions of the scientific revolution."[26] Delighted that Jimmy had come to similar conclusions based on his experiences as a worker at Chrysler, Ferry got in touch with Leo Huberman and Paul Sweezy, the editors of *Monthly Review*, who decided to publish Jimmy's manuscript.

From then on we were in regular contact with Ferry. Born and raised in Detroit not far from our house—his father had been the chairman of Packard—the future of the city was very dear to Ping's heart. So we kept him abreast of our struggles in Detroit and of our efforts to move the black movement beyond the integration-versus-separation debate to the struggle for revolutionary transformation in our human relationships and in our concept of work made necessary by the technological revolution. Ping was not only concerned with the impact of technology on society but actively involved in struggles for nuclear disarmament and racial justice, tirelessly receiving and disbursing information about people and developments in all kinds of movement activities. An independent thinker and visionary, he was also constantly advising and encouraging everyone with the courage and imagination to challenge and propose alternatives to the conventional wisdom. He and his wife, Carol, were famous for their readiness to support innovative and relatively unknown causes. In the course of more than thirty years we must have exchanged thousands of clippings and memos.[27] Jimmy was a member of the Ad Hoc Committee on the Triple Revolution in Cybernation, Weaponry, and Human Rights that Ferry organized in 1964 at Princeton, under the auspices of J. Robert Oppenheimer. In 1976 we were among the approximately two dozen of Ping's old friends (POF) who spent a week with Ping and Carol at Branscombe in England.[28] Ping's good friends included individuals whom I had long admired from a distance: for example, Lewis Mumford, the visionary architect and urbanist; Joseph Needham, author of the forty-two-volume history of science and civilization in China; E. P. Thompson, the British cultural historian and main spokesperson for END (European Nuclear Disarmament), the movement that in the early 1980s demonstrated to Mikhail Gorbachev that he could undertake nuclear disarmament initiatives because public opinion in Europe and the United States would not accept military aggression by Ronald Reagan and company against the Soviet Union.

In the mid-1980s Ping was the catalyst for EXPRO (the Exploratory Project on the Conditions of Peace), which convened a small band of scholars and activists periodically to explore a peace system to replace our present war system. In the late 1980s Shea Howell and I joined EXPRO, bringing with us our experiences of the ongoing struggles of Detroit mothers, sisters, and grandmothers to build a peace system by organizing protests, reclaiming our streets, rebuilding our communities, and demanding a renewed respect for life.[29]

Some of the most cherished books in my library are Ping's copies, inscribed to him by their appreciative authors.[30] One of his (and my) favorite publications was *Manas*, the eight-page weekly exploring the relationship of ideas to urgent practical questions of work, education and the environment, which our friend, Henry Geiger, put together practically single-handedly (without a typo) from 1948 to 1988. *Manas* was one of the first American magazines to publish articles on "Buddhist Economics" by E. F. Schumacher, the author of *Small Is Beautiful*.[31]

The response to *The American Revolution* far exceeded our expectations. Ossie Davis summed it up in his remarks at the memorial celebration for Jimmy in October 1993:

> This little book came into my life. I read every word of it and it opened my mind, my thoughts. It was immediately apprehended by me in every possible way. When I read it, I said, "Yes, of course. Amen. Even I could have thought of that." Immensities of thought reduced to images so simple that coming away from the book I was indeed born again. I could see the struggle in a new light. I was recharged, my batteries were full and I was able to go back to the struggle carrying this book as my banner. Ruby and I bought up copies and mailed them to all the civil rights leaders, Martin Luther King Jr., Malcolm X, Whitney Young. We thought all of them should have access to this book. It would give them an opportunity to be born again.

As movie and TV actors and writers, Ossie and Ruby have been part of the lives of millions of black Americans for more than forty years. *The American Revolution* brought them into our lives. From time to time they visited us in Detroit and Maine. In 1982 KERA (Dallas/Ft. Worth) filmed an animated four-way conversation in our living room on Field Street for the *With Ossie and Ruby* series on public broadcasting. They are national endorsers of Detroit Summer, the youth program that we started in 1992, and Ossie has done some great benefit performances for the youth program and Ruby for SOSAD (Save Our Sons and Daughters).

To our amazement Jimmy received a letter, dated August 20, 1963, from Bertrand Russell, the world-famous philosopher and peace activist, saying "I have recently finished your remarkable book *The American Revolution*" and "have been greatly impressed with its power and insight." The letter goes on to ask for Jimmy's views on whether American whites "will understand the negro [*sic*] revolt because "the survival of mankind may well follow or fail to follow from political and social behavior of Americans in the next decades." On September 5 Jimmy wrote back a lengthy reply saying among other things that "so far, with the exception of the students, there has been no social force in the white population which the Negroes can respect and a handful of liberals joining in a demonstration doesn't change this one bit." Russell replied on September 18 with more questions that Jimmy answered in an even longer letter dated December 22. Meanwhile, Russell had sent a telegram to the November 21 Town Hall meeting in New York City at which Jimmy was scheduled to speak, warning Negroes not to resort to violence. In response Jimmy said at the meeting that "I too would like to hope that the issues of our revolt might be resolved by peaceful means," but "the issues and grievances were too deeply imbedded in the American system and the American peoples so that the very things Russell warned against might just have to take place if the Negroes in the U.S.A. are ever to walk the streets as free men." In his December 22 letter Jimmy repeats what he said at the meeting and then patiently explains to Russell that what has historically been considered democracy in the United States has actually been fascism for millions of Negroes. The letter concludes:

> I believe that it is your responsibility as I believe that it is my responsibility to recognize and record this, so that in the future words do not confuse the struggle but help to clarify it. This is what I think philosophers should make clear. Because even though Negroes in the United States still think they are struggling for democracy, in fact democracy is what they are struggling against.

This exchange between Jimmy and Russell has to be seen to be believed. In a way it epitomizes the 1960s—Jimmy Boggs, the Alabama-born autoworker, explaining the responsibility of philosophers to The Earl Russell, O.M., F.R.S., in his time probably the West's best-known philosopher.

Within the next few years *The American Revolution* was translated and published in French, Italian, Japanese, Spanish, Catalan, and Portuguese. To this day it remains a page-turner for grassroots activists because it is so personal and yet political, so down to earth and yet visionary. The first paragraph of Jimmy's introduction demonstrates his gift for getting to the heart of matters:

> There are two sides to every question, but only one side is right. I believe in democracy, but I don't believe in being too damn democratic. In other words, I believe that everyone has a right to his opinion, but I don't believe he has a right to be hypocritical or sly about it, and I believe that it is my responsibility to fight and right those opinions that are wrong.

Before long Jimmy began to receive requests for articles and speaking engagements that he struggled to fill while never missing a day's work at Chrysler. For example, on the day before John F. Kennedy was assassinated in November 1963, he flew to New York after work to make the Town Hall speech, flying back at midnight so that he could be in the plant the next morning at six o'clock. In his speeches he began raising the need to struggle for Black Power years before the slogan was made famous by Willie Ricks and Stokely Carmichael on the 1966 march to Mississippi. But Jimmy stayed out of the limelight. He was "The Man Who Wouldn't Be King." For example, when Stokely came to speak at the Shrine of the Black Madonna in 1967, Jimmy was among those acting as bodyguards to escort Stokely to the pulpit. Out of the blue Stokely used to call periodically. Hanging in my hall there is a picture of him with his arm around and looking down fondly at a very young-looking Jimmy.

The break with CLR removed the last barrier to my rooting myself in Detroit. For nearly a decade I had been struggling and quarreling and fussing with Jimmy and at the same time learning from him. In the process I had grown in self-confidence because I felt that I was living my convictions and not just talking them. My ideas were beginning to come from reality and not just from books. I had voted in every election, something that, as a radical, I had previously disdained to do. I was no longer a nomad but a citizen. Detroit had become my home, the place and the city for which I felt responsible. Armed with the ideas in *The American Revolution*, I was ready for action.

5
"The City Is the Black Man's Land"

At the beginning of the 1960s the word *black* was an epithet. If you called someone black, you had to be ready to fight. At the end of the decade if you didn't identify yourself as black, you were called an Uncle Tom or an Oreo. Detroiters twenty-one or younger have only known a black mayor, a black school superintendent, a black police commissioner, and a predominantly black City Council. They do not realize that before Detroit exploded in July 1967, the idea that the city should be run by blacks was regarded as outlandish by blacks as well as whites.

In the 1960s blacks in Detroit created a movement to take over the city, to make it their turf. They were no longer just protesting. They were contesting the control of the city by the diminishing number of whites and especially by the overwhelmingly white police force. This force, acting like an occupation army, routinely stopped and frisked blacks. It was encouraged in this behavior by the mayor, Louis Miriani, who in 1960 outraged the black community by ordering a "crackdown" on "Negro crime." In 1961 blacks got a taste of their potential political power when their votes played a key role in Miriani's defeat by Jerome Cavanagh, a young lawyer with no public record. During the campaign Miriani labeled Cavanagh the "Negroes' candidate" because he had come out for "equal rights for Negroes."

In 1961, however, no one was talking about Black Power. It would take a decade of practical and theoretical struggle, culminating in the 1967 rebellion, to establish the idea. To build the Black Power movement people coming from different backgrounds and with differing points of view had to work together, for the most part ignoring or smoothing over differences because of our sense of urgency and also because we could feel our humanity stretching as we organized for a common cause. I felt blessed that because I had made the personal decision to marry Jimmy years before the black movement got under way, I now had the privilege of being intimately involved in the struggle on a daily basis. Twenty years earlier, when I joined the March on Washington movement, I was a political neophyte just getting my feet wet. That movement lasted less than a year. Now I felt like a player in an unfolding drama. I had no goal beyond the empowering of blacks, no idea how things would turn out or how long the struggle would take, but I was confident that we were moving in the right direction and I felt myself growing and learning as the days, weeks, and years passed.

I remember the decade as a flood of myriad activities, each with its distinct flavor but interconnecting with all the rest. I was working most of the time, first as a secretary in law offices and then as a elementary schoolteacher. My main interest, however, was in organizing and participating in demonstrations. I went to meetings practically every night. Jimmy called me "meeting crazy," and he was not far off. I loved going to all kinds of meetings and still do. I am fascinated and energized by the interaction of the participants, by the way that diverse types are able to come together and agree on an action and work with one another for a while, until differences, which at one point appear unimportant, fester and develop into antagonisms. Jimmy was much more selective about his involvement, partly because he had to get up every morning at five to go to work at Chrysler, and partly because, after the publication of *The American Revolution*, he was writing articles for national magazines like *The Liberator*, *Negro Digest*, *Revolution*, and *Monthly Review*, projecting the concept of Black Power and challenging blacks to make it more than just a change in the color of those in charge.

In the 1950s I rarely went to a community meeting without Jimmy and would usually just listen or ask questions. Now, having worked in the city and socialized with Jimmy's friends and *Correspondence* readers for years, I felt I had something to contribute. I was beginning to feel comfortable with the *we* pronoun, so comfortable that in FBI records of that period I am described as Afro-Chinese.

The leaders of the struggle for Black Political Power in Detroit, the ones most in the public eye, were Rev. Albert B. Cleage (pronounced *Clague* with a long *a*), Richard and Milton Henry, and Edward Vaughn.

Jimmy and I worked closely with the four of them but stayed out of the spotlight by choice. We were all very different with different political agendas.

Rev. Cleage, in his midfifties at the time, was the oldest. His parishioners and colleagues in the struggle called him "Rev." After the 1967 rebellion he was called "Jerimoge" by the members of the Black Christian Nationalist Movement, which he founded.[1] I shall call him Cleage or Rev. Cleage. Cleage was the eldest in an old Detroit family that had been brought up in the Tireman neighborhood on the West Side, the enclave of the light-skinned elite who were longtime residents of the city rather than recent migrants from the South. His father had been the first "colored" doctor on the staff of Receiving Hospital. He had three brothers: Henry was a lawyer, Louis a doctor, and Hugh a printer. Louis's office was across the hall from Hugh's print shop in the same building on Scotten. One sister, Edith, was a teacher. The family was very close-knit. Mother Cleage was the matriarch; she even looked a little like Rose Kennedy, slight and very fair. Louis and Hugh still lived at home with her, and after his divorce Rev. Cleage ate dinner with his mother and brothers every night. Meanwhile, Doris, Rev's ex-wife and the mother of his two daughters, married his brother Henry because, according to sister Barbara, she "couldn't bear not being a part of the Cleage family." Rev. Cleage spent Sunday evenings at the home of Henry and Doris, reviewing the past week's developments and plotting strategy for the coming week. I sometimes joined them.

Pink-complexioned, with blue eyes and light brown, almost blonde hair, Cleage was a charismatic and dynamic speaker (whites called him a demagogue), master of the sound bite. A TV reporter once told me that Cleage could say more in five seconds on TV than the average person could say in five minutes. When things heated up, he was not inclined to cool them down. His response to those who asked him to do so was that he had been trying to cool things down for years by trying to get the power structure to yield to the just demands of his people. His younger daughter, Pearl, who was a child in the 1960s, is now a well-known playwright and writer living in Atlanta. I remember her sitting with her sister in a front pew and listening rapt as their father exposed the crimes of racism. She has learned her lessons well. In her book *Deals with the Devil*, she is as relentless against sexism as he was against racism.[2]

Milton and Richard Henry came from an old Philadelphia family. Their father was a preacher. Milton had been a pilot in the Second World War and had become a brilliant and successful lawyer. A good friend of Malcolm's, he visibly enjoyed the opportunities provided by the struggle to outwit the power structure and recorded almost everything in pictures and audiotape. Today Milton is a Presbyterian preacher.

Richard Henry was a technician who worked at the Detroit Arsenal with a number of thirtysomething young men like himself. With these young men Milton and Henry organized GOAL, the Group of Advanced Leadership. Richard was a natural publicist. At the drop of a hat, he would issue a press release, sometimes creating a new organization on the spot. One day at a mass meeting that had attracted lots of media, he announced the formation of the Republic of New Africa (RNA), renaming himself Brother Imari while Milton became Brother Gaidi. I am not sure but I think the meeting was one that GOAL called to celebrate Malcolm's birthday on May 19, 1965, a few months after he was assassinated. Richard had undoubtedly been planning to form the RNA for some time, but I recall wondering whether the presence of so many reporters just seemed too good an opportunity to miss. Today, Richard teaches in a southern college.

Edward Vaughn was a businessman who ran Detroit's first black bookstore on Dexter Avenue. Before the 1967 Rebellion it was the only place in the city where you could buy black literature. Today he is a Michigan state representative and recently announced his intention to run for mayor of Detroit in the next election.

I first met Rev. Cleage at a debate in 1962. The Detroit Board of Education was campaigning for an increase in the millage, with the support of the teacher's union and of both black and white teachers. Cleage opposed any increase because he said the Detroit public schools were not educating our children and it would be a crime to give them more money to continue to sell our children short. In the late 1950s and early 1960s the Detroit schools were just beginning to experience the crisis that has continued and deepened over the years. Today's public school system works for the children of middle-class families on their way to universities and lucrative professions. For most black kids, who in the 1960s were fast becoming the majority in the inner city as whites moved to the suburbs, the schools have been mainly custodial, a place where they could be kept off the streets for six hours a day. As a teacher, I was discovering this for myself. In the teachers' lounge white teachers openly talked about black kids as less than human. One old redheaded woman used to say that her dog could get more out of her class than her pupils. The black teachers weren't much better. Teaching was mainly a job for them. At three o'clock they would leave the inner city behind and go back to their own neighborhoods where all too many of them enjoyed middle-class lives, playing bridge, drinking scotch, and going skiing. As someone who was essentially a substitute teacher with no experience, I didn't argue with them. Instead, during the day I did my best to get my pupils to excel, especially in spelling and arithmetic, and at nights I would go to the debates on millage where Cleage was ruthlessly attacking the system and its supporters. Backing him up at these meetings, where teachers, parents, and administrators squirmed as he ripped through their defenses, was Helen Kelly, a community person with seven children. Helen was a heavy, dark-skinned woman, who intimidated her opponents by her size and her lack of decorum. She would shout at you until you either shouted back or shrank down into your chair, wishing that you were someplace else. After the 1967 Rebellion Helen became a community representative of New Detroit, started wearing a stylish Afro, cleaned up her act, and was rarely seen without a briefcase.

I agreed with Cleage and Helen that more money was not the answer to the crisis in education and that teaching black history and having black principals in the schools were needed to increase the self-esteem of students. So I began accompanying them to meetings, attended Cleage's church occasionally, and read *The Illustrated News*, the pink newsletter that was edited and written mainly by Cleage, printed by brother Hugh, and deposited in stores and churches all over town to be picked up free and chuckled over by tens of thousands of blacks. Printed on newsprint with plenty of pictures, short lively articles, lots of open space, and looking as if it had been put together in a basement, *The Illustrated News* was a perfect example of the kind of newsletter that you need to build a grassroots movement.

Cleage's Central Congregational Church was at 7625 Linwood, north of Grand Boulevard, just down the street from C. L. Franklin's New Bethel Baptist Church at 8450 Linwood, where it had moved after the Hastings Street neighborhood was demolished to build the Chrysler freeway. New Bethel's congregation was made up of mainly older blacks from the South. Jimmy's cousin Irene was a member of the Usher Board. Periodically, I would drive her to church. A few blocks north on Linwood was Muhammad's Mosque No. 1, which was attracting younger blacks who had been raised in the inner city. In the 1960s that quarter mile of Linwood, from Grand Boulevard to Davison, generated most of the religious leadership for the Black Power movement in Detroit. It was a lively strip with churches, markets, dry cleaners, apartment houses, and neighborhood restaurants. Today it is a wasteland. The Shrine of the Black Madonna and New Bethel Baptist Church are still at their old addresses, but Muhammad's Mosque No. 1 has moved to 14880 Wyoming on the Northwest Side. Linwood Avenue has been renamed C. L. Franklin Boulevard, but aside from the Shrine and New Bethel it is mostly vacant lots and gutted buildings. The neighborhood was one of the half dozen that suffered the most torching and looting in the 1967 Rebellion.

Central Congregational started out as a member of the United Church of Christ denomination, and its parishioners, like that of Plymouth Congregational Church, where City Councilman Nicholas Hood was the pastor, had at one time been mainly middle-class colored people. However, as Cleage became known over the city for his militancy, the complexion of his congregation darkened. In addition to Sunday services the church was the center of countless community meetings, attracting ambitious politicians like Russell Brown, a perennial candidate for state representative on the Democratic ticket, and William Bell, who was active in the Republican Party.

Black preachers, as a group, are without question the most gifted orators in this country. Each has his distinctive style. By now the whole world is familiar with the rhetoric of Dr. Martin Luther King Jr., the evangelical passion, the historic sweep, the rolling phrases, and the constant invoking of the dream of the Promised Land. Cleage's style was more analytical and agitational, more like Malcolm's. Listening to his sermons people could see themselves struggling against their own backwardness. Each sermon was a lesson in revolutionary politics. It is hard to lead an oppressed people, Cleage would tell his congregation, because they are not used to accepting responsibility for making their own decisions or for organizing and developing their own ideas. Instead, they are always looking for a messiah. During slavery black preachers had used the theme of escape from Egypt based on the Old Testament book of Exodus. To create a theology for urban blacks Cleage decided to develop the theme of the New Testament Jesus as the black revolutionary or Black Messiah, who went from town to town, city to city, creating a movement and an organization to build the Nation. He warned his congregation that "shouting and screaming did not yet constitute a Nation," that blacks "were still divided, still individuals, each fighting for his own little prestige, for the things he wanted for himself." Jesus's twelve disciples, Cleage said, were his cadre among whom, as in every cadre, there were those like Peter who would deny him and those like Judas who could be bought for thirty pieces of silver. His parishioners, visualizing themselves fighting in the streets, would break up in laughter as he described how effective black folks are "at tearing up things." He would then try to persuade them to develop more disciplined ways of fighting, forming caucuses, and joining the church.[3] The imagery of the revolutionary organizer building solidarity and developing strategy was perfect for Detroit, the city that had given birth to the labor movement.

Step by step, through his sermons and through the leadership he was giving in community struggles, Cleage established Central Congregational Church as the center of the struggle for black political power and of the Black Christian Nationalist Movement in Detroit. By 1966 the image of the church had been so transformed that its name was changed to the Shrine of the Black Madonna.

In 1962 and 1963 we enjoyed ourselves hugely in a number of actions that were mostly the brainchild of Milton Henry. For example, when we picketed the Apprentice Training School for admitting so few blacks, we were so noisy and disruptive that we were given a $5 traffic ticket for disorderly conduct. Milton then fought the $5 ticket in traffic court, calling so many witnesses that Judge Woods finally dismissed the case. (To impress the court I wore the suit that CLR and Selma had had custom-made for me in London for my forty-second birthday in 1957. I still wear it periodically.) On another occasion the police refused to give us a permit to use the loudspeaker for a Saturday meeting on the Old County Building steps. So Milton entered the building in the morning, hiding in a broom closet until after the building closed at noon. Then at two o'clock, while Jimmy spoke on the steps in front of the building flanked by bodyguards in helmets, Milton climbed to the roof and spoke through a loudspeaker. The police on the ground, unable to figure out what was happening or how to get into the locked building, ran around like Keystone Cops. "He'll be walking on water next," we taunted them.

During this period I also began exploring the Nation of Islam (NOI). Malcolm had reorganized *Muhammad Speaks*, the NOI paper, and every week one of the members would drop it by the house. I invited Minister Wilfred, Malcolm's oldest brother who was and remains an extraordinarily gentle, soft-spoken man, to hold a meeting at our house to explain to me and others what the Nation of Islam stood for. Kathleen Gough and I went to a huge NOI meeting at the old Olympia Stadium where Elijah Muhammad gave the main address and Malcolm the organizing speech. Ferry invited me to address a roundtable forum at the Center for the Study of Democratic Institutions in Santa Barbara, and I stunned the all-white male audience by saying that not all blacks are for integration and that the Nation of Islam is the vehicle through which many blacks have assumed the responsibility for creating a new concept of themselves. Black support of the NOI, I said, is a sign that we are entering a new age, the age of "dialectical humanism," when all of us are being challenged to define what it means to be a human being. Robert Hutchins, the center's president, who chaired the meeting, advised the participants not to respond immediately but to take time for reflection.[4]

Nineteen sixty-three was the turning point, the year when Detroit became conscious of itself as the spearhead of the Northern black movement and the rest of the country began to become aware of the movement emerging in Detroit. In May 1963 the nationally televised brutality of Bull Conner turning fire hoses and police dogs on black women and youth in Birmingham outraged people all over the country. In response the UAW and CORE (Congress of Racial Equality) called a protest meeting outdoors in downtown Detroit. The meeting was attended by only fifty or so people and was so lifeless that a few of us began shouting "We want Cleage! We want Cleage!" Cleage as usual tore the whole thing up. "This meeting is a disgrace," he shouted. "The organizers should be ashamed of themselves. We should be marching down Woodward Avenue with so many tens of thousands of people that the police would be afraid to show their faces!"

That night we began meeting in small groups to plan the kind of mass march down Woodward Avenue that Cleage had projected. Cleage got together with Rev. C. L. Franklin just up the street to form the Detroit Council for Human Rights (DCHR), which issued the call for the march. The DCHR began preparing for a mass turnout by holding weekly meetings in different churches across the city. Headquarters were set up in a building owned by James Del Rio on Grand River Avenue with Tony Brown, now host of national *Black Journal*, as coordinator. Dr. Martin Luther King Jr. agreed to lead the march. On June 23 approximately 250,000 people participated in a massive March for Freedom down Woodward Avenue, more than would join the much better known I Have a Dream national March on Washington two months later. Flint, Pontiac, and other Michigan cities sent delegations. From side streets up and down Woodward Avenue thousands of marchers fed into the main body. Until the 1995 Million Man March there has been nothing like it.

When the march ended at Cobo Hall near the Detroit River, Cleage made a ringing speech, urging Detroiters to boycott supermarkets until they hired black managers and department heads. So effective was his speech that on the next Monday, only a couple of us picketing at supermarkets were enough to persuade people to turn around, and within a week the supermarket chains were ready to negotiate. Cleage was a genius at this kind of strategizing, as was Jimmy. They both understood that every march, every demonstration has to conclude with something very specific, very concrete for people to do. Otherwise, you are just getting people all fired up and disempowering them because you are not providing them with a way to make a difference and thereby discover their own powers.

Meanwhile, the anger and resentment among young people and street people against the police occupation army were growing. Articulating their rage were people like Charles (Chuck) Johnson, John Williams, General Baker, and John Watson who were members of the group UHURU (the Swahili word for freedom). These young people, in their early twenties and mostly from working-class families, had been around the Socialist Workers Party and tended to think and speak in terms of imperialism, colonialism, the working class, and revolutionary social forces. They would later form the nucleus of the League of Revolutionary Black Workers. In this period they were loosely affiliated with RAM, the Revolutionary Action Movement led by Max Stanford (aka Muhammad Ahmed) who had dropped out of college to work in the movement. Originally from Philadelphia, Max moved around the country organizing in support of the armed self-defense and the "by all means necessary" positions of Robert Williams and Malcolm X. In Detroit he stayed at our house, absorbing revolutionary analysis of capitalism and imperialism from Jimmy. In New York, between 1962 and February 1965, he met regularly with Malcolm, keeping him abreast of developments in the Student Non-Violent Coordinating Committee (SNCC) and other youth groups, giving him RAM documents for review and following closely Malcolm's transformation from a religious nationalist, viewing white people as devils, to a political internationalist attacking the global capitalist system as the main enemy of black people. In 1962 when Max asked Malcolm whether he should join the Nation of Islam, Malcolm advised against it, saying that he "could do more for the Honorable Elijah Muhammed by organizing outside the Nation."[5]

Like the UHURU youth, Max was from a different generation and class background from the Cleages and the Henrys, whose friends and associates were middle-class professionals. They always wore suits and ties to meetings. Jimmy wore a suit only when he was scheduled to be the main speaker or a panelist at a meeting. Otherwise he wore a sports shirt, sweater, and oxfords. Max, who spent his time organizing among street youth, always wore jeans and white gym shoes and looked so antiestablishment and threatening that on a couple of occasions police at the local precinct called to say that they had picked up a young man who said he knew me and would I please come down to the precinct and identify him. Today, Max teaches political science at Capitol University and Cuyahoga Community College in Cleveland, Ohio, and is a member of AFSCME Local 100.

A few weeks after the peaceful June 23 march down Woodward Avenue, Detroit got a glimpse of the rising anger of young people against the Detroit police. Outrage against the murder of Cynthia Scott, a prostitute, by a white cop on Edmund Place near downtown Detroit brought about five thousand, mostly young people, to police headquarters at 1300 Beaubien. Over and over again they marched around the building chanting "Stop Killer Cops! Stop Killer Cops!" while the police manned the doors and windows, prepared to shoot if the marchers tried to storm the building. As the crowd became larger and more agitated and it looked as if we were in for a bloody massacre, Cleage, Milton, and I had a brief consultation and decided to call on the marchers to caravan to the nearby corner of Edmund Place where Cynthia Scott had been killed. A couple of months later, as we were mailing out invitations to the Grassroots Leadership Conference, a black woman with a good white-collar job confided that she would never forgive us for having diverted them from storming the building. Some people, including herself, might have been killed, she said, but it would have been worth it if they could have taken some of the cops with them. How they would have done this with only their bare hands, I have no idea. But her readiness to give up her life in a physical confrontation with the police indicated the depth of the pent-up rage. It is therefore not surprising that four years later a police raid on a "blind pig" (an after-hours bar) on 12th Street would trigger the Detroit Rebellion.

Prior to the June 23 march the DCHR had sent out a call to national Negro leaders to come to Detroit over the November 8–10 weekend for a Negro Summit Leadership Conference. I had known Rev. Franklin ever since 1955 when we worked together on promoting Kenya Sunday and he had shared with me his hopes for building a political community in Detroit to help blacks from the South cope with the isolation and individualism of city life. In early June, knowing that I was going on a visit to Boston, Franklin asked me to invite folks from the East Coast to the Summit Conference. However, suddenly on October 21, less than three weeks before the scheduled conference, Franklin told Cleage that he wanted nothing to do with eastern radicals, socialists, and/or supporters of the principle of self-defense, and that unless Cleage got rid of them he would have nothing to do with Cleage.

Franklin's turnabout was the result of national developments and national pressure. All summer long the Kennedy administration had been moving heaven and earth to contain the escalating black movement. In the wake of the mass demonstrations and arrests in Birmingham in the spring, spontaneous demonstrations all over the South were becoming increasingly violent. The youth activists of SNCC were growing impatient with the administration's policy of compromising with local whites and its failure to protect black militants, and some were beginning to question King's nonviolent strategy. In an attempt to pacify them President Kennedy acknowledged the existence of the "Negro revolution" on June 11 and called on all citizens to help in its completion. At the same time, however, the administration was trying to rein in King by threatening to expose information about his private life that had been acquired by FBI wiretaps. Meanwhile, angered by white violence in the South and inspired by the gigantic June 23 march in Detroit, grassroots people on the streets all over the country had begun talking about marching on Washington. "It scared the white power structure in Washington, D.C. to death," as Malcolm put it in his "Message to the Grassroots" and in his *Autobiography*.[6] So the White House called in the Big Six national Negro leaders and arranged for them to be given the money to control the march. The result was what Malcolm called the "Farce on Washington" on August 28, 1963. John Lewis, then chairman of SNCC and fresh from the battlefields of Georgia, Mississippi, and Alabama where hundreds of blacks and their white student allies were being beaten and murdered simply for trying to register blacks to vote, was forced to delete references to the revolution and power from his speech and, specifically, to take out the sentence, "We will not wait for the President, the Justice Department nor Congress, but we will take matters into our own hands and create a source of power, outside of any national structure, that could and would assure us a victory." Marchers were instructed to carry only official signs and to sing only one song, "We Shall Overcome." As a result, many rank-and-file SNCC militants refused to participate.[7]

Meanwhile, conscious of the tensions that were developing around preparations for the march on Washington and in order to provide a national rallying point for the independent black movement, Conrad Lynn and William Worthy, veterans in the struggle and old friends of ours, issued a call on the day of the march for an all-black Freedom Now Party. Lynn, a militant civil rights and civil liberties lawyer, had participated in the first Freedom Ride from Richmond, Virginia, to Memphis, Tennessee, in 1947 and was one of Robert Williams's attorneys.[8] Worthy, a *Baltimore Afro-American* reporter and a 1936–37 Nieman Fellow, had distinguished himself by his courageous actions in defense of freedom of the press, including spending forty-one days in the Peoples Republic of China in 1957 in defiance of the U.S. travel ban (for which his passport was lifted) and traveling to Cuba without a passport following the Bay of Pigs invasion in order to help produce a documentary. The prospect of a black independent party terrified the Democratic Party. Following the call for the Freedom Now Party, Kennedy twice told the press that a political division between whites and blacks would be "fatal."

These were the forces behind the breakup of the DCHR, which had organized the June 23 March. I have a very vivid recollection of the split. That evening Milton Henry and I were in someone's basement working on a preamble to an all-black International Trade Unions Council when Cleage burst in with the news of Franklin's ultimatum and his own refusal to accept Franklin's conditions for continuing collaboration. Milton's immediate response was typical: "If that's the way they want to play, who cares? We'll have our own Conference that same weekend, and we'll get Malcolm to speak."

So that is what we did. Milton called Malcolm who got Mr. Muhammad's permission, and we immediately sent out our own call for a Grassroots Leadership Conference to take place on the same weekend as Franklin's Summit Leadership Conference. We made arrangements to hold the workshops at Mr. Kelly's, a cocktail lounge on Chene Street, and to hold the Sunday night rally at King Solomon's Baptist Church on 14th Street with Malcolm as the speaker. In the workshops we discussed and projected a number of actions: a Christmas boycott to protest the September church bombing that had killed four little girls in Birmingham, Alabama; a nationwide boycott of General Motors; and a campaign for the all-black Freedom Now Party. Gloria Richardson, the leader of the struggle in Cambridge, Maryland, came to our conference and pronounced it much livelier and more interesting than the Summit that was being held in a downtown hotel. There were some serious disagreements and heated discussions. Jimmy and I vigorously argued for the Christmas boycott, which was opposed by GOAL members who had already started a business designing and selling Christmas cards with black themes and characters. But at the plenary session we finally adopted all the proposed actions and elected Jimmy conference chairperson and myself as secretary.

At the mass rally on Sunday night, November 10, we presented Malcolm with an audience of more than three thousand people. The majority of them were not religious Muslims. This is the main reason, I believe, why Malcolm, who was extremely sensitive to his audiences, was able to make a speech so different from any other speech I had ever heard him make up to that point. He began by placing the Black revolution (as contrasted with the Negro revolution) in the historical tradition of other revolutions for land and, using the March on Washington as an example, went on to draw his famous class distinction between house Negroes who had become part of the master's establishment and field Negroes who wanted nothing to do with the master. His speech began with his usual homage to the Honorable Mr. Muhammad, but suddenly his style changed, and leaning forward to look straight into the minds of his audience he began what he called his "off-the-cuff chat between you and me, us." It was as if he had stopped looking backward and was ready to move forward. The tribute to Mr. Muhammad was so nominal and mechanical as contrasted with the passion and urgency in his "off-the-cuff, down-to-earth chat" that I whispered into the ear of Rev. Cleage who was sitting next to me on the platform, "Malcolm's going to split with Mr. Muhammad." This was on November 10, nearly two weeks before the assassination of John F. Kennedy and Malcolm's "chickens come home to roost" remark that led to his suspension by Mr. Muhammad. At the time I had no idea that Malcolm was questioning Mr. Muhammad's conduct toward young women in the Nation of Islam, but after two decades of attending political meetings my ear had become sensitized to the rhetorical changes that suggest that a radical political change is in the offing.

As the person who had just been elected chairman of the Grassroots Leadership Conference, Jimmy made the collection speech after Malcolm spoke. It was a disaster. From that huge and inspired audience he was only able to collect $131. After that, we teased him mercilessly on how much more money one of his "shyster preachers" would have collected.

In the November 1963 issue of *Correspondence*, I summed up the significance of the Grassroots Leadership Conference:

> The Black Revolution in the North is less than six months old. Beginning after Birmingham as a sympathy movement for the South, it has now begun to work out its own philosophy and strategy based upon the specific grievances which face the Northern Negro. . . .
>
> The majority of those attending this conference were young people, men and women in their 20s and 30s, most of whom have been born or reared in the big Northern cities: rank and file factory and office workers, teachers, young professionals and students, mainly from working class backgrounds. . . .
>
> The Black Revolution in the North is also confronted more directly with economic issues than the revolution in the South. In the South Negroes are still fighting for the right to equal access to public accommodations and for the right to register and vote. To gain even these rights they may have to take public

> power. But in the North, Negroes already have these rights, at least officially. Therefore, *whether* they work (i.e., whether they eat) and *why* they work, *whether* they vote and *why* they vote, become crucial questions.
>
> This was made abundantly clear by both Malcolm X and Cleage at the rally. A Negro Revolution and a Black Revolution are not the same thing, explained the Muslim minister in an analysis that will be argued over for a long time to come. A Negro Revolution is the kind which liberal whites could accept because it would simply incorporate the black man into the corruption of existing white society. A Black Revolution, however, would center around struggle for control of "land" (economic resources) and would have to take the steps necessary for such control.
>
> Speaking for the Freedom Now Party, Cleage made essentially the same point in terms of political struggle. If Negroes simply keep on voting for the Democratic or Republican Parties, he explained, they waste their votes because these parties are essentially white parties organized to keep the Negro in his place begging for concessions. However, by organizing and voting for the All-Black Party, Negroes can put themselves into an independent and controlling position of power that will force whites to negotiate with them.

As 1963 was coming to an end, I sensed that we had reached a turning point in the black movement, that the hopes of a future for black people in this country that had inspired the civil rights movement in the South and the June 23 Freedom March down Woodward Avenue in Detroit were being replaced by the hopelessness and frustrations of black youth in the inner cities of the North. I was so convinced that we were at a defining moment that for Christmas that year I sent two records to our close friends as gifts: *Between Heaven and Hell* by composer and lyricist Oscar Brown Jr., which came out in 1962, and "A White Man's Heaven Is the Black Man's Hell" performed by Louis X (now known as Farrakhan), which I first heard in 1963.[9]

The album *Between Heaven and Hell* is sassy and sexy, full of fun and laughter, at the same time that it conveys the hard life that blacks live and the hard work they do. Every cut on the album swings and soars. Even the "Elegy (Plain Black Boy)," based on a poem by Gwendolyn Brooks (it was Jimmy's favorite), has an upbeat blues quality. "Sam's Life" expresses this hope:

There's a fellow I know
Folks call him Sam.
He never gets as much as he gives.
But if you'll give a listen, "Please sir, please ma'am,"
I'll tell you something about how Sam lives.

Sam's life is not the sort of life you'd wish.
Sam's life is wash another dirty dish.
Sam's life is just another floor to mop,
Harvesting somebody else's crop.
Sam's life is common labor every day.
Nothing but trouble comes the easy way.
Sam's life is weary muscles, aching back
Praying to God and facing facts.

Fact is this life of his
Is too much pain and sorrow.
But Sam's strong and still has a song
and hope for tomorrow.

Sam's life is a bright-eyed girl and boy
Working to make a way so they'll enjoy
A little better opportunity
Than ever was given to Sam or me.
And I believe he can
Because I believe in Sam.

By contrast, "A White Man's Heaven Is the Black Man's Hell," a forty-five single, while sung and played with a haunting beauty by Louis X, is unadulterated bitterness and hostility toward both the black preacher misleaders and the white man. Here are some verses:

Why are we called Negro?
Why are we deaf, dumb and blind?
Why is everybody making progress
Yet we seem to be lagging so far behind?
Why are we mistreated?
Why are we in this condition?
Stripped of our name, our language, our culture, our God and our
religion?

Here in America all of our religious training has been gotten by the
preacher
Who has told us of a heaven way up in the sky

That we can't enjoy now but rather after we die.
All of the years we are living
Are nothing but hell, torture and misgiving.
Yet the preacher tells us of a heaven, full of material luxury
Which the white man and the preacher have right here as we see.
So my friends take it for what it's worth.
Your heaven and hell are right here on this earth.

When the white man came to America
He told the Indian I am your white brother.
He said, "Red man, I teach you the best."
Yet instead he pushed the Indian further west.
With his white woman and fire water,
With tricks and lies he stole America.
The original owner of this nation
Is cooped up on a reservation.
So my friends, it's easy to tell.
White Man's Heaven is a Black Man's Hell.

He needed someone to work the land.
His back was too weak, he needed you, black man.
So he commissioned Sir John Hawkins
To commit the world's most grievous sin.
To take a man who's born to be free
And sell him into slavery.
To sell a man as merchandise,
On his body put a price.
Oh, my friend, it's easy to tell.
A White Man's Heaven is a Black Man's Hell.

When the slavemaster wanted to have some sport
He would heap on our parents cruelties of the worst sort.
Burn them at the stake, hang them on trees, indifferent to our parents' pleas.
Although you were pregnant, black woman, you pulled the plow
Like a horse, like a dog, even a cow.
He filled your womb with his wicked seed,
His half-white child you were made to breed.
Oh, my friend, it is easy to tell.
White man's heaven is a black man's hell.

So-called Negro open up your eyes.
Black man everywhere is on the rise.
He has kicked the white man out of Asia
And he is going fast out of Africa.

With every ounce of strength and breath,
He is crying "Give me liberty or give me death!"
The whole black world relies on you
To see what the so-called Negro is going to do.
So, my friends, it is easy to tell
Our unity will give the white man hell.

In 1964 this bitterness and anger began erupting in a few scattered communities in the North. Then in 1965 Los Angeles exploded in the Watts "Burn, Baby, Burn" rebellion.

Meanwhile, in Detroit we continued our struggles to organize the black community for political power as the best way to prevent needless violence. From my participation in the Grassroots Leadership Conference I had acquired a reputation as an organizer.[10] So a couple of weeks after the conference Cleage and Joe Barron came to see me and asked me to be the coordinator for the all-black Michigan Freedom Now Party. To get on the ballot we had to gather more than eleven thousand signatures in eleven counties of the state, at least one thousand in each county, by a set date. I gladly accepted the challenge. It gave me an opportunity to drive all over the state in our new red Galaxy, with Joe Barron, Chris Alston, and others, and get to know Michigan cities with fairly large black populations like Muskegon, Grand Rapids, Flint, and Pontiac, and others with black populations so small we practically had to sign up every black citizen. That was not at all easy in a period where so many folks would respond to our request for their signature with "I don't want to be part of anything all black." But we were able to gather enough signatures to get on the ballot in Michigan, while in other states internal disputes over whether whites should be allowed to participate were so divisive that organizers were unable to even get started petitioning. Through the statewide Freedom Now campaign we met Barbria and Jim Jackson who became lifelong friends and comrades. Jim is a Muskegon osteopath who as a boy in Springfield, Massachusetts, was introduced to the movement when Rev. Cleage organized a youth group at a local church.

After we were certified to be on the ballot, we put up a complete slate and published it with pictures of all the candidates in *The Illustrated News*. Rev. Cleage headed the ticket, running for governor. Dr. Jackson of Muskegon was our candidate for lieutenant governor. I was a candidate for some educational office. When voters challenged our all-black ticket, supporters would point to my picture. In September, two months before the election, Milton Henry had a brainstorm. Robert Kennedy had recently decided to run for senator from New York, taking advantage of the provision in the U.S. Constitution that says a candidate must reside in the state from which he is elected *at the time of his election*. Milton suggested that we call Malcolm in Cairo, Egypt, and ask him to run on the Freedom Now Party ticket for senator from Michigan. We did and he declined.

The night of the general election we were delirious with joy when early reports showed the Freedom Now Party getting tens of thousands of votes. Later we were told that it had been a technical error, that we had received only about twenty-five hundred votes. Some folks suspected that we had been victims of a racist plot. But considering that the election was in the fall of 1964, before the Watts uprising, at a time when "black" was still a no-no in the community, I was not surprised at the result.

In 1964 a half dozen members of the Revolutionary Action Movement (RAM) stayed in the basement of our house for a week putting together an issue of *Black America*, which to this day, although not widely known, remains an excellent introduction to the ideas that went into the creation of the Black Power movement. On the cover is a reproduction of a charcoal drawing of Max Stanford, the original of which hangs on my living room wall. The illustrated magazine contains six pages of quotations from the creators of revolutionary nationalism, including Marcus Garvey, Elijah Muhammed, W. E. B. Du Bois, Robert Williams, Malcolm X, Harold Cruse, Rev. Cleage, Max Stanford, and James Boggs. There are also full-length articles by Max, Jimmy, Rolland Snellings (later known as Askia Toure), Don Freeman, and Chuck Johnson, as well as a poem, "Song of Fire," by Rolland and a letter of "Greetings to our Militant Vietnamese Brothers."

Housing the RAM brothers in our basement was a first-class headache. They would stay up all night laughing and talking, indifferent to the fact that Jimmy needed a good night's sleep so that he could get up at 5 A.M. to go to work at Chrysler. When Jimmy would chide them for their lack of simple technical skills, they would say that they weren't worried about such matters, that after the revolution the brothers from Africa would take care of things like that. In those days people had a lot of illusions about Africa. One night a young man on the run from some incident involving a cop came to the house, seeking help on how he could find sanctuary in Africa!

After the publication of *Black America* we drove to New York for a meeting with Malcolm that Max had arranged. Our purpose was to ask Malcolm, now that he had split with Mr. Muhammad, to work with us to build an organization to struggle for Black Power. Together with Bill Worthy and Patricia Robinson from Third World Women's Press, we met with him in a Harlem coffee shop. Bill and Pat were present as friends and comrades, not as reporters. We were right on time. Malcolm started the conversation by emphasizing that people who are serious about struggling to better the condition of black people have a responsibility to be punctual and not to break the law, even on something as simple as illegal parking and driving through a red light. Folks who use racism as an excuse for irresponsible social behavior, he said, are not serious about struggle. He requested a little time to think about our request and suggested that we send someone to get his answer at an affair he was attending that night. I was the one designated to get his reply. It was that we should go ahead and form the organization without him because he saw his role as being an evangelist. Personally, Malcolm impressed me as a very open-minded and thoughtful person. But I also had the sense that politically he was very much alone and uncertain about what he should be doing and where he should be taking the movement.

In 1964 Malcolm came to Detroit a couple of times to speak, on one occasion giving his "Ballot or the Bullet" speech. His audiences were relatively small, about one to two hundred people, but Malcolm was his usual challenging self, provoking uneasy but appreciative laughter in his audience as he chided them for their lack of militancy and their acceptance of the white man's values. On February 14, 1965, he was scheduled to speak at a meeting in Ford Auditorium, which seats two thousand people. That morning his home in Elmhurst, New York, had been bombed and we wondered whether he would be able to keep the engagement. As we were waiting for him to appear, I spoke to Milton Henry in the lobby. "Malcolm's dead," he said. He meant that Malcolm was exhausted, but I took the comment literally and was devastated. When Malcolm finally appeared on the platform and began to speak, he rambled so much that most people, including myself, began drifting out of the auditorium. It was too painful.

The next Sunday, February 21, Malcolm was gunned down as he spoke to an audience at the Audubon Ballroom in New York City. Patricia Robinson telephoned us with the news. We had just returned from a CORE demonstration outside the church of Rev. Ray Shoulders, who was denouncing black youth for their militancy. One of the winter's worst blizzards had already started. Milton flew to New York for the funeral, which was televised. With Richard Henry, Reginald Wilson, Gwendolyn Mallett, and a few others we organized a Detroit memorial for Malcolm on Friday night at a hall on Gratiot on the East Side. It was so cold and the snow was so deep that only about fifty people showed up, but we all pledged to build the organization that Malcolm had finally recognized was necessary. After the assassination we explored with Pat Robinson, Bill Worthy, and others the question of asking individuals like Bertrand Russell and Jean-Paul Sartre to convene an international commission to investigate Malcolm's assassination for possible or probable CIA or FBI involvement but decided against it.

A few months later we founded the Organization for Black Power in our basement with representatives from Washington, D.C., Philadelphia, Chicago, Cleveland, and New York. We did not invite Cleage, Vaughn, or the Henry brothers to the meeting. We didn't talk about it and it didn't stop us from working together, but we were beginning to sense the differences between us. When you are involved in real struggles that are likely to influence events, the tendency is to minimize rather than exacerbate differences, allowing them to take their natural course. On the other hand, when you cannot influence events, as in the case of the Stalinists and Trotskyists debating Soviet policy in the 1930s, differences are more likely to lead to bitter vendettas.

Meanwhile, in the wake of the televised funeral services for Malcolm and the media blitz, thousands of black people were showing up at Malcolm X meetings, and black would-be leaders, some of them still in their teens, were starting their speeches with the words "Malcolm said," each hoping to inherit the mantle of Malcolm by reducing him to simplistic political slogans. I found it very troubling. If Malcolm had lived, there is no doubt in my mind that he would have continued developing, as every great leader does. In the last year of his life he had more questions than he had answers.[11] Following his assassination, Bill Worthy used to say that it would have been better for the movement if Malcolm had spent the year after his split with Elijah organizing and studying with us in Detroit rather than running all over the country and the world.

In the summer and fall of 1965 I worked with Cleage on the Vote 4 and No More campaign for City Council. By that time blacks were nearly half of the Detroit population, but there was still only one black councilman, hand-picked by the white power structure. By asking voters to "plunk" their votes, we thought we could elect more blacks. But the strategy didn't work. It took the 1967 Rebellion to upset the status quo and create the present situation in which the membership of the council, six blacks and three whites, is more representative of the ethnic composition of the city.

Meanwhile, Jimmy was writing and speaking. Most of his work in this period is reprinted in *Racism and the Class Struggle: Further Pages from a Black Worker's Notebook*, published by Monthly Review Press in 1970. In these speeches and articles you can hear Jimmy struggling to get black militants to deepen the meaning of Black Power to include the question of class and the revolutionary reorganization of American society. In those days when whites would ask how Black Power would differ from white power, most blacks would respond, "It can't be any worse than white power," as if only white people would ask such a stupid question. Patiently and respectfully, especially after Malcolm's death, Jimmy tried to enlarge the vision of those involved in the movement, struggling to make people see the need to take the question beyond separation or integration (who would want to be integrated into a burning house?) to the level of transforming the society, grappling especially with the issue of how we will all make our livings in the new era of automation.

One of the most important pieces in *Racism and the Class Struggle* is "The City Is the Black Man's Land," which explains how Black Political Power would reorganize the economy in the cities where blacks were fast becoming the majority. Jimmy and I worked on this together for a engagement that he had accepted from Morgan State College in 1965.[12] Because Jimmy could not get off from work, I traveled to Baltimore to make the speech. It was my first encounter with faculty members at a black college, and I was amazed at the protocol and ritual courtesies at dinner. The response to my speech was enthusiastic. To this day people still come up to me to say how much that article and that title meant to them. Referring to it in his remarks at Jimmy's memorial celebration, Ossie Davis said,

> At that time we thought of the Land as a source not only of power and wealth but of identity. We thought we had to own some land in this country and there was the claim that the government should cede black folks some land of our own on which we could build our factories and establish our communities and let the rest of the world go hang. Then I came across this article and once again my mind was opened. The title simply said "The City Is the Black Man's Land." I was disenchanted with my romantic concept that we had to go out and establish our flag on some of God's territory. Rather we had to struggle for what was meaningful, and in that instance and at that time and to this day it is in our cities where the struggle is the most intense. So the city is indeed the black man's land.

During this period a *New York Post* columnist—it may have been Jimmy Breslin or Murray Kempton—wrote that what was happening in Detroit was going to have a powerful effect on the whole country because not only activists but theoreticians were engaged in the local struggle.

Early in 1967 Jimmy and I organized the Inner City Organizing Committee in Detroit to develop rank-and-file comrades for leadership through a combination of political education and practical activities. Meetings were held at the Shrine of the Black Madonna, and Cleage was named president and Jimmy vice president, but Cleage, who was more interested in organizing the Black Christian Nationalist Movement, rarely attended the meetings and Jimmy actually led the group. Jim Hocker, our good friend and a GM worker, assumed responsibility for organizing a boycott of Sears because it limited black salespeople to small ticket sales. To struggle for community control of schools we organized students in an Inner City Students Council and parents in an Inner City Parents Committee. Jimmy also began to explore the new role that the police would play under Black Political Power and characteristically started with a historical study of the police in urban society.

In July 1967, as tensions in the city were mounting, we decided to drive to Los Angeles to spend our vacation with Freddy and Lyman Paine, taking along Jimmy's teenage daughter and another teenager. Before we left Detroit, Jimmy advised members of the Inner City Organizing Committee that if an eruption should take place, it would be best if they did not get involved. Sure enough, on Sunday, July 20, in Santa Barbara where we were staying overnight with the Ferrys on our way home, we heard over the radio that Detroit had exploded and that whole sections of the city were in flames, including Mack Avenue in our neighborhood. Since there was nothing we could do about it and since it would take us several days anyway to drive back to Detroit, we decided to continue with our plan to visit San Francisco and stay with Connie Williams at her calypso restaurant in Haight-Ashbury. When we returned to Detroit, we learned that Louis Lomax, author of *The Negro Revolt*, had written an article in the *Detroit News* alleging that six people were responsible for the rebellion: Rev. Cleage, the Henry brothers, Ed Vaughn, and Grace and James Boggs.

By the time we got back to Detroit, dignitaries of all kinds, including John Doar from the attorney general's office, Henry Ford II, and others were seeking an audience at the Shrine of the Black Madonna, where in order to get to Cleage they first had to pass inspection by Beverly Williamson, an intimidating tall dark man with dreads. In the community everybody was calling himself or herself black and giving the Black Power handshake. When folks would call Jimmy "Brother" and reach out their hand for the handshake, he would hold back, saying quietly but firmly, "I don't know how long this brotherhood thing is going to last." By this time I knew Jimmy fairly well. We had been together for fourteen years. But I was still awed by his ability to stand alone and speak his own mind when all around him people were being swept up in a tidal wave of blackness.

Anxious to capitalize on the nationwide interest that had been created by the Detroit Rebellion, NBC planned a one-hour special and invited some of us to come down to the studio to be filmed. Jimmy and I declined, even though Milton telephoned to urge us to join him. As we had expected, the special turned out to be a portrayal of the Rebellion as a conspiracy.

The week after the Rebellion, members of the Detroit establishment, including Joseph L. Hudson Jr., president of Hudson's department store, Chrysler and Ford executives, and UAW leaders, announced the formation of New Detroit, an organization ready to assume the responsibility for reconstructing Detroit in the wake of the Rebellion. The day before New Detroit was scheduled to meet, a tumultuous citizens' meeting took place in the auditorium of the City-County Building. During the meeting Cleage declared that "We are the new Black Establishment! New Detroit will take orders from us!"[13] He called on blacks to organize. On the spot the City-wide Citizens Action Committee (CCAC) was set up with representatives from all the different groups and tendencies in the city, including those who wanted to be elected to political office, those who wanted to prepare for armed struggle, those who wanted to organize black workers, those who just wanted higher-paying jobs for themselves, and those who wanted to establish their own turf in some part of the city. Before long, the CCAC was receiving enough media attention and funds so that the different tendencies were clashing with one another and the coalition soon fell apart.

For a brief period I worked with the CCAC, doing the news releases for its weekly radio program. Meanwhile we organized two conferences to explore how community control of schools would transform public education: a Community Control of Schools conference to which all kinds of big shots in the Detroit public school administration came, and a Black Teachers' Workshop, attended by Preston Wilcox and Rhody McCoy from the Ocean Hill Brownsville struggle in New York, which brought out hundreds of teachers, many of whom were waiting impatiently at the door when we arrived to set up registration. But it soon became obvious that there was more interest in getting elected to the Board of Education than in struggling for community control of schools. For example, a member of Cleage's congregation who was running for the board told a reporter that he was not for community control of schools, even though he had declared his support for this demand before the Inner City Parents Council and the Black Teachers' Workshop. When we brought the question up at an Inner City Organizing Committee, Cleage said that it wasn't important.

Jimmy responded by asking for a convention where the membership could discuss and decide the issue. Cleage was not interested, and we left the meeting. We never worked together again.

While our relationship with Cleage, with whom I had worked closely for six years, was disintegrating, chaos was spreading in the country. On April 4, 1968, King was assassinated. His murder was the final proof to blacks that the American Dream was dead, and uprisings like the Detroit Rebellion erupted in a hundred cities across the country. In the wake of King's death, black youth by the thousands began joining or forming Black Panther branches, attracted by the revolutionary rhetoric and the image of black youth carrying guns for self-defense and convinced that King's assassination signaled the beginning of a genocidal war by white America against blacks. In Detroit, people in the community started stockpiling canned goods in basements in anticipation of an assault by white suburbanites. At the same time the UHURU brothers and sisters were publishing their own newspaper, called the *Inner City Voice*, which carried a column by Jimmy and reprinted speeches by C. L. R. James. They were also beginning to organize black autoworkers in particular plants into DRUM (Dodge Revolutionary Union Workers), FRUM (Ford Revolutionary Union Workers), and so forth, together constituting the League of Revolutionary Black Workers.

Obviously, we were coming to the end of a period and it was no longer clear to Jimmy and me where we should be going and what we should be doing. So we were glad to accept the invitation from Roberto Giammanco for Jimmy to spend a week speaking to university students in Rome, Pisa, Florence, Trento, and Milan. Roberto was an Italian TV producer and publisher who had arranged for the publication of *The American Revolution* in Italian and was preparing to publish an Italian edition of *Racism and the Class Struggle*. Jimmy's speaking tour would help promote the book.

En route to Italy in early June 1968 we spent a few days in Paris where we stayed in the apartment of William Gardner Smith, the American novelist who was working for *Agence France Presse*.[14] Observing the young people torching billboards in Paris and talking with some of Smith's friends in the communications field, we were able to get some sense of the May-June revolt. From Paris we took the overnight train to Rome. In Rome Italian students were also in an uproar, and we had to go through police barricades to get inside the university where they were holed up. Throughout Italy students were intensely interested in the Black Power movement. Many had read *The American Revolution* in the Italian edition and thousands turned out to hear Jimmy, even though few could understand his Alabamese. In Trento, unaccustomed to the rich Italian food, Jimmy got sick and I had to speak for him. It was a whirlwind tour during which we mainly moved in and out of hotels with no opportunity to see the sights or talk with grassroots Italians.

After that, we flew to Conakry, the capital of Guinea, where we spent a week with Kwame Nkrumah before returning to the United States at the end of June. As we landed at the airport in Detroit, I had no idea what lay before us. All I knew was that it would be different from the decade that was coming to an end.

玉平

6
Beyond Rebellion

As we arrived back in the United States in June 1968, I was very conscious of how the relationship between Jimmy and myself had changed. We were still very different. For example, at the Detroit International Airport Jimmy breezed through Immigration and Customs while I was subjected to the close scrutiny and search reserved for suspected Asian drug smugglers. But having lived and worked together for fifteen years, our eyes and ears were beginning to see and hear the same things.

What we saw and heard was that Americans were thinking and talking and wondering about revolution as they had not done for nearly two hundred years. In the wake of the assassination of Dr. King and Robert Kennedy, the increasingly militant opposition to the war in Vietnam, and the black uprisings of 1967–68, Americans were beginning to feel that the bottom had fallen out of the society. Old beliefs were crumbling, existing institutions were no longer working, and even more than in the Great Depression of the 1930s great numbers of people were looking for new ways to think and act for themselves.

Closer to home on Field Street what we saw and heard was that "Jimmy's boys" had become outlaws, consciously and proudly at war with the institutions and legalities of white America. No longer willing to tolerate the racist abuse that had been a routine part of their lives, conscious that they were being made expendable by advancing technology, and energized by the uprisings that had eliminated their invisibility, black youth had become a street force and a growing threat to the white power structure. At the same time, because looting had been such a visible part of the uprisings and consumerism had become so entrenched in our culture, tens of thousands had turned to crime as a way of life. For example, Harvey Deering was one of Jimmy's boys who grew up across the street from us on Baldwin. Soon after our return he came by the house to show off some jewelry that he had stolen and was planning to sell. The eulogy that I gave at his funeral service after he was killed by a policeman in 1985 could have been given for thousands of others. The day before he was killed, he had borrowed the *Autobiography of Malcolm X* from me. This is what I said at the church:

> Like most of you here I have known Harvey since he was a kid. I particularly remember how mixed up he was after the 1967 rebellion. Because there was so much looting in the rebellion, Harvey and his friends began to see ripping off as a way of life. One thing led to another, and before long he was sent up to Jackson.
>
> After his release this year, it took Harvey a while to get himself together, but in the last few months he was really trying. He walked all over town looking for a job. After all these years cooped up with thousands of inmates, he wanted to live alone. But when he got together a week's rent for a room, the landlady wanted a month's security. He had decided to go back to school to get some skills. Then last week, after working all day rebuilding the porch for the man next door, he learned he would only be paid $11.
>
> I don't know all the details of what happened the night the police killed him, but whatever he was doing, Harvey didn't deserve to die—because he didn't have a gun.
>
> But Harvey's death doesn't have to be in vain. In South Africa the community knows how to use funerals to make the community stronger.
>
> Harvey wasn't trying to be Mayor or president of a bank. All he wanted was to work and become a respected member of our community. So many of our young people are out there, trying to do what's right but frustrated at every turn. We should be forming community support groups for our people coming out of prison. We can't be so busy with our own lives that we can't hear their cries for help. Not only their deaths but their lives must have meaning for us.
>
> In the words of Gwendolyn Brooks:
>
> > we are each other's
> > harvest:

we are each other's
business:
we are each other's
magnitude and bond.[1]

Thousands of black youth, fascinated by the militaristic image of Huey Newton in his black beret and black leather jacket, sitting on a throne-like chair with a gun in one hand and a spear in the other, were joining or forming Black Panther Party branches all over the country, hungry for both ideology and action, seeking a cause that would invest their lives with social and historical meaning and direct their energies into revolutionary political channels. In the month of June 1968 alone the Panthers recruited nearly eight hundred members in New York City, and by 1969 they had branches in forty-five cities.[2]

None of the individuals or groups in Detroit who had been so militant during the 1960s seemed even remotely conscious of the potential for transformation *and* self-destruction inherent in this new street force. They were too busy doing their own thing, implementing their particular ideology, competing with one another for the foundation grants and the positions that the white power structure was making available in order to defuse the movement, getting ready to run for political office, or going into business for themselves.

Like everyone else, the founders of the Black Panther Party were not prepared for this flood of aspiring revolutionaries. Even if they had wanted to, they had not had the time to create a revolutionary philosophy and ideology and a structure and programs to develop the thousands who were knocking at their door. So they borrowed virtually intact Mao's *Little Red Book,* without distinguishing between what is appropriate to China, or a postrevolutionary situation, and what is appropriate to the United States, or a potentially revolutionary situation. Forced into a virtual civil war with the police both by the impatience of members and by provocateurs sent into the organization to destroy it, the party began to fall apart. Countless party members were killed in raids or shootouts with the police, the FBI, and all too often with one another. Under the stresses of the struggle, many turned to drugs or alcohol.[3]

Today, nearly thirty years later, despite the loss of hundreds of thousands like Harvey to street violence, drugs, and prison, this street force is even larger than it was in 1968. It is also more desperate because with the export of production jobs overseas, more and more of our young people are seen and see themselves as expendable. At the same time, there is no longer the same readiness to sacrifice, the same confidence in themselves as agents for revolutionary change that moved thousands of black street youth to join the party in the late 1960s and early 1970s. That is why today, even more than in those years, black youth and an increasing number of other Americans need a vision and programs that can invest their lives with social and historical meaning. Until and unless this need is met, this country will continue to deteriorate socially and morally, no matter how much it expands economically and technologically.

Beginning in 1968 Jimmy and I began to focus our energies on meeting this challenge. To do this, the first thing we needed to do was to grapple with the theoretical question of the difference between rebellion and revolution. By 1968 we had been in the radical movement for a combined total of fifty-eight years, but we had never felt the need to make this distinction. Now, however, the great numbers of young people who had been driven by desperation to join the Black Panther Party, the party of organized rebellion, were not only being supported but encouraged in this rebellion by radicals, even though it was obvious that the end result could only be disaster and demoralization. Were these young people ready to provide revolutionary leadership? If so, what kind of a revolution would they make? If not, why not?

To explore these questions we needed to get away from fast-moving events in Detroit. So in 1968 we decided to spend our vacation with our old comrades, Freddy and Lyman Paine, on Sutton Island in Maine where Lyman had been spending summer vacations since he was a baby. There, in their summer home—called the Schoolhouse because it was where the children on the island went to school in the days when farmers worked the island—the four of us began the wide-ranging conversations in Maine that have since become a tradition. Every summer since 1968 we have carried on these conversations, even after Lyman died in 1978 and Jimmy in 1993—although not with the same sense of urgency as in the late 1960s and early 1970s. In 1979 Sharon Howell, popularly known as Shea, became a regular participant. Shea comes from a Welsh coal miner's family in South Greensburg, Pennsylvania. In 1977, after years of activism in the civil rights, antiwar, and women's movements, she was the first Euro-American to join our organization in Detroit and soon became a pivotal player in all our activities. One of the brightest people I have ever known, she also has a great sense of humor, is unflappable, indefatigable, and invariably willing to volunteer for more than she can do. While Jimmy was alive, we were inseparable. She was Jimmy's fishing buddy on Sutton and my moviegoing buddy in Detroit. Since 1980 she has been a professor of communications at Oakland University.

Lyman, Freddy, Jimmy, and I were a strange foursome—one Alabama-born African American and one New England Yankee man, one Jewish and one Chinese American woman. Tall, lean, blue-eyed, with small features and thin lips, Lyman looked like the WASP that he was. As a child he had played and sailed with the Rockefeller brothers in Maine (like him, they received an allowance of ten cents a week). After graduating from Harvard in 1922, he became a practicing architect. During the Great Depression he joined the radical movement and since then had committed not only his physical and intellectual energies but his financial resources to the movement.

Lyman and Jimmy had a special relationship. They both hated what this country had done and was doing but at the same time they always made it clear that they were American revolutionists who wanted to change this country because they loved it. Together they reminded me of Wendell Phillips, the New England abolitionist, and Frederick Douglass, the former slave who became an abolitionist leader and whose autobiography is must-reading for every American. In the magazine-sized *Correspondence*, which I edited in 1963–64, Jimmy's and Lyman's columns and pictures faced each other. Lyman's column was called "Before Pleasure Comes Paine" and Jimmy's was called "What It Means."

Freddy used to be a waitress, a dancer, and an artist's model. She started organizing in the garment district of New York in 1928 when she was sixteen and joined A. J. Muste's Conference for Progressive Labor Action (CPLA) in 1930. In the early 1930s she attended the Bryn Mawr Summer School for Women Workers, a program designed to give rank-and-file women workers a broad liberal education,[4] and in 1936 she became a part of the Trotskyist movement when the CPLA, which had become the American Workers Party, merged with the Communist League of America to form the Workers Party. She and Lyman got together in the mid-1930s soon after he joined the radical movement.

In an earlier chapter I have described Freddy's close relationship with CLR. Freddy knew everybody who was anybody in the radical movement and they all seemed to convene at 629 Hudson Street and later, when the Paines moved to Los Angeles, at their home on Holgate Square, both of which she ran like a top sergeant. She was only three years my senior, but when I came around in the early 1940s, Freddy viewed me as a pipsqueak intellectual (which I was), giving me instructions on how to dress and behave, as she did everybody else. Yet periodically because she thought that the political work I was doing was important, she worked in an office so that I could be engaged in politics full-time.

Freddy's genius has been in creating beautiful surroundings at the Paine home, first at 629 Hudson Street in Greenwich Village, then at Holgate Square in the Chicano community of Los Angeles, and also at the Schoolhouse on Sutton Island, organizing everything so that the hundreds of very diverse people who have gathered in these places over the years could easily interact with one another. In each community, including the one on Sutton, which consists mainly of university families, she is the one whom everyone calls when anything goes wrong. Freddy is a survivor. Since the 1950s, as a result of two bouts with tuberculosis she has functioned with one lung. In the early 1980s she had a heart bypass operation and in the late 1980s a mastectomy. In 1995 a malignant tumor was discovered in her left lung. But at the Schoolhouse in the summer of 1996 she was still the perfect hostess.

Our conversations were not planned in advance. In the course of dinner or over an after-dinner drink, questions and ideas would begin pouring out, especially from Lyman, as if a volcano had suddenly become active. The first two years I did not record the discussions, but beginning in 1970 I kept a reel-to-reel tape recorder ready to switch on as the discussion developed momentum. Back in Detroit I would transcribe the conversations, first in shorthand and then on the typewriter. Then I would edit and reproduce them on a spirit duplicator and circulate them to about a dozen friends and comrades. After the conversations were published in 1978, some readers complained that they do not make clear who said what. As the one responsible for the transcripts, I consciously left out such identification because I felt so strongly that the conversations were a collective activity, born out of our many years of struggle and very diverse backgrounds as movement activists whose lives had been profoundly influenced by our years of close association with and painful break from C. L. R. James. Occasionally, we would be joined by a close friend like Kathleen Gough, an anthropologist with a special interest in the development and decline of the family and the state. Her remarks are reprinted practically intact in the section on the "The Triple Revolution."[5]

There is no way that I can reproduce the flavor of these conversations, carried on in the peace and tranquillity of Sutton Island but also permeated with a sense of urgency because we were so conscious of the young people fighting for their lives on the streets of Detroit, Los Angeles, Oakland, Philadelphia, and all over the country. To this day they remain a priceless example of the passion and the joy with which profound philosophical questions can be pursued and new truths created at critical stages in the development of a society. I recall especially the persistence with which Lyman would keep raising tough questions: What is the purpose of revolution? To restore the sense of time? To create a new relationship between necessity and choice? Can we say anymore that man's social being determines his consciousness? Can a worker or a black be exonerated from responsibility because of his class or underclass? Are the ideas and contributions of whites and aristocrats to be rejected out of hand because of their class origins? Or are ideas and actions to be judged on their merits in relation to advancing humanity, regardless of class origins? How should people spend their lives? What is the relation between wants and thoughts? Between masses and revolutionists? What kind of vision of themselves and of society could transform rebels into revolutionists?

Jimmy never tired of saying that just coming out of your mother's womb does not make you a human being. He insisted that people become human through the choices that they make. Malcolm, he reminded us, had transformed himself from a hustler to a man ready to take responsibility for his own life and the lives of his people. What would it take to transform street rebels like Harvey into leaders like Malcolm? Jimmy would explain patiently that blacks had been able to create a movement for a higher form of human relationship between people, relations not yet shared or even believed in by most people, because they had maintained their humanity through centuries of oppression. That is why, for a brief period, it seemed that the whole country, despite the obvious divisions and opposition of many, would be lifted to a new plateau. Yet by the 1970s, even though most blacks were better off materially, all over the country we were experiencing the most dehumanized, blackmailing interactions between blacks and whites and between blacks and blacks that we had ever known. Why had this happened? Is it because we began to conceive freedom as "doing your own thing" and to view blacks as "oppressed masses" rather than as human beings capable of making moral choices? Or is it because those who today claim to be leading blacks are too intimidated by the angry black street force to chide and challenge them, as Malcolm used to do? What kind of philosophical leap do we need to make to get the movement back on the human track? What changes do we have to make in how we ourselves think about revolution in order to act as revolutionists? Masses have wants; revolutionists must have thoughts. They can't just rely on the wants and spontaneity of the masses. As we talked way into the night, especially between 1968 and 1974, I felt a liberation comparable to that which I had first experienced back at Bryn Mawr when the study of Hegel had helped me to see my own struggles as an integral part of the evolution of the human race. Inside my mind and heart the materialist concept of revolution as chiefly a redistribution of goods, property, and power was being enriched by a moral and spiritual dimension.

We didn't only talk. During the day Freddy and Jimmy especially would do the things that are necessary to keep up a house, like puttying windows, cutting wood, cleaning out a wasp's nest. Jimmy would work on "his" path, the quarter-of-a-mile-long hilly strip from the beach to the house, filling it in and smoothing it out with pebbles and underbrush so that a wheelbarrow, packed full of luggage and/or groceries, could be pushed up and down. Lyman's emphysema kept him from doing much physical activity. I would read to Freddy while she worked. Almost every afternoon there would be a walk around or across the island to pick mushrooms, cranberries, and/or apples and to see the osprey nest. There are no cars on the island, which is only a half-mile wide and a mile long, and most of the paths are too rough even for bicycles. At least once during our vacation we would "build" a chowder with the mussels that are so abundant at low tide that two people can easily pick up a hundred on the beach in a half hour. Now and then a fishing expedition would result in a good catch of tinker mackerel. We went swimming infrequently because the water was so cold that we used to rub vaseline on our ankles, knees, and elbows to keep them from freezing.

We talked about jazz as the distinctively American music created by blacks because their experience in this country was one of suffering *and* hope and as the music of liberation that says you can be different today from what you were yesterday. But we didn't only talk about it. Over and over again we played our favorite records, particularly Duke Ellington's *First Sacred Concert*, Errol Garner's *Concert by the Sea*, Leonard Bernstein's *Mass*, and Oscar Peterson's *Brotherhood of Man*. On our final night, while the popovers were swelling in the oven and the water was boiling for lobsters, we would play *Fiddler on the Roof*, especially enjoying "Tradition," "If I Were a Rich Man," and "To Life." Then at dinner over lobsters we would retell old stories, for example, how streetwise Freddy fared in her first encounter with her New England in-laws on Sutton thirty to forty years ago or how lobsters once were so abundant and cheap that the servants went on strike because they were tired of having to eat them all the time. The next day we would set out early in the morning to drive back to Detroit, stopping on the way overnight with Carol and Ping Ferry for our annual reunion.

In order to clarify the fundamental difference between rebellion and revolution, we had to come to grips with Marx's concept of the revolutionary process or scenario. Writing in the last half of the nineteenth

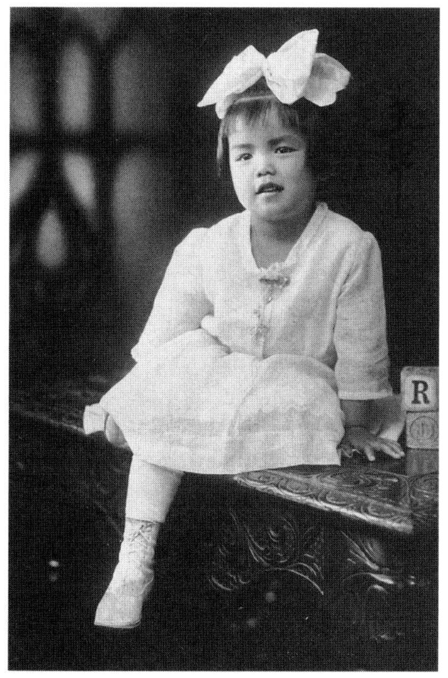

Grace at four or five

Left to right:
Harry, Grace, Eddie

Back row, left to right: George, Bob, Eddie;
front row, left to right: Kay, Chin Lee, Grace, 1945

Grace at fourteen

陳利

廣東台山六村人，到美行將六十年，向在紐英倫各地發展餐館事業，一九二一年，在紐約最繁盛戲院區域一六零四號布律委街，創陳利樓，規模宏大，座位凡八百餘，每月樓租三千元，一九廿六年在同街一五零六號再創陳氏餐館，堂皇富麗，設備華貴，規模更爲偉大，座位達一千一百餘，月租亦數千元，計兩餐館，每月樓租六千餘元，音樂手劇員六千餘元，電火五千餘元，煤火九百餘元，洗檯布茶巾白衣等四千餘元，每年營業總額數百萬元，其規模之大可想見，爲華僑餐館最大者，陳君一生勤勞奮鬥，熱心公益，經營餐館，是其所長，不愧爲華僑中之餐館王。

Excerpt on Grace's father from *The Chinese in North America: A Guide to Their Life and Progress* by Ling Lew. He is described as the "king of the restaurant businessmen among the Chinese."

Grace's paternal grandmother in China at 101 years

Grace at eighteen
Photo by Edward Lee

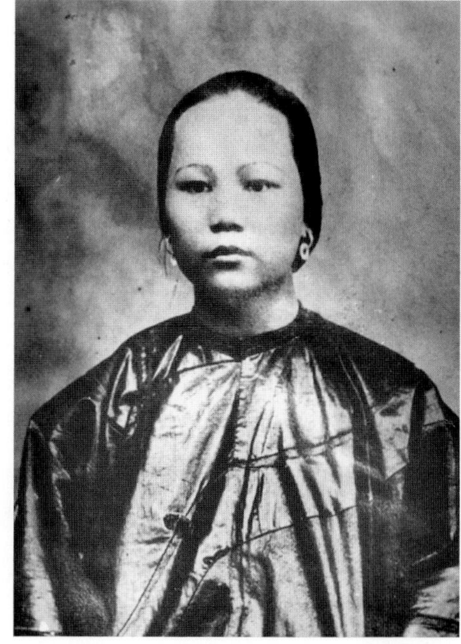

Grace's mother, Yin Lan, at twenty-one, arriving in the United States

Grace's mother at fifty-five

C. L. R. James, 1960

Kwame Nkrumah, July 1950

Grace and Selma James in London, 1957

C. L. R. James with Raya Dunayevskaya (*left*) and Grace in the 1940s

Jimmy, 1975
Photo by Kenneth Snodgrass

Kitchen politics
Left to right: Jimmy, Grace, and Ted Griffin, 1957

Left to right: Jimmy and Grace, Ruby and Ossie, at the Twentieth Anniversary Celebration of *The American Revolution*, 1983

Jimmy Boggs (*standing*) at the Grassroots Leadership Conference, November 1963. On the wall are pictures of Delores Wilson, Helen Kelly, Richard Henry, Reginald Wilson, and Grace.
Photo by Milton Henry

Dorothy (Mama G) Garner, leader of We the People Reclaim Our Streets (WE-PROS)

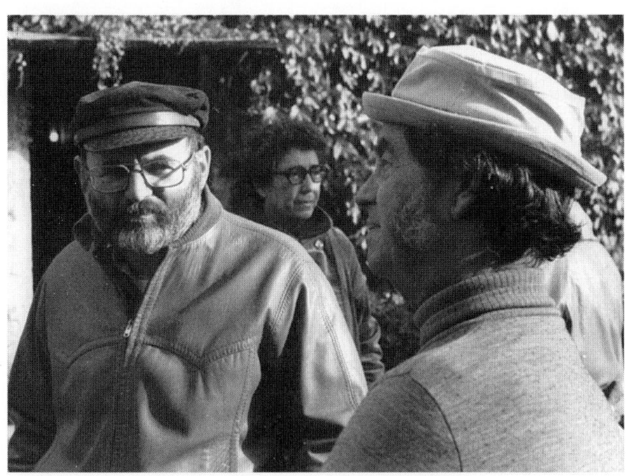

Ping Ferry *(right)* with Vic Navasky and Mae Churchill at Branscombe, England, gathering of Ping's Old Friends (POF)

Photo by Robert Churchill

Left to right: Grace, Lyman, Freddy, and Jimmy at the Sutton Island boathouse

Photo by Chrissie Nevius

Grace, 1980s

Grace protesting casinos

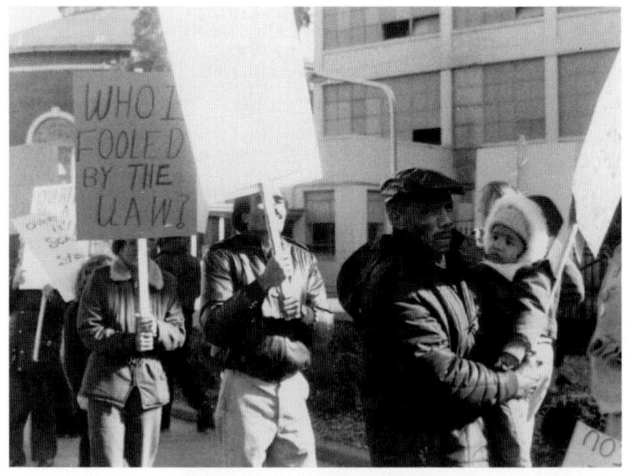

Jimmy *(right, holding child)* protesting the United Auto Workers

Grace marching down Woodward Avenue in the 1980s

Grace on her seventy-seventh birthday in 1992,
with Jimmy and Shea Howell

Grace and Jimmy with his niece and friends
in their living room, April 1992

Detroit Summer volunteers planting the Circle of Life Garden

Photo by Hank Kryciuk

Gerald Hairston, Gardening Angel

Photo by Hank Kryciuk

Grace, opening ceremony of Detroit Summer, 1996

Photo by Hank Kryciuk

Grace at the Temple of Heaven, Beijing, October 6, 1984

century when people in progressive circles were adopting science as the religion of the future, Marx was determined to create a theory of "scientific socialism," that is, to develop laws of social movement for the achievement of a just society as rigorous as those of the physical sciences and therefore excluding morality, choice, or politics. In many passages in Marx and especially in his early *Economic and Philosophic Manuscripts*, you can feel his moral outrage at the way that capitalism has turned all our relationships into economic or commodity relationships. But the main message that radicals have taken from him is his economic determinism. The only thing that matters is the material base—all the rest is superstructure. The revolution is inevitable because it is inherent in the laws by which capitalism develops. Thus in the famous passage in the chapter on "The Historical Tendency of Capitalist Accumulation" in *Capital*, Marx insists that the working class is disciplined, united, and organized by the very mechanism of the process of capitalist production. Therefore, there is no need for the workers to transform themselves. All that is required to bring socialism into existence is for the working class to revolt and break through the capitalist integument that is preventing socialized labor from manifesting itself.

For more than a century Marxist radicals have lived by this analysis, convinced that their only role was to expose the crimes of capitalism in order to increase the anger and militancy of the workers and get them into physical motion so that they can sweep away the capitalist shell and allow the invading socialist society to emerge. When the Russian workers did not exhibit these socialist qualities after the revolution, we were persuaded that it was because the revolution had taken place in a backward country where the working class was a minority. In a highly developed capitalist country like the United States, we were assured, Marx's analysis would be vindicated. Few people dared to question this prognosis. If you did, it was a sign that you no longer believed in the working class and were about to "leave the movement."

In *The American Revolution* Jimmy had challenged the validity of Marx's scenario for a highly developed country like the United States. In order to make an American revolution, he insisted, all Americans, including workers and blacks or the most victimized, will have to make political and moral choices. It was perhaps easy for him as a black man to insist on the need for white workers to transform themselves. But Jimmy was equally demanding of blacks. Being a victim of oppression in the United States, he insisted, is not enough to make you revolutionary, just as dropping out of your mother's womb is not enough to make you human. People who are full of hate and anger against their oppressors or who only see Us versus

Them can make a rebellion but not a revolution. The oppressed internalize the values of the oppressor. Therefore, any group that achieves power, no matter how oppressed, is not going to act differently from their oppressors as long as they have not confronted the values that they have internalized and consciously adopted different values. Precisely because the United States is so advanced technologically, precisely because it has developed an economic apparatus so productive that not only our needs but our wants can be satisfied, we cannot make a revolution without developing our human capacity to distinguish between needs and wants and to make responsible choices. Americans will not "regain their membership in the human race until they recognize that their greatest need is no longer to make material goods but to make politics," he used to say. The contrast between Jimmy's emphasis on the need for moral and political choices and the focus of Marxists on economic development could not be more stark. It was Jimmy's boldness in reconceptualizing the relationship between politics and economics and his effrontery in challenging Marx at this profound philosophical level that had infuriated CLR and provoked him to break off all relationships with us in 1962.

For twelve years, ever since his unhappy visit with CLR in London in 1956, Lyman had been struggling with Marx's economic determinism, recognizing the power that it had had over generations of radicals, including himself, and also recognizing that we could not just reject Marx's concept and scenario of revolution without replacing it with an equally powerful new philosophy as well as an equally powerful but fundamentally different concept and scenario of revolution. Lyman called this philosophy "dialectical humanism" to sharpen the contrast with the dialectical materialism of Marxism. If those victimized by capitalist exploitation are not necessarily revolutionary, if morality and choice play a critical role in making a revolution, if a revolution represents a leap to a new stage of being a more *human* human being, then the role of revolutionists is profoundly different from that which radicals have played. It cannot just be to rub raw the sores of discontent in order to get oppressed masses to rebel. Recognizing the damage that a highly developed capitalist system, pouring out goods from its assembly lines, has done to the humanity of all of us, victims as well as villains, revolutionists have a responsibility to create strategies to transform ourselves as well as the victims of oppression into human beings who are more advanced in the qualities that distinguish human beings: creativity, consciousness, self-consciousness, and a sense of political and social responsibility.

This is the key to the distinction between rebellion and revolution. Rebellion is a stage in the development of revolution but it is not revolution. It is an important stage because it represents the standing up of the oppressed. Rebellions break the threads that have been holding the system together and throw into question its legitimacy and the supposed permanence of existing institutions. A rebellion disrupts the society but it does not provide what is necessary to make a revolution and establish a new social order. To make a revolution, people must not only struggle against existing institutions. They must make a philosophical/spiritual leap and become more *human* human beings. In order to change/transform the world, they must change/transform themselves.

Year after year in our conversations, we peeled off, layer after layer, the Marxist assumptions that we had been accepting, not in order to attack Marx or to find excuses for leaving the movement, but in order to make clear that revolutions are made in order to advance the evolution of humankind and therefore require struggles not only against the external enemy but also against the enemy within.

As we come to the end of the twentieth century Marx's economic determinism and his concept of politics, morality, and spirit as mere superstructure are no longer as appealing as they used to be. As we have become more knowledgeable about the rest of the world, we have learned that other cultures do not accept the separation between spirit and matter that has become entrenched in European thought. The rise of the women's movement with its insistence that "the personal is political" has also dealt a death blow to the sharp dichotomy between the subjective and the objective, which began with Cartesian rationalism in the seventeenth century and which still influenced Marx's thinking. The collapse of the Soviet bloc has also created confusion in Marxist circles; the radical groups who still live by Marx's prognosis and are still mainly concerned with escalating the militancy of the oppressed have become marginal to ongoing struggles.

In the late 1960s and early 1970s, however, most liberals and radicals were hailing the Black Panthers as the vanguard of the revolution. We were more skeptical because the Harveys who formed the mass base of the Panthers were our friends and neighbors. The distinction between rebellion and revolution had also been implicit in our split with CLR in 1962, although it did not become explicit because CLR refused to submit his views for discussion.[6] In insisting on the need to transform ourselves in order to transform the world, we were encouraged by the knowledge that

Mao in China, Ho Chi Minh in Vietnam, and Amilcar Cabral in Guinea-Bissau, while identifying themselves as Marxist-Leninists, were actually struggling to develop and implement a "build as you fight" strategy for revolution that went beyond Marx and Lenin. In the 1917 revolution the Bolshevik Party had seized state power first and then faced the question of transforming the workers and peasants into politically conscious, socially responsible citizens after the revolution. Mao, Ho, and Cabral, struggling to make the revolution in economically undeveloped societies where the workers are the minority and having learned from the postrevolutionary problems faced by Lenin and the Bolsheviks, recognized that *before* the seizure of power the revolutionary struggle has to be conducted on two fronts. The revolutionary party not only has to mobilize the masses to fight against the external enemy. It also has to create structures and programs to transform the masses into representatives of the New Man and the New Woman. Thus, after they were forced to abandon the cities to the Kuomintang, the Chinese Communist Party struggled to build a society in remote Yenan based on alternative concepts of the economy, fighting against militarism and adventurism, and carrying on unceasing criticism and self-criticism. Amilcar Cabral, the leader of the revolution in Guinea-Bissau, kept urging his members to "oppose tendencies to militarism and make each fighter an exemplary militant of our party. . . . Tell no lies. Expose lies wherever they are told. Mask no difficulties, mistakes, failures. Claim no easy victories." As he put it, "Our experience has shown us that in the general framework of daily struggle this battle against ourselves, this struggle against our own weaknesses—no matter what difficulties the enemy may create—is the most difficult of all, whether for the present or for the future of our people."[7]

Different people can hold differing views on how successful or unsuccessful Mao, Ho, and Cabral were in actually transforming their revolutionary social forces. But there can be no question that all three of them viewed the struggle for transformation as an integral part of the revolutionary process. They were an inspiration to us during our conversations. To this day I continue to learn from Mao and to marvel at the audacity with which he accepted the challenge to create a billion New Men and New Women. I have read and reread my favorite articles in the one-volume edition of the *Selected Readings from the Works of Mao Tse Tung* so often that my copy is falling apart.[8]

We did not know it at the time, but in the last two years of his life Martin Luther King Jr. had also been grappling with the question of how to go beyond rebellion to revolution. King's leadership was always rooted in a profound appreciation of the need for human transformation. But the Watts uprising in the summer of 1965, his incursion into Chicago in 1966, the eruption of the Black Power slogan during the 1966 march into Mississippi, the war in Vietnam, and the rebellions of 1967—all had made him painfully aware of the need to go beyond the civil rights movement. Convinced that the only outcome of continuing rebellion would be continuing chaos, he struggled heroically to organize a nonviolent revolution of the dispossessed that would combine a revolution in values against what he called the "giant triplets" of racism, materialism, and militarism with a revolution against the structures that doom millions to poverty and powerlessness. Recognizing the need to go beyond technological progress ("we have guided missiles and misguided men") and beyond both traditional capitalism and communism (capitalism was too "I-centered," too individualistic, too thing-oriented; communism too collective, too statist), he explored strategies that would involve young people in "direct self-transforming and structure-transforming action" in "our dying cities" and mobilize the nation's poor in a sustained massive freedom march on Washington, D.C., that would force "the legislative and executive branches of the government to take serious and adequate action on jobs and income." Acutely aware that the United States and the world were at a historical watershed, he was struggling to create this new movement under the tremendous pressures of making three to four hundred speeches a year, merciless FBI surveillance, and opposition from most of his closest associates to his stand against the Vietnam War. Hence the frustration and even demoralization that are unmistakable in his "Free at Last" speech the night before he was assassinated. How King might have developed had he not been cut down in his prime we will never know. But like Malcolm he had already manifested one of the most important qualities of revolutionary leadership, the ability to evolve as reality changes and as you learn from your own experiences and the experiences of others.[9]

Based on our new understanding of the revolutionary process as transformational, our conversations in Maine emphasized the need for projections rather than rejections. It is not accidental that traditional Marxists come across as so negative. If the new social relations of community already exist in the working class and the capitalist integument only needs to be swept away for this positive movement to emerge, if workers in power have already been organized, disciplined, and socialized in the process of capitalist production, then the main responsibility of the revolutionist is to expose the crimes of capitalism so that the workers will get mad, rebel, and seize power. If, however, those who need to make a revolution also need to transform themselves into more socially responsible, more self-critical human beings, then our role as revolutionists is to involve them in activities that are both self-transforming and structure-transforming, exploring and trying to resolve in theory and practice fundamental questions of human life more complex than anything Marx could possibly have dreamed of. What kind of an economy, what kind of technology would serve both human and economic needs? What kind of transformation do we need in our values, institutions, and behavior to reconnect us with the rhythms and processes of nature? Should we do something just because we can do it? What is the difference between needs and wants? How do we meet people's psychic hungers? What does it mean to care? What is the purpose of education? How do we create community? What is the difference between a community and a network? Why is community a revolutionary idea? How do communities start?

Today, even more than in 1968, confusion, uncertainty, frustration, anger, hopelessness, and fear permeate every section of the population, as traditional beliefs about work, family, community, and education crumble in the face of relentless technological changes that are both liberating and alienating. For a revolutionary organization to talk about revolution and call for revolution without grappling with these questions would be the height of irresponsibility.

The more we talked in 1968, the clearer it was that even deciding what questions need to be asked, let alone discovering the answers, would take years, extending far beyond our lifetimes. One of our favorite sayings was "Things take time!" But in view of the spreading chaos it was also urgent that we get started on finding ways and means to develop these ideas further by putting them into practice. It was ridiculous to think that Jimmy could do this and at the same time work eight hours a day at Chrysler, spending his evenings writing, speaking, and going to meetings and then getting up in the morning at 5 A.M. to go to work on the motor line.

So at the end of our first conversation in 1968 we agreed that Jimmy would resign from his job at Chrysler—two years short of the thirty years required for retirement on pension—and Lyman would send us a modest quarterly stipend from the trust fund he had inherited after his father's recent death. Because we had both grown up during the Depression, Jimmy and I have always lived frugally. We bought practically all our furniture and clothing at thrift shops and took pride in our ability to live on very little. (Shea called me a tightwad.) Our cost of living was low because Jimmy did most of the fix-it jobs around the house that most city-dwellers pay others to do. In all our years together we never once argued with one another about money. From time to time the Ferrys would send a check. Things eased up a bit when I became eligible for Social Security in 1977 and Jimmy in 1981, although our monthly checks were minimal because both of us had stopped work when wages were still low. But we felt that we had made a great leap forward in our concept of revolution and we welcomed the challenge to make this new concept real through practice.

The first thing we heard when we arrived back in Detroit from Maine in 1968 was that small groups of armed black youth, declaring themselves to be Black Panthers, were holed up in several houses in Detroit, anticipating a shootout with the police. We also learned that in the wake of the Rebellion, Cleage's Shrine of the Black Madonna and Black Christian Nationalist Movement (BCNM) were expanding rapidly. Cleage had been renamed Jerimoge and new bishops were being trained to give leadership at the Linwood location and at other shrines, not only in Detroit but in cities like Atlanta and Houston. A nearby apartment building was being taken over to house church members who wanted to live together. One of Cleage's main objectives had always been to become a force in local politics. With the growth in membership of the Shrine and BCNM he was well on the way to influencing elections and even electing members of his own organization to positions on the City Council, the Detroit School Board, in the state legislature, and in Congress.

Edward Vaughn was managing a cooperative store on Linwood not far from the Shrine. Russell Brown, along with countless other blacks, was campaigning for election to the Michigan House of Representatives. Richard Henry (Brother Imari) and Milton Henry (Brother Gaidi) were busy organizing the Republic of New Africa (RNA) with the goal of acquiring territory somewhere in the southern United States for an independent nation. They had contacted Robert Williams in exile, inviting him to return home to become RNA president. Rob, Mabel, and their two sons had been forced to leave the country in 1961 and had spent the decade, first in Cuba and then in the Peoples Republic of China, garnering international support for the black struggle in the United States.[10]

The UHURU comrades, General Baker, John Watson, John Williams, and others, together with Mike Hamlin and Ken Cockrel, were organizing black autoworkers into the League of Revolutionary Black Workers, consisting of DRUM (Dodge Revolutionary Union Movement), FRUM (Ford Revolutionary Union Movement), among others, challenging not only management but the union bureaucracy. Outside the Dodge plant DRUM members and their supporters from the community were playing bongo drums and shouting demands for a black plant manager, black plant doctors, and equal pay and job opportunities, while inside the plant white workers were turning on their machines to drown out the beat of the drums and their own fears. At Wayne State University members of the League for Revolutionary Black Workers were getting ready to take over *South End*, the student daily, proclaiming on its masthead that "One class-conscious worker is worth a hundred students."[11]

We soon began hearing from people we had worked with in the Organization for Black Power and the Inner City Organizing Committee asking what we were going to do and what we thought they should do. We were also contacted by Dan Aldridge, a Detroiter who had been involved with the Student Non-Violent Coordinating Committee (SNCC). He had heard about our visit with Nkrumah whom he very much admired. Locally he was in touch with a number of young people who in the wake of the Rebellion were looking for a way to become active politically. Dan had a job on Mack Avenue not far from our house that gave him a lot of free time. He spent most of this time absorbing information and ideas from us.

As a result of these developments we decided to write the *Manifesto for a Black Revolutionary Party*, the purpose of which was to lead black youth beyond rebellion to revolution or to make revolutionists out of rebels. Toward this goal the party would

> 1) Make clear that Black liberation cannot be achieved except through a Black Revolution, and that the goal of the Black Revolution in the United States, like the goal of every revolution, regardless of color, is to take power for the purpose of bringing about a fundamental change in the social, economic and political institutions of the society.
>
> 2) Establish and keep before the movement and society as a whole the revolutionary humanist objectives of the Black Revolution in this country, a country which is both the technologically most advanced and the politically and socially most counter-revolutionary in the world.
>
> 3) Develop a revolutionary strategy and a revolutionary leadership to achieve these objectives, building on the struggles, sacrifices and achievements of the past, and learning from previous mistakes and shortcomings how to struggle more effectively towards victory in the future.

We presented the *Manifesto* in April 1969 at the National Black Economic Development Conference, convened by the Interreligious Foundation for Community Organization in Detroit, where Jimmy was one of the keynote speakers. His subject was "The Myth and Irrationality of Black Capitalism."[12] The *Manifesto*'s striking black and gold cover, designed by Philadelphia comrades Bill Davis and James McFadden and displaying a black hand holding up the world, contrasted sharply with the black fist commonly accepted as the symbol of Black Power. The strategy for a black revolution put forward in the *Manifesto* was also in sharp contrast with the much better-known *Black Manifesto* presented during this same conference by former SNCC organizer James Forman, which demanded a half billion dollars from white churches to finance black projects. Our *Manifesto* challenged blacks to assume the awesome responsibility of making a revolution to reorganize all the institutions of the country for the benefit of the entire society. The *Black Manifesto*, by contrast, put blacks back into the posture of supplicants playing on the guilt of white liberals to extract reparations.

I will never forget the meeting at which Forman presented his *Black Manifesto*. The meeting was not a regular session of the conference; it was more like a caucus of activists. Jimmy had gone home with a headache. When the demand for half billion dollars was projected to the fifty or more people gathered in a relatively small room, the audience gasped, eyes popped, and someone said "$15 a N----r." I was horrified—into my mind popped the lines from "The White Man's Heaven" that called putting a price on a man's body the "world's most grievous sin"—and raised my hand to speak. When I was not recognized immediately, I dropped my hand, thinking to myself that discretion is the better part of valor. I don't know what Jimmy would have said if he had been at the meeting. When people asked him later what he thought of the *Black Manifesto*, he didn't attack it. That was not his style. Instead, he said that his own view had always been that the more money the black movement demanded and received from white America, the more individuals would be bought off and pacified. What blacks needed most of all, he insisted, was not money but political development to prepare them for the awesome responsibilities of revolutionary leadership. Personally, I rarely get involved in discussions of reparations because my experience has been that when African Americans demand reparations, what they are talking about is not the future but the past, the millions of lives lost on the Middle Passage and the unspeakable degradation of slavery. And those are not things that you can debate.

Jimmy and I worked together on the *Manifesto for a Black Revolutionary Party*, which was obvious from the varying styles of different passages. But no one said anything and I don't think anyone cared, because by that time we were pretty much accepted as a team. Eventually, the *Man-*

ifesto went through five printings of five thousand copies each. Many young people carried it proudly in their vest pockets as a symbol of black pride and power. Dan Aldridge formed a group of young blacks, based on the *Manifesto,* calling itself the All African Peoples Union. After about a year the group dissolved. Dan eventually joined the Coleman Young administration and went to theology school to become a preacher.

In 1970 Jimmy and I gave a series of lectures "On Revolution" at the University of Michigan Extension in Detroit. Frank Joyce, who was then the organizer of People Against Racism and has since become UAW public relations director, arranged for the series and was on the platform with us. In these lectures we emphasized the distinction between rebellion and revolution and traced developments since the Russian Revolution in the theory and practice of revolution itself, as exemplified in China, Vietnam, and Guinea-Bissau.

At the same time, we began using the *Manifesto for a Black Revolutionary Party* to bring together black militants, not only in Detroit but in other cities where we had contacts, who were ready to commit to the discipline and political education necessary to develop themselves into the kinds of revolutionary leaders who could take the black struggle beyond rebellion to revolution. Our aim was to build local organizations that would be very different from the kinds of organizations blacks had known. The black community was accustomed to loosely knit organizations like the NAACP that emphasize legal and electoral struggles. They were also familiar with the black church, in which women are subordinate to men and do all the Jimmy Higgins (or grunt) work, and everyone follows the charismatic leader. These dynamics had been imported virtually intact into the Black Power movement. By contrast, our goal was to create the kind of organization in which women are the equal of men and every member is developed into a theoretical and practical leader, participating in creating the ideas and prepared to lead struggles at the community level.

Instead of depending on government or foundations for funds, we were determined to build an organization that supported itself by substantial membership dues and literature sales. Membership would be restricted to those who, after an extended period of revolutionary study and an orientation process, accepted the philosophy, ideology, and structure of the organization. Meetings would start on time; proceedings would be faithfully recorded in minutes so that members would develop a sense of historical responsibility. The organization's work would have three prongs: (1) internal political development, including the continual updating of the ideology; (2) propaganda or the promotion of ideas through public speaking and publications; and (3) programming or the projection and organizing of external struggles.

To carry out these three tasks, each local would consist of three committees: the Political Education Committee, the Propaganda Committee, and the Program Committee. The Central Committee would be made up of one or two representatives elected from each of these committees. Each year the membership would meet as a whole in convention to decide by majority vote its program for the coming year or what we called the "Political Line." Following the majority vote all members were committed to carrying out the Line in accordance with the principles of democratic centralism. Absence from the convention would automatically mean removal from the organization.

Special measures were taken to ensure that the locals were locally based. The founding convention of each local began with a founding document analyzing the history of the city. The political line of each local was based on the circumstances in the particular city and the composition of the members. For example, the Philadelphia local always included Dojo or training in the martial arts in its political line. The Syracuse local produced a noteworthy statement on fishing and pollution in New York.

This structure was mainly the creation of Bill Davis, a streetwise Philadelphia teacher who had been around Marxist organizations. Today it seems incredibly rigid, too reminiscent of the vanguard party structure that Lenin had created in prerevolutionary Russia and that had been duplicated, more or less, in China, Vietnam, and Guinea-Bissau. For example, members were not allowed to abstain from voting because it might encourage waffling, which to Jimmy was a grievous political sin. But in order to understand why we decided to go this route, you need to imagine yourselves living in either the Detroit or Philadelphia black community back in the late 1960s and early 1970s. No longer needed by capitalism as producers in the labor process but still exploited as consumers, black street youth were in a state of unceasing rebellion, demanding and taking, challenging and defying, deepening the sense of crisis and insecurity inside the community. Meanwhile, the only organizational forms available to blacks were those of the NAACP, social agencies, and/or the black church. At the same time organizations like the Black Panthers were structuring themselves with Ministries of Defense, Education, Finance, and so on, as if blacks had taken over state power. Our structure, by contrast, was created to emphasize commitment, responsibility, and the transformation of every member into someone whom the community could depend on for theoretical and practical leadership.

In the midst of the rampant confusion and disorder of those days and the haphazard and sloppy functioning of most organizations, there was something immensely satisfying about the organizational discipline and ideological unity of the organization. Membership in the organization was very demanding, but in putting demands on ourselves we felt that we were not only becoming more human human beings but creating living models of the kind of creative, politically conscious, and socially responsible human beings that a revolution, as distinct from a rebellion, would create. One of our first publications was a pamphlet titled *The Awesome Responsibilities of Revolutionary Leadership* with a sketch of Lenin, Castro, Cabral, Nkrumah, Ho Chi Minh, and Mao Tse-tung on the front cover. The introduction to the third printing was written by Kenny Snodgrass, who was a teenager when he joined the Detroit local. *Awesome* was one of his favorite words. The conclusion of his introduction reads:

> "We must become philosophical in our approach to politics. We must struggle not only against the system but against our own weaknesses, such as Individualism, Sexism, Idealism, Opportunism and Adventurism. Not until black people have struggled against their own weaknesses will we be able to lead the struggle to eradicate the old corrupt society and build a new, more human one."

In retrospect, it seems to me that although we did not misjudge the urgency of the situation, we did overestimate the revolutionary energy still in the black movement. By the midseventies, we had been able to organize only four small groups based on the ideas in the *Manifesto* and the structure that we had adopted: Advocators in Detroit, Pacesetters in Philadelphia, the Committee for Raising Political Consciousness in Muskegon, and the Committee for Political Development in New York City. Except for myself, membership in these groups was restricted to African Americans because the explicit purpose was to create the leadership to transform the rebels in the black street force into revolutionists. Hundreds and perhaps thousands of African Americans in their twenties and thirties read our literature, came to our public meetings, and resonated to our ideas. But most of them felt that they had to take advantage of the newly available job opportunities or to go to school in preparation for making a living and could not see themselves making the commitment in time and energy required for membership.

At the same time, our programs were not action-oriented enough for the young people who were attracted to the Black Panthers and had plenty of time on their hands. For example, before a person could even apply for membership, she or he was required to participate in a weekly Revolutionary Study Group (RSG), which began with the study of the *Manifesto for a Black Revolutionary Party* and continued for six more sessions on revolution and evolution, dialectics and revolution, and the revolutions in Russia, China, Vietnam, and Guinea-Bissau. If you applied for membership after completing the RSG, you had to go through six more sessions of orientation, followed by a entire day of postorientation, inducting you into the structure and political line of the local. Shea used to joke that an elephant could be born in the time it took to become a member. In Detroit these sessions were held in our downstairs recreation room, where the walls were decorated with quotations from Mao, Ho Chi Minh, and Cabral, side by side with a poster with the message "Since World War II, we have known that the old man—the consuming man, the purely technological man, the wholly materialistic man—must die. Our problem has been that no one better has come forward to take his place."[13]

Because comrades were imbued with such an enlarged view of revolution and their own role as revolutionists, our output was prodigious. We published more than a dozen statements that we sold for a dime and an equal number of pamphlets that we sold for fifty cents to a dollar. Mostly written by the members, these publications put forward advanced ideas in a straightforward and powerful way that everyone could understand. Each statement addressed a current crisis and had a clear structure. The first part described the crisis so graphically that everyone in the community could identify with it. The second explained how we got to this point. The conclusion projected actions that people in the community could undertake *on their own*. Every statement was a challenge to the reader to transcend the victim mentality that was impeding us from making the moral and social choices that were necessary for our own survival and the health of our communities. Their analyses and projections remain valid and challenging to this day.[14]

Our most popular statement was *Crime among Our People*. We decided to call it *Crime among Our People* rather than *Crime among the People* because we wanted to break with the radical tendency to objectify the masses. The proposals at the end of this statement included a call to everyone in the community to pledge with neighbors, family, and coworkers not to buy hot or stolen goods. "Thus in our practice," it read, "we can educate our communities, including the criminal elements, to understand that we are not going to tolerate inhuman, anti-social behavior any longer." It took a lot of courage to publish and sell this statement in a period when many blacks were using racism as an excuse for crime and others were afraid to challenge criminals who were often family members. The statement went through seven printings of five thousand each. Jim Embry came across a copy in Lexington, Kentucky, and got in touch with us. It was the beginning of a comradeship that has lasted more than two decades.

What Value Shall We Place On Our Selves? demonstrated our unique approach to the Woman Question. In the wake of the Rebellion many young girls were being persuaded to have babies by black nationalist men, using the argument that the more babies born to blacks, the more power blacks would have in their negotiations with whites. As a result, "a growing number of young girls, from the age of 12 onwards, are today having sex relations and getting pregnant." At the end of this statement we urged every young girl

> to make a conscious effort *not* to be swept off her feet by any man who views her just as a sex object or as a vessel for bearing children; *not* to bear a child for any man who is not ready to take responsibility for supporting and raising the children he conceives; and *not* to become a Welfare client in order to satisfy the ego or greed of any man.

This statement was a direct and necessary challenge to the sexism in the black movement, and we received many bulk orders for it from groups working with young girls. Later we also published three pamphlets dealing with the women's movement: *Women and the New World; Women and the Movement to Build a New America*; and *Beyond Socialist Feminism*.

Beyond Welfare, written by the New York comrades, was way ahead of its time. The statement begins by describing the degrading lives of people on welfare and the vested interest that slumlords, merchants in poor communities, and social workers have acquired in the welfare system. It concludes by urging welfare recipients not to focus on the struggle for more money but to struggle for jobs doing the socially necessary work of rebuilding our communities, paid at the same rate as other workers.

Three of our most popular pamphlets were *A New Outlook on You, on Me, on Health; Education to Govern*; and *But What about the Workers?* The health pamphlet, written by our Muskegon comrades, exposes the "healthlessness" that the present system is creating in the American people. It concludes by urging community people not to depend on the medical-industrial complex that profits from the increasing helplessness, medication, and hospitalization of sick people. Instead, we should be taking back control of our bodies and ourselves by changing our lifestyles and making our neighborhoods more healthy, by planting trees and gardens in our neighborhoods, among other activities.

Education to Govern links the question of education to "The City Is the Black Man's Land." Our school system, it says, has been organized to prepare people to fit into the present economic and political system, to prepare the great majority for labor, and to advance a few into the governing elite. What we need instead is an educational system that prepares the great majority to govern. This pamphlet, based on one of my speeches that was reprinted in *Monthly Review* and in a special issue of the *Harvard Educational Review*, went through three printings.[15]

But What about the Workers? by James Hocker and James Boggs begins by describing the dynamism of the labor movement in the days when it was part of the community, and its loss of vitality after it became concerned chiefly with the economic interests of its members. For their own survival and the survival of this country, workers are urged to go beyond seeing themselves only as workers demanding more for themselves and to accept responsibility as citizens and as human beings for grappling with the new questions of work, the environment, the family, and community that are now posed by the technological revolutions in production. This pamphlet attracted Rick Feldman, a Ford worker, to us in 1974. He is still using it to educate workers in his plant where he has worked for more than twenty years and has been a shop committeeman.

We also wrote and distributed leaflets on current events. In response to the TWA hijacking in the Middle East, we published a leaflet that remains timely to this day. Titled *We Must Break the Cycle of Pain*, it says that "our vulnerability to terrorist attacks began with the terrorism of U.S. support of the counter-revolution in the Third World—and will continue until, we the American people, clearly dissociate ourselves from the racist-terrorist policies of our government." As Christmas approached each year, we distributed a leaflet titled *How Shall We Spend Our Holidays?* urging our readers to spend time building our relationships in our homes and neighborhoods instead of on shopping sprees; to struggle for peace on earth by joining and supporting those struggling for nuclear disarmament; to "exchange gifts of friendship and share our fortune, no matter how small, with others who have basic needs for food and clothing." In response to the 1973 oil crisis, we issued *The Energy Crisis and You* statement in which we said that the energy crisis provides us with an exceptional opportunity to confront the American people with the need to struggle for a new society. Such a society, we said, could not be built by the American people as we are today: "Always wanting more things—whether we need them or not:

seizing every opportunity to evade responsibility for social decision-making, we are a people who have been damaged by the fruits of constantly expanding capitalism."

In our internal development programs we discussed wide-ranging topics critical to revolutionary theory and practice: for example, how to think dialectically, that is, to recognize that reality is constantly changing and therefore that ideas and paradigms that were once progressive can become reactionary; the need to go "beyond rationalism" and to understand history as the interpretation of the past in the light of the present and future; how to see "economics as a branch of wisdom," that is, to recognize the critical importance of human-scale economies to human development. These programs were especially enriched by the contributions of Xavier Nicholas (Nick), Ilaseo Lewis, and Nkenge Zola. Nick's *Questions of the American Revolution: Conversations with James Boggs* was published by the Institute of the Black World in 1976. He now teaches at Tuskegee Institute. Ilaseo is a Detroit police officer. Zola, who joined right out of college and was a member for ten years, is today an award-winning public radio broadcaster. Recently, when I asked her what our organizing activities had meant to her, she wrote back:

> Ten years later I am in possession still of these talismans: The struggle against our own weaknesses is the most difficult of all. Seeking rather than the real or the ideal, "the truth uniting both." Change myself to change the world. Economic or technological development to the subordination of social, political, spiritual, human development? Nix. United States? Love them enough to change them. Better to live for the revolution than die for the revolution. The yearly conventions I most looked forward to. Cloistered for the weekend to discuss our political year, exacting review and examination of our "Line," preparing for discussion and voting motions which we would carry out the coming year and resolutions which embodied the spirit in which we would carry out our work, then deciding who among us should serve as leadership to guide us through. It all engendered a feeling of being able to "make choices," as we were wont to say, in the belly of the chaotic beast.

Through a series of propaganda workshops we developed a historical overview of propaganda and the concept of propaganda as persuasive education. We analyzed the "significance of the spoken and the written word," distinguished the ingredients of revolutionary propaganda from those of counterrevolutionary propaganda, studied great speeches and great preambles, and practiced writing preambles for community organizations of all types. Kenny Snodgrass was the comrade most concerned that we deepen our analysis of propaganda, especially after he read Hitler's *Mein Kampf*. He and I often clashed, and Jimmy occasionally challenged his sexism. But Kenny was always one of "Jimmy's boys," the comrade who in his eagerness to assume the awesome responsibilities of revolutionary leadership most resembled the youth who had been drawn to the Black Panther Party. Kenny's eulogy of Jimmy in the *Michigan Chronicle* after his death described their relationship as a father-son, mentor-mentee one.

Writing, publishing, and selling these statements and pamphlets and creating these workshops took a lot of time and discipline. But comrades were proud of the work that we were doing and the way that we were breaking with the traditional practices of black organizations. Meetings started on the dot instead of when people got there ("colored people's time"). We were self-reliant; we didn't have to beg for money or depend on government and foundation handouts. Membership dues set by each local and literature sales financed our publications. Leadership was demystified. The structure was consciously organized to involve every comrade in the creation of our programs, literature, and ideas, to develop everyone to assume the awesome responsibilities of revolutionary leadership. Everyone received a copy of every document. In our small organization we were determined to put into practice Lenin's vision of "Every cook can govern," to demonstrate that Black Power means black empowerment. The contrast, not only with black organizations but with traditional radical organizations where the ideas and the line came down from the top, could not have been sharper.[16] Comrades acquired an ability to think philosophically and dialectically, to discuss and debate complex questions, and to explain them to their friends and colleagues in a way that made sense. To this day, they are often the ones to whom people come for clarity on current issues.

In 1974 Monthly Review Press published the lectures "On Revolution" that we had given in 1970 at the University of Michigan Extension as *Revolution and Evolution in the 20th Century*.[17] The final chapter, "No Promised Land," asserts that an American revolution must begin by our recognizing how down through the years we have retarded our evolution into more human human beings by separating ethics from politics and by interpreting "freedom as an evasion of political responsibility to ourselves and the rest of the world" and "democracy as a ritual for evading responsibility or delegating it to others," instead of seeing democracy as "a process whereby the great majority of the people engage in the political struggles necessary to arrive at important political decisions." Before we can confront the external enemy, the book concludes,

> a significant section of the masses must have abandoned their concept of themselves as victims and acquired confidence in their own capacity to govern. They must have come to the realization that there is no utopia, no final solution, no Promised Land, and that humankind will always be engaged in struggle, because struggle is in fact the highest expression of human creativity. They must have reached the conclusion that the only belief worth struggling for is the belief, not in gods or messiahs, but in humankind, because human beings have only themselves to rely on in their unending struggle to become more profoundly human.

Ron Karenga sent us a copy of the review of *Revolution and Evolution* that he had written for publication in the *Black Scholar,* along with a letter saying that he had studied it "like a textbook." His review was a masterly summation of its significance.[18] The book, Karenga said, would gain Brother and Sister Boggs

> no new friends among the primitive nationalist, abstract pan-Africanists, African atavists and all the other seekers of simple solutions who reduce revolution to demonology, traditional dress, social withdrawal and running of bars of abstractions about being black.... They refuse to pamper us or hide the fact that we fear each other, rob, rape and kill each other also, and have adopted to a self-destructive degree the vulgar, vicious individualism of this society which advocates and urges "get yours regardless of the cost to others." Leaving us no illusions, they tell us we have a pivotal role in the struggle for serious social change in this country not because of our color, inherent goodness or imagined incorruptibility, but because of our historical and present role in the construction of this country and its economy. And they challenge us to dare greatness, dare to defy and defeat the oppressor, dare to abandon all illusions about separate or simple solutions and prepare for a difficult and protracted struggle in alliance with all oppressed and progressive people.

We had first met Karenga at a conference in Chicago in 1967. After he was incarcerated in 1973, he sent Jimmy a paper he had drafted, and Jimmy wrote back commending him for

> using his time to reflect on the past, the present and begin to project rather than just bemoan your present plight. In this I

> feel very proud of you. . . . Now that you have negated a contradiction in yourself which came out of the past movement and struggles, don't stop. Keep on asking yourself the difficult questions, not the popular ones. . . . From now on we must be constantly reflecting, correcting and project how are we going to take men and women up the high road which they are very reluctant to take. It will demand the best from us. Nothing less will do.

This exchange is typical of the kind of correspondence that Jimmy carried on with very diverse movement activists like Karenga or Max Stanford or William Strickland, former head of the Northern Student Movement, advising, encouraging, and challenging each one to keep developing and to think more grandly.

Over the years we were in regular contact with Rosemary and Vincent Harding whom we first met in the mid-1960s at a demonstration against the Vietnam War, when their children, Rachel and Jonathan, were toddlers. In the 1960s the Hardings went South to work with Martin Luther King Jr. In the 1970s Vincent was the director of the Institute of the Black World in Atlanta. In 1981 he went to Denver to become professor of religion and social transformation at the Iliff School of Theology. A nationally known historian, Vincent is the author of many books, including *There Is a River,* and a regular consultant to documentary filmmakers on the black struggle for freedom in America.[19]

In July 1979 the Hardings brought movement activists together at Pendle Hill outside of Philadelphia to discuss the question "Martin Luther King Jr.: Where do we go from here?" I vividly recall that gathering because it was my first meeting with Bob Moses, whom I had long admired for his organization of Mississippi Freedom Summer. In 1964, recognizing the role that students play in taking a movement to a higher level and also recognizing that the nation would remain indifferent to the struggle as long as only blacks were risking and losing their lives, SNCC activist Moses issued a call for northern white students to come to Mississippi to help in the Voter Registration campaign. Scores of young people volunteered. While they were in training for the perilous mission, James Chaney, Michael Schwerner, and Andrew Goodman were brutally murdered in Philadelphia, Mississippi. Recognizing the doubts and fears that were tearing at the young people, Moses called them together and told them that anyone who decided not to go on would not be considered a coward. To those who chose to continue, all he could promise was that he would be at their side. No one withdrew. Mississippi Freedom Summer was the culmination of the civil rights struggle in the South, forcing the U.S. Congress to write into law the rights that grassroots activists had already won on the ground.

My first encounter with Moses was not auspicious. For most of the 1970s he and his family had been out of the country in Tanzania, where Julius Nyerere was president, and seemed to me to be out of touch. For example, on the night that Jimmy Carter was scheduled to make his now-famous speech on the spiritual crisis of this country, I asked that we delay the scheduled meeting so that I could listen to the president's speech. Moses's comment was of the kind with which black nationalists in those days withered anyone in the movement who dared to suggest that what happened in this country was more important to blacks than what was happening in Africa. "Nyerere," he said, "was *my* president." Since then, Bob and his family have resettled in the United States, and he has developed a new, evidently very effective method to teach algebra to inner city kids so that they will be able to compete for the jobs created by today's computer technology.

Also at the Pendle Hill gathering was Bill Sutherland, who served for many years as the representative in Africa of the American Friends Service Committee. Sutherland had accompanied C. L. R. James on his visits to Nyerere to persuade him to hold the Sixth Pan-African Congress in Tanzania in 1976. One afternoon he gave Jimmy and me an engrossing account of how disoriented the delegates from the United States had been. While they still saw themselves relating to African leaders as brothers and comrades because of their biological identity, these leaders had become heads of state and some of them, like Idi Amin, had become little better than thugs.

A few weeks before joining the Hardings at Pendle Hill, Jimmy, Jim Hocker, and I had a series of conversations on religion that for once did not end in heated argument. Hocker's views on religion and the church were very similar to Jimmy's. Recently, however, in the GM plant where he had worked for more than thirty years, he was discovering that he could relate to a black worker who was not a churchgoer but was constantly reading the Bible. Since the 1967 Rebellion, Hocker said, he had found it difficult to talk with most blacks in the plant because they saw themselves as "holier than thou," refusing to distinguish between right and wrong and blaming whites for everything. By contrast, this Bible-reading worker "really feels like he is struggling with himself and other people."

Hocker's stories gave me an opportunity to distinguish between the church and religion, and to analyze religion as something that human beings down through the ages have created to help us understand our place in the universe and provide us with the moral energy to carry on internal struggles between right and wrong. In our insistence on the urgent need for individuals to stretch their humanity by struggling against opportunism and greed, I said, we need the passions of religion, and not just the ideas of politics, because we are really talking about our souls. To my delight, Jimmy did not argue with his usual ferocity against my defense of religion. At the October 23, 1993, memorial celebration, Vincent described Jimmy as a sacred humanist: "What I valued so deeply in him is that he saw the sacred in us. He saw that we are indeed filled with divinity. Even though he would not be caught using the word, he knew our capacity to create, to love, to think unthinkable thoughts, to see the unseen. He knew that we are sacred and that we have a great capacity to struggle, to change, to transform ourselves, to change our world."[20]

The publication of *Revolution and Evolution* brought us to the attention of young whites who in the course of the civil rights and anti-Vietnam War movements had turned their backs on the values of capitalist America and were looking for an alternative. In the early 1970s, many of these young people, conscious that their activism lacked a theoretical foundation, were coming together in revolutionary study groups all over the country to study Marxist-Leninist theory and the revolutions in the Third World, hoping that out of this study they would be able to create or discover a philosophy and ideology to guide their practice. Some of these activists were attracted to our ideas, especially the distinction between revolution and rebellion, the relationship between dialectical thinking and revolution, and the concept that the main contradiction in the United States is that between economic and technological overdevelopment and human and social underdevelopment.

These young people wanted to become a part of our organization because we were the only group who had taken Marx's fundamental ideas seriously enough to see the need to go beyond them. But we were still trying to develop black revolutionary leadership, and we did not believe that people living outside the black community could feel the same urgency or relate to the street force. So we encouraged them to organize separately, and in Detroit, for example, Rick Feldman, John Gruchala, and others organized a group calling itself Alternatives.

However, after blacks joined the coalition that elected Jimmy Carter president in November 1976, we decided that blacks, like labor and women, had become incorporated into the system as a self-interest group, so that blacks had lost their moral authority. Therefore, the black movement and the period in which a black revolution might have been made under black revolutionary leadership had come to an end.[21] The black street force was growing in numbers and desperation every day. But it was going to take a new movement based on much more than the history and grievances of blacks to reverse the trend. Our challenge was now to begin creating the humanity-stretching vision and strategy for this revolution. On the basis of this new reality, we embarked on the struggle to build the National Organization for an American Revolution (NOAR), eventually forming new local groups with both white and black members in a number of cities across the country: in Syracuse, Boston, Lexington, Kentucky, Milwaukee, and on the West Coast in Seattle, the Bay Area, and Portland.

The decision to recruit whites was preceded by a lively discussion within the organization. The question at issue was not whether blacks and whites could get along. It was whether it still made sense to talk about a black revolution. It was not an abstract political question. Political consciousness for most of the comrades had begun with the black movement. Their lives and their hopes were so tied up in it that it was hard to admit that new contradictions had emerged, necessitating the creation of a new vision and a new movement. You could see the pain on their faces as Jimmy kept insisting that the black movement was dead. Just as the labor movement had been superseded by the black movement, the black movement would now have to be superseded by another movement. If we tried to evade the reality that was all around us and that we knew to be there, the reality would remain and keep developing, but we would become irrelevant. Fortunately, we had all been struggling with the challenge to think dialectically. Otherwise, the debate over whether to recruit white comrades might easily have led to a split.

Every August we continued to vacation in Maine, carrying on the conversations that we had started in 1968 but focusing less on getting rid of old ideas and more on projections for the future—for example, what is community and how do we build it? In 1974 the news of the death of James P. Cannon, the leader of the U.S. Trotskyists, prompted a comparison of his leadership with that of Max Shachtman and CLR, and a somewhat nostalgic review of our association with CLR.[22]

At the same time Lyman's health was declining. In 1968 he used to walk around the island and down to the boathouse. By 1975 he was on oxygen and would stay in bed until late afternoon. His illness created a lot of stress in the Paine household. All the work of maintaining both Holgate Square and the Schoolhouse fell on Freddy's shoulders. In the few hours that Lyman was sitting up, all he wanted to do was explore the future. He used to say that the only thing that kept him alive all year was the anticipation of our August conversations. Freddy, on the other hand, wanted him to build up his strength. At dinner she would insist that he eat and not talk, which would lead to bitter arguments during which we, or anyone else who was present, would sit by not knowing what to do or whether to intervene. When we left for Detroit in 1977, it was clear that Lyman was dying. His last words to me were, "Carry on." After his return to Los Angeles in the fall, he spent most of his time in a Los Angeles hospital with tubes attached all over his body.

Meanwhile, Rick Feldman and a number of the young people with whom he had been active in the anti-Vietnam War movement and who had been reading *Revolution and Evolution* had made arrangements with South End Press to publish the *Conversations in Maine* with an introduction by Rick. In the spring of 1978, while Lyman was lying barely conscious in a Los Angeles hospital, we were able to put in his hands a copy of the published conversations.

The morning of July 1, 1978 Freddy called us in Detroit to say that she had just brought Lyman back home from the hospital and that if we wanted to see him alive we should come at once. By the time we arrived in Los Angeles that evening, his body had been sent to the crematorium. Freddy told us that shortly after she phoned and while she was putting "Going Home" by Yusef Lateef on the turntable, Lyman had called out "Mouse" (one of his nicknames for Freddy) and died. On July 4, about fifty comrades, friends, and neighbors gathered at Holgate Square to celebrate Lyman's life. Freddy spoke about the good times they had enjoyed but also referred to the times when she and Lyman rubbed each other the wrong way. Lyman's son Michael Paine sang "Sailor Home from the Sea." We laughed as Ceil Lang, who had been a Johnsonite, talked about Lyman's sometimes interminable toasts and told her favorite story about how the same person is seen differently depending on whether he is "your friend or my husband." Ernesto Barrio, an elder from across the square, talked about what a good neighbor Lyman had been. Lewis Suzuki, our artist comrade from San Francisco, created a scroll of the toast that I wrote and that Freddy subsequently sent out in a card with Lyman's picture and the excerpt about Lyman from Rick Feldman's introduction to the *Conversations in Maine*:

A TOAST TO LYMAN PAINE
born November 18, 1901
died July 1, 1978

> It is altogether fitting that on this
> Fourth of July, 1978, we should be gathered here to
> drink this toast to you.
>
> Ten score and two years ago your ancestors
> were among those who brought forth upon this
> continent a new nation, conceived in liberty
> and dedicated to the proposition that all men
> are created equal.
>
> Over the last forty years you have struggled to
> make this vision a reality. You have also struggled
> to enlarge it by challenging each of us to
> realize that freedom involves the exercise of our
> distinctively human capacity to make
> responsible choices.
>
> Thank you, Lyman, for always giving a damn.

In Detroit we convened a small memorial. Nick opened it with these words:

> I just want to say
> a brave American died the other day.
> However great is our loss, even greater is our gain
> for having known Lyman Paine.
> We are the seeds which he planted.
> The voice of his vision
> speaks through us.
> He dared to give a damn
> and for this
> we have come to celebrate
> the end of his life as a beginning.

While we were building the organization and carrying on our conversations in Maine, Jimmy and I were also speaking to university students. My speeches usually dealt with education, being American, the challenge of self-government, and the women's movement, which was beginning to become more important to me and to the organization. In 1980 Shea Howell, Freddy Paine, Vivian Hall, a former Johnsonite and a Vassar alumna, and I participated in the Organization of Women Historians Symposium at Vassar College. The affair brought home to me the tremendous impact that the women's movement was having on intellectual life in this country. There were more than a hundred workshops, each with two to four presenters, on an incredible diversity of topics. Together with some of Vivian's friends, we formed a little group to attend and report back on different workshops. I especially recall a workshop on Asian American history in which a Filipina gave a paper on why Italian and Polish women in Chicago often married the Filipino men they met at dance halls, followed by a blue-eyed blond Minnesota woman reading a paper on the correlation between wealth and the family prospects of Chinese immigrants to this country. At one point I initiated a heated discussion in our little group by proposing that since one of the most important contributions of the women's movement has been its critique of scientific rationalism, we should propose a ten-year moratorium on scientific research so that the world can grapple with the fundamental question of whether we should do things just because we have the know-how and power to do them. One of my favorite essays is Starhawk's "The Burning Times: Notes on a Critical Period in History," which explains the sixteenth- and seventeenth-century witchhunts as the method used by the British power structure, which included philosophers like Francis Bacon, to expropriate the land of the villagers and replace the immanent knowledge of women with the scientific rationalism of the intellectual elite.[23]

Meanwhile, watching high school dropouts hanging around on corners as our communities deteriorated, I began to talk less about education to govern and more about creating a system of education to address the needs of these young people and of our communities at the same time. Instead of seeing our schools as institutions to advance individual careers, I argued, we must start turning them into places to develop our children into responsible citizens—by involving them in community-building activities, such as planting community gardens, preparing school and community meals, building playgrounds, cleaning up our rivers and neighborhoods. In this process our children will be learning through practice—which has always been the best way to learn. While they are working and absorbing naturally and normally the values of social responsibility and cooperation, they will also be stimulated to learn the skills and acquire the information that are necessary to solve real problems.

In the early 1970s Jimmy's speeches emphasized the need for blacks to go beyond rebellion and beyond nationalism, and to "think dialectically, not biologically." At Jimmy's memorial celebration Ossie Davis recalled one such speech:

> I remember he was at Columbia University and Ruby and I were in the audience. He was talking about our love of Africa. The movement for freedom on the African continent had had

> a tremendously inspiring effect on the struggle over here. And some of us were so moved that we changed our hair styles, we had our dashikis. Some of us thought that everything in Africa had been golden and marvelous and beautiful until the time they had taken us from Africa and brought us over here. James was talking about Africa and the culture and the country, and he mentioned the leadership and the rulership and some of the great kings of Africa. And he wound up saying, "A king is a son-of-a-bitch even if he is an African king." And all of a sudden my mind opened up, lightning struck. I saw the dashiki and the hairdo in an entirely different light. It wasn't that it made me ashamed. But James was saying that when you look back and look forward and you see the truth, you declare that particular truth.

On the recommendation of Ping Ferry, Jimmy sent an edited version of one of his "Beyond Rebellion" speeches to the *New York Times*, and it was printed on the op-ed page.[24]

Jimmy's speech at the Black Consciousness Conference at the University of Detroit in 1972 was especially important because it anticipated the focus on rebuilding the cities that would become our main concern in the 1980s and 1990s. In this speech Jimmy warns that blacks are taking over urban institutions, including schools and city government, at the time when they are all falling apart: "Our cities will continue to decline, our young people will become increasingly hopeless and desperate, and our lives will continue to be precarious until we struggle to transform our concept of Work and thereby our cities." He continued:

> We must face the challenge of building the city as a new form where people can relate to each other on the basis of what they give each other in the form of service and where they can make decisions together to benefit the community. Instead of the city being the place from which profits are taken to expand technology outside the city, it must become the place where decentralized communities decide what should be done with any surpluses, always bearing in mind that the main goal of all our decisions is to enable more of our people, and particularly more of our young people, to contribute their energies, their imaginations, their creativity, to the building of the community.

The speech also included a devastating attack on American schools, which, Jimmy said, have become an industry providing more than fifty million people with jobs:

> How long can we keep pretending that schools are preparing masses of black youth for jobs when we know that these jobs are constantly being eliminated by technology? How long can we hide from ourselves the fact that schools today chiefly serve the purpose of providing jobs and careers to teachers, administrators, project directors and custodians? Only when we face up to this reality can we begin the long hard struggle to redefine the fundamental purpose of education—to make clear that in the future *learning* cannot be just for jobs or careers or for earning power, and schools must serve a better purpose than providing jobs for teachers. Rather all future learning must be for the purpose of serving the community, governing the cities, and governing the country.[25]

Every November, beginning in the early 1970s and for more than twenty years, Jimmy and I spoke to James Chaffers's class on urban design and social change in the University of Michigan Department of Architecture. Chaffers had first come to see us after reading the *Manifesto for a Black Revolutionary Party* in 1968. With his students we mainly discussed community building and citizenship. Jimmy would make the initial presentation and I would field the questions. A pamphlet by Jimmy titled *Towards a New Concept of Citizenship*, based on his speech to Jim Chaffers's class a few days after the 1976 presidential election, concludes with these words:

> This nation was founded by a great revolution which inaugurated an age of revolutions all over the world because it gave men and women a new concept of themselves as self-governing human beings, i.e., as citizens rather than subjects. In other words, instead of being masses, who think of themselves as victims and only make demands on others, they were ready to make demands on themselves. This country is still in its infancy. The ancestors of the overwhelming majority of today's Americans were not among the few millions who founded this nation 200 years ago and established the political and social patterns which have brought us to our present crisis. The ancestors of today's blacks were here—but they were excluded from participation in the political and social process, even though their labor was building the infrastructure which made possible this country's rapid development. Thus the people now living in the United States have had no real experience of the great revolutionary struggles by which any great nation is created. That political and humanizing experience still lies before us all!

While we were building the organization, writing pamphlets, and making speeches, rapid changes were taking place in American society and the world. By the 1970s new developments in transportation and communications and the fragmentation of the production process into a host of component operations were making it easy for corporations to abandon plants and cities and move to other parts of the country or the world where they could make greater profits with cheaper labor and fewer social or environmental regulations. Corporations were abandoning cities and/or blackmailing city governments by demanding tax abatements and other concessions, making it increasingly difficult for municipalities to supply normal city services.

Coleman Young, the charismatic organizer and politician who had been elected the first black mayor of Detroit in 1973, was totally unprepared for this development. When Young became mayor, the main contradiction facing Detroiters was racism, especially the racism symbolized by STRESS (Stop the Robberies, Enjoy Safe Streets), the decoy system set up to reduce street crime that in two and a half years had resulted in twenty-two deaths, all of them of black people. During his first term Young's disbanding of STRESS, his appointment of a black police commissioner, and his affirmative action programs that transformed the racial composition of the police force and other departments had generated a new spirit of hope in the city.

At the same time Young began wooing and being wooed by the big-business interests in Detroit because, as he said in an interview with Studs Terkel,

> I realize that the profit interest is what makes things work in America. If Detroit is not to dry up, we must create a situation which allows businessmen to make a profit. That's their self-interest. The more they invest in Detroit, the more their interest becomes ours. That's the way the game is played in America today. I don't think there's going to be a revolution tomorrow. As a young man I thought it. I think the revolution's for someone else.[26]

What Young did not realize was how much the game had changed. By 1974, the year he was inaugurated, U.S. corporations were going multinational and deindustrializing Detroit. In the 1970s and early 1980s Parke-Davis closed its pharmaceutical plant that had employed two thousand people; Uniroyal closed down its tire plant, idling five thousand workers; auto-related shops closed or moved, laying off one hundred thousand more workers. Hudson's Department Store, the mecca of downtown shopping for Detroiters, was getting ready to turn off the lights.

The first big crisis resulting from Young's misplaced confidence in the corporations erupted in 1980 when he joined with General Motors to announce that the city was demolishing an entire neighborhood, bulldozing 1,500 houses, 144 businesses, sixteen churches, two schools, and a hospital in Poletown so that GM could build a Cadillac plant, with Detroit assuming the costs of land clearance and preparation. The endangered community, an integrated neighborhood of Poles and blacks, carried on a heroic struggle to save their homes and their community, but the UAW supported Young and GM because they promised that the new plant would employ six thousand workers. Ralph Nader sent in a team of five members to work with the Poletown protesters for six months. But in vain. All the homes, businesses, churches, schools, and the hospital were leveled. After the demolition I could not bear to drive around the site that was not far from our house. It was like a moonscape, so desolate that I could not tell east from west or north from south.[27]

When the new Poletown plant finally opened in 1984, it was so automated that it only employed 2,500 workers, and it has never employed more than 4,000—this despite the fact that the two older Cadillac plants that the Poletown plant replaced had employed 15,000 people as recently as 1979. Meanwhile, the situation in Detroit was so desperate in the wake of plant layoffs that in 1981 Young had to declare a state of emergency and create a hotline so that citizens could call in for food, shelter, help in paying utility bills, and so forth.

Jimmy and I only attended a few protest meetings during the Poletown struggles, and NOAR did not participate in organizing the resistance. However, we were very clear about the significance of the struggle. In August 1980 we issued a leaflet titled *What's Good for GM Is Not Good for America,* pointing out that "GM comes like a knight in shining armor to revitalize our communities when, in fact, it is destroying the few communities that still remain. GM, like other large corporations, tells us that progress is its most important product. But does uprooting our families and tearing down our homes, churches and hospitals represent progress?" It went on to ask, "How long will we allow multinational corporations to have this power over us?" and to urge that we "begin to think and discuss our future as citizens of communities and of our country who are no longer content to be slaves and subjects."

We did not get involved in organizing the Poletown resistance for a number of reasons. One reason was that we were busy trying to organize locals in many parts of the country in order to form a national organization. But there was also some reluctance among black comrades in Detroit to challenge Young, not only because his ruthlessness against any opposition was legendary but because it seemed like a betrayal of black unity. Noting this reluctance, Jimmy decided that what the organization needed was a new American manifesto making unmistakably clear the need to go beyond the black revolution projected in the 1969 *Manifesto* and laying the theoretical basis for creating a new movement.[28]

This Manifesto, which we called the *Manifesto for an American Revolutionary Party*, was written mostly by me, in close collaboration with Jimmy and Jim Ellis of Syracuse NOAR, and published in both English and Spanish in 1982. It was the beginning of the Reagan-Bush era during which multinational corporations were given free rein and the United States was transformed into a nation of winners and losers, the fabulously rich and the desperately poor.

The American Manifesto begins by naming capitalism as the enemy:

> In its limitless quest for profits capitalism has defiled all our human relationships by turning them into money relationships: Health, Education, Sports, Art and Culture, even Sex and Religion, have all become Big Business. It has transformed Work from a precious human activity into Jobs which are done only for a paycheck and which have become increasingly meaningless and increasingly scarce as the profits from our labor are invested in increasingly complex machines. By unceasing innovations which render obsolete the lessons of the past, capitalism has undermined the Family ties by which human beings down through the ages have absorbed naturally and normally the elementary standards of conduct and the sense of continuity with the human race which make us human. By encouraging us to value material things more than social ties, it has turned us into a society of selfish individualists and materialists, seeking to compensate for the spiritual emptiness of our lives by the endless pursuit of distractions. By exploiting the natural resources of our planet with the same single-mindedness as it has exploited our human resources, it has despoiled the Land, Waters and Air on which our lives and those of future generations depend.

It goes on to point out that capitalism has entered a new stage, the stage of multinational capitalism, which is even more destructive than finance and monopoly capitalism because it threatens our communities and our cities:

> Up to now most Americans have been able to evade facing the destructiveness of capitalist expansion because it was primarily other peoples, other cultures which were being destroyed.... But now the chickens have come home to roost. While we were collaborating with capitalism by accepting its dehumanizing values, capitalism itself was moving to a new stage, the stage of multinational capitalism.... Multinational corporations have no loyalty to the United States or to any American community. They have no commitment to the reforms that Americans have won through hard struggle.... Whole cities have been turned into wastelands by corporate takeovers and runaway corporations.
>
> That is why as a people and as a nation, we must now make a second American revolution to rid ourselves of the capitalist values and institutions which have brought us to this state of powerlessness—or suffer the same mutilation, the same destruction of our families and our communities, the same loss of national independence as over the years we have visited upon other peoples and cultures.

As a revolutionary alternative to multinational capitalism, the American Manifesto projects a vision of a New Self-Governing America based on local Self-Government, strong families and communities, and decentralized economies. To move toward this goal the revolutionary party should encourage people to begin

> organizing committees to create communities out of our neighborhoods which today are little more than geographical areas where we live behind barred doors and windows, more afraid of one another than we used to be of wild beasts.... Committees for Crime Prevention that will establish and enforce elementary standards of conduct, such as mutual compacts not to buy "hot goods," Committees to Take Over Abandoned Houses for the use of community residents who will maintain them in accordance with standards set by the community; Committees of Family Circles to strengthen and support parents in the raising of children; Committees to Take Over Neighborhood Schools that are failing to educate our children or to take over closed-down schools so as to provide continuing education for our children; Committees to Resist Utility Cutoffs by companies which, under the guise of public service, are in reality private corporations seeking higher profits to pay higher dividends to their stockholders; Committees to Take over Closed Plants for the production of necessary goods and services and for the training and employment of young people in the community; Anti-

> Violence Committees to counter-act the growing resort to violence in our daily relationships; Committees to Ban All Nuclear Weapons that will rally Americans against the nuclear arms race as the anti-war movement rallied Americans against the Vietnam war in the early 1970s. . . .
>
> These grassroots organizations can become a force to confront the capitalist enemy only if those involved in their creation are also encouraged and assisted by the American revolutionary party to struggle against the capitalist values which have made us enemies to one another. For example, in order to isolate the criminals in our communities, we must also confront the individualism and self-centredness which permits us to look the other way when a neighbor's house is being robbed.

The American Manifesto concludes with a call to build the movement and the revolutionary party simultaneously.

The publication of the American Manifesto energized the organization. Jimmy went on a speaking tour, including a visit to Tennessee with Rick Feldman and one to Louisiana with Rick and Kesho Scott. Talking about "our country" and "our communities," working together to develop ideas and programs for building communities, listening to the stories of everyone's lives and hopes, comrades discovered a new patriotism, a deeper rootedness and sense of place both in their communities and in the nation. This enlarged sense of ourselves was unmistakable at the cultural event of the second NOAR convention in 1982, which was emceed by Zola and Margie Carter of the Seattle Local. It comes across especially in the poem "We Are the Children of Martin and Malcolm," written by John Gruchala, Ilaseo Lewis, and myself for the June 1982 Great Peace March in New York, and read by John and Ilaseo at the convention. John, a poet and an urban agriculturist, is a Detroiter of Polish descent who was a member of Alternatives prior to joining NOAR. Ilaseo Lewis is an African American who became a police officer because he believed that blacks needed not only to demand power but to accept the responsibilities of power.

> We are the children of Martin and Malcolm
> Black, brown, red and white
> And so we cannot be silent
> As our youth stand on street corners
> and the promises of the 20th century pass them by.
>
> We are the children of Martin and Malcolm
> Our ancestors,

Proud and Brave
  Defied the storms and power
  of masters and madmen.

We are the children of Martin and Malcolm.
  So when money-eyed men remove the earth
  beneath our feet and bulldoze communities,
  While Pentagon generals assemble weapons
  to blister our souls and incinerate our planet,
We cannot be silent.

We are the children of Martin and Malcolm.
  Our birthright is to be creators of history,
  Our glory is to struggle,
You shall know our names as you know theirs,
  Sojourner and Douglass, John Brown and Garrison.

We are the children of Martin and Malcolm,
  Black, brown, red and white.
Our Right, our Duty
  To shake the world with a new dream.

Inspired by the American Manifesto members of the Detroit local began organizing in the community. Some members organized the Michigan Committee to Organize the Unemployed (MCOU) and began a struggle to obtain continuing health insurance for laid-off workers. Others organized Committees to Resist Utility Cutoffs. After MCOU failed to rally laid-off workers, comrades began helping residents in the Marlborough neighborhood, where MCOU had been holding street corner meetings, to close down crackhouses. Later, we joined the "cheese lines," which during the Reagan years provided millions of Americans with basic commodities. On the cheese line we discovered that the elderly and disabled were being trampled on by the young and able bodied. So we organized them into a group calling itself Detroiters for Dignity and waged a successful campaign for an extra distribution day for them.

During the 1984 Jesse Jackson campaign for president, NOAR members in locals across the country distributed leaflets challenging both white and black Americans to seize the opportunity to create a new movement. We urged white Americans to "take a chance and go to a Jesse Jackson meeting. Ask yourself whether the issues he is raising are important to your life and the life of our country. . . . Contrast the human questions Jesse is raising with the emptiness and absence of challenge to corporate America of the other candidates." We challenged black Americans to go forth from Jesse Jackson rallies to struggle over the issues that he was raising. "We can't leave it all to Jesse," we said. "In this way we can create a new movement that goes beyond Jesse and the Democratic Party because the issues he is raising cannot be resolved by him or by the Democratic Party." After Reagan and Bush won the November election we called on all citizens to "Love America enough to change it. Our Communities and our Country are now up to us!"

In 1983 John Gruchala, Nkenge Zola, and I, as members of the Detroit NOAR Program Committee, began publishing *The Awakening* to report on our organizing activities against crime and among the unemployed, victims of utility shutoffs, and the elderly. "Every great movement needs a newsletter to spread the word of its activities and to inspire others to join," we said. *The Awakening* kept coming back to the crime and violence that were spreading among inner city youth, wondering how and what could be done to start a movement among these young people. All around us, young people were losing their lives and limbs to street violence in such numbers that many of them, including two of Jimmy's grandchildren, were joining the military as the best way to stay alive. "We can't let crime be normal," we kept saying. In one issue Trinidad Sanchez's poem "Let Us Stop This Madness" was our lead:

> Let us take a stand
> let us stop the bullets
> from the guns
> Let us stop teaching the
> children that the bullets
> from the guns
> are the only way
> to deal with life.
> Let us destroy the factories
> that make the guns
> that destroy the children.

Then, suddenly, despite or perhaps because of all this external activity, NOAR began falling apart. Differences that had been viewed as enriching became sources of tensions. Meetings became so fractious that even I, with my notorious love of meetings, found excuses to stay away. Members began resigning, citing personal concerns (family, jobs, whatever) that demanded their time and energy. But political questions, even if unspoken, were also at issue. For one thing, members had committed themselves to building an organization with people who shared their views. Going out into the community to try to build a movement from scratch required a different kind of commitment. Another troubling undercurrent was the decision the organization had made to go beyond the black revolution. Intellectually, no one could refute the analysis that the black movement was dead, but it was clear that for some black comrades going beyond the black movement was in a sense betraying the black movement. So, looking for someone to blame for this betrayal, one comrade wrote a letter saying that even though "Jimmy used to be black, he had become gray, no doubt because he had been painted with a yellow brush." It was the first time that my position as a Chinese American in the leadership of the organization had ever been challenged publicly. When Jimmy read the letter, Shea recalls, "he was so mad that he shook." Yet nobody, including myself, suggested that the issue be addressed directly, probably because any fruitful discussion at that point was not really possible. In any case, on several occasions I was the target of remarks by black comrades so ugly that I could scarcely believe my ears. Yet other comrades remained silent. Looking around me for someone to protect my back, I saw no one—which made me wonder for the first time in my movement experience whether comrades would have intervened if the organization had included more Asian American members.

At the same time, the work we were doing outside the organization was invigorating. The Michigan Committee to Organize the Unemployed had crossed over into community organizing, and we were making new grassroots friends, like Steve Hamilton from the Marlborough Block Club and Geneva Smith of Detroiters for Dignity. But inside the organization it was as if we had become enemies to one another. The worst part of it was that we had no vocabulary to discuss what was happening to us. We didn't want to talk about personalities because we took pride in our commitment to ideas, not to persons. But the ideas that we had developed were of no help to us in understanding what was taking place in our relationships. We could freely discuss the work we were doing outside the organization, but we couldn't talk to one another about the organization to which we had devoted and were still devoting so much of our time and resources. During the hundreds of hours that Jimmy, Shea, and I spent together, we never discussed NOAR's collapse. To this day, I don't know what they were thinking or how they explained what was taking place. Maybe, like me, they blocked it out of their minds because it was too painful. When friends like Ping Ferry asked me what was happening to NOAR, I didn't know what to say.

The National Organization for an American Revolution never formally dissolved. Between 1985 and 1987 it just faded away as members resigned or became so much involved in community activities that they had no time for organization meetings. Our total membership was never more than seventy-five to a hundred. But between 1970, when we first began organizing for the black revolution, and 1983–84, when NOAR ran out of steam, these few comrades did a prodigious amount of work. Our comradeship, based on our willingness to commit our lives to the revolutionary transformation of American society, was both precious and energizing. Overall, anyone who was a NOAR comrade or was exposed to its ideas felt that his/her humanity had been enlarged by the challenge to go beyond rebellion to revolution, beyond Us versus Them thinking, and beyond our personal grievances and identity struggles to thinking about and taking responsibility for the whole society. The audacity of Jimmy's challenge to blacks to assume leadership for an American revolution lifted black comrades beyond victim thinking and empowered them to use their anger in a positive way, uncovering talents and energies that would otherwise have been wasted. Our emphasis on the contradiction between economic and technological overdevelopment and political and human underdevelopment enabled us to tackle questions of crime and welfare with proposals and positive programs for building community, as well as to explore a wide range of social, political, cultural, and artistic questions. As a result, we attracted people from the grassroots level as well as people with artistic sensibilities that enriched both us and them.

Almost everyone who was ever a member of NOAR remains active in some way—mostly working with young people or in the environmental movement or as artists. Many still share the literature that we published. Some use a modified form of our Convention procedure to help community groups collectively decide their programs. In Lexington, Kentucky, Jim Embry has taken the lead in organizing a group of Million Men March veterans that calls itself CRUCIAL (Committee for the Redevelopment and Unification of Community Involvement and Leadership). In Oakland, California, Dennis Terry has started to create videos in the belief that film can become a means for transforming behavior and restoring fraternity and community in our violence-torn inner cities. Articles by Kenny Snodgrass frequently appear in the *Michigan Chronicle* and the *Michigan Citizen*, Detroit's two black weeklies. Rick Whaley, an environmental activist in Milwaukee, Wisconsin, is coauthor with Walt Bresette of *Walleye Warriors: An Effective Alliance against Racism and for the Earth*.[29]

As NOAR was obviously coming to an end, I proposed a process of more formal dissolution so that we could evaluate the shortcomings of the organization as well as its positive contributions. But I received no support for my proposal, especially not from Jimmy, who tended to see evaluations as postmortems in which individuals blame each other for failure. At the time he was probably right. There was so much pain in the disintegration that any discussion would undoubtedly have led to bitter recriminations as in any divorce.

Nevertheless, as the years have passed, I often ask myself, and I imagine other comrades who went through the NOAR experience do the same, "What lessons can we learn about the development of grassroots revolutionary leadership and the limitations of the Vanguard Party from NOAR?" If, as I believe, the structure of NOAR was too internal, too rigid, too hierarchical, and too much modeled on Leninism (which grew out of very different conditions in czarist Russia), what other more flexible forms can we create in the United States to develop grassroots revolutionary leaders—using the experiences of the women's movement and other movements, but always bearing in mind the experiences of the Black Panther Party and the reality that the rebellious street forces of the 1960s are now much larger and more desperate? Should we have been struggling to develop an organization to give revolutionary leadership to a particular social stratum like the black street force? Or should revolutionary leadership be based on a more holistic approach to the diverse needs of our society? Should a revolutionary organization seek to recruit mainly from the most oppressed strata of society? Or should it consciously aim at social and ethnic diversity, especially in a country like the United States, at the same time creating special forms, like the Third Layer School developed by the Johnson-Forest Tendency, to nurture grassroots leadership? Should the tens of thousands of desperate young people like those who flocked to the Black Panther Party in the late 1960s and early 1970s and who are all around us today be called on to assume the awesome responsibilities of revolutionary leadership? Or do they urgently need organizations and programs that develop and empower them by engaging them in collective, community-building activities?

These are only a few of the questions that analysis of the NOAR experience might help to illuminate. Nancy Vogl, a NOAR comrade from the Bay Area, has suggested that concepts of science developed in the twentieth century offer a clue to new forms of less hierarchical, less static organizations. In *Leadership and the New Science*, for example, Margaret Wheatley writes,

> Our concept of organizations is moving away from the mechanical creations that flourished in the age of bureaucracy. We have begun to speak in earnest of more fluid, organic structures, even of boundaryless organizations. We are beginning to recognize organizations as systems, construing them as "learning organizations" and crediting them with some type of self-renewing capacity. These are our first tentative forays into a new appreciation for organizations. My own experience suggests that we can forego the despair created by such common organizational events as change, chaos, information overload and cyclical behaviors if we recognize that organizations are conscious entities, possessing many of the properties of living systems.[30]

In retrospect, I can think of many reasons for NOAR's collapse. One obvious factor was that whereas Jimmy and I had already settled into our life's work of movement building, most comrades were at the age when they were facing life decisions about family, children, jobs. The recruitment of white comrades into a black organization may also have played some part because the literary and organizational skills of white comrades at that time were higher than those of most black comrades. I was especially aware of the tensions created by the sexism of the main founders of the organization, who, except for myself, were black men. Under the leadership of Patricia Coleman-Burns, who had joined NOAR after being active with the National Black Feminist Organization, the Detroit local especially tried to challenge this sexism. But it was too deeply rooted in the black community and in the patterns of the black church and of the Black Power/Black Nationalist movements of the 1960s, which had reproduced these patterns virtually intact. The Black Power movement, especially as it was covered by TV, had been a very heady experience for black men. I suspect that our emphasis on creating leadership also encouraged ambitions that were beyond the capacities of individuals or the opportunities provided by the objective situation. The peer rivalry between men in NOAR created a climate of competition that, I am glad to say, is not as prevalent in today's community organizations, which are more likely to be led by women. Had it not been for the presence of Jimmy, an older black man whose political personality had already been shaped when the black revolution erupted, NOAR probably would not have lasted as long as it did.

But the main reason for NOAR's disintegration, I believe, is that the organization we had created had outlived its usefulness. Even though we went through various stages with different names, we had essentially come out of the rebellions of the late 1960s. Our goal was to do what the

Black Panther Party was not doing—to develop revolutionary ideas and a revolutionary leadership for the exploding black movement. When that movement came to an end, we kept trying to adapt ourselves to the changing situation. It is no accident that our internal development programs and our publications were our major achievement. They directly addressed the changing reality, dealt not just with symptoms but with fundamental causes, were visionary in their projections, and, in the words of Nkenge Zola, opened wide the consciousness of every member and supporter, "permitting symphonic ideas, plastic arts, music, principle, responsibility, choice, creative lunging to spill and bump against any, all and none." By contrast, our organizational forms were created to correct the shortcomings of a movement that had already peaked, was on the decline, and came to an end in the mid-1970s as the black middle class moved out of the inner city, leaving behind only the very poor and the elderly. A new leadership would have to come out of a new movement whose hopes and dreams were still undefined.

7
"Going Back" to China

One morning in the fall of 1983 I woke up thinking that I would soon be seventy and I still had not "gone back" to China. For most of my life "going back" had been precluded — either by the civil war or by the sanctions imposed by the United States against the Chinese because they decided to go their own way. However, for more than a decade, ever since President Nixon's stunning visit in 1972, trips to the People's Republic of China had become possible and popular. People were returning with glowing reports and asking me when I was going. My younger brothers Harry and Eddie had gone back. But I kept putting it off, mostly because I was so involved in building the organization but also because I was concerned about the effect it might have on my political life after all these years. Would it open up a Pandora's box? Oblige me to become more involved in U.S.-China Friendship Association activities? Reawaken my hopes that I could learn how to read, write, and speak Chinese? Meanwhile, I was not getting younger. If I was ever going back, I had to do it soon. I didn't want to go on the usual three-week tour because I wanted to stay in one place long enough to feel comfortable moving around on my own. Around this time I heard about a Canadian program providing six weeks of study at the Beijing Language Institute followed by a two-week tour of the country. I signed up and left San Francisco on September 20, 1984.

Ever since my college days I had been studying Chinese off and on, sometimes taking a class, for example, in the 1930s at Columbia University and in the 1970s at the University of Detroit and at the University of Windsor. But mostly I studied on my own because until relatively recently few universities gave language courses in Chinese. I kept at it because I was embarrassed and ashamed that I was more at home in German, French, and Spanish than in the language of my forebears. Also, since studying Chinese as a child, I have been fascinated by the written language. Western languages are phonetic so you can make a stab at pronouncing a word even if you don't know the meaning. For example, man is *homme* in French, *Mensch* in German. By contrast, written Chinese is made up of ideograms or picture-ideas. For each word there is a separate symbol. The simplest characters suggest that they were originally created by people drawing objects. For example, the character for moon resembles a crescent and the one for man appears to be someone on two legs. More complex characters combine a radical that suggests the meaning of the word and a phonetic that indicates the pronunciation. Thus, characters having to do with language contain the radical for speech, those having to do with marriage contain the radical for women, and so on. The average reader recognizes approximately twelve hundred characters, every one learned individually. As a child I learned a few dozen characters, some very simple and others relatively complex, and I have never forgotten them.

Studying Chinese has been the hardest thing I have ever attempted and perhaps the greatest disappointment of my life. I didn't have an ear for the language because we did not grow up in Chinatown or a Chinese community. At home we spoke English among ourselves and to my mother and father, and except for elementary commands, they soon began to respond in kind. Complicating the situation was the fact that as immigrants from Toishan in southern China, my parents and the workers in my father's restaurants spoke a Cantonese dialect very different from Mandarin, the national and official language taught in university classes. So I was constantly vacillating between studying Cantonese, which was much easier for me, and Mandarin, which would be more useful in wider circles. I would pursue one for a while, give up, and then after some months or even years, start up on the other. Or I would throw up my hands altogether. As a result, I have accumulated dozens of tapes, dictionaries, and textbooks in both dialects—and a record of failure.

Growing up I had been ambivalent about being Chinese, occasionally taking pride in my ancestry but more often ignoring it because I disliked the way that Caucasians reacted to my Chineseness. It bothered me that my almond-shaped eyes and straight black hair struck people as "cute" when I was a toddler and that as I grew older I was always being asked, even by strangers, "What is your nationality?"—as if only Caucasians or immigrants from Europe could be Americans. So I would put them in their place by telling them that I was born in the United States and therefore my nationality is U.S. Then I would add, "If you want to know my ethnicity, my parents immigrated from southern China." Whereupon they would exclaim, "But you speak English so well!" knowing full well that I had lived in the United States and had gone to American schools all my life.

I hated being viewed as "exotic." When I was a kid, it meant being identified with Fu Manchu, the sinister movie character created by Sax Rohmer who in the popular imagination represented the "yellow peril" threatening Western culture. When I was in college, I wanted to scream when people came up to me and said I reminded them of Madame Chiang Kai-shek, a Wellesley College graduate from a wealthy Chinese family, who was constantly touring the country seeking support for her dictator husband in the Kuomintang's struggles against the Japanese and the Chinese Communists. Even though I was too ignorant and politically unaware to take sides in the civil war in China, I knew enough to recognize that I was being stereotyped. When I was asked to wear Chinese dress and speak about China at a meeting or a social function, I would decline because of my ignorance of things Chinese and also because the only Chinese outfit I owned was the one my mother wore on her arrival in this country.

Shortly after I joined the Workers Party in the early 1940s, I was encouraged by Marty Abern to write a piece on China for the *New International*, the party's theoretical journal. For the first time in my life I did some research on China, producing a series of four articles titled: "China: The Colossus of the East. The National Revolution and the Imperialists"; "The China of Chiang Kai-Shek: The Kuomintang and the Classes"; "China under the Stalinists: National Revolution and Peasant Revolt"; and "China under Japanese Domination: Japan and the Capitalists in Eastern China." The series was informational, especially for me, but it lacked passion because it was based on books and newspaper and magazine articles and I didn't have the background to evaluate what I read. The third article in the series, on "China under the Stalinists," is particularly revealing. The news about the Communists organizing the peasants in the interior of China had excited me but I muted my excitement because I was aware of the Worker's Party's anti-Stalinism and devaluation of the peasantry as a revolutionary social force. In fact, the article ends with a 1928 quote from Trotsky giving the party position that "with a new rising wave of the proletarian movement . . . one will be able to speak seriously about the perspective of an agrarian revolution." In the text I refer to "Mao The Tung" (*sic*) as the "Communist leader," not the "Stalinist leader." The title was probably given by the editor. After the series was published,[1] I gave a presentation at a branch meeting of about ten people. But no one showed any interest, and I myself was soon swept up in the work of the Johnsonites.

I did not fall in love with the Chinese Revolution until the 1960s when information about what was happening in China together with Mao's writings became available in this country. I liked Mao's philosophic approach to revolutionary politics. I identified with the way that he was always talking about learning from practice, struggling against contradictions, and correcting mistaken ideas and/or ideas that have become subjective because the objective situation has changed. One of my favorite documents by Mao is his "Correcting Mistaken Ideas in the Party" written in 1929 as a critique of militarism and adventurism in the Chinese party. It not only impressed me as applicable to the Black Panthers, but it struck me as very Chinese and in some ways reminded me of my father.[2] I think that is because, like my father, Mao was carrying on the centuries-old Chinese cultural tradition that, since the time of Confucius, has stressed moral rather than legal force as the foundation of political authority and legitimacy, and that conceives goodness in terms of a relation between people rather than as a moral quality that an individual can have on his/her own. For example, *politics* is conveyed in the Chinese language by two characters, pronounced *zheng zhi*. *Zheng* means "to straighten or correct" while *zhi* means "to heal or cure." The character for humanity or benevolence is made up of two radicals, the radical for *ren*, meaning "man" or "human being" and the radical for *er*, meaning two or more than one. I could also hear my father's voice in Mao's 1936 document titled "The Important Thing Is to Be Good at Learning." To be wise and courageous, according to Mao, "one must acquire a method of learning. . . . The method is to familiarize ourselves with all aspects of the enemy situation and our own, to discover the laws governing the actions of both sides and to make use of these laws in our own operations"; "the crux is to bring the subjective and the objective in proper correspondence with each other."[3] In other words, political development takes place through correcting mistaken ideas and straightening out your relations with others.

At the same time I could appreciate the profound difference between my father's use of the Chinese cultural tradition and Mao's. My father's approach had been Confucian. Goodness inside our family required our acceptance of the patriarchal tradition in which the wife is subordinate to the husband and the children to the father. By contrast, Mao's approach was driven by a revolutionary vision of those at the bottom of society assuming the rights and responsibilities for social decision making, which had theretofore been the exclusive responsibility of the rich and powerful. So he was always challenging the members of the party and the Chinese peasants and workers to transform themselves by struggling both against the internal limitations stemming from their position in the social structure and against those holding power in the structure that limits them. Mao did not visualize Communism as a utopian society, an objective thing that can be achieved only after a society has reached material abundance through economic development. Communism, for him, was a process combining self-transformation and structural transformation—"mankind consciously remolding itself and the world," creating a new stage in the evolution of the human race.

In the 1950s and even into the 1960s, it was incredibly difficult to find out what was taking place in China. The U.S. power structure, furious that "we lost China" to the Communists, outlawed travel to the country and resorted to outrageous measures to uphold the ban. For example, when a group of reporters from *Look Magazine*, including our friend William Worthy of the *Baltimore Afro-American*, traveled to China in 1957, the government lifted their passports.

Under these circumstances, along with the many other Americans eager to know what was happening in China, I became dependent on individuals like Felix Greene and Maud Russell for information. Greene, a British-born journalist and businessman who began visiting China in 1957, wrote books[4] and produced exciting TV documentaries that were shown on public television. He also went on lecture tours around the United States, describing the historic developments in the New China. Because he was so debonair and spoke with such a well-bred British accent, blue-haired ladies at Town Hall meetings found Communist China less frightening. For people born in China or of Chinese descent what he told us was like manna from heaven. I will never forget my father, then in his nineties, beaming as he listened to Greene speak at a meeting in our house in 1964 or 1965. He could die happy, he said, because Mao was bringing to villages like his the kind of progress he had always dreamed of.

In Detroit we used to look forward to Maud Russell's annual visits. A native of northern California, born the same year as Mao, Maud had gone to China as a YWCA worker after World War I around the time of the Chinese students' demonstrations against imperialism. During the 1920s she conducted literacy and health programs for Chinese women, encouraging them to participate in political struggle. In the 1930s she was with Mao in Yenan. In 1944 she returned to the United States but her heart remained in China. So in 1960 she defied the government ban and returned for a visit. After that, she began publishing the *Far East Reporter* to inform Americans of developments in China, and every spring she would set out alone from New York in a car loaded with books and slides to talk about China to small groups in Cleveland, Detroit, Chicago, and wherever people were ready to set up meetings for her. Even when she was in her eighties and both her hearing and her driving had become undependable, Maud persisted. One year, driving west on the New Jersey Turnpike, she was involved in an accident. But after pulling over to the side and determining that the damage was minor, she kept going because a group in Cleveland was expecting her to speak that night. Maud died at the age of ninety-six in 1989. Two years before her death I received a card from her in Nicaragua. She had gone there to show her support for the revolution.

In 1970 when Asian Americans were inspired by the black and anti-Vietnam War movements to organize themselves, I was one of the founders of the Asian Political Alliance (APA) in Detroit. There were only six of us, three Japanese and three Chinese, including my brother Harry and myself. To the average Caucasian we may have all looked alike, but we were very aware of the differences in our backgrounds. American-born and Asian-born, we stayed together for less than two years, but it was one of the most enjoyable periods of my political life. Our program was very modest. We discovered things about each other and about ourselves by studying Chinese history and Japanese history. Each month we showed films like *The East Is Red,* which attracted a varied group of Asians, especially Chinese from China who had been fearful of showing too much interest in the Chinese revolution but who in the darkness of a movie hall would break into smiles as they witnessed the tremendous changes taking place in their homeland. We held workshops to help young American-born Asians discover and create their identities. We also participated in anti-Vietnam War demonstrations locally and nationally, shouting "Yellow Is Mellow" and blasting the racism and imperialism of U.S. aggression in Asia. We called those Asian Americans who did not get involved in the anti-Vietnam War movement "bananas"—yellow on the outside but white on the inside.

Working with Asians was unlike anything that I had known in the white or black community. This was the first and only period in my life that I was meeting regularly with political people who shared my background as an Asian American. The experience made me much more aware of how Asians have been marginalized not only in American society in general but in movement circles because, until very recently, we have been so few and far between. The most striking difference was the respect that young people showed for me as an elder. Thus, when I attended the Asian American Reality Conference at Pace University in New York in 1970 as a representative of APA, I was asked to make the closing speech, something that had never happened to me in all the years that I was involved in the black movement. In my speech, which was off the cuff, I found myself speaking like an elder to the mostly college-age audience, drawing lessons from my experience in the movement. Rereading the speech, I am amazed at how didactic I was.[5]

Until we formed APA, I had had only two Chinese friends—Louise Chin, my classmate at Barnard, and Tom Quock. After graduation Louise married an overseas sociology student, C. K. Yang (later the author of *Chinese Communist Society: The Family and the Village*) and traveled with him to China, Japan, and the many cities all over the United States where he was invited to teach.[6] Until 1995, when we attended a Barnard College alumnae reunion together, our only contact over the years had been our exchange of Christmas cards. Tom Quock was born in China, where his brother was a cadre in the Chinese Communist Party, and came here as a teenager in the late 1930s. During World War II he was a member of the all-Chinese Service Unit in which my brother Harry served. He eventually moved to Detroit where he married an African American and worked in the Ford plant for more than thirty years.

Out of the APA experience I developed my only two close friendships with Chinese born in China, Itty Chan and Chung-lu Tsen (known as Louis) whose parents had been active in the Left Kuomintang. Louis was the son of Tsen Tsong Ming who was assassinated by Chiang Kai-shek's gunmen in Hanoi in 1939. His mother was the painter Fan Tchun Pi who studied painting in both France and China. Her works, which wed Western naturalism with a Chinese sensibility, hang in both French and Chinese museums. Itty and Louis grew up in China together as children. After the 1949 Revolution Louis's mother left China and settled in Paris with her three sons while Itty's parents took their children to Thailand. As a result, Itty has the erect carriage and delicate beauty of a Thai woman, while Louis sometimes reminds me of an ebullient Parisian.

Itty teaches in an elementary school in Boston's Chinatown, has a graduate degree in education from Columbia University, and has written and spoken widely on the differences between the American and the Chinese approach to education. Education in China, she says, is based on the Chinese belief in human educability: "By nature men are pretty much alike; it is learning and practice that set them apart," according to Confucius. So the Chinese emphasize the ways in which children are alike rather than unalike—in their inquisitiveness and in their potential to become caring and socially responsible individuals. In the United States little children are often heard to say "I can run faster" or "This is mine." In China the focus is on the social self, the child's sense of who he or she is in relation to other people and their interrelationship in society.

Louis is a philosopher, a cultural historian, and a filmmaker who is fluent in Chinese, French, and English and recently retired from the UN in Geneva after twenty years as a Chinese interpreter, during which he spent substantial periods on "home leave" in China. In 1968 Louis came to see Jimmy and me after coming across a copy of the *Manifesto for a Black Revolutionary Party*. At the time he was teaching philosophy and cultural studies at Monteith College, a special branch of Wayne State University in Detroit. His unique background has given him a fascinating insight into different cultures. A descendant of a distinguished Chinese family, he has a Chinese intellectual's appreciation of Chinese history and culture. Having been raised in France by his artist mother, he enjoys the Western intellectual's familiarity with European culture. Living and teaching in Detroit during the 1960s and early 1970s, he had substantial contact with Americans; his wife, Ann Herbert, is an American. While he was teaching Shakespeare at Monteith, he gave a special class that he called "From Tao to Mao" for our mostly African American friends and comrades. In 1976, after our week with Ping Ferry's old friends in Branscombe, England, we arranged to meet Louis, Ann, and Louis's mother in Paris where they took us on a two-hour tour of the Louvre to gain an overview of the historical development of Western art. In 1986, when I was in England for the C. L. R. James Tribute, I flew over to Geneva where Louis and Ann took me on a quick visit to three churches—Russian Orthodox, Roman Catholic, and Calvinist—so that I could experience the steady loss of sensual stimulation in church architecture. His letters from his home leave visits to China and his trips to Africa and the Middle East in the course of his work as a UN interpreter are priceless in tracing the changes that have been taking place in the past twenty to twenty-five years and the differences in the spirituality of different cultures. I knew abstractly that Chinese culture is a dialectical interplay between Taoism ("doing nothing" while "ten thousand things rise and fall without cease") and Confucianism (the politics of correcting/straightening things). But Louis made it come alive for me when he called my attention to the way that in China the sword is always accompanied by the tassel.

Over the years I have come to rely on Louis for a long-range understanding of developments in China. For example, after the confrontation between the democracy movement and the government in Tiananmen Square in June 1989, Louis wrote to say that he had received a stream of sympathy from Americans consoling him for the recent catastrophe, but that he was not as impressed as Americans seem to have been by the Chinese students:

> The more I know about these Coca Cola Red Guards, the more I am appalled by their naïveté. They are a Me generation á la chinoise, with no sense of society, history or politics, moved only by frustrations and vague longings.[7] Totally alienated from China, they say they are "world citizens" and support their claim with idiocies. They argue that China would have been better off if, instead of making revolutions, it had been colonized by foreign powers. Then it would have become like Hong Kong or Taiwan. Disdaining anyone who doesn't live in the cities, they despair of China ever "making it" unless half its population is wiped out "by nuclear war, famine, AIDS, doesn't matter what." If these kids were to come to power, they would probably bring another brand of demagoguery. However, they have paid for their fantasies with their lives. There is no call to be harsh on them. My ire is reserved for the old fogies in the Forbidden City.
>
> These men have been dealing with power for half a century. They are not cultivated people but they have dreamed, fought and lived for nothing but power. One would expect some sophistication from them when it comes to its exercise. Confronted by a month-long sit-in, a rational government would have either consented to a dialogue with the demonstrators or waited it out until they got bored. The clever way would have been to engage the students in a well-publicized marathon dialogue, show them confidence and overwhelm them with the long list of China's problems. But the old men have no such statecraft.... For them it was a choice between standing pat and surrender. They rejected dialogue because it was too humiliating and they rejected waiting it out because they had no patience. So, in the end they followed their most primitive instinct and threw the tanks at the students in full view of a horrified world. In a global village, where everybody can see into everyone else's bedroom, they still imagined they could get away with beating their kids without the neighbors raising hell.... There was no thinking through, no idea how to proceed from this mess. For spite, they have wrecked their own reform policy of the last ten years and turned China into an international pariah. Now they can nei-

> ther go forward into capitalism (no human rights, no investment) nor back into socialism. (Having trashed Mao, they can't credibly re-invoke him). They are stuck in a dilemma of their own making.

Over the years I have shared Louis's letters with my friends who invariably ask if they can share them with others. This letter on Tiananmen Square made its way through Carol and Ping Ferry to Harrison Salisbury, former *New York Times* China correspondent. Salisbury wrote back: "This is simply the most sophisticated and understanding analysis of the many I have seen and it sets the affair in the context of Chinese reality as nothing else."

In 1995 Louis sent me a brief paper he had written on "China in Transition: Nation Facing a Moral Vacuum." He has always understood, as few Westerners can, the ideological and moral void in China following the Opium Wars and the Taiping Rebellion. The ensuing chaos destroyed the value system of Confucianism, which rested on three basic obediences—the inferior should obey the superior, the young should obey the old, and the woman should obey the man—and which also sanctioned the rule of the emperor through something known as the Mandate of Heaven. Mao was able to lead the liberation struggle because he filled this vacuum with the Mandate of the People and the concept of serving the people. It was on the basis of this new mandate that the Chinese Communist Party built the liberation movement and claimed its right to govern.

Now, however, by telling the people that "to get rich is glorious," the party has in turn negated the Maoist doctrine of serving the people and thus undermined its own legitimacy.

> So at the moment China is neither Confucian or revolutionary. It faces a very real vacuum. Having no sure grip on its mandate, the Party keeps one jump ahead of crisis by promising the good life to many if not to all. Amazingly, against all predictions it has managed to deliver for the last seventeen years. The question is, can it keep on delivering? The Party itself is far from confident.

Louis left China when he was a teenager. Going back for the first time in 1973, he was shocked by the strident sounds and teeming streets of "wall-to-wall people," so different from his images of serene landscapes derived from books and paintings. Since then he has gone back nearly a dozen times. In the spring of 1997 he shared with me his culture shock on returning to Europe:

I was in Beijing in March on a consultancy job with Nestlē China. After that I met Ann in Hong Kong to bask, so to speak, in the last sunset of the Empire. Coming back to Geneva after spending one month in Asia was a stunning experience. Flowers in bloom everywhere. No pollution, no dust, very little noise. People don't crowd, don't talk much in public, don't throng the stores and bazaars. The parks manicured. The city as tidy as a toy. This is truly urban living at its most civilized. Yet something is wrong.

Asia is all abustle and aboom. Cities are in a continual process of being built and being demolished. Every day new constructions go up—new highways, new bridges, new rail stations and airports. The horizons never remain static. Going beyond bare survival up to the next phase of acquisition and consumption, people work with amazing energy, look around themselves with a lot of greed and not a little pride and eat and buy with abandon. There are more children who play, study and work. A few beg in Beijing.

By contrast, Europe is so perfectly regulated. There is a rule for every activity. Each job pays half again as much in benefits. Social services ensure decent living to the jobless. Infrastructures are not being built so much as being rebuilt, refurbished and carefully maintained. This quality of life is quite costly. Europe's outlays are too high, its returns too slim. The only way out for it is to invest heavily elsewhere—like in Nestlē China—to subsidize its own well-being. In Europe it is the multinationals that call the tune now, for they are the ones who have the efficiency and bring in the profits. They also push hardest for European unification so Europe can hold its own in global competition.

But the key are the Europeans. They live well. They take vacations. They are environmentally conscious. They hang on to their acquired rights. They don't gamble or take risks. They feel threatened by the new yellow peril and desperately hope to hold it at bay. It may be for this reason that so many of them identify with the plight of the Tibetans. But it's a ruthless world out there. With such expensive habits and so little vitality, I don't see how they can expect to beat the Asians.

How do I feel about all this myself? I'm not sure. I have always consciously chosen quality over quantity. But I must admit I feel a deep thrill when I watch the teeming masses of a whole continent on the move.

Fortuitously, Louis was in Beijing when I arrived there in September 1984. So I was able to meet and socialize with some of his friends. I was particularly anxious to discuss the Cultural Revolution that Mao launched in the late 1960s, and I had an opportunity to do so both with a young Chinese couple and with Westerners who have lived in China and been supporters of the Chinese revolution for decades. Louis and I had a delicious meal with the Chinese couple in their one-room quarters. The dinner was cooked by the husband who had taken off work to prepare it. Their attitude to the Cultural Revolution was ambivalent. On the one hand, they felt that their careers had suffered because they would never regain what they had lost during those years. At the same time, they didn't denounce the revolution because, it seemed to me, to deny any value to the Cultural Revolution meant denying one-third (nine years) of their lives. They were anxious to come to the United States to study, and perhaps even to live, and had little idea of the negative aspects of life in the West. When I told them about crime, their immediate response was, "Why doesn't the government do something about it?"

The Westerners whom I visited a number of times were Israel Epstein and David and Isabel Crook who had witnessed the preliberation and postliberation struggles in China and lived through the Cultural Revolution. Israel was editor in chief of the English edition of *China Reconstructs*. Isabel and David are the authors of *Revolution in a Chinese Village: Ten Mile Inn*, a ten-year history of the period immediately before the setting up of the Chinese Peoples Republic, and *The First Years of Yangyi Commune*, dealing with the period from 1958–61.[8] It was a joy to meet them because I had learned a lot from these books, which are in my library. Isabel and David had raised their children to adulthood in China. Like other "foreign experts," they now lived in the Friendship Hotel, which I believe was built by the Russians. Their apartment was comfortable and well equipped, with a modern bathroom and central heating. The rooms where we met were so warm that for the first time in Beijing I began to perspire. From our discussion I gathered that they had all had a very rough time during the Cultural Revolution and were still struggling to gain a historical perspective on it. In general, they thought there were a lot of good things about the revolution, for example, the effort to bridge the gap between the workers and the intellectuals, but that it had been taken to extremes. They were also glad that the party was admitting its mistakes and reevaluating. I thought they were very sincere, very committed people, and I admired their dedication. Previously, I had been somewhat envious of the opportunity they had enjoyed to witness firsthand events of such historical magnitude. But I was glad that I was not in their present situation and that I had the struggle in Detroit to go home to.

Through Israel Epstein I met Frank Su Kaiming, who was born in northern Henan province in 1903 and in 1927 was sent to study in the United States where he received an M.A. from Harvard and also worked on behalf of the revolution. In 1953 he returned to the People's Republic of China with his American wife and daughter in order to help build the new China. His history of modern China, published in 1985, is fascinating because it is written from the viewpoint of a Chinese who has lived in three different worlds: semifeudal and semicolonial China, capitalist America, and new China, where he was experiencing the joys and pains of building a new society.[9]

At the Beijing Language Institute I shared a sparsely but adequately furnished dormitory room with another student, using the washrooms and squat toilets down the hall. We ate three meals a day family style and there was always plenty of food, although most of it was too greasy for my taste. I woke up every day early enough to see the spectacular sunrise—the East is really red! Classes were in the morning. After lunch I would take the bus or walk to various neighborhoods and poke around the stores to see what kinds of things were available for sale. During the last two weeks we traveled by train, mostly by night, sleeping on three-tiered bunk beds. From Beijing we went to southwest China ending up in Chongqing, the Kuomintang capital during World War II, which is hillier than San Francisco. Then we spent three days on the boat traveling southeast down the Yangtze River to Wuhan, ending up in Guangzhou. I was proud of the fact that although I was the oldest person in our group, I was never ill and was able to carry my own luggage everywhere. The only exception was on the morning when we were getting ready to take the boat at Chongqing and I looked down at the one hundred steps leading to the river and panicked.

The most important thing I learned during my two months in China was that I am more American than Chinese. At first it was confusing and overwhelming to be Chinese and yet not be able to talk Chinese. I felt ashamed, almost as if I were being rebuked by my kinfolk (all one billion of them) for not returning to China sooner and for not having learned the language of my ancestors. I also gained a deeper appreciation of what it must have been like for my mother to be in a foreign country unable to speak the language (in her case, unable to read or write any language).

As I walked around by myself, however, it was obvious that based on my body language people perceived me as American but at the same time different enough from other Americans that they felt free to come up and ask me all kinds of personal questions about where I came from, what kind of work I did, whether I was married, how many people there were in my family. Back in the 1930s when I asked personal questions like these of a Chinese student at Bryn Mawr, she reprimanded me for being too personal. I'm not sure whether that was because she came from a higher social class or because the revolution has opened things up. I answered their questions as best as I could in my limited Chinese.

The ingenuity and energy of the Chinese reminded me of my father, for example, the way that they used bicycles, often transformed into tricycles, for transporting all kinds of things: little children (sometimes in a sidecar), bricks and concrete, beds and furniture. I was amazed at the number of entrepreneurs lining the sidewalks with little sewing machines ready to alter or make a garment, barbers with stools and scissors, knife sharpeners, shoe repairmen, vendors selling food and other kinds of merchandise from carts. Everywhere I went I saw women knitting, as they waited for a bus or walked along the street, as if they couldn't waste a minute. I had never seen such an industrious people. It was unlike anything that I had witnessed in England, France, the West Indies, Africa, or the United States.

The only time people appeared to be resting was when they were squatting—to converse, to eat a meal, or to play cards. Squatting was obviously something that you learned very early in life. (Every now and then my knees got a little weak from the unaccustomed use of my squatting muscles, for instance, in the toilet.) Little children squatted to pee almost anywhere or were set down by their parents even on a bus floor for that purpose. Yet, surprisingly, there was no smell of urine on the buses or streets. The offensive smell of shit was in the vicinity of public toilets because fecal matter is used as night soil and therefore not chemically treated. Someone in my group, which was mainly Canadian, suggested that the Canadians should export disposable diapers to China and make a lot of money. My response was that it would make more sense for Americans to import the idea of split pants from China.

I was humbled by how little the Chinese I talked to knew or cared about Detroit. It was clear that for them Detroit was no longer the auto capital of the world. Most taxis I saw were from Japan or were made in China. I also had the impression that the Chinese cared and knew little or nothing about social struggles in the United States. I think this has a lot to do with what has always been a kind of self-centeredness in the Chinese, except in periods like the Tang dynasty (600–900 A.D.). No wonder that the Chinese party never created an international like the Third International founded by the Soviets after the 1917 Revolution. The Chinese see the world in terms of China's interests. This was obvious to me as I read the English-language *China Daily*.

Most people moved about either on foot, by bike, or on buses—which were fantastically crowded, even though they came very frequently, especially on Sundays when hundreds of thousands of people would go to the center city to visit Tiananmen Square, the parks, or to shop. You had to fight to get on. I had a seat only a few times, usually when someone took note of my gray hair or a conductor yelled "lao ren" (old person) to shame someone into giving up his or her seat. Considering how jam-packed the buses were, it was amazing to see so many people pushing their way to the conductors to buy a ticket. You paid according to where you got on and intended to get off, giving this information to the conductors who usually sat at a counter, selling tickets and calling out the stops. This honor system worked, it seemed to me, mainly because the fare was so cheap (a few cents for most rides and rarely more than ten fen, which is less than a nickel). If the price had been higher, or if they charged a dollar flat no matter where you were going, as in Detroit, a lot more people might have tried to get away with paying nothing or lied about how far they intended to ride. It struck me as a unity of idealism and materialism.

The bus conductors were mostly women who seemed to have more moral authority than male conductors, for example, to ask that seats be yielded to women or men carrying children or to the elderly. However, when the buses were jammed as they are most of the time, there was little or no leeway for such courtesies.

I found it hard to believe the abundance of goods for sale in the stores and the amount of shopping that people did for food and commodities (TVs, books, shoes, stereos, cookies, clothes). I saw thousands of Chinese going into stores and coming out with shopping bags, like last-minute Christmas Eve shoppers.

Construction was going on everywhere. Cement mixers sounding like marching bands blared at you from right and left. I was impressed by the designs built into the most utilitarian structures—flowers, fish, dragons, birds—in concrete walkways or the eighteen-foot metal fences around a building. Apparently, when you are living in a country with so many historical sites and magnificent structures from the past, design and function are conceived of inseparably. I was surprised that bamboo is used for scaffolding since I had always thought of bamboo as fragile.

While we were still in Beijing, we visited the Temple of Heaven, a miracle of construction from the fourteenth century with fantastic pillars made of huge tree trunks transported (like the stones at Stonehenge) from many miles away. The acoustics were incredible. At one place you could stand on the stone in the center of a huge circle and your voice resonated as with a loud speaker because of the way the sound waves are reflected from the circular stone wall.

Among the historical sites we visited outside Beijing, I especially recall Datong, Xian, and Dazu. Datong is a coal-mining town where under the Japanese occupation ten thousand Chinese died in the mines because they were worked so relentlessly. It was a dreary place with no redeeming features. Xian is a textile center that is a little like Beijing. It has been the capital of eleven dynasties, and the city has eleven of Shaanxi province's universities, so there was a cosmopolitan atmosphere and a sense of historical continuity. The inhabitants carry themselves like citizens of a metropolis. In the Tang dynasty Xian was the beginning of the Silk Road to the Middle East associated with Marco Polo. Hence the brightly colored art objects, yellow, orange, and green camels, and other figurines associated with this dynasty. It is also the site of Hot Springs, which Chiang Kai-shek was visiting in 1936 when he was kidnapped (he lost his teeth as well as his "face" trying to escape) and was forced to negotiate with Chou En-lai, representing the Chinese Communist Party, to create the United Front against the Japanese. Xian is also famous as the city where peasants digging a well in 1974 discovered the thousands of life-size terra cotta warriors standing guard at the tomb of the First Emperor who unified China two thousand years ago.

At Dazu we saw nearly fifty thousand sculptures carved by Buddhist monks out of rock on mountainsides wherever there was a protective shelf. We were told that in the ninth century A.D., when China was falling apart because of peasant revolts and wars between the states, Buddhist monks came to Dazu because it was so remote and protected by mountains. From the sculptures we could see how in the course of a thousand years after its introduction into China, Buddhism became "Sinosized." Confucian ideas of right relationships within the family and within the state were incorporated in the figures, making them very different from the more meditative, contemplative, otherworldly Buddhist figures at Datong or in temples.

What I found in every section of Chinese society was an attempt to "walk on two legs." The most visible example of this is the use of both Western and traditional medicine. In hospitals the pharmacy for Western medicines and the one for traditional medicines were on opposite sides of the front lobby. The Chinese also seemed to be very conscious of the contradictions developing from the one-child family—the child is spoiled and the traditional language that provides different words for younger and older aunts and uncles, for example, is being impoverished. At the same time, it seemed to me that the Chinese were getting practice in making the hard choices that everyone on this planet will have to make in the next century. An important part of our underdevelopment as Americans, which is weakening us for the future, is that we think our rights are unlimited, that all possibilities are or should be open to us. This makes it difficult for us to think holistically.

I spent only a few days in Guangzhou (Canton) in southern China where the dialect and food were more familiar and I felt more at home than in Beijing. The Cantonese I observed in restaurants and on the streets seemed more outgoing and spontaneous than the people I had encountered in Beijing and elsewhere in China. Still struggling with the Cantonese-Mandarin dilemma, I thought that if I had spent six weeks in Guangzhou instead of in Beijing I might have ended up speaking the language. I had hoped to visit my father's village two hundred miles from Guangzhou. But I gave up the idea after talking with a Chinese Canadian man in our group. Two years ago he had visited relatives in the same area. It took him two days of travel by bus, down dusty roads and across countless ferries to reach his village, and he ended up with only two hours to spend with his relatives. He knew who they were because he didn't leave China until he was ten and he had been corresponding with them. If I had made it to the village I wouldn't even have known whom to ask for because my parents left China nearly a century ago and my father, who was our only link to his family in China, had been dead for nearly twenty years.

By the end of November I was ready to return to the United States. Even though I had not made much headway in my Chinese class, I had learned a lot from moving about and I was glad that I had "gone back." But if previously I had had any doubt that I was more American than Chinese, two months in China had erased them.

On my way home I stopped in Honolulu to eat Thanksgiving dinner with my brother Bob and his family. When I got back to Detroit, I toyed around for a few weeks with the idea of continuing my study of Chinese and established contact with a Chinese student at Wayne State as a possible tutor. But it made no sense. Although I had spent hours each day for six weeks in Beijing, in and out of class, listening to tapes and practicing my reading and writing, I was still as far from fluency in the language as I had been at home. I did develop a little skill in using Chinese dictionaries and learned more about the structure of the language, but that was about it. Helping me to make my decision was the flippancy with which the Chinese student I had contacted as a possible tutor talked about the Chinese revolution and Mao. Among the younger cadres in China, I had found the same lack of respect, the same indifference to the sacrifices and struggles that had liberated the Chinese people from the Japanese occupation and the Kuomintang dictatorship. The shamelessness with which they spoke about enriching themselves literally made me sick. Their attitude to Mao and the liberation struggles reminded me of the contempt that the overseas Chinese students in the 1930s had for women, cab drivers, and waiters. So after all these years, I finally concluded that with more than a billion Chinese in China speaking Chinese, I didn't have to feel guilty about not speaking it myself. It was a very liberating conclusion.

玉平

8

New Dreams for the Twenty-First Century

Coming back from China at the end of November 1984 I found Jimmy, Rick, Shea, and Marilyn Schmidt, a NOAR supporter, working with the Marlborough Block Club in one of Detroit's most devastated East Side neighborhoods to close down a crackhouse. The National Organization for an American Revolution was beginning to fall apart, but members were in good spirits because they sensed a new wind blowing in the community. Shortly thereafter we began going out to the cheese lines where every Thursday, in neighborhoods across the city, tens of thousands of Detroiters lined up in the snow and the sleet to get the cheese and other free commodities that they needed to survive. Overhearing the grumbling of the elderly at the way they were being trampled and pushed around by younger recipients, we brought a few of them together to organize a demonstration demanding that Neighborhood Services schedule a special day for the old and disabled. It was a very simple demand (which we won), but the enthusiasm of the demonstrators and the self-assurance with which the women especially confronted the Neighborhood Services director were impressive. There was also something catchy about the name, Detroiters for Dignity, which was suggested by Emma Davis, one of the demonstrators. Members began to call themselves Detroiters for Dignity and paste the little orange sticker with the name on their food bags and windows. People who had never spoken in public before got up proudly at meetings and made statements or asked questions in the name of the group. Jimmy began adding Detroiters for Dignity to his signature on his letters to the editor. A new voice, that of women elders, was clearly emerging in the city. To celebrate the appearance of these new players in the unfolding drama of Detroit and to show our support for the Navajos resisting relocation, we organized a trip of Detroiters for Dignity to Big Mountain in the spring of 1985.

By this time I had participated in enough movements to know that no one can tell in advance what form a movement will take. Movements are not initiated by revolutionaries. They begin when large numbers of people, having reached the point where they can't take the way things are anymore, see some hope of improving their daily lives and begin to move on their own. I have also learned that if you want to know what a movement is going to be about, you should keep your ears close to the grassroots to hear the "why" questions that people are asking. For example, during and after World War II when black folks had acquired a new self-confidence from working in the plant and fighting overseas, they began asking, "Why do white folks treat us this way?" with a new urgency, and so the civil rights movement was born. In the 1960s, when white flight to the suburbs made blacks the majority or near-majority in cities like Detroit, people began asking, "Why are all the political leaders in our city still white?" giving rise to the Black Power movement. In the mid-1980s the main questions people in Detroit were asking were about young people and violence.

Violence among young people had been growing in Detroit since the 1967 Rebellion. But it was in the early 1980s that it began to reach epidemic proportions. By then, with the election and reelection of Ronald Reagan, all hope that the rebellions of the 1960s would bring about an improvement in the life of inner city youth had evaporated. Because of high-tech industry and the export of jobs overseas, young people could no longer drop out of school in the ninth grade and get a job in the plant making enough to raise a family. Then in the mid-eighties crack was invented, creating the basis for a crack economy. All over town young people started saying, "Why continue going to school in the hope that eventually you'll get a degree and make a lot of money when you can make a lot of money right now rollin'?" As a result, turf struggles erupted and our neighborhoods became war zones where children walking to and from school risked being shot and killed.

In 1986 forty-three young people were killed and 365 wounded in Detroit. At some funeral homes young folks laid out in caskets outnumbered the elderly. One funeral home installed a special window for drive-by viewing. All during the year, whenever two or three adults came together, the discussion invariably ended up with folks asking, "What is happening to our young people? Why are they killing one another?" On the last day of the year Ray Cooper, who had graduated from Eastern High School just up the street and had been active in the late 1960s, stopped by with his sister and aunt. As the discussion turned naturally and normally to the question of youth violence, I decided to switch on the tape recorder because I was so sure that what was being said in our living room was being duplicated in living rooms all over the city. Later I learned that on the same day, on the other side of town, Clementine Barfield, whose sixteen-year-old son had been killed and fourteen-year-old wounded the past summer, was bringing a few parents of murdered children together to talk about how they could go beyond mourning to create positive programs for young people.

A few days later I saw a small item in the paper announcing a meeting to organize against youth violence at the Church of the New Covenant-Baptist on Puritan Avenue. I immediately decided to attend. At the first meeting there were several hundred people. At the second there were even more. Compared to what had been happening for the past dozen years in Detroit, that in itself was promising. Usually out of the hundreds who might turn out in the heat of the moment to protest a senseless death, only a handful return to the second organizing meeting. There were even more surprises. At the second or third meeting, with several hundred people present, Clementine Barfield, a tall, powerfully built woman, took issue with the preacher, Rev. Randall, who was chairing the meetings. When the question of naming the organization came up, he proposed that the organization call itself The Group With No Name because the phrase had been used in an article about the group by Susan Watson, the popular *Detroit Free Press* columnist. Clementine was adamant that the organization be called Save Our Sons and Daughters or SOSAD and stuck to her guns even after the chair called for a debate on the question, with people lining up to take sides. This was the first time I had ever seen a black women not only question the preacher presiding at a public meeting (I later learned that Randall was her preacher) but refuse to back down even after he had turned it into a power struggle. Clearly, we were on the threshold of something new.

Subsequently, I learned that Clementine Barfield had been born and raised in the South, the thirteenth child of a Mississippi sharecropper and had been a teenager during the civil rights struggle. In 1987 she was in her midthirties, had divorced her preacher husband, and was a Detroit city employee raising four children. Soft-spoken but a woman who obviously knew and spoke her own mind, she had attended Wayne State University and had some organizing experience.

The media, always sensitive to the emergence of a new public personality, began circling around Clementine whose quiet composure, while she was taking very clear stands, was in sharp contrast to the militant rhetoric of the 1960s. The *Detroit Free Press* published a full-length article on her in its Mother's Day Sunday Magazine. The papers, TV, and radio spread the word that SOSAD was asking Detroiters to wear red ribbons during the first week of February and assemble on Sunday, February 8, at St. Paul's Cathedral for a candlelight service. As a result, more than fifteen hundred people showed up for the memorial. It was the largest movement meeting in Detroit since the early 1970s. To commemorate the occasion John Gruchala, Nkenge Zola, and I, now organized as New Life Publishers, published a booklet titled *Loving Them to Life,* containing a photo essay of the memorial service and interviews with local activists working with young people.

After the St. Paul's memorial SOSAD called for a mass march down Woodward Avenue. I volunteered to help with preparations for the march and began talking with Clementine who told me that her goal was to build a movement that would do for our time what the civil rights movement had done for its. Soon thereafter I began working with the economics committee of SOSAD and also editing the monthly SOSAD newsletter, which was widely distributed locally, nationally, and internationally. The newsletter not only reported SOSAD activities and programs but also other community-building activities that SOSAD was associated with or encouraged. Every issue featured a front-page article by Clementine calling for community mobilization against violence and on behalf of young people. In almost every issue I would include sayings like "If you're not part of the solution, you're part of the problem," or Martin Luther King's statement that "our scientific power has outgrown our spiritual power. We have guided missiles and misguided men," or Malcolm's "We can work together with all other leaders and organizations, in harmony and unity, to eliminate evil in our community." The saying "It takes a whole village to raise a child" (which I had seen in a little newsletter identifying it as an African proverb) really caught on. After about a year organizations all over the country began using it, and Hillary Rodham Clinton recently adapted it for the title of her book. Jimmy also began writing a regular column for the newsletter, raising all sorts of questions, such as, "Why are we at war with one another?" "How will we make a living?" "What Time is it in Detroit and the World?"[1] Clementine's deeply felt appeals, Jimmy's challenging questions, and my inclusion of news of community-building activities all helped to create the image of SOSAD as not just another organization but the spearhead of a new movement.

Jimmy and Clementine related to one another like members of an extended family. They had both been raised in the South and shared a skepticism about black preachers. Jimmy treated Clem like a younger sister, encouraging and instructing her. She treated him like the grandfather or older uncle who acts as historian or griot, passing on wisdom and information to younger generations. She also enjoyed mimicking his Alabamese. At the July 31 memorial for Jimmy, she described how Jimmy would call her at all hours of the day or night and say, "Gal, I loves you." Jimmy's relationship with black women, especially those raised in the South, was very moving. Geneva Smith of Detroiters for Dignity called him "the best friend I ever had. He showed me how to talk up for myself." Ellen Richardson felt that "we could always talk to him about anything and everything. He was our lawyer, our counselor, our big brother, anything but a minister. He was a mother figure, a father figure, a brother figure." They knew that my southern cooking left a lot to be desired. So they always put his name in the pot. Whenever SOSAD had a party at the office, Clem and the other mothers made sure that I took home some collard greens and a piece of sweet potato pie for Jimmy.

Behind my back Clementine used to call me Mama because, she said, I was always giving advice. I saw myself as an activist (and still do), but apparently I had become an elder in the eyes of others. Through SOSAD I met Alice Jennings, whose legal and financial help made it possible for SOSAD to get off the ground. Alice and her husband, Carl Edwards, are partners in their own law firm. Together they are the parents of seven children, the youngest in elementary school. Old enough to have caught the tail end of the black movement of the sixties but too young to have been shaped by it, they are among the very few black professionals who, having benefited from the civil rights and Black Power struggles, feel a responsibility to help build the new movement that will empower young people. For example, Alice headed a SOSAD committee that prepared *A Conflict Resolution Curriculum for Elementary Age Children*. Emphasizing the relationship between peace education and caring for the community, the curriculum is used in a number of public schools. In 1993 her in-depth analysis of the Malice Green murder by Detroit police officers, written from a community perspective, was published as a special supplement to the SOSAD newsletter. The article ends with concrete proposals for reforming the Detroit Police Department and for building a community movement for justice and hope. She is an inspiring example of a young black woman who is nurturing and giving leadership to younger black women.

The formation of SOSAD was the turning point in Detroit. The determination of Clementine and other mothers of murdered children to involve young people in positive change aroused in everyone the hope that is necessary to the building of a movement. The humanity of everyone was stretched as we witnessed mothers whose children had been killed reaching out to the mothers whose children had done the killing because they recognized that both had lost their children. Outstanding among the mothers has been Vera Rucker, whose daughter Melody was killed on the front porch of her home at her sweet sixteen party. Also from the South, Vera has supported Clementine with the quiet strength and day-by-day assistance that every person in the public eye needs to keep going.

Over the years SOSAD has sponsored a number of programs, including the Harvest Program that engaged young people in planting community gardens; Bereavement Support Groups for Survivors, with separate sessions for families, children, women, and men; Crisis Response teams to go into a community that has been traumatized by violence; and Violence Prevention and Gun Control Programs. For more than six years it has been part of the Cease Fire Coalition, led by Father Tom Lumpkin, that conducts a weekly vigil at noon in front of the Spirit of Detroit statue at the City-County Building, rain or shine, bitter cold or sweltering heat. As the end of every year approaches, the coalition mounts a campaign to urge Detroiters to break with the tradition of shooting guns into the air at midnight to usher in the New Year. Save Our Sons and Daughters is also building a peace movement among young people in the schools, which includes students adopting and reciting a Peace Pledge. In schools where the peace movement is being built there is noticeably less disorder. Students stand taller, speak more respectfully to one another and to the teachers, and take more responsibility for their school.

As a result of Clementine's high visibility, the organization's activities, and the newsletter, SOSAD has received literally hundreds of appreciative plaques, more than it can possibly hang on its walls. Ron Allen, founder of Horizons in Poetry, has organized two twenty-four-hour marathon "Words Against Weapons" readings by local poets in support of the organization. Mothers from SOSAD have appeared on national TV programs, including the *Oprah Winfrey Show.* TV, magazine, newspaper, and radio reporters from all over the United States and Europe come to the SOSAD office to interview Clementine and the other mothers and to spread the word about the movement. Every year hundreds of students from dozens of college spend their "Alternative Spring Break" with SOSAD working with schoolchildren to build the peace movement. Clementine receives more invitations to speak and to attend conferences locally, national, and even internationally than she can possibly accept. As a result, SOSAD is probably better known than any other antiviolence organization in the United States.

The following excerpts from two poems that have appeared in the SOSAD newsletter give a sense of the passions that drive the organization. Scholar and poet aneb kgositsile, also known as Gloria House, was an SNCC volunteer in the 1960s and now teaches at Wayne State University. Errol Henderson, raised in a Detroit housing project, was a leader of student struggles for black studies at Wayne State University. He received his Ph.D. from the University of Michigan, has taught classes on gangs, and now teaches at the University of Florida in Orlando. Both poems have been reprinted countless times. "Calling All Brothers" anticipates the October 16, 1995, Million Man March.

Calling All Brothers

Calling all brothers!
Calling all brothers!
Calling you out
from the hushed kingdoms
of corporate comfort:
calling you out of
your cognac bottles.
Calling all my brothers
to break out of
your laid-off/unemployed blues,
break out of your videohypnosis:
Calling all brothers, precious
as you are to your women,
Cherished as you are by your sisters
calling you out of your daze
or disgust with the family who sustains you—
your mothers, your sisters, your own brothers....

This is our Vietnam, our South Africa,
our Grenada, our Nicaragua,
in the streets of Motown, Philly,
New York, L.A.—
on our block, in our 'hood.

Calling you to dare
the monster death dealers who hustle the children
to face you down.

Calling all brothers,
crying for all brothers,
moanin' for a brother,
Ain't no brothers nowhere?
Calling the makers of babies
to become their saviours.

—aneb kgositsile

SOSAD—The War Zone

It's SOSAD when they die so young
in a city where no one cares
there are too many funerals and too many guns
too many swords and not enough ploughshares.
I've never held ill feelings to anyone
until I found my child was dead
until I found my child was dead
until I found my child was dead. . . .

there was a time when it was different than now
BK's and Flynns ran the streets
you didn't hear no hip-hop
like stuff they play now
Parliament Funkadelic was the dominant sound
and the east side was booming back then
this was before YBI, before Uzis and Mac-10s
and spraying was what you did from a can
writing names like Co-cheez, P-Funk, and Dirty Flynns
and a gang was a gang not a crew
stealing Borsalinos, leathers, not killing for Troop suits
and rolling cane didn't mean a thing
it was heroin, j's, maybe some mescaline
it was tight but it was nothing like this
cats got beat down in the street,
but I mean, they would live
to tell it after the deal was done
but too many niggers got triggers
too many triggers got guns
too many triggers held fingers and hands
too many superniggers didn't try to understand

too many kids was rolling 51's
So the fingers pulled triggers and mothers just lost sons
and daughters cried in funeral pyres
Poets read poems then they ran for their lives
and they blamed the whole game on rap music and slang
sat on their asses, didn't do a damn thing
but talk about the days when they marched with King
told little kids from the back of limousines
"now, we're doing what we can, but you don't stop trying"
the kid walked home and brutally died brutally died
brutally died brutally died
Derik Barfield brutally died brutally died
Melody Rucker brutally died. . . .
200 kids brutally died brutally died
it's SOSAD when they die so young
in a city where no one cares
there are too many funerals and too many guns
too many swords and not enough plowshares. . . .

—Errol Anthony Henderson

Sometimes a growing movement needs the whip of a countermovement to take it to a new plateau. In Detroit this countermovement took the form of a proposal by Mayor Coleman Young to bring casino gambling to Detroit. The idea of casino gambling had already gone down to defeat twice in Detroit, in 1976 and 1981. But the continuing deindustrialization of the city and the connection that more and more Detroiters were making between violence and the lack of jobs for young people prompted Young to renew the proposal in 1988. Casino gambling, he promised, would produce fifty thousand jobs.

For most of his adult life Coleman Young has been a progressive and militant. Quick-witted, fearless, and feisty, he had distinguished himself as an organizer for the National Negro Labor Council and the National Negro Congress and had become a hero in the black community after he accused the House Un-American Activities Committee itself of being Un-American. Coleman was so bright and so sharp that had he not been black, the idea of him sitting in the Oval Office in the White House would not have seemed far-fetched. But his past had not prepared him for the kind of crisis that today's cities are in. Having received most of his political education in left-wing circles, he took pride in reducing everything to economics and in minimizing human and social relations. He seemed to think that this added to the image, which he has consciously cultivated, of a hard-nosed, streetwise radical who is always realistic, can't be pushed around, and doesn't care what white middle-class people think of him. "Education, drugs, homelessness, unwed mothers, crime, you name it . . . every social issue is about jobs," he has written in his autobiography. "Jobs built Detroit, and only jobs will rebuild it."[2] No longer able to count on the industrial corporations for jobs, Young had no hesitation about turning to casino operators. Any jobs would do, even if these jobs were created by a crime-producing industry like casino gambling.

To defeat the newest proposal for casino gambling, Jimmy, Shea, and I joined a coalition of community groups, blue collar, white collar, and cultural workers, clergy, political leaders, and professionals calling itself United Detroiters Against Gambling (UDAG), led by the Rev. William K. Quick, a United Methodist minister, and Rev. E. D. Cobbin, a black Baptist minister. The coalition turned the city into a continuing town meeting with demonstrations, rallies, meetings, and debates on TV and radio. The SOSAD newsletter featured a front-page article by Clementine headed "No to Casinos! Yes to the Future!" "The problem in Detroit is not the lack of jobs," wrote Clementine. "It is the lack of hope. We have lost the will to struggle and fight together for one another. We have lost the bond between downtown and the community. The issue of Gaming is creating further division among the people. But the search for alternatives could unite us."[3]

Despite Young's popularity and his hold over the Baptist preachers, who either supported him or remained neutral, we were able to defeat the proposal for casino gambling for the third time. The main reasons for our victory, I believe, were that we emphasized the need of young people not only for jobs but for hope and the fact that Detroit remains a working-class city where the majority (at least of the voters) have a gut-level belief in honest toil. After our victory, we decided to stay together as Detroiters Uniting (DU). "Our concern," Jimmy wrote in the DU brochure,

> is with how our city has been disintegrating socially, economically, politically, morally and ethically. We are convinced that we cannot depend upon one industry or any large corporation to provide us with jobs. It is now up to us — the citizens of Detroit — to put our hearts, our imaginations, our minds, and our hands together to create a vision and project concrete programs for developing the kinds of local enterprises that will provide meaningful jobs and income for all citizens.

To engage Detroiters in the creation of this vision, DU embarked on a campaign for open government in the city, issuing a series of leaflets calling on citizens to examine the whole chain of developer-driven megaprojects with which Young had tried and failed to revive the city (including Poletown and the People Mover) and to assume responsibility for envisioning and implementing alternative roads of development based on restoring neighborhoods and communities.

During the debate over casino gambling Young had challenged his opponents to come up with an alternative, accusing us of being naysayers without any solutions of our own. Jimmy welcomed the challenge. There was nothing he liked better than using crisis and breakdown as an opportunity for renewal and transformation. His forte was devising solutions that were visionary and at the same time so down-to-earth that people could almost taste them. For more than fifteen years he had been writing and talking about the crisis developing in our cities and the need to redefine work, especially for the sake of our young people. In October 1986, at a meeting in Oakland, California, which the Bay Area NOAR sponsored to present "a vision of 21st century neighborhoods and communities," Jimmy had declared that it was now "idealistic" to expect the government or corporations to do the work that is needed to keep up our communities and to provide for our elementary safety and security. Multinational corporations and rapid technological development have turned our cities into graveyards. "Efficiency in production," he argued, "can no longer be our guiding principle because it comes at the price of eliminating human creativity and skills and making millions of people expendable." He continued: "The residue of the last 100 years of rapid technological development is alienation, hopelessness, self-hate and hate for one another, and the violence which has created a reign of terror in our inner cities." Realism now demands that we

> begin to practice doing for ourselves — or collective self-reliance. And as we do this, starting out with relatively simple things — like creating support networks to look out for each other and moving on to community gardens and greenhouses, community recycling projects, community repair shops, community day care networks, community mediation centers — we will discover that we are not only controlling and improving our space but that we are also transforming ourselves and our young people from faceless masses who are afraid of one another into socially responsible, mutually respecting and politically conscious individuals who are systematically building the power to change our whole society.[4]

I also spoke at the Oakland meeting, saying that

> In the 19th century those few Americans who rejected the mainstream culture had to leave the city to create communities like Brook Farm. In the late 1960s and early 1970s those young people who saw the need to create a counter-culture created communes and collectives made up mainly of their peers and those who agreed with them philosophically. But today creating communities wherever we are, of all those who live in the same neighborhood, of varying ages and ethnic backgrounds and regardless of ideological differences, has become a necessity for our very survival.

In Oakland, California, we had been outsiders, projecting ideas. But in Detroit we were an integral part of the ongoing debate about the future of our city. This was the opportunity Jimmy had been waiting for. As he said in a public speakout on casino gambling,

> To rebuild Detroit, we have to think of a new mode of production based upon serving human needs and the needs of the community and not on any get-rich-quick schemes.... If we are going to create hope especially for our young people, we have to stop seeing the city as just a place to which you come for a job or to make a living and start seeing it as the place where the humanity of people is enriched because they have the opportunity to live with people of many different ethnic and social backgrounds.
>
> The foundation of our city has to be people living in communities who realize that their human identity or their Love and Respect for Self is based on Love and Respect for others and who have also learned from experience that they can no longer leave the decision as to their present and their future to the market place, to corporations or to capitalist politicians, regardless of ethnic background. We, the People, have to see ourselves as responsible for our city and for each other, and especially for making sure that our children are raised to place more value on social ties than on material wealth....
>
> We have to get rid of the myth that there is something sacred about large-scale production for the national and international market.... We have to begin thinking of creating small enterprises which produce food, goods and services for the local market, that is, for our communities and our city. Instead of destroying the skills of workers, which is what large-scale industry does, these small enterprises will combine craftsmanship, or the preservation and enhancement of human skills, with the

> new technologies which make possible flexible production and constant readjustment to serve the needs of local customers....
>
> In order to create these new enterprises we need a view of our city which takes into consideration both the natural resources of our area and the existing and potential skills and talents of Detroiters....
>
> We also need a fundamental change in our concept of Schools. Since World War II our schools have been transformed into custodial institutions where our children are housed for 12 years with no function except to study and get good grades so that they can win the certificates that will enable them to get a job.... We have to create schools which are an integral part of the community, in which young people naturally and normally do socially necessary and meaningful work for the community, for example, keeping the school grounds and the neighborhood clean and attractive, taking care of younger children, growing gardens which provide food for the community, etc., etc.[5]

It is hard to overestimate the importance of the struggle with Coleman Young over casino gambling. It forced us to articulate an alternative, helped us to focus the emerging movement around the rebuilding of our cities, and started a lot of thinking in the community. It is through struggles like these that the humanity-stretching vision necessary to all movements is created. As a result of the struggle, Jimmy began insisting that the main question facing us is "How Can We Re-Civilize Our Society?"[6] and that the key to "re-civilizing our society" is building communities. "Communities," he said, "have always been and will always be the basis for developing and maintaining human values and building personal character. Those who recognize this are still very few. But all great historical movements were started by a minority."

I was very much involved in the struggle because I was passionately opposed to casino gambling. In fact, I was the vice president of Detroiters Uniting. But I doubt that I could have conceived or projected the alternative with Jimmy's self-confidence. Having been raised in a poor agricultural community in the South, Jimmy knew from experience that people can start from scratch and make do if they relate in a human way to one another and utilize the natural resources all around them. Thinking this way is much more difficult for people like myself who, having lived all our lives in cities, have become dependent for our survival on food and clothing that come from the store.

I was more sure of myself on the need for a new system of education, which had been my special interest since teaching school in the 1960s. Speaking in the Martin Luther King Jr. Forum Series at the Schomburg Center in New York on December 8, 1990, I said,

> I like to think that if King were alive today, he would be struggling to apply Gandhi's philosophy of education to the crisis in our cities with the same courage and far-sightedness as forty years ago he struggled to apply Gandhi's philosophy of Non-Violence in the civil rights movement. Gandhi knew that education in India had been structured mainly to supply the next generation of clerks to sign, stamp and file all the paperwork needed to run the British Empire. Meanwhile, the villages where the vast majority of the people lived were left untouched. . . . Against this system of education set up to serve British interests, Gandhi proposed a system of popular education to serve the Indian people. Teach people those things which will truly help them, he said, not to become servants and bureaucrats but in all the little things of village life. Education should be of the Heart, the Hand and the Head. It should give people an understanding of themselves and where they stand in the world, and from there, their obligations towards their neighbors. The three main resources of this popular education, he said, are the Community, the Natural Environment and the Work Environment.

I was fascinated by the light that the debate over casino gambling threw on the differences between Coleman and Jimmy. Coleman was only a year older than Jimmy. He had also been born in the South, worked in the plant during World War II,[7] been active in labor and antiracist struggles, and moved in and around radical circles. But the differences between Coleman and Jimmy were more important than the similarities. Coleman had been brought to Detroit by his parents when he was a toddler; he grew up on the rough streets of the big city. Jimmy did not come to Detroit until he was a young man. Coleman was an unabashed politician who not only knew how to bully and charm his way to power but obviously enjoyed the rough-and-tumble of party and machine politics. He prided himself on his "realism." Jimmy prided himself on being a movement builder. As a result, Coleman, with all his political power and prestige, began to look more and more like an old man trapped in the culture of the receding twentieth century, while Jimmy, "the man who wouldn't be king," began to take on the image of a prophet with a vision for the fast-approaching twenty-first century and practical proposals on how to realize it.

Throughout the struggles of the 1980s and the early 1990s over the very immediate issues involved in revitalizing Detroit, the differences between the personalities of the two men took on concrete political form. While Young was willing to create jobs by any means necessary, Jimmy insisted that although jobs had originally brought us to the city, high-tech and global corporations are now eliminating jobs, forcing us to begin thinking about work and economics in a new way. While Young was constantly showing his contempt for social ties (during this period, for example, he was sued by a former city worker for support of the child he had allegedly fathered, refusing to admit paternity until it was finally established by a blood test), Jimmy kept insisting that the main thing all of us, and especially our young people, need is love and respect for one another. Therefore, especially for the sake of our young people, we need a new vision of the city as the organized cooperative form that people can use to serve one another more effectively. The only way we can reduce crime, he insisted, is by creating a new spirit of hope in young people based on a new attitude toward work and on redefining or recivilizing the city as a collection of communities.[8]

As Shea, Jimmy, and I drove to Maine for our vacation in 1988, we were jubilant. The emergence of SOSAD had created in the city the sense of hope that is necessary to build a movement, while the confrontation with Coleman Young over casino gambling had provided us with not only a victory but a deeper understanding of how rebuilding our cities would stretch everyone's humanity as every great movement must do. On our way back from Maine we made our annual stopover with Ping and Carol Ferry to share our good news and hopes for Detroit's future.

Back in Detroit Jimmy started to paint the house and garage as he had done every other autumn for twenty-five years, climbing up and standing on the ladder hour after hour and day after day, as I held my breath afraid that he would lose his balance and fall. This year, however, he complained of a pain in his back and was unable to finish. After many visits, first to his primary doctor, a Korean woman at the Conner Center of the Metro Medical Group, and then with a urologist, we learned that he had bladder cancer and that surgery would be necessary. The urologist assured us that it could be done on an outpatient basis and that there was no cause for concern. Instead, the experience turned out to be a nightmare. On the appointed day we arrived early in the morning at the Metro Medical Group Northwest Center, and Jimmy went into surgery around nine o'clock. A few hours later I was told that he was still bleeding and that the doctor would have to operate again. At four o'clock the center began closing down for the day, and only one nurse was left in the room with Jimmy and in the whole building. Although he was obviously weak from loss of blood, she insisted on his getting dressed and into the wheelchair so that she could go home. In the wheelchair he immediately lost consciousness. Fortunately, just at that moment Jimmy's son Tyrone arrived. With his help we were able to get Jimmy onto a gurney and rush him to Emergency where he was revived and remained hospitalized for a couple of days.

I was furious at the surgeon and the hospital administration for having allowed this situation to develop. If Tyrone had not been there, I don't know what would have happened. But when I called both the surgeon and Jimmy's primary doctor to ask what steps they were going to take to prevent a recurrence with somebody else, they acted as if nothing out of the ordinary had occurred. So I contacted a doctor friend of ours, Howard Schubiner, who had been in a NOAR Study Group, and on his recommendation we applied for a transfer to the Henry Ford Senior Center where Howard's friend Dr. Marybeth Tupper is the director. As a result, Marybeth became our doctor and good friend. It was a blessing. Because of Medicare and our Health Alliance Plan insurance, we didn't have to worry about medical expenses, but I shudder to think of what our lives would have been like over the next four years and especially during Jimmy's last few months if we had still been dependent on the doctors at the Metro Medical Center.

Over the next few years Jimmy would be tested every few months and undergo nearly a half dozen bladder operations until they became so routine that he got into the habit of going to meetings or demonstrations right from the hospital. This was fortunate because in the fall of 1988, inspired by the example of SOSAD and our victory in the casino gambling struggle, things began jumping in Detroit.

For years the night before Halloween has been known as Devil's Night in Detroit because young people took advantage of the holiday to burn down abandoned houses and in general to turn the city into a cauldron. In 1988 the city declared a No Devil's Night campaign, and people all over the city mobilized to take back their neighborhoods. Soon thereafter I read in the paper and heard over TV that a group on Sharon Street on the southwest side of Detroit had succeeded in getting rid of a crackhouse on their block by mobilizing the neighbors and that they were holding a meeting in the Patton Recreation Center. At the meeting the Sharon Street group urged other neighborhoods to organize similar actions so that crack dealers, having been driven out of one neighborhood, could not relocate in another. At the same time we heard of a group in Pilgrim Village on the northwest side headed by Dorothy Garner that had organized a march to the local police precinct carrying a coffin to symbolize death to the crack trade. After some phone calls we were able to call together a meeting of the two groups at the Core City Neighborhood office where participants agreed that our main task was to break the cycle of fear. We then decided that the best way to do this was to hold regular marches in different neighborhoods all over the city. Jimmy wrote a leaflet explaining *Why We March,* and for three years, calling ourselves WE-PROS (We the People Reclaim Our Streets) at the suggestion of Sister Theresa, executive director of Core City Neighborhood, we carried on weekly marches in different neighborhoods, undeterred either by the heat of summer or the below-freezing temperatures of winter. At one point there were eight neighborhood groups marching together as WE-PROS. All over the city we chanted "Up with hope! Down with dope!"; "Pack up your crack and don't come back!"; "Dope dealer, dope dealer, run and hide! People are uniting on the other side!" Before the WE-PROS marches people had been afraid of one another, afraid to sit on their front porches, afraid of being laughed at if they took a stand against crackhouses. The WE-PROS marches broke that cycle of fear, replacing it with a new spirit of hope and unity in the neighborhoods where we marched. In Dorothy Garner's Pilgrim Village neighborhood the police reported an 80 percent drop in crime in the wake of our marches.[9]

In most neighborhoods our WE-PROS marches began and ended at churches. A few preachers and priests, mostly white (Rev. Luther Wright of Truth Evangelical Lutheran Church and Father Tom Lumpkin were WE-PROS regulars) joined our march, but black preachers were conspicuously absent. Jimmy kept pointing out that with more than two thousand churches in the Detroit area, we could rout the crack dealers in our city if only 10 percent of them conducted anticrackhouse marches in the surrounding four-square-block area. But to no avail. Nowadays, few congregations care about the neighborhoods in which their churches are located. Parishioners drive to services from across town, and church parking lots, staffed by security guards, take up more space than the church itself. Some of the newer churches even build huge fences to protect themselves against the neighborhood. The failure of black Baptist preachers to respond to the WE-PROS call reinforced Jimmy's conviction that the black church cannot be counted on in the life-and-death struggles now going on in the black community.

I refused to give up on the church. In 1990 Sister Cathy DiSantis, who often marched with us, invited me to speak to the Detroit Catholic Pastoral Alliance on how the church can help to "recivilize" Detroit. I jumped at the opportunity. The church, I said, is in a unique position to help build the movement to restructure our city both practically and conceptually:

> Man/Woman, it has always insisted, does not live by bread alone. The weakness of the church is that it has too often accepted the separation between the material and the spiritual . . . leaving the material to the economic and political power structure. . . . The crisis of a city like Detroit provides the church with an extraordinary opportunity to develop and practice a vision of a new economy and a new educational system which meets both the material and spiritual needs of human beings. . . . Churches are . . . in an excellent position to develop small enterprises that provide models of how to meet the needs of the community and the city and at the same time teach young people the importance of skills, process and respect for Nature. All over the city churches are surrounded by vacant and unused land. If Detroiters, and especially young Detroiters, could see this land being used by churches for organic gardens to supply produce for local needs or to plant Christmas trees for sale at Yuletide or greenhouses where vegetables are grown year round, the idea of a self-reliant living economy to meet the material and spiritual needs of people could come alive.[10]

Through WE-PROS we got a sense of how concerned grassroots community people, especially older Detroiters like Norma Mayfield, president of Mound-Outer Drive-Ryan Block Clubs (MORS) in northeast Detroit, and Dorothy Garner, president of the Reach Community Group in northwest Detroit, are about young people and also how determined they are to rebuild the city from the ground up to save the homes that they had worked all their lives to own. Jimmy and Dorothy became especially close friends. Like Jimmy she had been born and raised in Alabama. Her sense of self was also inseparable from her sense of community. She also believed that

> we have to learn how to relate to one another again, to smile and laugh again, to fall into one another's arms and love each other again. We have to live with less and be happy baking bread, restoring a house. We need more control over how things are made, more self-reliance. We need to be closer to the source of what things are made of and how they are made. We need to stop thinking that every problem has to be solved by an expert and to depend more on ourselves and one another.

One of the main reasons for today's violence, Dorothy used to say, is the stress on individual upward mobility: "You can work hard and get good grades in high school, go to college, and yet when you get your degree there is no job for you. So under the pressures of your house note and car note you explode." Before she met Jimmy and me, Dorothy had never spoken in public. "He encouraged me," she said at the service we held for Jimmy a week after his death, "and I haven't shut up since."

In May 1990 under the auspices of SOSAD a community celebration honoring Jimmy and me was held at the Detroit Association of Women's Clubs. Freddy Paine came from Los Angeles to talk about our common radical foundations. James McFadden and Ken Snodgrass testified to our efforts to develop African American leadership. Jim Jackson and Lizette Chevalier spoke about revolutionary vision and art. Dorothy Garner, Clementine Barfield, Trisha Arndt, and Ruth Hicks emphasized our contribution to rebuilding communities. Councilman Mel Ravitz presented a resolution from the Detroit City Council.

The diversity of the celebrants was heartwarming. To my surprise Conrad Mallet Jr. showed up. He had just been appointed Michigan Supreme Court justice to fill the unexpired term of Dennis Archer, who had resigned to begin his (eventually successful) campaign for mayor of Detroit. Since our close collaboration with his parents on *Correspondence* in the early 1960s, we had seen very little of Conrad. On one occasion when he was Mayor Young's chief aide and Detroiters for Dignity was holding a protest sit-in the mayor's office, he had whispered in "Uncle Jimmy's" ear before helping to throw us out of the office. Conrad has recently been elected chief justice of the Court.

I have a thick album of letters sent to SOSAD for the celebration. They are interesting because they say as much about the writers as they do about Jimmy and me. Carol and Ping Ferry wrote to say, "Human progress is not progress at all, it is moving around, sometimes toward more cruelty and injustice, sometimes toward more equity, individual freedom, and social cooperation. But every move that either Grace or Jim has made over their lives has been toward decency of the human race. That is true progress." Louis Tsen wrote, "After a lifetime, Grace and Jimmy can truly claim two histories and two traditions: the activist tradition of the Afro-American and the teaching tradition of the Asian-American."

Jimmy's speech at the celebration was an example of how he never stopped using his own life experiences to challenge others to go beyond victim thinking:

> I grew up in a little town called Marion Junction, Alabama, where folks were gentlemen and ladies by day and Ku Klux Klanners by night. They hung somebody almost every weekend so that we would be nice fellows the rest of the week. But I'm still saying that the challenges facing us today are far grander than those facing us then. Because our parents told us "You have to make a way out of no way." You don't hear anyone saying that now. All of us go around saying "I can't do this or that because of this racist society, this capitalist society and white folk messing with me." So that most of us are frozen. Most black folks are locked in the word *racism*. We don't see it as a challenge to take us to another plateau. We see it as an excuse for not doing anything. That is the most devastating thing that has happened to us.
>
> I'm going to have to depend on everyone who's younger than me. But don't go out there looking for no cheap-ass victories. There ain't going to be no easy victories. There's going to be blood and sweat and tears. There's going to be defeat after defeat, and yet you're going to get up the next day and try all over again. All I would try to urge you is don't lose your spirit, don't lose hope because you're going to need lots of hope. You got to believe in yourself and just look at the world around you and what you have to change.

A month later Jimmy and Freddy gave me a seventy-fifth birthday party in the parlor of the First Unitarian-Universalist Church. My special birthday gift was a little booklet with my picture on the front cover. Simply titled *Grace*, the booklet includes five of my speeches, a brief introduction by Jimmy, and a longer one by Freddy. The booklet had been "prepared with love by James Boggs, Joseph Eggly, Richard Feldman, John S. Gruchala, Sharon Howell, Freddy Paine and Nkenge Zola." At the party aneb kgositsile read a poem, which she called "Lessons in Grace":

> Face like stone sculpture
> features rounded, softened by wind,
> The flesh concedes to weathering,
> But the eyes will not relinquish
> their keen measuring of the world
> where you have chosen
> to put down roots.
>
> From you we learn
> the costs of commitment
> the clarity of courage;

how, even, to withstand
the trivia that assails
a spirit in search of saneness.

You are the lesson of balance, grace;
where to invest—
to forward battle or fashion beauty,
where to withhold;
bold when strength is wanted
silent when words will be futile;
knowing when to be gentle
because there is pain,
where to object
because there is deceit.
Your work inscribes
this terrain of human striving
for those who would travel
the road you have braved.

You planted your life
in African-American soil.
Now it seems
China and Africa
are married in you.
The example of your life
weds us to the whole world.

Louis Tsen sent a poem from Switzerland:

On the Anniversary of Grace

There comes a time in life
When hope turns into memory.
We remember afresh
Our past strivings for a future,
Which kept revealing itself
To be different from our argument,
But sure of life's repetition
As we are of earth's turning,
We go on shaping new visions,
Fervently believing
That to say what we see
Carries an import
For those who bestir after us.

You were the kiva woman
Who laid down her tool
To marvel at the firmament.
You were the sailor
Who espied a new island
And took it to be India.
In race with life,
You run ahead,
Leaving life,
As always,
Slowly to catch up with you.

I felt blessed to be celebrating my seventy-fifth birthday in such good health and surrounded by such loving comrades. Raya Dunayevskaya had died in 1987 at the age of seventy-seven. We had not exchanged a single word for thirty-one years, but Jimmy, Freddy, and I sent a telegram to her husband, John Dwyer, expressing our appreciation of her commitment to the struggle. In May 1989 CLR died; he was eighty-eight. Marty Glaberman, Gloria House (aneb kgositsile), and I organized a tribute to him at Wayne State University on October 9, at which we showed the one-hour documentary produced by Tariq Ali and CLR's nephew, Darcus Howe, for the BBC. I also spoke at a C. L. R. James memorial celebration in New York City.

Shortly after my seventy-fifth birthday party our old friend Kathleen Gough Aberle called to wish me many happy returns of the day. She was her usual spirited self and seemed in good health. Less than three months later, incredibly, she was dead from bowel cancer. It was a terrible blow. Jimmy and I had taken the deaths of Raya and CLR in stride because we had been estranged for years and they were in their upper seventies and eighties. But Kathleen was only sixty-five. She was the author of two *Correspondence* pamphlets, *The Decline of the State and the Coming of World Society* and *When the Saints Go Marching In*. We had visited Trinidad together in 1960 and had many friends in common: Freddy and Lyman, Filomena, Marty and Jessie Glaberman, Conrad Lynn, Bill Worthy, Frances Herring. Kathleen was on Sutton several times and participated in our conversations. For thirty years we had visited back and forth. When she was living in Ann Arbor and teaching at Wayne State in Detroit, we would lunch together several times a month. On Jimmy's forty-first birthday she gave him a wonderful party with all his children. From Ann Arbor she and her husband, David, also an anthropologist, went to Brandeis University to teach, leaving for the University of Oregon after a demonstration led by Kathleen during the Cuban missile crisis ("Kennedy to Hell, Up with Fidel") upset the Brandeis authorities. Determined not to support the Vietnam War by grading students, she and David moved to Canada in the late 1960s to teach at Simon Fraser University and the University of British Columbia, respectively. A distinguished anthropologist, specializing in the study of imperialism and the resistance to imperialism, Kathleen was also actively involved in the struggle. After her death *Anthropologica*, sponsored by Wilfred Laurier University in Waterloo, Ontario, published a special memorial issue in which fellow scholars paid tribute to her work and life.[11]

Meanwhile, in Detroit, Coleman Young, for lack of a vision, was making deals with the developers who were pouring money into his campaign chest. Downtown Detroit was already a wasteland with more than seventy empty office buildings. Every new and fancier building enriched the developers but emptied an older but still perfectly good building in a costly game of "musical buildings." Nevertheless, in 1990 Young tried to ram through a proposal to demolish Ford Auditorium in order to build a new bank building for Comerica. By this time, after fifteen years of Young's multimillion-dollar deals, community people were beginning to see through him. Ford Auditorium had a sentimental value for Detroiters because it had been given to the city by the Ford family, and many had walked across its stage during high school graduation exercises. To defeat the Comerica proposal, DU created a new organization, Detroit USA, and organized a petition drive to force a referendum on the issue, taking advantage of a little-known ordinance discovered by Curtis Blessing, an attorney whose father had once been head of the City Planning Commission and who is himself deeply committed to Detroit's revitalization. We had only three weeks to gather seventeen thousand signatures in the dead of winter. But all over the city, grassroots folks stood outside department stores and supermarkets in below-freezing weather, gathering more than enough petitions so that we were able to force and win the referendum vote in April 1991.

By the spring of 1991, with the wind of the WE-PRO marches and the casino gambling and Save Ford Auditorium victories in our sails, we decided that it was time for the community to celebrate itself. So in November we brought together community organizations from across the city in a People's Festival, describing it as "a Multi-Generational, Multi-Cultural Celebration of Detroiters, putting our hearts, minds, hands and imaginations together to redefine and recreate a city of Community, Compassion, Participation and Enterprise in Harmony with the Earth." At the urging of Curtis Blessing, Dennis Archer, who had resigned from the Michigan Supreme Court to run for mayor of Detroit, came to the festival.

The success of the People's Festival confirmed our belief that a new movement to rebuild Detroit by rebuilding communities was already in the making. What could we do to accelerate its growth? Thinking back to how Mississippi Freedom Summer raised the civil rights movement to a new plateau by bringing young people from the North to assist in the Voter Registration Drive in 1964, Jimmy came up with the idea of bringing young people to Detroit to work with local youth in order to dramatize the idea that rebuilding our cities is at the heart of the new movement that is emerging as we come to the end of the twentieth century.

So in January 1992 Jimmy, Clementine Barfield, and Paul Stark of the Detroit Greens issued a call to university youth to come to Detroit and become a part of Detroit Summer, "an Intergenerational Multicultural Youth Program/Movement to rebuild, redefine, respirit Detroit from the Ground Up." Detroit Summer has now completed its sixth season. Through its four-week sessions Detroit Summer has helped to develop a rebuild-the-cities-movement consciousness in the fifty to sixty young people, out of town and local, who each year work with community elders and children on projects such as community gardens and public murals during the day, and in the evening, after a community dinner, grapple with challenging questions in intergenerational dialogues or develop media or organizing skills in workshops.

At the ceremony that opens Detroit Summer every year participants are given a sense of the unique questions that their generation faces. What kind of technology would be the most beneficial in human and environmental terms? Why can't the purpose of our economic and educational system be the development of our people, our communities, and our country? "As we approach the twenty-first century," I said at the 1994 opening,

> these are the very tough and very real questions we have to grapple with and the choices we have to make if we want to cut back on crime and violence, homelessness, cancer and birth defects. We can't leave these decisions to multinational corporations who have no loyalty to our communities or country—or to the politicians who serve these corporations.... There are no quick or easy answers to these questions. Twenty years ago the Black Panthers captured the imagination of people all around the country with the saying, "If you're not part of the solution,

> you're part of the problem." In becoming a Detroit Summer volunteer you have become part of the solution.[12]

One of the main reasons why Detroit Summer youth see themselves as part of a movement is that they are all volunteers. The significance of this was pointed out by Tracey Hollins, who at the age of fifteen was one of our first volunteers in 1992. After her first year's experience, she wrote:

> When most people heard about Detroit Summer, their initial statement was "You don't get paid?" To them working for no money was crazy, and volunteerism seemed to be a foreign language. They didn't understand that a smiling child's face and friends for life were better compensation than wages. A paycheck continues to cloud the minds of young adults who have been taught that money is everything. Teens continuously walk the street not noticing the trash and not caring about the graffiti. Most don't realize the importance of putting a piece of paper in the right place. They have kept the mentality that one person can't make a difference. Detroit Summer was the perfect cure. Detroit Summer had a special way of making you forget that you weren't getting paid. It filled your head with answers to questions that you'd had all of your life and questions that no one can answer. It made you feel that you were an important part of the changing and molding of future generations. It made you feel that the hole you dug, the garden you watered or the swing set you painted, made a difference.

The adults who make Detroit Summer possible are also volunteers. Co-coordinators Shea Howell and Michelle Brown provide imaginative leadership. Gerald Hairston is the link to the Gardening Angels, a loose network of mainly African American southern-born elders who plant gardens not only to produce healthier food for themselves and their neighbors but to instill respect for nature and process in young people and to stop crime. Night after night Joni Kryciuk with the help of Mary Brown miraculously creates delicious community dinners for vegetarians who don't eat dairy foods and those who do, vegetarians who eat poultry and those who don't, as well as those who like myself eat everything. Hank Kryciuk takes photos that capture the magical ways in which Detroit Summer grows people as well as vegetables. Jane Kyriacopoulos, a retired schoolteacher, keeps the books and is always ready to run an errand. The First Unitarian-Universalist Church provides Detroit Summer with an office and meeting spaces.[13] The funds for supplies and programs come mainly from small donations from hundreds of concerned citizens.

Detroit Summer is an example of the self-transforming/structure-transforming actions that Martin Luther King Jr. in the last year of his life projected for young people in "our dying cities." In the process of developing themselves, Detroit Summer youth help to make community dreams come true. For example, eighty-year-old Jessie Thomas, a Gardening Angel, and her neighbors on Beniteau Street on the East Side of Detroit were fed up with looking at the seven vacant lots on their block littered with an accumulation of old cars, tires, and other trash. So in 1992 Detroit Summer youth turned the lots into Beniteau Children's Park with a swing and sandlot for the kids and a vegetable and flower garden for the adults, and every year we return to spruce things up.

The emphasis on intergenerational cooperation between Detroit Summer youth and the Gardening Angels has given the movement to rebuild Detroit a unique quality that the national and international media has recognized. For example, a new national magazine called *Hope* carried a five-page article in its May-June 1996 issue titled "Roots Revival: The Gardening Angels Bring Neighborhoods Back to Life." On August 3, 1996, a long article appeared in the *London Daily Telegraph* describing how the moral decline of Detroit has been arrested through the activities of Detroit Summer and the Gardening Angels. The caption under the picture of Detroit Summer volunteers working to create a community garden with the "Cucumber Kids" reads, "Weeding out: Inner city youngsters eschew the drug culture for horticulture."

Detroit Summer volunteers work on six or seven projects each summer. In southwest Detroit they have painted four murals. Outside the Cass Corridor Neighborhood Development Corporation office not far from the First Unitarian-Universalist Church, two murals overlook a community garden for the homeless. In 1997 they are creating a memorial garden of fruit trees and flowers on the grounds of Genesis Lutheran Church at the corner of Field Street and Mack Avenue, a few hundred feet from my house. Individual trees will be dedicated to members of the community and alumni of Eastern High School, which once stood on the site. Every year Detroit Summer receives more proposals for community projects than we can possibly work on. Instead of expanding Detroit Summer, we hope that others will be inspired to initiate similar projects to engage an ever-widening circle of young people. That is how movements develop.

When Detroit Summer began in 1992, most people were talking about young people only as a problem. Today all over Detroit and other cities young people are being seen as creators of community change. Detroit Summer, with very limited funds and no paid staff but with community support, has played an important, though by no means the only, part in bringing about this transformation. It is an example of how people inspired by a vision can contribute to the building of a movement.

In 1991 an X ray disclosed a tumor in Jimmy's left lung, which he stubbornly refused to connect with a lifetime of smoking. After forty radiation treatments the cancer went into remission, but in 1992 another tumor showed up on a CAT scan. In February 1993, on what we had viewed as a routine visit to Dr. Tupper, he was put on oxygen. A few days later she came by the house to explain the hospice program, and he decided to enter it.

Some years ago I saw a documentary on dying whose main theme was that people die as they lived. That was Jimmy. For five years, since he began undergoing operations for bladder cancer and even after his lung cancer was diagnosed, he continued the activities that he considered important, marching against crackhouses, campaigning against the demolition of the Ford Auditorium, organizing Detroit Summer, making speeches, and writing letters to the editor and articles for the SOSAD newsletter and *Northwest Detroiter*. In 1992 while he was undergoing the chemotherapy that cleared up his bladder cancer, he helped form the Coalition against Privatization and to Save Our City. The coalition was initiated by activist members of a few AFSCME locals who contacted Carl Edwards and Alice Jennings who in turn contacted us. Jimmy helped write the mission statement that gave the union activists a sense of themselves as not only city workers but citizens of the city and its communities. The coalition's town meetings and demonstrations were instrumental in persuading the new mayor, Dennis Archer, to come out against privatization, using language from the coalition newsletter to explain his position.

At the same time Jimmy was putting out the garbage, keeping our corner at Field and Goethe free of litter and rubbish, mopping the kitchen and bathroom floors, picking cranberries, and keeping up "his" path on Sutton. After he entered the hospice program, which usually means death within six months, and up to a few weeks before his death, Jimmy slowed down a bit, but he was still writing and speaking and organizing. He used to say that he wasn't going to die until he got ready, and because he was so cheerful and so engaged it was easy to believe him. A few weeks after he went on oxygen we did three movement-building workshops at the SOSAD office for a group of Roger Barfield's friends who were trying to form a community-action group following a protest demonstration at a neighborhood sandwich shop over the murder of one of their friends. With oxygen tubes in his nostrils and a portable oxygen tank by his side, Jimmy spoke for almost an hour on one of his favorite subjects, the need to "think dialectically, rather than biologically." Recognizing that this was probably one of Jimmy's last extended speeches, I had the session videotaped by Ron Scott. At the end of this workshop we asked participants to come to the next session prepared to grapple with three questions: What can we do to make our neighborhoods safe? How can we motivate people to transform? How can we create jobs?

In the second session, which I conducted, I used Kenneth Burke's paradigm to describe movement struggle as a drama with five main elements: the Purpose or why we do it; the Act or what we do; the Scene or where and when we do it; the Actors or who does it; the Agency or the means or methods.[14] One of the main purposes of any movement struggle is to give hope to the people who are suffering. The acts must be ones that are appropriate to the time and place and must be the kind that grassroots people can identify with and easily duplicate, for example, the sit-ins at the Greensboro, North Carolina, Woolworth's in 1960. The actors must earn the respect of those whom they want to lead. At the end of this workshop participants suggested possible actions, for example, community gardens, neighborhood clean-up crews, neighborhood lookouts/watches, messages of love and peace. The third workshop, conducted by Shea, outlined the elements of a strategy that included establishing your identity through your name, mission statement, and a identifying activity; building organizational strength and legitimacy; using a variety of forms to get out your message.

As soon as the weather got warm enough, Jimmy began holding court on our front porch, talking to people in the neighborhood and receiving visitors. On May 29, we gave him what he and we knew was his last birthday party in our backyard. A lot of people came, including Annie, his first wife; Marie Lawson and Virginia Jackson, his first cousins; my brother Eddie; City Council President Maryann Mahaffey; and Clementine Barfield. Shea, Ann Perrault, and Jackie Victor scrubbed the house in advance and barbecued the chicken. A snapshot of Jimmy at the party shows him looking gaunt and frail, but that didn't stop him from making a long and spirited speech in which, among other things, he thanked Annie for the work that she had put into raising their children.

On June 23 the *Detroit Free Press* printed Jimmy's last letter to the editor under the title "Race: The Issue Isn't Black and White." This letter said:

> It is no longer useful to look at the racial climate of this country only in terms of black and white. People from more than 100 ethnic groups live here. By 2040 European Americans and African Americans will be among the many minorities who make up the United States.
>
> Blacks in Detroit are a majority; they need to stop thinking like a minority or like victims. Both African Americans and European Americans should be thinking of how to integrate with Detroiters of Latino and Arab descent.

To the very end Jimmy was striking out at two of his favorite targets: racial (or what he called biological) thinking, and blacks viewing themselves as a minority.

When Ossie and Ruby stopped by to see us in June, he met them at the door with a three-page memo suggesting things for them to work on. The next week Ruby sent him a big batch of rich dark gingerbread that she had baked. A few weeks before his death he called Clementine to alert her to the killing of children that was going on in Liberia and to instruct her how to intervene. A few days later he spoke at a Detroit Summer gathering. The next day he went out with a friend (without his oxygen tank) to supervise the moving of a refrigerator. The week before he died he did a two-hour interview with a local radio reporter. Up to two days before his death, he was grooming himself as carefully as always. Then, suddenly on Tuesday night, July 20, he began to stumble, sat down in a bedroom chair, and never got up or spoke again. I was all alone and wasn't sure what I should do. There didn't seem to be any point in calling anybody. So I kept stroking him and saying to him over and over:

> You are a helluva guy.
> You raised a whole lot of hell—and a helluva lot of questions.
> You made a helluva lot of friends—and a helluva lot of enemies.
> You had a helluva lot of ideas—
> And wrote a helluva lot of books and pamphlets.
> You made a helluva lot of difference to a helluva lot of people.

Early Wednesday morning the hospice nurse, with whom he used to carry on all kinds of discussions, came by to give him morphine to ease the pain. During the day a long poem "For James, Writer, Activist, Worker" arrived from Ruby Dee, who I am convinced is psychic. He did not try to speak but it appeared that he could hear and understand what people were saying to him because he smiled at all the right places as I read Ruby's poem to him.[15]

All that day and the next morning he was surrounded by friends and family, playing his favorite music and reading his favorite poems to him. People from the neighborhood drifted in and out of the house. Wednesday night his youngest daughter, who is a doctor, and his granddaughter, Ernestine, spent the night with him and me. Finally, at 11 A.M. on Thursday, July 22, he passed away peacefully and painlessly.

Because Jimmy's body was cremated, I was not planning any kind of funeral service. I had in mind a memorial celebration later in the fall so that friends and comrades could attend from out of town. But his children wanted a service that would provide closure for themselves and their friends. So on July 31 we held a small family service in the parlor of the Unitarian-Universalist Church, followed by a much larger gathering in McAllister Hall, which people had learned about through word of mouth. At this gathering, where Nkenge Zola acted as emcee, family members and dozens of friends spoke.

On October 23, his friends and comrades from Detroit and all over the country held a joyful memorial celebration in the sanctuary of the Unitarian-Universalist Church. As folks entered they were given a copy of the twenty-eight-page tribute booklet compiled by New Life Publishers. The program began with the first showing of the eleven-minute film *James Boggs: An American Revolutionary*, produced by Academy Award nominee cinematographer Frances Reid, which has since been shown countless times. It continued with remarks by Jimmy's youngest daughter, Dr. Delois Berrien-Jones; actors Ruby Dee and Ossie Davis; historian Vincent Harding; electrician, poet, and urban agriculturist John Gruchala; community activist Dorothy Garner; and Detroit Summer youth volunteers Julia Pointer and Tracey Hollins; as well as music by a jazz combo. I acted as emcee and also shared the story of how Jimmy and I got together. The part of the celebration that I suspect he would have liked best was when individuals stood up and were introduced according to how many years they had known him, beginning with Faye Brown who had worked with him at the Chrysler-Jefferson plant in the early 1940s and Ping Ferry who had known him since 1962. Those who had known him the shortest time were the young people of Detroit Summer. Julia Pointer spoke for them when she said,

> On Opening Day of Detroit Summer he stepped to the mike and challenged every youth in the audience. He told us that kids our age wanted to get paid to use the bathroom these days. Next he commended us for volunteering. He said we proved to him that there were young people around who cared about the

city. Now it was up to us to make a difference in our communities. The time had come to stop waiting for GM and Ford to supply jobs and create our own. It was time to stop waiting for the city to beautify our neighborhoods and do it ourselves.

That, he said, is what Detroit Summer is all about. Its purpose is to empower and inspire youth to reclaim some responsibility in rebuilding our cities. And we wanted to—because Jimmy made it clear that afternoon and every day afterwards that he was proud of us. And that made us proud of ourselves. Because this thin, wiry man who a moment ago was a stranger became our friend.

玉平

9 On My Own

I knew that Jimmy was going to die, but I didn't expect it. The difference is subtle but real. When you expect something, you imagine it. But Jimmy remained so alert and active almost to the very end that I never imagined being on my own. If he had been in bed suffering excruciating pain for months, as happens with many lung cancer patients, I might have spent more time wondering and perhaps worrying about the future.

The night after he died I spoke at a Detroit Remembers Malcolm X Conference at Wayne State University in his place. General Baker had called early in the week while Jimmy still seemed his old self to confirm that he would be there, and I decided to take his place because it was an opportunity to tell people that he was no longer with us. Carl Edwards arranged for a brief video clip of Jimmy to be shown after I spoke. The next morning, for the same reason, I conducted the workshop on the 1963 Grassroots Leadership Conference that I had been scheduled to do. Max Stanford was present and went out of his way to talk about the contributions I had made to building the black movement.

A couple of weeks later, Shea and I drove to Maine for our vacation as usual. Before Jimmy died, the three of us had been planning to make the trip together. Freddy had been particularly anxious that Jimmy have one last summer on Sutton and had already made arrangements for oxygen to be delivered to the island, as she had done for Lyman in the 1970s.

The first twenty-four hours on Sutton felt right. Louis Tsen was in the United States to visit his in-laws, and he and Itty Chan came up by bus from Boston to spend the night. It was like being with family. Looking around the dinner table, it suddenly struck me that of the five people present, the majority (Louis, Itty, and I) were Chinese and the minority (Freddy and Shea) Caucasian. I can't remember ever thinking that way before, and I'm not sure why it happened or why I thought it necessary to call attention to it. Perhaps it was a sign that with Jimmy gone I was beginning to reclaim my Chinese American identity.

The rest of the stay in Maine was very tough going. I saw Jimmy everywhere—on the beach, at the dock, at the boathouse, on "his" path, at breakfast, lunch, and dinner. Yet except for the ceremony when we buried his ashes in the tiny island cemetery and the session during our conversations when we discussed the program for the October 23 memorial celebration, nobody talked about him. The only one who seemed to understand how I felt was Micah, Rick Feldman's eight-year-old son, who during the few days that they were on Sutton, would sit down close to me and say, "I miss Jimmy, too." I couldn't wait to get back to Detroit.

In Detroit, wherever I went, not only at meetings but at the market or downtown, it seemed that someone, often a person whom I didn't even remember, would come up to me and say how much an article or speech or something Jimmy had said or done had meant to him or her. Quite a few said that they remembered sitting on the couch in our living room on Field Street. In Detroit there was always someone whom I could call or who would call me to talk about Jimmy: Dorothy Garner, Ellen Richardson, Clementine, even our eighty-three-year-old landlady, Marjorie Anderson, who lived upstairs and whom Jimmy looked out for. They seemed to miss him as much as I did. From time to time, usually on holidays or Mother's Day, I would hear from Jimmy's grandchildren and children, especially Thomasine, who was the one who used to call him most often, and from Bill Boggs, his nephew in El Paso, Texas. William, Jimmy's oldest brother and only remaining sibling, sent postcards from Chicago. Following a tracheotomy he used a voice box and avoided phones. Jesse, Jimmy's other brother, died the year before he did. I would occasionally call or be called by Jesse's widow Addie.

The first thing I had to do back in Detroit was take responsibility for the chores that Jimmy used to do: vacuuming, mopping the kitchen and bathroom floors, rubbing down the car after it rains. Out of sheer necessity I learned to do these things, not with Jimmy's fervor or frequency but, as time passed, without the feeling that he was looking over my shoulder. My brother Eddie, who had been the closest to Jimmy, has been a great help with house and car problems. So I have gotten into the habit of eating dinner with him every Sunday, during which he gives me what I call "my weekly scold," reminding me of how Jimmy "spoiled" me, my lack of self-reliance in household and car maintenance, and the contradiction between my "politics" and my practices. Although he is five years my junior, he reminds me of my father at Sunday dinner, taking justifiable pride in his cooking and figuratively, if not literally, sitting at the head of the table. The visit has also become an opportunity to discuss his weekly letter from Bob in Hawaii, which often triggers family reminiscences. (Our recollections rarely jibe, which is to be expected considering the difference in our ages, which means a lot when you're growing up. There is also the matter of gender. Americans tend to view Chinese females as exotic and Chinese males as threats.) Bob never ceases to amaze me with his energy and zest for life. A year older than I and with an aortic aneurysm, he continues to seek and get jobs to supplement his Social Security, does major repairs on his unreliable cars, and swims a mile in the ocean once a week. Recently, as the Senior Volunteer of the Week, he was featured on Honolulu's Channel 4 conducting exercise classes at a senior center. Bob's resilience stems, I believe, from his generosity of spirit, which Jimmy often noted. In that sense he also reminds me of my father.

After a meal that tastes remarkably like the ones my father used to cook for our Sunday dinners in Jackson Heights, Eddie sends me home with a doggie bag containing food enough to last me almost all week and, in season, Chinese cabbage, Chinese winter melon, tomatoes, and cucumbers from his garden.

The hardest thing during the first year was not having someone to share the things I was seeing and doing. One of the greatest rewards of a long and close relationship is the opportunity it provides for experiencing everything twice—the doing or the seeing and then the retelling, for example, how an old friend or a neighborhood has changed. "You'd never guess who I met this afternoon!"

I especially missed our discussions, which often became struggles, about what was taking place in the city. Jimmy died a few months before Dennis Archer replaced Coleman Young as the Detroit mayor. So I never knew how he would have related to the new administration. Fortunately, I was able to discuss these matters with Dorothy Garner who, since retiring from her job as a corrections officer working with young prisoners, was able to spend more time at the Thurgood Marshall Elementary School in her neighborhood, motivating students to excel in their schoolwork and working especially with the sixth graders to give them the sense that the neighborhood and the city are theirs to build and rebuild. She was constantly creating ways to enlarge their belief in their capabilities, for example, encouraging them to write letters to the members of the City Council. One day we took a busload of her sixth graders to Oakland University to hear a talk by Lani Guinier, the lawyer whom President Clinton nominated as assistant attorney general for civil rights and then abandoned under pressure from the Right. Their participation in the discussion from the floor was a delight, especially to Ms. Guinier. Because Dorothy's main concern, like mine, was developing young people, we formed a Council of Elders, one of whose aims was to bring back the "granny porches" where youngsters could go for comfort and advice.

With Dorothy I could also discuss how much or how little difference the new mayor was making and compare the community meetings in her Pilgrim Village neighborhood with those in mine. I hadn't been enthusiastic about Archer as a mayoral candidate but voted for him because his opponent, Sharon McPhail, was endorsed by outgoing Mayor Young, and her election would have meant a continuation of at least some of his appointees and approach. The first few months of the Archer administration were encouraging. His inaugural speech was a passionate statement of concern for our communities and a call to Detroiters to get involved in the rebuilding of the city. The transition team that he appointed included people like Clementine Barfield, Errol Henderson, and Michelle Brown, co-coordinator of Detroit Summer. For his executive assistant he chose Angela Brown, a community activist in her thirties living not far from me, whom I had supported for City Council and who sometimes introduces me as her mentor. Archer's vision for Detroit, that it become a "world-class city," is very vague, but his energy and impression of openness have been refreshing after the rigidity and defensiveness of the Young administration in its last three terms.

As 1994 began, I sat back, waiting for the new opportunities to build the grassroots movement to recivilize Detroit, which I was sure would be forthcoming, not knowing what form they would take or how I would respond now that I was on my own, but confident that the same combination of chance, fate, and character that had blessed my life thus far would continue to lead me to make the right choices. In the past few years I have gotten into the habit of referring to one of my favorite passages in *The Sayings of Confucius*: "At fifteen I thought only of study; at thirty I began playing my role; at forty I was sure of myself; at fifty I was conscious of my position in the universe; at sixty I was no longer argumentative; and now at seventy I can follow my heart's desire without violating custom."[1]

I did not have to wait long. In February 1994 I was invited to an Environmental Justice Symposium in Washington, D.C. I decided to go because it suggested a new arena of struggle to build the movement. The Environmental Justice Movement was founded at the First National People of Color Environmental Leadership Summit held in Washington, D.C., in October 1991. At the gathering three hundred African American, Native American, Chicano, and Asian-Pacific Islander grassroots activists from all over the country gave a new definition to "the environment"—one that goes beyond land, air, and water to include all the conditions that affect our quality of life, including crime, unemployment, failing schools, dangerous working conditions, pesticide-filled foods. Through passionate struggles over the course of three days the delegates developed and adopted seventeen wide-ranging principles of environmental justice, among which are the right to participate as equal partners at every level of decision making, including containment at the point of production; opposition to the destructive operations of multinational corporations; and our responsibilities as individuals to make personal and consumer choices to ensure the health of the natural world for present and future generations. The coordinator of the planning committee was Rev. Charles Lee, the Chinese American research director of the United Church of Christ Commission for Racial Justice. One of the cochairs was Benjamin Chavis, at that time a member of the same United Church of Christ Commission and later executive director of the NAACP.

Because of Jimmy's illness I did not attend the October 1991 Summit. But the February 1994 symposium blew my mind. Participating were more than five hundred grassroots people of color from toxic hot spots all across the country, aggressively pressing their demands on the various government agencies responsible for environmental and health issues, including the Environmental Protection Agency (EPA), National Institute of Environmental and Health Services, and Center for Disease Control. At one point the delegates became so unmanageable that EPA director Carol Browner was forced to tear up her prepared speech and open the mike to statements from the floor. My roommate was a member of Jesus People Against Pollution in Columbia, Mississippi. That will give you an idea of the grassroots character of the gathering.

Back in 1987 Jimmy and I had participated in the Greens Conference at Hampshire College, but after the conference I stopped going to Greens meetings because I found the group too middle class, too rootless, too abstract. So it was good to find myself at an environmental gathering where grassroots people were fighting for their own lives and communities. I participated in the caucuses of the Asian American/Pacific Islander delegates who were particularly concerned with issues like the jellyfish babies born on the islands where the United States has conducted nuclear tests, the working conditions of Korean workers in Silicon Valley, and the polluted waters where Vietnamese and other Indo-Chinese communities fish for food. The energy of the plenary sessions was very different from that in black/white meetings where other people of color are absent or marginal. Black/white meetings carry the tremendous historical burden of past oppression and struggles against oppression and all the political tendencies that have emerged in the course of these struggles. So every word is loaded. By contrast, in meetings where African Americans are one people of color among others, there is the sense of the unknown and of a future still to be created, a twenty-first century America that is going to be dramatically different because we are becoming a nation of minorities in which the old Euro-American majority will be one minority among others. I had the same feeling when I was the keynote speaker at a Women of Color Symposium in Ann Arbor in 1994 where the planning committee included African Americans, Korean Americans, Chinese Americans, Latinos, Filipinos, and East Indian Americans. In the multicultural gathering I saw no sign of the competition to be the "most oppressed" that began to cripple the struggle in the 1970s.

I am awed by the potential in the Environmental Justice movement for deconstructing conventional concepts of knowledge, racism, and how we should make our livings. The enthusiastic participation of Native Americans especially brings a respect for elders and for traditional ways of making a living and relating to the universe, which is missing in most social change organizations. Because of their belief that every decision should be weighed in the light of its effect on seven generations, even a few Native Americans can change the character of a gathering. With every year Native Americans seem to speak with greater certainty that we are on the threshold of a great sea change because the West can no longer continue on its suicidal path of human and environmental destruction. For example, I shall never forget the dead silence at a breakout session during the February 1994 symposium after Tom Goldtooth, a Native American, stood up and put the experts and scholars in their place with a single sentence: "Your knowledge is based only on humans while ours includes that of animals and plants." Moreover, because the Environmental Justice movement emphasizes how people of color and poor people have suffered disproportionately from the toxic consequences of industrial production and expansion, it frees those at the bottom of our society to think about a more just society, not mainly in terms of a higher standard of living or more things but in terms of new ways of producing and new ways of living.

Prior to the emergence of the Environmental Justice movement, the "environment" was regarded by people of color and poor people as a white middle- and upper-class concern. Now, all over the country, people of color are using the principles of Environmental Justice to demand the cleaning up of toxic sites in their neighborhoods and to defeat the blackmailing attempts of corporations to place dioxin-producing incinerators in deteriorating neighborhoods in exchange for a few jobs.

Returning to Detroit, I began working with the local delegates to the 1991 and 1994 gatherings to organize Detroit's First Environmental Justice Gathering, which we convened in June 1994 with more than two hundred participants. Since then we have founded Detroiters Working for Environmental Justice (DWEJ), whose goal is to build a grassroots movement to challenge the threats to our daily lives where we live, work, and play *and* to rebuild Detroit safer, healthier, and more self-reliant. The core group of DWEJ, I believe, has the potential to develop into a new generation of "organic leaders" in the Detroit community. Predominantly African American women in their thirties and forties, they have more confidence in their ability to provide leadership and are therefore more open and less defensive than the generation that came to maturity at the peak of the Black Nationalist period. Many are college graduates but, unlike the intellectuals with Ph.D.'s who move from one city and one university to another in pursuit of their careers, they are rooted in Detroit and committed to using their skills and education to rebuild the city. My hope is that DWEJ can become a movement organization mobilizing local Detroiters, especially young people, to reclaim and rebuild our turf. For that to happen, however, it must avoid becoming a service provider as has happened to all too many so-called community-based organizations whose survival depends on foundation and agency funding.

Up to this time DWEJ has been chiefly occupied with getting itself organized, but we have also provided support and some assistance to local groups in struggle. We supported the Highland Park Citizens Empowered for a Clean Environment in defeating the attempt to site a medical incinerator in their impoverished community and West Side Concerned Citizens in defeating the siting of a hazardous soil remediation facility in their densely populated community. Alice Jennings worked with the Sugar Law Foundation and local activists in Flint, Michigan, to win a landmark consent judgment that provides for monitoring a $100 million incinerator endangering a predominantly African American and poor community. Environmental Justice principles were used to educate the judge in the case. In June 1995 we hosted an all-day conference on urban revitalization as one of a series of conferences cosponsored by the National Environmental Justice Advisory Council (NEJAC) and the EPA in five cities—Detroit, Oakland, Atlanta, Philadelphia, and Boston. In each city community residents were asked to present a community vision of urban revitalization to city, county, state, and federal officials. After touring Detroit and being presented with our vision, sponsors from the NEJAC and EPA agreed that, although Detroit was the most devastated of the five cities, it was also the most hopeful because we had the most far-reaching vision of a new kind of community-based economy, based on self-reliance and people power. One EPA sponsor said that our presentations changed her way of thinking so much that it stretched her humanity. In chairing the session I projected Detroit as a "Movement City." The presenters included Donele Wilkins, DWEJ chair; John Gruchala, former NOAR member; Julia Pointer, Detroit Summer Youth Volunteer; and Kaleema Hassan, poet and community activist.

Based on this vision, DWEJ is preparing for an Environmental Leadership Summit by bringing together community activists to organize around local environmental issues. In the process we are discovering the unique strengths of Environmental Justice organizing. It is holistic organizing because all the issues affecting local residents—health, safety, housing, economic development, education—are tied together by the principles of Environmental Justice. It renews society from the ground up because it is rooted in the places where people live, work, and learn—their homes, streets, neighborhoods, workplaces, schools—and depends on the knowledge that comes from daily experience.

In September 1995 I conducted an Environmental Justice Workshop at the AARP Empowering Minority Elders Conference in Buffalo, New York. Two months earlier, in July, more than seven hundred people had died in Chicago during the heat wave, most of them elders whose bodies were sometimes not discovered for days. The media emphasized the medical and social reasons for the tragedy. For example, as we get older, our body's ability to sweat, cool, and regulate heat deteriorates. Also nowadays the elderly poor often live alone in sweltering apartments in the inner city, many of them so fearful of being robbed of their few possessions that they keep their windows barred and closed. In the workshop I emphasized the special vulnerability of children and elders to increases in the ozone level due to smog and soot, which are created by excessive heat, and therefore the need for us to become active in the ongoing struggle around federal ozone-level standards. I also encouraged participants to get involved with schoolchildren in "greening" activities like creating community gardens and planting trees, which filter small particles and absorb harmful pollutants like ozone and sulfur dioxide out of the atmosphere. The discussion was very lively and empowering.

One of DWEJ's board members is Bunyan Bryant, whom I have known since the 1970s when he participated in a NOAR study group. Bunyan was one of the co-coordinators of the February 1994 symposium and has been a national endorser of Detroit Summer since its inception. A professor in the University of Michigan School of Natural Resources, he trains his students for environmental justice work in the community. Largely because of his efforts, University of Michigan students are anxious to work with Detroit community people on various projects, such as developing urban agriculture, preparing an Environmental Justice Report Card on Detroit, and making neighborhood assets surveys.

Toward the end of 1994 I was invited to become a stakeholder in Healthy Detroit as a representative of Detroit Summer. Healthy Detroit is part of the Healthy Cities Movement, a movement based on a broad definition of health to include the community, environment, education, transportation, the economy, and governance. The movement was launched by the World Health Organization in 1986 and reportedly has a presence in fifteen hundred cities around the world. In Detroit Mayor Archer is the honorary chairman, and the approximately one hundred stakeholders represent a variety of city departments, agencies, and community organizations. After the opening reception I was hesitant about becoming involved because overall the stakeholders struck me as briefcase-carrying types. But I decided to go to the first meeting and I am glad I did. When I rose to say that I was troubled by the absence of youth and grassroots participants, I was asked to submit a list of new invitees, and Angela Brown, the Mayor's executive assistant, suggested that we take special steps to reach young people. So, together with Allen Martin, former youth worker with SOSAD, we convened several youth meetings, one of which created its own Youth Vision of a Healthy Detroit.[2]

At this first meeting the stakeholders, in small groups of eight to ten, drew or wrote their dreams and hopes for a healthy Detroit on templates. A subcommittee, on which I served, then created a draft vision out of these ingredients, which was revised after discussion by the whole body. As in every group with any diversity, not everyone is equally passionate about every section of the vision that spells out goals for community, health, economy, education, environment, transportation and communication, art, culture and recreation, and governance in a healthy Detroit. But the preamble, which I drafted, gives a sense of what unites us and of the new spirit that is emerging in Detroit:

> We hold these values to be the foundation of a Healthy Detroit:
>
> We believe in the inherent worth, dignity and equality of every person and in the right of every person to our basic needs as human beings: love, good housing, food, health care, a clean and nurturing environment, meaningful and purposeful work, quality education, recreation, safety of person and property.
>
> We are proud of the rich ethnic and social diversity of our city and its environs and we pledge to promote mutual respect and cooperation and to build bridges between various ethnic groups and between Detroit and surrrounding communities.
>
> We are committed to live in harmony with one another in vibrant communities; to place special emphasis on the unique needs of our Youth and Elders; to respect our different beliefs; and to protect our natural environment for the sake of ourselves and future generations.
>
> At the beginning of this century, Detroit pioneered mass production. In the 1930s we pioneered the labor movement. During World War II we were the "Arsenal of Democracy." Now we gladly accept the opportunity and the responsibility to pioneer in making Detroit the model of a 21st Century Healthy City.

After developing our vision, assessing current reality, and setting priorities, the group divided into four self-selected Action Teams. Each team was challenged to develop action initiatives that were "trend-bending" and also met six criteria: systems changing, doable, understandable, not duplicative of existing efforts, leading to improved quality of life, and creating linkages and connections.

My team, the Youth Involvement/Citizen Activism team, is generally acknowledged to be the most dynamic. This is because, unlike the other teams, it includes the grassroots activists added as stakeholders at my suggestion, especially Norma Mayfield who was a member of WE-PROS and Gerald Hairston who is the live wire behind the Gardening Angels. Renaming our action team the Green Zones Initiative, we conceive our mission to be the creation of a movement whereby youth supported by the community take the lead in neighborhood-based community-building activities, such as reclaiming vacant lots and/or parks for gardening, street theater, playlots, cooperative markets, or other activities. I am the team's convener.

It is too early to tell how Healthy Detroit will develop. Sometimes at the general meetings I am troubled by the number of briefcase-carrying types who are present only or mainly because of their jobs. But then I think about the devastation of Detroit and the struggles that it is going to take to make it a healthy city. Experience has taught me that in order to create a movement, people of widely differing views and backgrounds need to come together around a vision, submerging ideological differences that will undoubtedly surface and create splits after the movement declines or succeeds. Meanwhile, I am encouraged by the fact that up to this time my suggestions have been well received and that there has been consensus on the vision and on the need for the initiatives to be trend bending and systems changing. It also interests me that none of the traditional radical groups is involved. Radicals will spend years working with workers and/or blacks with very backward ideas because according to their ideology these are the revolutionary social forces, but even though they themselves very often come from the middle classes they are unable to exercise the same patience with people like themselves. On the other hand, I am increasingly convinced that to create twenty-first-century cities and a twenty-first-century civilization out of the chaos in which we are now engulfed, it is going to take the imaginations, the skills, and the commitment of very diverse people from many different ethnic groups and very different backgrounds.

At this point our Green Zones Initiative is the only one that explicitly sees its mission as creating a movement. That is because our vision and our activities did not just begin with Healthy Detroit in 1995. They go way back to the struggles of the 1980s and the early 1990s out of which Jimmy and I, along with other Detroiters, began to sense that the only realistic future for the city lies in developing collective self-reliance. Long before Healthy Detroit was formed, thousands of Detroiters were taking over vacant lots to plant gardens and the youth volunteers of Detroit Summer were working with the Gardening Angels. All over the city people have been saying for years that we have to bring life back into our neighborhoods by producing for ourselves and creating our own community markets. We can't keep going to the suburbs to purchase our basic needs. We have to restore reverence for life in our young people by involving them in nurturing living things.

The embodiment of this vision is Gerald Hairston who was born in Martinsville, West Virginia, raised in Detroit, and graduated in the 1960s from Eastern High School just down from our house on Field Street. A former foundry worker who recently turned fifty, Gerald makes his living doing odd jobs because he wants to be free to do what is closest to his heart, literally rebuilding Detroit from the ground up. Over the years Gerald has become the nucleus of a wide-ranging informal network of community-minded people who are convinced that Detroit's revival begins with community gardens and that the more than eight thousand vacant lots in the city are a boon rather than a disaster because we can take them over to grow our own food. With Jim Stone, his Finnish American buddy who is my upstairs neighbor, he is a transmission belt between elders and youth, tilling the land of the elders, driving them to meetings, and introducing young people to the excitement of growing and making things for yourself. With Gerald's aid and encouragement, parents and teachers at the Howe Elementary School in my neighborhood are creating the Kwanzaa Gardens based on the seven principles of unity, self-determination, collective work and responsibility, cooperative economics, purpose, creativity, and faith. Other schools are beginning to follow suit. It is clearly an idea whose time has come.

Working with Gerald and the Gardening Angels, I feel that I am part of and helping to renew the hope that made Detroit so vibrant in the 1940s, 1960s, and early 1970s and that withered away in the course of Coleman Young's five terms as mayor. Individual hope was what once brought generations of Detroiters to the city to work in industry. Now it is becoming collective. Our network of believers and practitioners is multicultural and intergenerational. Coming from all different backgrounds, with diverse religious beliefs, we are united in our conviction that revitalizing Detroit begins with producing our own food in community gardens and developing community markets. So we cooperate, interact, overlap, interlock. Several months ago David Hacker of the Hunger Action Coalition brought about a half dozen of us together to form the Detroit Growers Support Group (DGSG), including the Kwanzaa Gardeners who are preparing to produce and market a Kwanzi-Q Sauce based on the recipe of a Howe science teacher. The DGSG will provide technical support and financial assistance to the student, teacher, and parent creators of the Kwanzaa Gardens so that they can organize themselves as a cooperative and become the springboard for other co-ops.

The enthusiasm of these groups is infectious. It comes mainly from our commitment to Detroit. But it is reinforced by the realization that we are part of a national movement. In the 1980s civic leaders in Chattanooga, Tennessee, brought together residents from all sections of the city, including high school students, to project a vision of Chattanooga 2000.[3] One of their most important conclusions was that to save the city we have to bring the country back into the city. Nationally, there is also a growing recognition that education needs to be turned around to combine theory and practice in community building along lines that I have long advocated. Our present system based on preparing children for individual upward mobility into the system by making "us" like "them" is destroying our communities because those who succeed in the system leave the community while those who don't take out their frustration and sense of failure in acts of vandalism. It is leaving too many children behind, labeling too many as suffering from attention deficit disorder and therefore requiring Ritalin, and widening the gap between the very rich and the very poor. The main cause of youth violence and addiction to drugs, I believe, is youth powerlessness. We have turned young people into parasites with no socially necessary or productive roles, nothing to do for eighteen years but go to school, play, and watch TV. Rich and poor, in the suburbs and the inner city, they are, as Paul Goodman pointed out years ago, "Growing Up Absurd,"[4] deprived of the natural and normal ways of learning the relationship between cause and effect, actions and consequences by which the species has survived and evolved down through the millennia. Then we wonder why teenagers lack a sense of social responsibility. Schoolchildren need to be involved in community-building activities from an early age, both to empower themselves and to transform their communities from demoralizing wastelands into sources of strength and renewal. Their heads work better when their hearts and hands are engaged. Thus, students at El Puente for Peace and Justice in Brooklyn, New York, are working to improve their communities by cleaning up vacant lots and planting community gardens. "It gets their cognitive juices running," according to Chester Pine, a university professor of education and public policy.[5] In south central Los Angeles, following the explosion over the verdict in the Rodney King beating trial in the spring of 1992, students at Crenshaw High School started restoring a weed-infested garden behind the football field in order to provide food for the hungry and homeless. With the help of their science teacher and a volunteer business consultant, this initiative has since blossomed into the Food from the Hood Company, producing and selling their own salad dressing using ingredients from their garden.

I have learned a lot from participating in the process by which the Healthy Detroit group moved from visioning to action initiatives. Ever since I participated in a Futuring Conference at the University of Michigan conducted by Bunyan Bryant during Martin Luther King Week in 1992, I have wanted to explore this process further. "Futuring," says Bunyan,

> is based upon Hope. Hope is the force that propels us through life, giving us nourishment, purpose, and energy for our actions. Futuring causes us to question assumptions we make about life. Through the techniques of writing and sharing stories, creating images and participating in role-plays, we can simulate events as though we are already in the future. Our objective in such visualizations is not to predict the future, but to perceive potential futures in the here-and-now and to conceptualize what it will take to get from here to there. . . . There is no monopoly on futurism. Every person has the childlike ability to spontaneously create.[6]

At the 1992 futuring conference I created a vision of Detroit Youth in the year 2032. A record-breaking snow storm had occurred on the eve of the celebration of Martin Luther King's 103rd birthday, I wrote, but people had no trouble getting to the celebration because young people, organized in Youth Block Clubs, had assumed the right and responsibility to keep the streets clean and safe for the community, especially elders. The vision goes on to describe how community work had been incorporated into the school curriculum, so that elementary schoolchildren working with elders were growing most of the food for the city while middle and high school students were doing most of the work of preparing and serving food in the community, and so on.[7] Having that vision in my head and heart since the futuring conference has helped me time and again to project youth activities that transform young people at the same time that they improve the community.

My participation in futuring has also given me a new insight into the role that visionary leadership can play in movement building and has helped me to move beyond the NOAR approach to leadership that was still deeply embedded in Marxist-Leninist concepts of the vanguard party. All over the world today we are obviously living in that in-between period of historical time when great numbers of people are aware that they cannot continue in the same old way but are immobilized because they cannot imagine an alternative. I am constantly impressed by the number of people from all walks of life who once they take time to think about it realize that community is the key to our survival as individuals and as a nation and who also suspect that our communities are being destroyed by the global economy.[8] However, I have also noticed that few people are ready to come right out and challenge the global economy, probably because the government and the multinationals are so aggressively propagating the myth that globalization is inevitable and sacred, making any resistance to it both futile and subversive, comparable to refusing to go along with anti-Communism during the Cold War. However, popular recognition that the global economy is depriving Americans not only of jobs but of control over our communities and even our country is growing, as was demonstrated by labor's opposition to NAFTA (the North American Free Trade Agreement) in the fall of 1994 and Patrick Buchanan's exploitation of the issue during the 1996 primary campaign for the Republican presidential nomination. Many labor leaders are aware that the global economy is robbing communities of control over our own destiny (former AFL-CIO president Lane Kirkland said as much during the anti-NAFTA struggle), but they do not link up with local communities to struggle against NAFTA and other legislation, because they do not understand or accept that the struggle to rebuild and control our communities is the wave of the future.[9] That is why they are on the defensive and behind the eight ball in so many struggles, for example, the recent Detroit newspaper strike. On the other hand, as so often happens, it is right-wing reactionaries like the Militiamen and Pat Buchanan who have their fingers on the pulse of the people.

Attacking these groups for their reactionary politics will only increase their defenders and supporters. As we wrote back in the early 1970s, "we must not allow our thought to be paralyzed by fear of repression and fascism. One must always think realistically about the dangers, but in thinking about the counter-revolution a revolutionist must be convinced that it is a 'paper tiger.'"[10] What we need to do instead is encourage groups of all kinds and all ages to participate in creating a vision of the future that will enlarge the humanity of all of us and then, in devising concrete programs on which they can work together, if only in a small way, to move toward their vision. In this unique interim time between historical epochs, this is how we can elicit the hope that is essential to the building of a movement and unleash the energies that in the absence of hope are turned against other people or even against oneself. That is why more and more I have been conducting and urging others to conduct visioning workshops using this basic format. When people come together voluntarily to create their own vision, they begin wishing it to come into being with such passion that they begin creating an active path leading to it from the present. The spirit and the way to make the spirit live coalesce. Instead of seeing ourselves only as victims, we begin to see ourselves as part of the continuing struggle of human beings, not only to survive but to evolve into more human human beings.

In December 1996, for example, the Detroit Growers Support Group hosted a "Visioning Urban Agriculture in Detroit" Kwanzaa Potluck that brought together a diverse group of forty-two people, including Gardening Angels, Master Gardeners from Michigan State University, and city workers in Farm-a-lot and Adopt-a-Park programs. Participants, divided into six groups, were asked to answer three questions: What would urban agriculture in Detroit look like in 2001? What programs do we need to make this vision a reality? What are you doing now to move Detroit toward this vision and what will you commit yourself to doing in 1997? Called on to use their imaginations and give free rein to their hopes, participants envisaged Detroit as a Garden of Eden and a gardening city rather than a gambling one; kids learning to think and developing a work ethic; children and elders working together; the weeding out of negatives like crime and hunger; cleaner, healthier neighborhoods; cleaner environment, and so forth. For the coming year participants mainly recommended more of what they were already doing, more networking, more outreach, especially to youth, more greenhouses, more visioning sessions. Two participants, already working with young people to create a Garden of Eden, committed themselves to creating ten more such gardens.

Since the Visioning gathering the Detroit Growers Support Group has hosted a potluck every other month, matching needs (gardening equipment, skills, seeds) with resources, developing a database, and attracting new individuals and groups. In the process we have been creating an urban agricultural network. Meanwhile, for the thousands of Detroiters affected by cutbacks in welfare and food stamps an alternative food system based on locally grown, processed, and marketed food is urgently needed. So, guided by our vision, we are developing food security and community sustainability programs to meet this need.

In 1995 I was invited to become a member of the New Detroit Race Relations Committee, one of whose goals is to celebrate the multicultural richness of Detroit and develop multiethnic leadership of the city. I was also asked to join the City of Detroit Youth Commission, which plans to use the seven Kwanzaa principles to nurture and guide our youth and empower young people through involvement in life-enhancing activities. As I accepted these invitations, I couldn't help wondering whether, if Jimmy had been alive, I would have been asked to serve and whether I would have answered affirmatively. My sense is that neither would have happened. I would not have been invited because Jimmy was seen as too confrontational and too threatening, and if they had invited me and not Jimmy, I would not have accepted, because I would have been convinced that they were disrespecting him.

As I have begun to work with insiders as well as outsiders, I have become more conscious of the difference between Jimmy's political style and mine. Jimmy had a gift for sharpening contradictions and for confrontation that I used to envy and still do. For example, I can't imagine myself standing toe to toe with Coleman Young, while there was nothing that Jimmy enjoyed more. For much of the 1980s and early 1990s that was what he was doing, not face to face, but through the media and letters to the editor. My tendency, as a woman and a Chinese American, is much more to intervene by trying to draw people outside the paradigm in which they are trapped by making a suggestion or asking a question, for example, "Don't you think that we ought to address the question of technology and the global economy?" or "I am concerned that we are not including young people." In general, I have been pleasantly surprised by how willing people are to listen, not only or even mainly because of my style but because so many people recognize that we cannot go on in the old ways and are looking for new ways to think and to act. For example, the media subcommittee of the New Detroit Race Relations Committee is now developing an innovative Eyes on the Media program to be cosponsored by New Detroit, WTVS (the local public broadcasting station), and Wayne State University School of Journalism. The program is based on the explicit recognition of the media as a player in the ongoing process of rebuilding Detroit and therefore the need to encourage the development and creation of new ways of reporting that will make it a more active and responsible player in this process. Sometimes I have the feeling that people who knew Jimmy and me see my conduct as a deviation or maybe even betrayal of Jimmy's more challenging posture. On the other hand, I am confident that if Jimmy had lived, he would have adapted his style to the new situation. He was very good at asking questions to open up the minds of people and also in proposing the strategies and tactics appropriate to different situations. As time has elapsed, however, what he might be doing is no longer the issue. I am on my own and have to do what comes most naturally to me.

This sense of being on my own was reinforced in the spring of 1995 when I went back to New York for my sixtieth (and first) Barnard College Reunion and to visit Jackson Heights, the neighborhood in Queens where I grew up. I had been reading about the expanding Asian American population. I had even been the keynote speaker at an Asian/Pacific Islander women's conference at the University of Michigan in 1992 where, among other things, I was amazed at the number of twenty-year-old Asian women named Samantha, Tiffany, and Melanie. But seeing so many Asian Americans with my own eyes on what was once my own turf affected me far more than "going back" to China had done in 1984. At the alumnae of color reception Judith Schapiro, the college president, told me that Asians are now 25 percent of the Barnard student body and that the percentage is even greater at Wellesley. When you have been a member of a minority so small as to be almost invisible, it is almost intoxicating to wake up one day and discover that your ethnic group is developing such a critical mass that what it does matters. Immediately upon my return to Detroit I sat down at my computer, typed in the title of the first chapter, and began writing the first draft of this autobiography.

Nineteen ninety-five was a very exciting year because I was creating my own identity as an activist in the Detroit movement and at the same time making new discoveries about my identity as an Asian American. It was also a very painful year. On Easter Sunday Dorothy Garner, who inspired our anticrackhouse marches, died suddenly of a blood clot. She was sixty-five. Since Jimmy's death we had become very close. In August Henry Richardson, Ellen's husband and the father of our goddaughter, Stephanie, had a fatal heart attack as he was sitting in the family room watching TV. Then in September Ping Ferry died at the age of eighty-four.

At Dorothy's funeral every seat in the large church was taken. It was even hard to find standing room. The young people with whom she had worked talked about how Mama G motivated them to do well in their schoolwork and to participate in the strengthening of their community. City Council President Maryann Mahaffey and Councilwoman Alberta Tinsley Williams lauded her activism and commitment to Detroit. Ozell Dupree, the principal of Thurgood Marshall Elementary School, announced that the new playground at the school would be named for her. I talked about Dorothy's vision of a Detroit made up of strong communities where we looked out for each other and depended on one another. There was a lot of sadness in the church, but there was also a lot of hope because during her lifetime Dorothy had done so much to combat violence and hate and greed.

Ping Ferry's death also left a big hole in my life. For years we had been exchanging notes, clips, papers, books. Because he was a native Detroiter and especially resonated to Jimmy's goal of recivilizing Detroit, I took great pleasure in sending him every little piece of news about the emerging movement. To countless progressives and activists he was known, in the words of a *New York Times* obituary, as "Muckraker, Peacemaker,

Curmudgeon, Champion of Justice, Kind Heart, Splendid Friend. To the very end he kept doing the impossible, the right thing." I had been expecting him to go on for a long time. When Shea and I made our annual stopover in Scarsdale on our way back from Maine in the fall of 1994, Ping seemed in his usual good health and humor. James Ward, a professor of American history at the University of Tennessee in Chattanooga, had undertaken to write his biography, and I was able to leaf through the thick file of letters that they had been exchanging. It bothered me when I heard that Ward expected to take eight years to finish the book. But it didn't seem to bother Ping—maybe because he was enjoying the correspondence so much and/or he expected to be around at its completion.

Speaking at Ping's memorial celebration at the Century Club in New York City on October 24, I recalled that Ping was not one to mince words. In 1968 he wrote an article in which he said "Farewell to Integration" because he had given up not on blacks but on whites.[11] He didn't flinch at backing unpopular causes. When most intellectuals were reluctant to challenge the dictatorship of technology, he suggested revising the U.S. Constitution to control technology. He could not be intimidated by the FBI. When FBI agents came to him seeking information about the radical activities of his friends or acquaintances, Ping would call the person involved to listen in on the conversation. Ping never decided which groups or causes to support on the basis of their chances for success. As he put it, "It is not necessary to succeed in order to strive."

In November 1994 I invited twenty-eight movement-oriented, theoretically minded African Americans to gather in Detroit to respond to the question, "What Fire Can a Younger Generation Catch from the Work of James Boggs?" The phrase *catch fire* was borrowed from a Sonia Sanchez poem with her consent. Joining the Detroit participants were Vincent and Rosemary Harding from Denver, Robert Lucas from Chicago (he led the 1966 march into Cicero), Jim Embry from Lexington, Kentucky, Marcia Brown from Newark, Jim and Barbria Jackson from Muskegon, and Bunyan Bryant and Jim Chaffers from Ann Arbor. Altogether there were six elders, seven young people under twenty-five, and the rest in their thirties, forties, and early fifties. I acted as facilitator. The discussion reminded me of the black community as it was prior to desegregation—multiclass and multigenerational where elders were respected and everyone was accepted and felt safe because unity was so necessary for survival in the face of the common oppression. One concrete idea that came out of the gathering was Alice Jennings's suggestion that we create a James and Grace Lee

Boggs Community Foundation to develop community leadership. Since then, the James and Grace Lee Boggs Center to Nurture Community Leadership has been incorporated with an interim board of directors. The interim cochairs are Shea Howell and Donald Boggs, Jimmy's youngest son who is also president of the Organization of School Administrators and Supervisors. So far the board has raised the money to purchase the house at 3061 Field Street, which has been the site of so many movement-building activities over the years, and a core group is now working on clarifying the mission and work of the center. We have decided on a five-year time frame and are generally agreed that the center will be a Community Think Place and Visioning Center that through dialogues and multimedia will honor the work of community people, bring together elders and young people, and open up the minds especially of young people and children to rethink fundamental ideas about revolution, politics, and citizenship because, as Jim Jackson puts it, "Ideas are the beginning of power. Ideas that enlarge people have been taken out of the struggle. Instead people use ideas to blame others for what is going on instead of to empower themselves."

After Minister Louis Farrakhan and Rev. Benjamin Chavis issued the call for the Million Man March in the fall of 1995 a number of people called to ask how I thought Jimmy would have responded. I said that he probably wouldn't have gone to Washington since he much preferred neighborhood marches, and that his main concern probably would have been how the spirit of the march would or could be embodied in concrete community-building activities. Personally, I rejoiced at the march because it seemed obvious to me that the overwhelming majority of those who went to Washington did so because they were looking for ways to renew and redeem themselves and begin accepting responsibility for transforming their relationships with their women, children, and communities.

Following the march several hundred Detroiters met and formed the Million Man March organization. Every morning Tom Pope began his four-hour talk show on WCHB 1200 AM, addressed primarily to the African American community, with the pledge shouted out by a million men on the steps of the U.S. Capitol Building on Monday, October 16, 1995.[12] (He still does.) Hundreds of men called in to report what they were doing with their children and families and in their communities, for example, organizing anticrackhouse marches. With the passage of time, participation and enthusiasm have declined. But changes in this popular talk show reflect developments in community thinking as a result of the march. There is less blaming of others and more sharing of constructive activities. When callers complain, the host challenges them to stop acting like victims and assume responsibility for creating positive changes in our communities, especially by organizing small businesses.

The weekend after the march I spent in Binghamton, New York, conducting a workshop in community renewal on Saturday and giving the Sunday morning sermon at two churches with predominantly white congregations. I am glad to say they greeted me enthusiastically when I said:

> This Sunday, in churches all across the country, African Americans are rejoicing over last Monday's Million Man March and the energy which it has generated for blacks to assume responsibility for rebuilding their families and communities. I believe that in this church we should be rejoicing with them because we have been talking this morning about reviving our souls, and the next hymn we will be singing celebrates "All who love and serve your city / All who bear its daily strife and stress / All who cry for peace and justice / All who curse and all who bless."

An article by Farrakhan, written before the march to encourage participation, ended with this declaration of self-reliance: "We will make the shoes and cobble our feet. We will make the suits and dresses to clothe our backs. We will make the underwear, shirts, socks and other necessities that are now being imported from China, Japan, Korea and Italy. We will take responsibility for food, clothing and shelter for our people, in a partnership with government, a partnership for mutual progress."[13] Since the march I have heard a lot of talk in Detroit about economic development but mainly in terms of individual entrepreneurship. I have heard practically no discussion of cooperatives or of the tremendous role that the black church could play in helping to build a neighborhood economy. For example, on Mack Avenue, up the street from my house there are more than a dozen churches and a few party stores surrounded by vacant lots on a one-mile strip. If each church made a survey of the productive skills of its members, I am confident they would discover plenty of cooks, bakers, hatmakers, dressmakers, and mechanics as well as carpenters and plumbers and bricklayers who could do the work necessary to renovate neighborhood houses and train young people in these skills. Using organizing skills that parishioners have honed over years of running bake sales and chicken dinners, these churches could begin organizing bazaars where neighborhood residents could purchase their needs inside the community instead of going to the suburbs to spend their money. Through this process, over a period of time, the human infrastructure of discipline and trust for a new cooperative economy could be built as well as the initial capital for more permanent enterprises that can be supplemented by loans from credit unions and community banks. But unfortunately, making this kind of contribution to the redevelopment of our communities appears to be the furthest thing from the minds of black preachers.[14] Like most Detroiters they cannot see us producing for our own needs. They would be happy with suburban-type malls in the inner city where we could purchase cheap consumer goods manufactured in Asia, Central America, and Eastern Europe. They do not realize that the freedom to make important choices begins with producing your own food and other basic necessities so that you are not dependent on external forces beyond your control. Ultimately, I believe, their eyes, minds, and hearts will not be opened up until they realize that the only way to save our children from drug addiction and violence, in the suburbs as well as in the inner city, is by involving them in productive work from an early age.

Meanwhile, there are some signs of progress. The Cass Corridor Food Co-op, Detroit's largest and oldest grocery co-op, has been doing so well in its present quarters with 2,300 square feet of selling and storage space that the board is looking for a new site providing 12,000 square feet. Co-op board president is Njia Kai, a cinematographer who runs the Cinema Cafe, a member of the Red Door Collective. Around the corner from the Food Co-op Ann Perrault and Jackie Victor, producers of Women's Coffeehouse, have just opened the Avalon Bakery. Organic breads baked on the premises will be sold retail at the site and wholesale to restaurants across the city. Herbs for the breads will be purchased from the Gardening Angels. Great Lakes Hours, which prints its own currency, is uncovering skills within the community and creating an economic network among approximately 140 Detroiters who use Great Lakes dollars to exchange services (for example, babysitting, word processing) and products (for example, baked goods, meals). The Inner City Subcenter conducts a Share Program whose members can purchase groceries at wholesale prices in exchange for two hours of volunteer work a month.

On March 6, 1996, I was proud to be in the first group of twenty-four community people arrested for civil disobedience at the Detroit News Agency organized by Readers United, a group of community activists formed in order to make clear the stake of the community in a just settlement of the Detroit newspaper strike. I was in good company. Our group included City Council President Maryann Mahaffey and three bishops. Ilaseo Lewis, a former NOAR member, was among the friendly arresting officers who treated us very gently because they seemed to understand that they also have a stake in struggling against huge absentee corporations like Gannett and Knight-Ridder. Since then, more than 250 other community activists have been arrested for putting their bodies on the line. In April 1996 I wrote an article for a community newsletter pointing to the need to develop new strategies to stop absentee corporations from destroying our communities in their limitless greed for profits:

> Corporations were not even mentioned in the U.S. Constitution and there was a time in our history when they were understood to be mere fictions, subordinate to the sovereign people, chartered by states and prohibited from functioning except as specifically permitted. Given this history we need to develop strategies to dismantle especially harmful corporations, to reduce their size, to prohibit them from owning other corporations, from making contributions to election campaigns and from all lobbying—with the goal of empowering local work forces and local communities. . . . [For example,] we have to question whether the Detroit police, who are paid by the taxes of Detroit citizens should be used *at all* to protect the property of absentee corporations who have no respect or loyalty to Detroit or to the unions and other institutions which have been won through the blood, sweat and tears of our parents and grandparents.[15]

Early in 1996 Jim Jackson called from Muskegon one night and suggested that I accompany him on his second trip to Cuba as part of the U.S./Cuba Labor Delegation to witness the May Day parade.[16] The Cuban revolution has always been close to my heart. I was with Kathleen Gough in spirit when she led the demonstration at Brandeis University shouting "Kennedy to hell, up with Fidel!" during the Cuban Missile Crisis. But I had never been to Cuba. The visit turned out to be more inspiring and thought-provoking than any of the movement-related overseas trips that I have made over the years. In part, this was because I went without any preconceptions or expectations. But mainly it was because our visit took place at a time when the Cuban people, by redefining and recommitting themselves to the struggle for socialism, have begun to recover from the crisis caused by the collapse of the Soviet Union. In the process they have been creating an alternative vision for Third World countries and perhaps even for deindustrialized cities like Detroit, which resemble Third World cities in so many ways.

The highlight of the one-week visit was attending the Seventeenth Cuban Trade Congress, the theme of which was *Se Puede Multos*

Juntos (Together We Can). As visitors we sat in a large hall with a huge screen so that we could view the proceedings while listening to simultaneous translations in English. The Congress gave me a sense of how real and how spiritual the struggle for socialism is in Cuba—how it is energized not only by the necessities of physical survival but by love and the profound conviction that working together we can resolve our contradictions, create a better and more just world for ourselves and especially for our children, and advance the evolution of the human race. It was awesome to watch the nineteen hundred multicolored Cuban delegates and the nine hundred black and brown revolutionaries from all over Latin America, women and men, listening intently so that they could take the message of revolutionary struggle back to their communities and homelands. The very thoughtful opening presentation was made by Pedro Rose Leal, the short, powerfully built leader of the Cuban Trade Unions whose physical appearance contrasts so sharply with Fidel's. While stressing the need for discipline and efficiency, he also made clear that Cuba was going to continue on the socialist path because it refuses to accept the capitalist view that selfishness and individualism are an irrevocable part of human nature. Sitting next to him on the dais throughout was Fidel, clapping, smiling, frowning, and intervening when he felt like it. In a brief greeting the president of the World Federation of Trade Unions, based in Brazil, contrasted the priority that Cuba, in the midst of economic crisis, has given to health and education, with the desperate struggle of workers in Western countries to maintain hard-won gains in health and education, the mushrooming individualism and violence throughout the capitalist world, and the millions of children reduced to homelessness and prostitution in Latin America and Asia. "Today," he said, "Cuba remains as the free territory of America."

Among the reports from the field was one by a young man, Amando from Guantánamo, who explained how he was able to produce milk for children in his area by building a mesh fence to corral some wild cows, recruiting some young people, and getting an old man to teach them how to milk. There was a delightful back and forth between Fidel and his brother Ramon (who looks like a somewhat absent-minded white-haired Fidel) debating whether it was better to use oxen ("take the bull by the horns," as Ramon put it) rather than tractors to increase the sugar harvest. At one point, after a delegate urged the development of more specialists, Fidel jumped in. "Everybody wants to be an intellectual, a university graduate," he said. He added:

> It is a vice, an invention of the devil. The Soviets built huge columns, consuming skills they could have used to build three factories. [This was the only criticism I heard of the Soviet Union.] Who is going to plant the potatoes, bury the dead, sweep the streets? In some schools they have a different janitor to wash the floors, the windows, the doors. There are at least 800 parts of the body. Do we need a specialist for each one?

I was reminded of Dorothy Garner's insistence that we have to stop thinking that every problem has to be solved by an expert.

The Congress ended with a two-and-a-half-hour speech by Fidel that was both philosophical and down-to-earth. It was the first time that I had heard him speak at length, and I felt enormously privileged to be watching the seventy-year-old bearded revolutionary, the only one of the great twentieth-century leaders who is still with us, still developing his ideas before our very eyes, still combining theory and practice. I was especially fascinated by Fidel's explanation of the difference between Socialism and Communism. It brought back to me Jimmy's critique of American radicals in *The American Revolution* for their failure to take seriously Marx's concept of Socialism as a particular stage in the revolutionary struggle when workers use state power to rapidly develop the productive forces in order to create the abundance necessary for Communism. "It was always understood," Fidel said, "that Socialism is one thing and Communism another." At the same time, he spelled out how "the Cuban people have acted in the spirit of Communism without an economy that could admit of Communism." As he spoke, I could visualize Marx, the theoretician, sitting at his desk in the middle of the nineteenth century and drawing a clear and distinct line between Socialism and Communism as systems or "isms" as contrasted with Fidel who has led a real revolution to power in the middle of the twentieth century. Through life-and-death struggles against U.S. imperialism, Fidel has learned that unless Socialism is imbued with the spirit of Communism, it is only property relations, and the people will not defend it. So the Cubans have not only struggled for economic development; they have manifested Communist spirit in stressing moral and not only material incentives, giving priority to the needs of the working people, and taking no measures without consulting all the people, especially the workers. This is the spirit of the revolution that cannot be defeated.

Listening to the Cubans talking about self-sufficiency, self-reliance, and the need to struggle against individualism and selfishness reminded me of Jimmy's conviction that the only realistic perspective for cities like

Detroit is collective self-reliance and making do with our own resources. It is clearly an idea whose time has come for people in the nations to the South (who were known as the Third World during the Cold War), a combination of decentralization and centralization that offers an alternative to the capitalist road of economic development imposed by the International Monetary Fund and multinational capitalism and causing such impoverishment and environmental devastation in Africa and Latin America. In Cuba, for example, the initiative to build a day-care center often comes from the people in the neighborhood, who then get some of the material resources from the state. It is a model that can be applied in the inner cities of the North as well as in Subsaharan Africa.

One evening we attended a block party and, as the community activist in the delegation, I was asked to make the presentation. I said that I had come to Cuba to learn how to make the revolution in the United States that would liberate people all over the world. I described the devastation in Detroit following our abandonment by multinational corporations, the struggles we are engaged in to rebuild our communities and our cities from the ground up, and said I wished I could bottle the spirit of love of people, love of community, and love of country that I found in Cuba and take it back with me. I really meant it. Unless we find a way to develop this spirit in the struggle to transform America, we are lost. I asked Nkenge Zola who went to Cuba to cut sugarcane some years ago what she sees as the difference between the Cuban and the black nationalist approach to self-determination. "When blacks in the United States talk about self-determination," she said, "they are talking from a victim mentality and about a way to remain capitalist and get more things for themselves." By contrast, "Cuban self-determination and self-reliance are imbued with a socialist, anticapitalist perspective." Jim Jackson says that

> when the Cubans talk about self-determination they are talking about the unity, the solidarity, the collectivity that make it possible to create a better world. Things aren't perfect but they are grappling with their contradictions and trying to resolve them. I am tired of black folks running around complaining about what we don't have and should have instead of how we can work together to make things bettter. It is becoming a question of survival. We are at the point where if we don't move, we won't have any country, any society left. We can't resolve our contradictions by negativity, by complaining.

At the same time we need to keep clear the difference between where we are in Detroit and where the people are in Cuba. In the first place, Cuba has never been industrialized; it is still primarily an agricultural country. The people still lack many elementary necessities. By contrast, Detroit, despite the desolation of many neighborhoods, is not a Third World city. It was at one time the crown jewel of the Industrial Revolution. Moreover, the large majority of Americans, including those living in poverty, have many more things than we need and are still chasing after more, even though the more that we already have has made us enemies to one another. Accepting the values of our capitalist consumer economy, we now identify freedom with the amassing of material goods and are unable to distinguish between needs and wants. Every day we are losing more of the sense of community and of what it means to be a human being that has made possible the survival of the human race. At the same time, we are threatening the biosphere by our excessive use and abuse of natural resources and widening the gulf between the very rich and the very poor, not only domestically but internationally, between the nations of the North and those of the South, in the process creating for ourselves problems and struggles over immigration that encourage the formation and expansion of fascist groups within our own country.

Second, the Cuban people have made a revolution; they have taken state power away from the Batistas who ruled Cuba on behalf of U.S. capitalists and U.S. imperialism. Their Together We Can spirit is the fruit of that revolution and the continuing struggle to defend it for nearly forty years. On the other hand, we have not made a revolution in the United States, and there is no possibility that we will do so unless we overcome our individualism and materialism and transform ourselves into socially responsible and mutually respecting individuals. The best way for us to do this is to create community-based economies to meet our basic needs, in the course of which we can learn how to make the crucial distinction between needs and wants and increase our people power so that we can eventually take power away from the multinational corporations that control the global economy.

In Detroit and other deindustrialized cities of North America, we increasingly face the choice between two roads of economic development. If we go along with the global economy, which means the export of jobs to wherever labor is cheapest, our deindustrialized cities will become increasingly dependent on casino gambling and new sports stadiums as our local "industries," both of which reinforce capitalist values, consumerism, and individualism and thus lead to more crime, violence, and disunity. The alternative is to build resistance to the global economy by producing for our own needs, growing our own food, and producing our own clothing and shelter in environmentally friendly worker-owned and cooperative enterprises, thus setting an example of productive work for our youth and at the same time creating community and empowering people.

When I became a movement activist more than half a century ago, the only two economic systems competing for public support were capitalism and socialism. Capitalism maintained hegemony because of its tremendous productivity but was suspect because of the Great Depression and the existence of poverty in the midst of plenty. After World War II, most newly independent countries looked to the Soviet Union as a model because it had achieved rapid economic and technological growth through state ownership of the means of production and central planning. Today the Soviet Union has collapsed, and a growing number of people are repelled by capitalism because it is so obvious that the transnational corporations controlling the global economy are only interested in amassing profits and have no loyalty to any community, city, country, or even the biosphere on which all our lives depend. But they see no alternative.

It is under these circumstances that what is going on in Detroit has grabbed the imagination of people all over the country. All kinds of people perk up their ears when I start describing what we are doing. I think this is because at a gut level many realize that the twentieth-century industrial city, symbolized by Detroit, is dead and that all Americans have a stake in our pioneering struggle to make Detroit the model of a twenty-first-century city. When I overheard a woman say recently, "I feel that God has Detroit in his plans," I thought to myself, "That is one way of putting it."

Witnessing and participating in the rebuilding of Detroit, I am often reminded of our conversations in Maine a quarter of a century ago when we wondered whether it was still appropriate to use the word *revolution* for the kind of struggles that we saw ahead for the American people, struggles that would have to begin from the bottom up, with changing ourselves first. In recent years, especially with the collapse of the Soviet Union, it is becoming clearer to me that just as we should not try to create twenty-first-century cities that look like twentieth-century ones, we should not try to make twenty-first-century revolutions on the model of twentieth-century ones. Twentieth-century revolutions have been based essentially on a Marxist-Leninist strategy of capturing state power and then struggling to involve the people in the reorganization of the economy from below. In pursuing this strategy what has obviously happened is that the state has swallowed up the energies of the people at the bottom, despite the best intentions and valiant efforts of gifted and committed revolutionary leaders like Lenin, Mao, and Castro who struggled unceasingly to mobilize the participation and leadership of the workers and peasants. As we approach the new century, we must have the courage to learn from their experiences.

We also need to learn from developments in Africa in the past three decades. In the 1950s and 1960s we rejoiced as African nations like Ghana, Kenya, Nigeria, and Guinea won their political independence from British, French, and Belgian colonialism. We were convinced that with leaders like Ghana's Kwame Nkrumah, Kenya's Jomo Kenyatta, and Nigeria's Nnamdi Azikiwe in political power Africans would finally begin to control their own destiny after centuries of being looted first for slave labor and then for gold, diamonds, and copper by Western imperialism.

Today, except for South Africa where apartheid has been abolished and Nelson Mandela is head of government, our images of Africa are almost all negative. In Rwanda hundreds of thousands of men, women, and children have been massacred in ethnic conflicts between the Hutus and the Tutsis. Warlords in Liberia and Somalia, competing for state power with guns and tanks, are committing unspeakable atrocities against the civilian population. Meanwhile, for everyone except a tiny elite, economic conditions are worse than they were under colonialism. In 1960 most African nations were producing their own food; today they are dependent on imports from abroad. Millions of children starve to death every year, and tens of thousands of others are being orphaned by the AIDS epidemic. Every year more forests are being destroyed and hundreds of square miles of cropland are being turned into desert. The situation is so terrible that some people are even thinking of the period under colonialism as "the good old days."

All of this has happened because over the past thirty years transnational corporations supported by the International Monetary Fund and the World Bank have taken over large sections of the African continent to grow coffee, bananas, peanuts, and the other commodities that consumers in the United States and Europe crave. But those governing the newly independent nations must also bear some responsibility. A mostly male elite who had been educated in the West, they have been preoccupied with achieving and maintaining state power. Their only model for economic development has been Western-style rapid modernization. With little respect for the villagers in the countryside who are still the overwhelming majority of the African population, most African governments have spent twice as much of their annual budgets on arms purchases from the United States, the Soviet bloc, and China as they have on agriculture.[17]

Precisely because their situation has become so desperate and so hopeless, millions of villagers have been struggling during the past ten years to take their future into their own hands and to create an African way of development. All over sub-Saharan Africa villagers are growing their own food, planting trees, creating better ways to use draft animals, discovering plants that grow more quickly, diversifying cereal, fruit, and vegetable crops, building village granaries. They are determined to eliminate hunger by the end of this century, and they are convinced they can do it. As Mamadou Cissokho, the Senegal peasant leader, explained, "We are optimists because we have experienced hunger. You in Europe allow yourselves the luxury of pessimism because you don't know what hunger is." In sub-Saharan Africa there are literally tens of thousands of grassroots groups that are practicing this kind of self-reliance. The size of the groups varies: fifteen to twenty in some cases, one to two hundred in others. Everywhere women are in the majority and providing the leadership because in Africa women are the ones who have traditionally been responsible not only for raising the children but for gathering and growing food for subsistence. In Kenya there may be fifteen to twenty-five thousand women's groups. These groups are also changing centuries-old social relationships—not only encouraging women and young people to speak up but regulating dowries and other costly ceremonies celebrating birth, marriage, and death.[18]

The African movement is so inspiring not only because of the huge numbers involved but because it is based on their own culture as expressed in their proverbs. First and foremost, they have consciously rejected the concept of themselves as victims. "We are not victims without a solution," they say. "Every problem has a solution." They quote the African proverb, "The only failure is not to try" and the Arab proverb, "He who wants to do something finds a way; he who doesn't finds an excuse." They are self-critical. They realize they have participated in creating erosion of the soil by not feeding the land as their ancestors did. They are wary of accepting money from foundations before they learn to stand on their own feet. They appear to be guided by the spirit of Patrice Lumumba, the leader of newly independent Congo who, before his assassination by CIA agents, warned that "It is easy to shout slogans, to sign manifestos, but it is quite a different matter to build, manage, command, spend days and nights seeking solutions to problems." Instead of seeing the movement in terms of mass demonstrations as we did in the 1960s, they see themselves building the movement individual by individual, small groups networking with one another. As Susan Kusema of Zimbabwe put it, "Self-reliance starts with yourself, by doing something for yourself and succeeding. Then your friend will come and ask you what you did and will join you, and then another, and then another, and one day you have a movement." They cite the African proverbs, "Many little people in many small places undertaking many modest actions can transform the world" and "When the ants unite their mouths, they can carry an elephant."

Reflecting on our activities in Detroit and on what I had been reading about agricultural and tree planting groups in sub-Saharan Africa and Grameen banks in Bangladesh,[19] I wrote an article in the spring of 1995 titled "The Look of 21st Century Revolution," which begins: "This is an exciting time for movement activists. All over the world ordinary people are engaged in initiatives to make the places where they live, work and play, safer, healthier and more life-centered." These initiatives, I wrote,

> are a new historical phenomenon. Going beyond rights, people are collectively and locally exploring new ways of meeting our material needs and at the same time living in harmony with each other and with nature. Therefore they have the potential for creating an alternative to both the state-controlled socialist economies which have manifestly failed and the competitive global economy which is proving so destructive to local communities and the natural environment.

In Detroit, I said, there has been an explosion of meetings and groups all over the city, all focused on the rebuilding of Detroit:

> These groups have certain qualities. The most important is hope. In the last 15 months there has been a rebirth of the hope with which all movements begin. . . . City-wide meetings are mixed, reflecting the ethnic diversity of the city. Those meeting seem to understand that the rebuilding of Detroit will take time—there is no quick fix—and that we cannot deal with issues in isolation. Community, environment, employment, education, culture, governance are all interconnected. There is a shared understanding that our basic needs are spiritual as well as physical. We need love and respect for one another and a renewal of our spiritual and civic lives, as much as we need a roof over our heads and food in our bellies. Our focus is Detroit, the local space for which we are responsible, but we are also aware that what we do in Detroit has national and even international implications. There is more humility than in other groups struggling for fundamental change that I have known in the past, a recognition that the challenge we face is so monumental that no one individual, no one group has the answer; we need to listen to one another. Also in sharp contrast to the civil rights and Black Power movements of the 60s, women play a promi-

> nent role in almost all groups, and even those convened by corporate sponsors recognize the need for community input. . . .
>
> Thus quietly but unmistakably out of the devastation created by de-industrialization and years of grasping at straws by an administration unprepared for corporate abandonment, a new concept of economics as if people, communities, nature and spirit matter is emerging in the center of the First World as it is emerging at the grassroots level in Africa and Bangladesh.[20]

As I move toward my mideighties, I thank my lucky stars (and my parents) for my continuing good health. (To stay in shape I do water aerobics at a local recreation center three times a week.) I still love going to meetings that are part of the ongoing movement to rebuild, redefine, and respirit our cities from the ground up. But I am not the prime mover and I know that if I were no longer around, things would continue. When you reach my age, that is a situation much to be desired. So while I am not thinking of cutting out, I know that if I were to fall ill or die tomorrow, there is a new generation already in place struggling for their own dreams of a better world, which will contain many of the ingredients of the vision that Jimmy and I have struggled to bring to life—and also expand it. I still make speeches and write articles. People still come to Field Street for information and materials. But I am no longer a coordinator or organizer. I am more a resource person, a connector, whose concerns and admonitions are listened to, although not necessarily accepted. My sense of urgency is undiminished, but I am more able to lay back like a Taoist, feeling less compelled to play the Confucian role of making sure that things are correct or straight.

I rejoice at the changing of the guard and at the fact that the new generation, which is beginning to discover its mission, is more open than the generation that led the movements of the 1960s. I wish Jimmy, Lyman, Kathleen, Dorothy, and Ping were here to rejoice with me. I am glad that I am still around not only as a participant but as a griot to pass on the story of how we got to this place—because, to paraphrase Kierkegaard, if the future is to be lived, the past must be understood.

Notes

Introduction

1. From "Reassurance," in Alice Walker, *Revolutionary Petunias and Other Poems* (New York: Harcourt Brace Jovanovich, 1973).

1. East Is East—Or Is It?

1. Jack Chen, *The Chinese in America* (San Francisco: Harper and Row, 1980), 26, 139; Loren W. Fessler, ed., *The Chinese in America, Stereotyped Past, Changing Present* (New York: Vantage, 1983), 86.

2. Ling Lew, *The Chinese in North America: A Guide to Their Life and Progress* (Los Angeles: East-West Culture Publishing Association, 1949). I am indebted to Bill Fishman and Jeff Stansbury for obtaining this book for me from the East Asia division of the University of California at Los Angeles Library.

3. *Los Angeles Times*, February 1, 1997.

4. Peter Nien-Chu King, "When Know-Nothings Speak English Only," in *The State of Asian America*, ed. Karin Aguilar-San Juan (Boston: South End Press, 1994), 125 ff.

5. "Among American-born married women ages 20–29 in 1990, 67 percent of Asian-Americans and 38 percent of Hispanic women married outside their ethnic group, according to Zhenchao Qian of Arizona State University." *New York Times Magazine*, September 29, 1996, 97.

2. From Philosophy to Politics

1. Recently I was delighted to find economist-ecologist Herman E. Daly and philosopher John B. Cobb Jr. using Whitehead's "fallacy of misplaced concreteness" to support the need for a paradigm shift in economics. Present-day economics, the two authors explain, is founded on the abstraction of economic man (*homo economicus*) who is only

interested in satisfying his own material needs, hence the need to return to concrete men and women who are many-sided human beings, living in communities and caring about others. Herman E. Daly and John B. Cobb Jr., *For the Common Good: Redirecting the Economy Toward Community, the Environment, and a Sustainable Future* (Boston: Beacon Press, 1989), 25–117.

2. "If Socrates had been reincarnated in New York's garment district, he would have turned out to be Weiss." Dick Cavett and Christopher Porterfield, *Cavett* (New York: Harcourt Brace Jovanovich, 1974), 95.

3. Kant's "principle that every man is to be regarded as an end in himself is a form of the doctrine of the Rights of Man, and his love of freedom is shown in his saying (about children as well as adults) that 'there can be nothing more dreadful than that the actions of a man should be subject to the will of another.'" Bertrand Russell, *A History of Western Philosophy* (New York: Simon and Schuster, 1945), 705.

4. G. W. F. Hegel, *The Phenomenology of Mind*, trans. J. B. Ballie (New York: Macmillan, 1931); Hegel, *Science of Logic*, vols. 1 and 2, trans. W. H. Johnston and L. G. Struthers (New York: Macmillan, 1929). I have two copies of *Phenomenology* because one has been thumbed through so often that it has fallen apart.

5. George Herbert Mead, *The Philosophy of the Act* (Chicago: University of Chicago, 1938); *The Philosophy of the Present* (Chicago: University of Chicago, 1932); *Mind, Self and Society* (Chicago: University of Chicago, 1934); *Movements of Thought in the Nineteenth Century* (Chicago: University of Chicago, 1936).

6. Grace Chin Lee, *George Herbert Mead: The Philosopher of the Social Individual* (New York: King's Crown Press, 1945).

7. Carl Sandburg, "Chicago," in *Complete Poems* (New York: Harcourt Brace, 1950).

8. St. Clair Drake and Horace R. Cayton, *Black Metropolis: A Study of Negro Life in a Northern City* (New York: Harper and Row, 1962).

9. See Philip S. Foner, *Organized Labor and the Black Worker 1619–1973* (New York: Praeger, 1974), 240.

10. Titled "A Labor Base for Negro Struggle," it put forward what I understood to be the party line that "to achieve even their democratic rights, the Negroes, under revolutionary working class leadership of Negroes and whites, must achieve the socialist revolution." *The New International*, August 1942. Reading the article today, I am amazed and ashamed at the arrogance with which I, a pip-squeak intellectual fresh from the university, pontificated on the Negro struggle. I probably would not have had the nerve to say such things to a live audience of blacks, but it was relatively easy to write them in a magazine read by other radicals. As I observe the certainties and the self-righteousness of young radicals today, I am reminded of myself in those days. We live and learn.

11. At my urging, for example, he wrote a series of articles reviewing the labor and revolutionary movement during World War I. Harry Allen and Ria Stone, "World War I in Retrospect: An Historical Examination," *The New International*, June-July, August 1942.

3. C. L. R. James

1. Preface, C. L. R. James, *The Black Jacobins: Toussaint L'Ouverture and the San Domingo Revolution* (New York: Vintage, 1963).

2. In those days we called C. L. R. James "Jimmie." In the many books and articles now being written about him he is usually referred to as James. However, because Jimmy Boggs was called either Jimmy or James, I have gotten into the habit of referring to CLR by his first three initials. He was called "Nello" by family members, intimates, and West Indian friends. I never called him that. Letters from me and other members of the

Johnson-Forest Tendency usually begin "Dear J:". Between 1938 and 1952 he wrote in party publications under the names J. R. Johnson, A. A. B., and J. Meyer.

3. C. L. R. James, *The Case for West Indian Self-Government* (New York: New York University Place Book Shop, 1967; originally published in 1933); *Minty Alley* (London: Secker and Warburg, 1936); *World Revolution, 1917–1936: The Rise and Fall of the Communist International* (New York: Pioneer Publishers, 1937); *A History of Negro Revolt*, Fact Monograph no. 18 (London, 1938); *The Black Jacobins: Toussaint L'Ouverture and the San Domingo Revolution* (London: Secker and Warburg, 1938); Boris Souveraine, *Stalin: A Critical Survey of Bolshevism*, trans. C. L. R. James (New York: Longmans, Green, 1939).

4. Frederic Warburg, *An Occupation for Gentlemen* (London, Hutchinson, 1959), 182. Vanessa Redgrave of the distinguished theatrical family takes sharp issue with C. L. R. James's politics but was also impressed by his passion for Shakespeare: "He loved and studied Shakespeare as did no Englishman I have ever met other than Tony. One evening he enthralled a group of writers at my house with a two-hour lecture on *King Lear*." Tony, Redgrave's first husband, is Anthony Richardson, the internationally known film and stage director. *Vanessa Redgrave: An Autobiography* (New York: Random House, 1994), 183.

5. C. L. R. James, *Mariners, Renegades and Castaways: The Story of Herman Melville and the World We Live In* (New York: C. L. R. James, 1953), chap. 7. This chapter, titled "A Natural but Necessary Conclusion," is CLR's story of his incarceration on Ellis Island in 1952 and his plea to be allowed to remain in the United States. It was omitted from the edition published by Bewick in 1978.

6. Karl Marx, "The Historical Tendency of Capitalist Accumulation," in *Capital*, vol. 1, chap. 33 (Chicago: Charles H. Kerr, 1906).

7. They have been published by Blackwell under the title *Special Delivery: The Letters of C. L. R. James to Constance Webb, 1938–1948*, ed. Anna Grimshaw (Oxford: Blackwell, 1996). Constance's originals are in the Schomberg Collection in Harlem.

8. The phrases "natural and acquired powers" and "be his payment high or low" and the descriptions of mutilation and degradation come from volume 1 of *Capital*, especially chaps. 15 and 25. I don't give page references because few people use the same edition of *Capital*. The one I use is an early-twentieth-century edition published by Charles H. Kerr, which is falling apart.

9. *Capital*, chap. 35.

10. This passage from part I of the *Communist Manifesto* is as challenging today as it was when it was first written in 1848.

11. Paul Romano and Ria Stone, *The American Worker*, 1st ed. (New York: Johnson-Forest Tendency, 1947; 3rd ed., Detroit: Bewick, 1972).

12. For details of this discussion see *Leon Trotsky on Black Nationalism and Self-Determination*, ed. George Breitman (New York: Pathfinder Press, 1978). The discussion is also reproduced in part in C. L. R. James, *At the Rendezvous of Victory* (London: Allison & Busby, 1984), 33–64.

13. See Nelson Peery, *Black Fire: The Making of an American Revolutionary* (New York: New Press, 1994) for a firsthand account of the uprisings by black servicemen and the violence between black and white soldiers and black soldiers and white civilians during World War II.

14. C. L. R. James, *The Future in the Present* (Westport, Conn.: Lawrence Hill, 1977), 126–27.

15. Marx, *The Economic and Philosophic Manuscripts of 1844*, 3rd ed., ed. Dirk Jan Struik (New York: International Publishers, 1967), 187.

16. *Essays by Karl Marx, Selected from the Economic and Philosophic Manuscripts* (New York: Johnson-Forest Tendency, 1947). The English translation of all the 1843–44 manuscripts did not appear until nearly two decades later. See note 15.

17. News and Letters, Raya's group, published her English translation of Lenin's notes on Hegel in a 1955 pamphlet, Raya Dunayevskaya, *Lenin's Abstract of Hegel's Science of Logic* (Detroit: News and Letters, 1955). Eight years later, an English translation by Clemens Dutt became available in V. I. Lenin, *Collected Works, Philosophical Notebooks*, vol. 38, ed. Stewart Smith (Moscow; Foreign Languages Publishing House, 1963).

18. V. I. Lenin, *The State and Revolution, Selected Works*, vol. 7 (New York: International Publishers, n.d.).

19. These notes were originally known as the "Nevada Document" because they were written in 1948 when CLR was in Reno, Nevada, fulfilling the six-week residency requirement to get a divorce from his first wife, Juanita, so that he could marry Constance Webb. Facing Reality, the name assumed by CLR's supporters after our split in 1962, published a first edition of CLR's *Notes on Dialectics* in mimeographed form in October 1966 and a second edition in May 1971. In 1980 they were published as *Notes on Dialectics: Hegel, Marx, Lenin* by Allison and Busby in London and Lawrence Hill in the United States with an introduction by C. L. R. James. There is an air of unreality about this introduction because Raya is not referred to by name but as "one collaborator" and there is no reference to any previous publication or any indication of deletions or additions. In fact, references to G. and Grace that appear in the original text were deleted. In the introduction CLR also says that when he wrote the notes he had been familiar with "Lenin's 1915 article *On the Question of Dialectics* [*sic*]" "for nearly fifteen years." This is contradicted by CLR's own account on page 99 of the same edition: "I remember on my journeys between Missouri and New York stopping at Washington and Rae calling out an at-sight translation from Lenin's Russian notes and my scribbling them down." That dates CLR's first encounter with Lenin's notes as 1941 or 1942 when he was traveling to and from southeast Missouri to work on the sharecroppers' strike.

20. See "Letter to the Congress," December 25, 1922, in Lenin, *Collected Works*, vol. 36 (Moscow: Progress Publishers, 1966), 597. This letter is sometimes referred to as Lenin's "Final Testament."

21. CLR's insightful analysis of the contrast between Trotsky's and Lenin's methodology begins on page 99 of his *Notes on Dialectics*.

22. In Lenin, *Selected Works in Twelve Volumes*, vol. 11 (New York: International Publishers, 1967).

23. I still keep a copy of Lenin's *Philosophical Notebooks* by my bedside. Excerpts from his notes on Hegel are appended to a speech I gave in 1982 to the NOAR (National Organization for an American Revolution) Cadre Training School titled "Developing Revolutionary Theoreticians."

24. James, *Notes on Dialectics*, 117.

25. *The Invading Socialist Society* (Detroit: Bewick Editions, 1972). (Bewick Publications can be ordered from Bewick Press, P.O. Box 14140, Detroit, MI 48214.) See also *Dialectical Materialism and the Fate of Humanity*, in C. L. R. James, *Spheres of Existence* (Westport, Conn.: Lawrence Hill, 1980), 70ff; and *State Capitalism and World Revolution* (Chicago: Charles H. Kerr, 1986).

26. Castoriadis, a practicing psychoanalyst since 1974, has become an internationally known French intellectual. His book *The Imaginary Institution of Society* was published by MIT Press in 1987. In 1987–88 more than two dozen intellectuals contributed to a volume dedicated to his work titled *Autonomie et auto-transformation de la société: La philosophie militante de Cornelius Castoriadis*, published by the Revue européenne des sciences sociales. A three-volume edition of his *Political and Social Writings*, translated and edited by David Ames Curtis, was published by the University of Minnesota Press in 1988 and 1993. I have not seen Cornelius since 1978, when he spent a couple of days with Jimmy and me in Detroit, but periodically he sends me a copy of the latest volume in his series on *les Carrefours du labyrinthe* (Crossroads in the Labyrinth) (Paris: Editions du Seuil).

27. *Indignant Heart* was subsequently reprinted twice, in 1978 by South End Press and in 1989 by Wayne State University Press. In both cases Charles Denby, which was the pen name assumed by Si Owens as the worker-editor of *News and Letters*, was named as the author. Although the actual writing of *Indignant Heart* was done by Constance Webb James, her contribution has never been publicly acknowledged. Jimmy deliberately pointed out Constance's contribution in a preface that he was asked to write for the Wayne State edition, but his preface was not published.

28. *Mariners, Renegades and Castaways*, 105.

29. This chapter was left out of the Bewick edition published in 1978.

30. C. L. R. James, Grace C. Lee, Pierre Chaulieu, *Facing Reality* (Detroit: Correspondence Publishing, 1958; reprinted by Bewick, 1974).

31. "Against this monster [state power] people all over the world, and particularly ordinary working people in factories, mines, fields and offices, are rebelling every day in ways of their own invention. Sometimes their struggles are on a small personal scale. More effectively, they are the actions of groups, formal or informal, but always unofficial, organized around their work and their place of work. Always the aim is to regain control over their own conditions of life and their relations with one another. Their strivings, their struggles, their methods have few chroniclers. They themselves are constantly attempting various forms of organization, uncertain where the struggle is going to end. Nevertheless, they are imbued with one fundamental certainty, that they have to destroy the continuously mounting bureaucratic mass or be destroyed by it." *Facing Reality*, 3.

32. Selma's influence on CLR during their long partnership has not been sufficiently recognized. A forceful personality with many years of experience working in the plant and in the Johnson-Forest Tendency, Selma had strong convictions about the role of women and how revolutionary organizations should function, and these are reflected in CLR's work during the 1950s and 1960s. At the same time she typed his manuscripts, organized his papers, and hosted luncheons for the many activists, writers, and dignitaries (including Martin Luther King Jr.) for whom a trip to London would be incomplete without a visit to the venerable Pan-African Marxist. After their separation Selma became the leader of the International Wages for Housewives Campaign. Her published works include *The Ladies and the Mammies: Jane Austen and Jean Rhys* (Bristol, England: Falling Wall Press, 1983).

33. Sometime in the 1970s, for example, I received a phone call from Harold Cruse expressing his concern because he had recently witnessed a collapse by CLR in a hotel lobby in Ghana and nobody seemed to know whom to contact.

34. My speech, titled "C. L. R. James: Organizing in the U.S.A. 1938–1953," is included in *C. L. R. James: His Intellectual Legacies*, ed. Selwyn R. Cudjoe and William E. Cain (Amherst: University of Massachusetts Press, 1995).

35. Eric Williams, *Capitalism and Slavery* (Chapel Hill: University of North Carolina Press, 1944).

36. See Walton Look Lai, "C. L. R. James and Trinidadian Nationalism," in *C. L. R. James's Caribbean*, ed. Paget Henry and Paul Buhle (Durham, N. C.: Duke University Press, 1992), 199. See also Ivar Oxaal, *Black Intellectuals and the Dilemmas of Race and Class in Trinidad* (Cambridge, Mass.: Schenkman, 1982), 182.

37. Kwame Nkrumah, *Towards Colonial Freedom* (London: Heinemann, 1962).

4. Jimmy

1. Charlotte Perkins Gilman, *Women and Economics* (Amherst, N. Y.: Prometheus, 1994).

2. Edgar Snow, *Red Star over China* (New York: Modern Library, 1944).

3. Quoted in Bill Moyers, *The Language of Life* (New York: Doubleday, 1995), 93.

4. Reprinted as one article titled "The World and the Jug" in Ralph Ellison, *Shadow and Act* (New York: Vintage Books, 1972).

5. Originally published in an abbreviated form in 1904, Robert Tressel's *The Ragged Trousered Philanthropists* has been reprinted in various editions in England and in the United States by Monthly Review in 1962. Jimmy's copy, a gift from Ping Ferry, was the Monthly Review edition. José Ortega y Gasset, *The Revolt of the Masses* (New York: Norton, 1993).

6. C. L. R. James, *World Revolution: 1917–1936* (New York: Pioneer Publishers, 1937).

7. Ruby shared an early draft of this poem with us in Maine during the 1991 Labor Day weekend. The latest version, which she reads in public performances, is titled "I Miss the Russians" and includes these verses:

I miss the Russians as they used to be.
How dare the evil empire leap into the arms of
"One nation under God"—so fast?
Flatten humanity's aspirations, dimensions.
How dare the Union of Soviet Socialist Republics
refuse to be the opposite pole—devil incarnate—
enemy of overproduction, unemployment,
recessions, depressions,
deep and high crime and all other glories of
multinational capitalism?

The world needs oppositions—
a decent agitator class, man,
to help keep some part of it honest, sister,
to—like that main thing in the washing machine,
the righteous agitator—get the dirt out.

Everybody on the same side of the ship—
or trying to get there
will sink the sucker.
You wasn't all bad, bro.
Wish you coulda hung in there and made your
commitment work.

Tell you something. Bet before long
you'll wish you'd stay on your side of the
human equation.
Stop thinking the grass on the football field is
always real grass. Stop being jealous of the cousins
who turned their noses up at you
when you were bleeding, sweating, overthrowing
czars and royalty and exclusivities.

You weren't all wrong.
You had a lot going for you.
You shoulda hung in there.
Then maybe this democracy business could
someday, really do
the of-the-for-the-by-the-
with-the people thing.
History is sure happening, honey.

8. In a perceptive chapter in *Race Rebels* titled "To Be Red and Black" (New York: Free Press, 1994), Robin Kelley describes how the African Americans who became

Communists brought their own politics to the party: "These black radicals created a kind of hybrid movement that combined Garveyism, Pan-Africanism, vernacular cultures and traditions, and Euro-American Marxist thought. Their actions and the ways in which they constructed their identities should lead us to question categories that we too frequently regard as mutually exclusive in African American communities: nationalism and communism, religion and communism, Pan-Africanism and internationalism" (11).

9. *Shadow and Act*, 234.

10. In his 1969 "Homage to Ellington on His Birthday," Ralph Ellison writes, "Even though few recognized it, such artists as [Duke] Ellington and Louis Armstrong were the stewards of our vaunted American optimism and guardians against the creeping irrationality which ever plagues our form of society. They created great entertainment, but for them (ironically) and for us (unconsciously) their music was a rejection of that chaos and license which characterized the jazz age associated with F. Scott Fitzgerald and which has returned once more to haunt us as a nation. Place Ellington with Hemingway, they were both larger than life, both masters of that which is more enduring in the human enterprise: the power of man to define himself against ravages of time through artistic style" (*Going to the Territory* [New York: Random House, 1986], 219).

In the same vein Columbia University professor Ann Douglas contrasts "Euro-American cultural pessimism" with the "Aframerican cultural optimism" expressed in the writers of the Harlem Renaissance. In a brilliant and moving chapter of *Terrible Honesty: Mongrel Manhattan in the 1920s* (New York: Farrar, Strauss and Giroux, 1995), she interprets the blues as a form of religion, tracing them back to the hopes and fears of the black masses in the post-Civil War period: "Although they were never propaganda, they were protest art, a protest both against the particular historical set of circumstances and tactics that relegated black men and women to the lowest ranks of American society, and against all such power arrangements as violation of the deepest truths the human spirit is capable of apprehending" (117).

11. The film produced by Frances Reid for Jimmy's memorial celebration opens with this classroom scene.

12. In *The City in History* (New York: Harcourt, Brace & World, 1961), Lewis Mumford stresses the critical role played by those who have been raised in agricultural communities in the development of the city: "The order and stability of the village, along with its maternal enclosure and intimacy and its oneness with the forces of nature, were carried over into the city; if lost in the city at large, through its overexpansion, it nevertheless remains in the neighborhood. Without this communal identification and mothering, the young become demoralized; indeed their very power to become fully human may vanish, along with neolithic man's first obligation—the cherishing and maturing of life. What we call morality began in the mores, the life-conserving customs of the village. When these elementary bonds dissolve, when the intimate visible community ceases to be a watchful, identifiable, deeply concerned group, then the 'We' becomes a buzzing swarm of 'I's,' and secondary obligations become too feeble to halt the disintegration of the urban community. Only now that village ways are rapidly disappearing throughout the world can we estimate all that the city owes to them for the vital energy and loving nurture that made possible man's future development" (15). The working class that Marx valued so highly in the nineteenth century still had close ties to the agricultural community. This was brought home to me in 1948 when riding through the French countryside en route from Le Havre to Paris we passed a factory at the end of the workday and witnessed hundreds of workers mounting their bikes to ride to their nearby homes.

13. From "Reassurance," in Alice Walker, *Revolutionary Petunias and Other Poems* (New York: Harcourt Brace Jovanovich, 1973).

14. Raya Dunayevskaya, *Marxism and Freedom* (London: Pluto Press, 1958).

15. For example, in *25 Years of Marxist-Humanism* by Raya Dunayevskaya, published in 1980 by News and Letters Committees, we learn that in 1949 CLR had waited

four months before acknowledging receipt of Raya's note pointing out the importance of "Lenin's new appreciation of the 'self-development of the concept'" and that when Stalin died in 1953, [Grace] Lee, "far from seeing any concern with that event on the part of American workers, made her point of departure the fact that some women in one factory, instead of listening to the radio blaring forth the news of Stalin's death, were exchanging hamburger recipes." This kind of postmortem polemics was one of the least savory legacies of the old Left.

16. *Guide to the Raya Dunayevskaya Collection* and *Guide to the Supplement to the Raya Dunayevskaya Collection, Marxist-Humanism: A Half-Century of Its World Development*, Wayne State University Archives of Labor and Urban Affairs (Chicago: News and Letters, n.d.).

17. See Robert Conot, *American Odyssey: A Unique History of America Told through the Life of a Great City* (New York: Morrow, 1974), 430, 454.

18. Reggie later became president and Conrad vice president of Wayne County Community College. Gwen and Conrad's children stayed with us on Field Street when she went to the Soviet Union with Women Strike for Peace in 1962. Today, Conrad Mallett Jr. is the chief justice of the Michigan Supreme Court.

19. James Boggs, *The American Revolution: Pages from a Negro Worker's Notebook* (New York: Monthly Review Press, 1963).

20. Ibid., 93.

21. Ibid., 43–44.

22. "A Critical Reminiscence" by James and Grace Lee Boggs in *C. L. R. James: His Life and Work*, ed. Paul Buhle (Chicago: Sojourner Truth Organization, 1981).

23. CLR's behavior was so weird that I was ashamed for him, especially since Kathleen was meeting him for the first time. He and Selma were returning from a visit to Ghana; Kathleen, Jimmy, and I, together with Conrad Lynn and his wife Yolanda, had come from the United States and were waiting on the patio of their home in Port of Spain for them to come from the airport. CLR was well known for his graciousness on meeting people for the first time or after a long separation, asking you questions about your work and family and listening avidly to your response. Imagine our surprise, therefore, when immediately upon their arrival, CLR barely exchanged greetings, demanding instead that Selma fetch a tape recorder so that we could all listen to the speech he had made in Ghana! From then on it was all downhill. We spent our time exploring Trinidad, keeping our distance from CLR and the house.

24. See James and Grace Lee Boggs, Freddy and Lyman Paine, *Conversations in Maine: Exploring Our Nation's Future* (Boston: South End Press, 1978), 281 ff.

25. See Grace Lee Boggs, "Thinking and Acting Dialectically. C. L. R. James: The American Years," *Monthly Review* (October) 1993.

26. W. H. Ferry, *Caught on the Horn of Plenty*, Center for the Study of Democratic Institutions *Bulletin* (January) 1962.

27. Ping would often share our materials with his friends who included Thomas Merton. A June 12, 1963, letter from Merton contained this comment: "The little Correspondence sheet struck me as admirable. Not consoling but alive and vocal and independent. Though a lot of things said in letters were wrong and absurd. But the basic underlying theme is there and no one can dispute it. I was almost tempted to write Boggs a letter about it, but I just have too many letters to write, and can't get involved in new correspondence if I can help it. But you might tell him if and when you write. His column was particularly good." A few months later, on October 28, 1963, he wrote: "I am always impressed by the stuff that emanates from Detroit. I think Jim Boggs is a great mind, a very promising political commentator. There is a real vision there." *Letters from Tom*, chosen and edited by W. H. Ferry (Scarsdale, N. Y.: Fort Hill Press, 1984).

28. Since it was the 1970s, the women at the Branscombe gathering met in a caucus and prepared this testimonial to W. H. Ferry: "In recognition of his extraordinary feat in moving from a Victorian view of women to his present stance, namely one in which his expectations of women are no less exacting than his expectations of men, which—God knows—few of either sex can meet. That he has made so major a turn-around well after reaching maturity while surrounded by men sot in the ways of an earlier age earns him even greater kudos."

29. See *Conditions of Peace: An Inquiry,* ed. Michael Shuman and Julia Sweig (Washington, D.C.: Exploratory Project on the Conditions of Peace, 1991). The collection contains essays on security, democracy, ecology, community, and economics by Grace Boggs, Robert Borosage, W. H. Ferry, Dietrich Fischer, Sharon Howell, David Orr, Arjun Makhijani, Michael Shuman, and Julia Sweig. Makhijani's essay on economy has since been expanded into a book providing a holistic theoretical analysis for a new generation of activists: *From Global Capitalism to Economic Justice: An Inquiry into the Elimination of Systemic Poverty, Violence and Environmental Destruction in the World Economy* (New York and London: Apex Press, 1992).

30. Some of these were sent to me by Ping. Others came into my possession after Ping's death when Carol invited some of his friends to pick and choose from his voluminous library. "He could never leave the house and return without a book," she said. Ping used to lend me single issues of *Resurgence,* the magazine of Small Nations, Small Communities and the Human Spirit, published in Britain, on condition that I return them. Now his file of *Resurgence* is in my library.

31. E. F. Schumacher, *Small Is Beautiful* (New York: Harper Colophon, 1975).

5. "The City Is the Black Man's Land"

1. *Jerimoge* literally means the "traveler." For Shrine members it means "Holy Patriarch" and "Leader of the Black Nation."

2. Pearl Cleage, *Deals with the Devil, and Other Reasons to Riot* (New York: Ballantine, 1994).

3. His sermons from the 1960s are collected in *The Black Messiah* by Albert B. Cleage Jr. (New York: Sheed and Ward, 1968). My audiotapes of some of his sermons are in the Boggs Collection of the Wayne State Archives.

4. The audiotape of my speech "Who Will Blow the Trumpet?" is available from the Center for Cassette Studies and is also in the Boggs Collection of the Wayne State Archives.

5. Muhammed Ahmed, "Malcolm X and the Black Liberation Movement," unpublished paper.

6. *Malcolm X Speaks,* ed. George Breitman (New York: Grove Press, 1963), 14; *The Autobiography of Malcolm X,* written with Alex Haley (New York: Grove Press, 1966), 278 ff.

7. See Clayborne Carson, "March on Washington," chap. 7 in *In Struggle: SNCC and the Black Awakening of the 1960s* (Cambridge, Mass.: Harvard University Press, 1981); also Taylor Branch, "The March on Washington," chap. 22 in *Parting the Waters: America in the King Years 1954–63* (New York: Simon and Schuster, 1988).

8. See Conrad Lynn, *Monroe, North Carolina: Turning Point in American History,* foreword by James Boggs, *Correspondence* pamphlet no. 5, 1962.

9. When I was in Boston in June 1963 I had coffee with Louis X at a restaurant on Blue Hill Avenue. He talked very movingly and I thought somewhat naively about Plymouth Rock and the importance of blacks having their own nationalist symbols. The

meeting had been arranged by Truman Nelson (author of *The Surveyor*, a novel about John Brown in Kansas), who had good relations with the Nation of Islam.

10. Recently I ran into Richard Henry for the first time for nearly thirty years at a memorial for veteran organizer Chris Alston. As we talked over old times, he told me that when people compliment him for organizing the Grassroots Leadership Conference, his response is usually, "I couldn't have organized that conference. Grace Boggs did."

11. "I'm a Muslim and a revolutionary," Malcolm told Jan Carew during their informal conversations in London in 1965, "and I'm learning more and more about political theories as the months go by. The only Marxist group in America that offered me a platform was the Socialist Workers Party. I respect them and they respect me. The Communists have nixed me, gone out of the way to attack me . . . that is, with the exception of the Cuban Communists. If a mixture of nationalism and Marxism makes the Cubans fight the way they do and makes the Vietnamese stand up so resolutely to the might of America and its European and other lapdogs, then there must be something to it. But my Organization of African American Unity is based in Harlem and we've got to creep before we walk, and walk before we run." He paused and added, "But the chances are that they will get me the way they got Lumumba before he reached the running stage." Jan Carew, *Ghosts in Our Blood: With Malcolm X in Africa, England and the Caribbean* (Westport, Conn.: Lawrence Hill Books, 1994).

12. James Boggs, "The City Is the Black Man's Land," first published in *Monthly Review*, April 1966.

13. For a detailed report of this meeting see "Birth of a Nation" by Grace and James Boggs, *National Guardian*, October 7, 1967.

14. In *Return to Black America* (Englewood Cliffs, N. J.: Prentice Hall, 1970), Smith describes James Boggs as "the man many observers consider to be the most original, and probably the most important, theoretician of black power" (135).

6. Beyond Rebellion

1. Gwendolyn Brooks, "Paul Robeson," in *The Broadside Treasury* (Detroit: Broadside Press, 1968, 1970).

2. George Katsiaficas, *The Imagination of the New Left: A Global Analysis of 1968* (Boston: South End Press, 1987), 74.

3. For a moving and informative account of the stresses and strains of Black Panther Party membership and leadership, see David Hilliard and Lewis Cole, *This Side of Glory: The Autobiography of David Hilliard and the Story of the Black Panther Party* (Boston: Little, Brown, 1992); also Assata Shakur (aka Joanne Chesimard), *Assata: An Autobiography* (Westport, Conn.: Lawrence Hill Books, 1987).

4. Freddy is a strong presence in *Women of Summer*, the award-winning documentary on the school produced by Suzanne Bauman and Rita Heller.

5. James and Grace Lee Boggs, and Freddy and Lyman Paine, *Conversations in Maine* (Boston: South End Press, 1978), 100.

6. In the absence of a clear distinction between rebellion and revolution, it is impossible to appreciate the philosophical/spiritual leap that is necessary to go beyond rebellion. A case in point is Robin D. G. Kelley's *Race Rebels: Culture and the Black Working Class* (New York: Free Press, 1994). Kelley introduces his closely researched and fascinating book with the passage celebrating rebellion from *Facing Reality* by C. L. R. James, Grace C. Lee, and Pierre Chaulieu (cited in note 31, chapter 3). In chapter 1, titled "Shiftless of the World Unite!," Kelley describes the thousands of ways (theft, sabotage, music, dance, dress, and so on) through which over the years blacks on the bottom rail of society have expressed their rejection of the dominant ideology. In chapter 7, titled "The Riddle of the Zoot Suit:

Malcolm X and Black Cultural Politics during World War II," he explains the zoot suit as a symbol of black and Latin refusal to be subservient and to accept the work ethic. He concludes by chiding Malcolm for using "narrow rigid criteria . . . to judge the political meaning of his life" instead of "recuperating the oppositional meanings embedded in the expressive youth cultures of his era."

bell hooks's analysis of Malcolm's transformation is more insightful. Commenting on the passage in the *Autobiography* where Malcolm describes how Allah and the religion of Islam "completely transformed my life," she writes: "Confinement in prison provides the space where Malcolm can engage in uninterrupted critical reflection on his life, where he can contemplate the meaning and significance of human existence. During this period of confinement he comes face to face with the emptiness of life, the nihilism. This time for him is akin to a 'dark night of the soul.' It is a time when he experiences deep grief for the past and an anguish of spirit." *Yearning, Race, Gender and Cultural Politics* (Boston: South End Press, 1990), 80.

Carl Upchurch in *Convicted in the Womb: One Man's Journey from Prisoner to Peacemaker* (New York: Bantam, 1996) tells the story of how he rediscovered his humanity while in solitary confinement at the federal penitentiary in Lewisburg, Pennsylvania. Going over his cell inch by inch one day he discovered by pure accident a copy of Shakespeare's *Sonnets* that had been stuck under one leg of a table to make it level with the other three. From there he went on to read everything and anything, including Thomas Paine, Mark Twain, Betty Friedan, Maya Angelou, Elijah Muhammad, the Bible: "My readings changed everything for me. . . . Literature gave me a vocabulary I could use to express my deepest feelings and the insight to understand that my situation was universal. I escaped in a way far more satisfying than any tunnel under a prison wall, into a completely new world."

Manning Marable identifies himself as part of the transformationist tradition in African American politics, which is "best expressed in the writings of Amilcar Cabral, C. L. R. James and Walter Rodney." But Marable's transformationist politics turns out to be little more than social democracy with a race angle. Transformationists, he writes, "basically seek the redistribution of resources and the democratization of state power along more egalitarian lines." There is no hint in Marable of the enlarged sense of one's humanity that is at the heart of the transformational process. *Beyond Black and White: Transforming African American Politics* (London: Verso 1995), 227–28.

7. Amilcar Cabral, *Revolution in Guinea* (London: Stage 1, 1969), 74.

8. *Selected Readings from the Works of Mao Tse Tung* (Peking: Foreign Languages Press, 1971).

9. See *Where Do We Go from Here? Chaos or Community* and *The Trumpet of Conscience* in *A Testament of Hope: The Essential Writings of Martin Luther King Jr.*, ed. James Melvin Washington (New York: Harper & Row, 1986), 555–653. Vincent and Rosemary Harding, who worked closely with King on his anti-Vietnam speech, have made it their special responsibility to let the world know that King "was not killed for wanting black and white children to hold hands" but because he was getting ready to mobilize a struggle not only against racism but against militarism, materialism, and anticommunism. See *A Way of Faith, a Time for Courage*, National Organization for an American Revolution pamphlet, 1984. Also Vincent Harding, *Martin Luther King: The Inconvenient Hero* (Maryknoll, N. Y.: Orbis Books, 1996).

10. Robert Williams died on October 16, 1996. On November 1, 1996, a tribute committee, including General Baker, Mike Hamlin, Gloria House, Marian Kramer-Baker, Ron Scott, Charles Simmons, Ken Snodgrass, and myself, assembled an intergenerational gathering of activists at Wayne State University to honor Robert and Mabel Williams. To mark the occasion we compiled tributes from all over the world in a booklet titled *A Legacy of Resistance*. "Robert Williams became a hero," I said in the booklet, "because he was willing to assume responsibility for grappling with the contradiction of his community and his generation. In the 1950s and 1960s the main contradiction faced by southern blacks was that NAACP leaders, mainly preachers and members of the middle class, were unable to

stand up to the KKK violence which was terrorizing their communities. Rob Williams, the offspring of a working class family and an ex-Marine, refused to accept that blacks who were sent all over the world to terrorize people should be terrorized at home. So, coming out of obscurity (as [Frantz] Fanon put it) he organized the grassroots members of his community to stand up against the KKK. As a result, he became a national leader who was admired and respected all over the world. We honor Rob Williams by doing for our generation and our communities what he did for his." Rob's *Negroes with Guns* is being reprinted by Wayne State University Press with a new introduction by Gloria House, aka aneb kgositsile.

11. For a lively account of their activities, see Dan Georgakas and Marvin Surkin, *Detroit: I Do Mind Dying. A Study in Urban Revolution* (New York: St. Martin's Press, 1975). A paper by my brother Edward Lee titled "Whoever Heard of Bongo Drums on the Picket Line?" is in the Boggs collection in the Wayne State Archives. Eddie was working in the Dodge plant during the DRUM demonstrations.

12. In James Boggs, *Racism and the Class Struggle: Further Pages from a Black Worker's Notebook* (New York: Monthly Review Press, 1970), 133 ff.

13. From an ad in the College and Universities section of the *New York Times*, Sunday, March 3, 1972.

14. For information on pamphlets, statements, and speeches, contact the James and Grace Lee Boggs Center to Nurture Community Leadership, 3061 Field St., Detroit, MI 48214, or go to *www.boggscenter.org*.

15. *Monthly Review* (September) 1970; *Education and the Black Struggle: Notes from the Colonized World*, ed. Institute of the Black World (Atlanta), Monograph no. 2, 1974.

16. Dorothy Healy, veteran leader of the Los Angeles Communist Party, has pointed out this weakness in the party: "There was, as I've noted, a lack of genuine theoretical understanding in the Party, for all of our talk about theory. We were so busy with day-to-day organizing that we could rarely consider the larger questions facing our movement; in the midst of the Party crisis in 1956 the charge that was made over and over again was that we had been deliberately kept so busy that nobody had time to think. Whether it was deliberate policy or not, it was certainly true that the Party lacked the kind of internal political structures that might have encouraged us to ask substantive questions about the meaning of our own experience." Dorothy Healy and Maurice Isserman, *Dorothy Healy Remembers* (New York: Oxford University Press, 1990), 58.

17. Not included in the book was the talk on Cuba that Phil Hutchings had given in the 1970 series. Hutchings, who was elected in June 1968 to succeed Rap Brown as the leader of SNCC, was active in the Venceremos Brigade. In those days he lived across the street from us.

18. For some reason not known to me, it was never published in *The Black Scholar*.

19. Vincent Harding, *There Is A River* (New York: Vintage, 1983).

20. Our discussion was published in a pamphlet: James Hocker, Grace Lee Boggs, and James Boggs, *These Are the Times That Try Our Souls* (Detroit: National Organization for an American Revolution, 1981).

21. African American novelist James McPherson provides a similar analysis for the demise of the black movement but dates it a decade later: "The legacy that once fueled the civil rights movement was a belief that *any* dehumanization of another human being was wrong. This moral certainty once had the potential to enlarge our humanity. Beneath it was the assumption that the experience of oppression had made us more human, and that this higher human awareness was about to project a vision of what a fully human life, one not restricted by color, should be." However, "preoccupations with fashionable individualism and with small-time politics, toward the end of survival during decadent times, invaded the very center of our lives. In order to make room for these fashions, we tore down, tossed out and discarded some of our most basic beliefs. But a very high price was paid for this trade-

off. . . . By the end of the 1980s black Americans had become a thoroughly 'integrated' group . . . no better than and no worse than anyone else." James McPherson, "Junior and John Doe," in *Lure and Loathing: Essays on Race, Identity and the Ambivalence of Assimilation*, ed. Gerald Early (New York: Penguin, 1993).

22. *Conversations in Maine*, 281–88.

23. Starhawk, "The Burning Times," in *Magic, Sex and Politics* (Boston: Beacon Press, 1982), 183 ff.

24. See the *New York Times*, September 23, 1972.

25. James Boggs, "Blacks in the Cities: Agenda for the 70s," *The Black Scholar* (November) 1972.

26. In Studs Terkel, *American Dreams Lost and Found* (New York: Pantheon, 1980), 368.

27. See Jeanie Wylie, *Poletown: Community Betrayed* (Champaign: University of Illinois Press, 1989), and the film *Poletown Lives*, which tells the story through the voices of the residents.

28. The fifth printing of the *Manifesto for a Black Revolutionary Party*, published in 1976, had included a new seven-page introduction pointing out the need to go beyond a black revolution to an American revolution.

29. Rick Whaley and Walter Bresette, *Walleye Warriors: An Effective Alliance against Racism and for the Earth* (Philadelphia: New Society Publishers, 1994).

30. Margaret J. Wheatley, *Leadership and the New Science: Learning about Organization* from an Orderly Universe (San Francisco: Berrett-Koehler, 1992).

7. "Going Back" to China

1. *New International*, February, March, April, May 1944.

2. In my dining room an oil painting of Mao hangs next to one of my father painted by my sister-in-law Julie Lee.

3. "The Important Thing Is to Be Good at Learning," in *Selected Readings from the Works of Mao Tse Tung* (Peking: Foreign Languages Press, 1971), 58, 59.

4. See Felix Greene, *China: The Country Americans Are Not Allowed to Know* (New York: Ballantine Books, 1961).

5. Reprinted as an APA pamphlet titled *Asian Americans and the U.S. Movement.*

6. C. K. Yang, *Chinese Communist Society: The Family and the Village* (Cambridge, Mass.: MIT Press, 1965).

7. An article by Patrick E. Tyler in the *New York Times* (September 4, 1996) reports that the same students who seven years ago were pro-democracy demonstrators are today channeling their "energy and their frustrations in other directions," including "Yankee bashing."

8. Isabel Crook and David Crook, *Revolution in a Chinese Village* (London: Routledge, 1959) and *The First Years of Yangyi Commune* (London: Routledge, 1966).

9. Frank Su Kaiming, *Modern China: A Topical History* (Beijing: New World Press, 1985).

8. New Dreams for the Twenty-First Century

1. Jimmy's SOSAD columns have been published by New Life Publishers under the title *What Can We Be That Our Children Can See?* The last issue of the SOSAD newsletter was published in February 1995.

2. Coleman Young and Lonnie Wheeler, *Hardstuff: The Autobiography of Coleman Young* (New York: Viking 1994), 8, 238.

3. SOSAD newsletter, no. 13, June 17, 1988.

4. James Boggs, "Going Where We Have Never Been: Creating New Communities for Our Future," presented at Bay Area NOAR meeting, Oakland, Calif., October 1986.

5. James Boggs, "Rebuilding Detroit: An Alternative to Casino Gambling," public speakout, Detroit, June 24, 1988.

6. Title of an unpublished speech to the Urban Design and Social Change class, University of Michigan, November 3, 1988.

7. Jimmy worked at the Chrysler-Jefferson plant throughout World War II. Coleman spent most of the war years in the segregated armed services, battling Jim Crow every step of the way, both as a Tuskegee air pilot trainee and as a bombardier.

8. "Civilizing what is left of the city, creating community in the city, is going to be the great social challenge of the next century," according to Peter Drucker, the nation's foremost management consultant. "There was only a comparatively short period in which cities were comparatively safe because the people who lived in them were still rural in their mentality. The family, the village, the church, these strong communities had an iron grip. The modern city has no communities in that sense." Interview in the *Los Angeles Times*, February 2, 1997.

9. The story of WE-PROS is told in a lively fifteen-minute video titled *Breaking the Cycle of Fear*.

10. My speech to the alliance on February 21, 1990, was included in the booklet of selected speeches published for my seventy-fifth birthday celebration a few months later. Recently, a two-page excerpt was reprinted in *The Witness* as "A Vocation for Churches," December 1996.

11. *Anthropologica* 25, no. 2 (1993).

12. "Each Generation Must Discover Its Mission," *The Commitment*, August 1994.

13. The historic First Unitarian-Universalist Church has become the center of a growing grassroots cultural movement in the heart of the city's Cultural Center. It now hosts seven groups: Black Folk Arts, Inc., Center for Women's Culture, Cinema Cafe, Detroit Summer, Detroit Women's Coffeehouse, Thick Knot Rhythm Ensemble, and Horizons in Poetry. The groups call themselves the Red Door Collective because it is through the red rear door that generations of artists and activists have entered the church theater. The pastor of the church is Rev. Larry Hutchison, who was active with Frank Joyce in the People Against Racism group in the 1970s and remains a community activist to this day.

14. See, for example, Kenneth Burke, *The Philosophy of Literary Form: Studies in Symbolic Action* (Berkeley and Los Angeles: University of California Press, 1973), 106n.

15. The following excerpt from the poem was reprinted in the brochure announcing the October 23 memorial celebration. The entire poem is reprinted in the tribute booklet given out at the celebration.

Are you shrugging your shoulders
Worker hands outstretched from arms
Elbows pressed to side, eyes wide
Proclaiming
WE ALL GOT TO DIE — THAT'S A GIVEN
NOTHIN' WE CAN DO ABOUT THAT.
THE POINT IS UNBEATABLE —
LET'S SPEND THE TIME DOING/SAYING
SOMETHING THAT CAN MAKE A DIFFERENCE.

You, dear James, you and Grace, represent
The nobleness of life
Stalwart cheerleaders of the
BETTER WAY contingent
Water on the seed bed of exciting and
Necessary choices
You have certainly opened us—Ossie and me
To horizons of thought and theory that
Underline and
Strengthen so much of what we have done and
Hope to do in our remaining minutes in the
Arts. You have taught us ways of thinking
And looking at Life and its challenges
That without you
May have escaped us.

So even tho I cry and want to
Tear out what's left of the hair as I
Think of you trying to ease out the door
Unnoticed, dazzling and stopping us all
With the enormous body of thought and
Instructions for future directions flying
Towards us,
My heart reaches through the event to hold
And hug you hard, swear and cry, before you
Smiling, with finger to lips,
Quietly close the door.

When you move through the glory tunnel
My heart will track the journey with you
Shouting
LOVE, LOVE, LOVE, WE TRULY LOVE YOU.
Best we so far know how.

If you won't be too busy
Come see me sometime
If you can.

9. On My Own

1. *The Sayings of Confucius*, trans. James R. Ware (New York: Mentor, 1955), 25.

2. See "Youth Identify Values for Healthy Detroit," SOSAD newsletter, Winter 1995.

3. The story of how residents from all walks of life, united by the vision that they had created together, were able to transform Chattanooga into one of our nation's most vibrant cities is told in the American Architectural Foundation documentary film *Back from the Brink: Saving American Cities by Design*.

4. Paul Goodman, *Growing Up Absurd: Problems of Youth in the Organized System* (New York: Random House, 1960).

5. See the *New York Times*, May 23, 1995.

6. See Bunyan Bryant, "Rehearsing the Future," *In Context*, no. 40.

7. See *The Future: Images for the 21st Century*, ed. Bunyan Bryant (Ann Arbor: University of Michigan Office of the Vice Provost for Minority Affairs and the Environmental Equity Institute, 1993), 44ff; also *In Context*, no. 40; and *The Commitment*, Detroit Summer Newsletter, March 1995.

8. For example, fourteen- and fifteen-year-old Detroit Summer volunteers, asked to list the positives and negatives of the global economy in a 1995 workshop, were unable to come up with even one positive. In "The Reconstruction of Community Meaning" (*Tikkun* 11, no. 3), Gar Alperovitz provides an insightful analysis of our present impasse, quoting Martin Buber and Hannah Arendt, two philosophers with whose ideas I have wrestled over the years. The 1996 *Detroit Summer Reader* included a copy of this article.

9. An enjoyable way to learn how the global economy works to destroy communities and the environment and how to devise collective strategies for struggle against transnational corporations is by participating in the video workshop/game on "The New Global Economy: A View from the Bottom Up," created by the Resource Center of the Americas in Minneapolis. Participants role-play different groups (the local union, the city council, the corporation's board of directors, a Green group, an activist religious coalition, and *maquiladora* workers in Tijuana) and simulate responses to three situations: the corporation's announcement that it is closing the local plant and moving to Mexico, anti-immigrant legislation, and the World Trade Organization's refusal to uphold a United States ban against importing produce with Toxol-9 residues. Having role-played and observed several different groups my impression is that the union holds the weakest hand in the struggle while Green and religious groups provide strong leadership by bringing new principles of universal human rights to the struggle.

10. *Revolution and Evolution in the Twentieth Century* (New York: Monthly Review Press, 1974), 22. During the 1960s Latin American revolutionist Adolfo Gilly shared with us his conviction that "Sin embargo estan perdidos" (whatever happens they—the reactionaries—are lost). It has never left me.

11. Ferry, "Farewell to Integration," *The Center Magazine*, March 1968.

12. The Million Man Pledge: "I, (say your name), pledge, that from this day forward, I will strive to love my brother, as I love myself. I... from this day forward, will strive to improve myself: spirtually; morally; mentally; socially; politically; and, economically, for the benefit of myself, my family, and my people. I... pledge, that I will strive to build business, build houses, build hospitals, build factories, and enter into international trade, for the good of myself, my family, and my people. I... pledge, that from this day forward, I will never raise my hand, with a knife or gun, to beat, cut, or shoot, any member of my family, or any human being, except in self-defense. I... pledge, from this day forward, I will never abuse my wife by striking her, disrespecting her, for she is the mother of my children, and the producer of my future. I... pledge, that from this day forward, I will never engage in the abuse of children, little boys or little girls, for sexual gratification. But, I will let them grow in peace to be strong men and women, for the future of our people. I... will never again use the "B" word, to describe any female, but particularly my own Black sister. I... pledge, from this day forward, that I will not poison my body, with drugs or that which is destructive, to my health and my well-being. I... pledge, that from this day forward, I will support Black newspapers, Black radio, Black television. I will support Black artists who clean up their acts, to show respect for themselves, and respect for their people, and respect for the ends of the human family. I... will do all of this, so help me GOD!"

13. *Afro-American Gazette*, October 1995.

14. Sixty years ago W. E. B. Du Bois called on Negro churches to become the core of a cooperative neighborhood economy: "It would mean a new kind of pastor. It would involve the elimination from the present church organization just as far as possible, of theology and supernaturalism.... Nevertheless the Negro church and even the white church faces grim alternatives: either it becomes a great social organ with ethical ideals based on reorganized economics, or it becomes a futile and mouthy excrescence on society which will always be a refuge for reaction and superstition." W. E. B. Du Bois, *Against Racism: Unpublished Essays, Papers, Addresses, 1887–1961*, ed. Herbert Aptheker (Amherst: University of Massachusetts, 1985).

In the spring of 1997 Hartford Memorial Baptist Church, one of Detroit's largest and most prestigious churches, made a deal with K-Mart to build a huge discount store on land owned by the church in northwest Detroit without consulting neighborhood residents. When large numbers of residents opposed the deal because it would bring heavy traffic and also ruin small local businesses, the pastor, Rev. Charles Adams, invoked religious authority to defuse their opposition. When the deal was brought to the City Council for approval, only one member, Mel Ravitz, voted against it.

The only black preacher with a holistic vision for community development that I know is Rev. Charles Willis, who works with Detroiters Working for Environmental Justice. A member of the Million Man March organization, he is convinced that within our communities are the material, physical, and intellectual resources, the "bootstraps," that we can utilize to develop jobs and the skills of our young people. He calls attention especially to the abandoned cars that the police now remove in the guise of cleaning up our communities. Why can't we recycle them to create an auto parts business that will provide jobs and at the same time teach car mechanics to our young people? Rev. Willis came from Mississippi to Detroit in 1946. His make-do thinking reminds me of Jimmy and Dorothy Garner.

15. Grace Lee Boggs, "People and Communities over Profits and Corporations," *The Exchange*, April 1996. The strategy for ending corporate tyranny by struggling to revoke state charters of corporations that have violated the public trust comes from the Program on Corporations, Law and Democracy created by Richard Grossman and Ward Morehouse. At Ping Ferry's memorial celebration Grossman talked about the encouragement and help he had received from Ferry in developing the program to end corporate rule.

16. See my article "Cuba: Love and Self-Reliance," *Monthly Review*, December 1996.

17. *Democracy and Development in Africa* by Claude Ake (Washington, D. C.: Brookings Institute, 1996) provides a devastating analysis of the limitations of the African elites who took over state power from the colonialists: "With a few exceptions the African elites have been more interested in political survival than in development, and the conditions of their survival have usually been inimical to development. Agriculture has not been given the importance it deserves, and agricultural policy and development have tended to disappear in the struggle between the state and political elites, who want to control the peasants' agricultural surplus, and the peasants, who resist expropriation" (96).

18. The story of this movement is told in a number of books, especially Pierre Pradervand, *Listening to Africa: Developing Africa from the Grassroots* (New York: Praeger, 1989); Paul Ekins, *A New World Order: Grassroots Movements for Global Change* (London and New York: Routledge, 1992); and Paul Harrison, *The Greening of Africa* (New York: Penguin, 1987) and *The Third World Tomorrow* (New York: Pilgrim Press, 1983). In 1987 Pradervand spent four and a half months visiting 111 villages in five countries (Senegal, Mali, Burkina Faso, Zimbabwe, and Kenya) during which he discovered that "literally millions of farmers have moved to take the future into their own hands, to reclaim the self-reliance that was theirs until the disruption of colonial occupation and the post-Independence era of rapid modernization." Pradervand concludes that "the time has come for us to realize that the material poverty of Africa has blinded us to its amazing human and cultural wealth, just as our own very recent material wealth seems to have blinded us to more insidious forms of spiritual, human and moral poverty" (213). *The Greening of Africa* is full of examples (many of them illustrated) of measures being taken by Africans (for example, microbasins, multilayer farming, alley cropping) to reclaim their land and vegetation. In *The Third World Tomorrow* Harrison describes the new approaches to production, health care, and education now emerging in the Third World because the Western model of development has resulted in so much inequality and poverty.

19. Andreas Fuglesang and Dale Chandler, *Participation as Process: What We Can Learn from Grameen Bank Bangladesh* (Norway: Norwegian Agency for Development Cooperation, 1986).

20. *Synapse*, no. 31, 1995.

玉平

Index

Addenda

The full text of C. L. R. James's statement mentioned on page 109, in which he declares, "I break all relations, political and personal, with all who subscribe to this resolution," has been reproduced in *Marxism and the Intellectuals*, a pamphlet published by Facing Reality Publishing Corporation. It is available from Bewick Editions, P. O. Box 14140, Detroit, Michigan 48214.

Following Lyman Paine's unhappy visit with C. L. R. James in 1956, referred to on page 152, Lyman spent years struggling to develop a philosophy of dialectical humanism to replace dialectical materialism. He argued with CLR and with himself, and jotted down his questions on hundreds of little scraps of paper. Freddy Paine had these notes organized and typed, and Larry Sparks has bound them in eight notebooks.

Grace Lee Boggs is a first-generation Chinese American who has been a speaker, writer, and movement activist in the African American community for fifty-five years. She has lived on the East Side of Detroit since 1953, most of that time in the same house. With her husband, James Boggs, she coauthored *Revolution and Evolution in the 20th Century*. Currently, as a volunteer, she is active with Healthy Detroit, Detroit Summer, Detroiters Working for Environmental Justice, and the Detroit Growers Support Group.

Ossie Davis, in addition to his roles as actor, director, and producer, prefers to be known foremost as a writer. Author of the Tony Award winning play *Purlie Victorious*, Davis has also published such plays as *Curtain Call, Mr. Aldridge, Sir*; *Langston*; *Escape to Freedom*; and his first novel about young people in the civil rights movement, *Just Like Martin*, published by Simon and Schuster.